RELIGIOUS LIFE
IN A NEW MILLENNIUM
VOLUME ONE

Finding the Treasure

Religious Life in a New Millennium
Volume One

Finding the Treasure
Locating Catholic Religious Life in a New Ecclesial and Cultural Context

Sandra M. Schneiders, I.H.M.

PAULIST PRESS
New York/Mahwah, N.J.

Procession of the Virgins, detail of gold leaf on glass and colored glass mosaic in Sant'Apollinare Nuovo, Ravenna, Italy, c. 568. ©Archivo Iconografico, S.A./CORBIS

Cover design by Cynthia Dunne

Series design by J. E. Pondo

Copyright © 2000 by Sandra M. Schneiders, I.H.M.

Library of Congress Cataloging-in-Publication Data

Schneiders, Sandra Marie.
    Finding the treasure : locating Catholic religious life in a new ecclesial and cultural context / Sandra M. Schneiders.
        p. cm.—(Religious life in a new millennium ; v. 1)
    Includes bibliographical references (v. 1, p.) and index.
    ISBN 0-8091-3961-8 (alk. paper)
    1. Monastic and religious life of women. I. Title. II. Series
BX4210.5.S36 2000
255'.9—dc21

                                                                00-026319

Published by Paulist Press
997 Macarthur Boulevard
Mahwah, New Jersey 07430

www.paulistpress.com

Printed and bound in the
United States of America

The Reign of God is like a TREASURE
hidden in a field
which a person FOUND...
and out of joy
SOLD ALL *she had to buy that field.*
(cf. Mt 13:44)

*This volume is dedicated
with love and gratitude*

*to
Margaret Brennan, I.H.M.
and
Constance FitzGerald, O.C.D.*

*who are
prophets in their own country.*

Table of Contents

Preface
to
Religious Life in a New Millennium
(Three Volumes)

In the twelve years since the publication of *New Wineskins*[1] the experience of Roman Catholic women Religious, who were the primary intended audience of that book, has broadened and deepened to an extraordinary degree. If, in 1986, it was appropriate and necessary to talk of new wineskins, that is, of new structures and procedures, and even of new theological categories and constructs, to hold and give shape to the new experience of the life that was emerging in the wake of Vatican II, today it is time to speak of the wine itself, the substance of the life, which has matured during the past decade, yielding both excellent vintage and some disappointing results. The new wine that demanded new wineskins a decade ago now needs decanting. It is time to pour, to taste, to analyze, to judge, to choose and reject, to blend and bottle, to store for the future. This task is already underway in a plethora of books and articles that have appeared during the 1980s and 1990s. This three-volume work, *Religious Life in a New Millennium,* is intended as a contribution to that lively discussion.

It is the underlying presupposition of this work that for Religious Life and those who live it in faith there is indeed a future full of hope (cf. Jer 29:11). But if that hope is to be realized Religious must do the difficult work of rethinking their life in the radically new context of a new millennium which many cultural critics are characterizing as postmodern. I say that this is a difficult work because the context is complex, the experience to be examined and integrated is extremely rich and varied, the dialogue partners who can no longer be ignored as irrelevant are numerous and diverse. If Religious Life is to continue to make sense, to be a compelling and energizing life choice for those who live it and an attractive possibility to those contemplating it for themselves, and finally to be able to be presented coherently to those who appreciate it as well as those who do not, it must be examined anew and in depth.

I have been struck in recent years by the qualitative difference between the types of questions Religious were asking two decades ago and those that are at the center of discussions today. It seems to me that the difference is essentially that virtually every question raised today leads directly into the issue of what Religious Life is and means. In other words, whatever the presenting problems or issues—celibacy, permanent commitment, formation, associates, community, vows, ministry, feminism, Church, or prayer—the real question is "What is this life really all about?" Whatever one has to say about the particular issues must originate in and be expressive of what one claims the life is and means. I think the explicit emergence of this question is a very positive development, even though it greatly heightens the stakes in every discussion. It manifests the realization that, finally, Religious Life is a life, not a collection of disparate and separable elements but a coherent whole. The question about the life itself is one about its wholeness, its integrity, its authenticity as a way of being in this world. Consequently, this work, and especially the first volume, is not an easy read. Anyone looking for a possible answer to specific problems will probably be disappointed.

What I am offering is an understanding of the life itself in its contemporary cultural context (volume 1) as the framework for a reconsideration of its constitutive dimensions, namely, consecrated celibacy lived in community (volume 2), and an exploration of the way in which the authentic and integrated living of this life can help to transform not only the Religious herself but also the society and culture of which Religious Life is a part (volume 3). This is a dangerous project for a writer because a comprehensive view of any reality invites not only agreement and disagreement with particular points (always a welcome source of both affirmation and improvement) but complete rejection of the project as a whole if the underlying presuppositions are found unacceptable. This is a danger I am willing to run because I am convinced of the value of Religious Life not only to the individuals called to it but also to the Church, which is called to be a light to the nations and therefore to the world itself. Recently someone asked me, "Does Religious Life need the Church?" and I replied that I thought the prior question is "Does the Church (and therefore the world) need Religious Life?" and I am convinced that the answer to the latter question is yes (and for other reasons so is the answer to the first). The realization of the potential of Religious Life, both for the Church and for our endangered cosmos, species, and culture, however, requires a theoretical basis that is clear and compelling. I am not arrogant enough to claim that this work supplies such a basis, much less the only one, but I hope it will generate focused discussion at the level on which I think this discussion must proceed at this point in history.

The primary intended audience of *Religious Life in a New Millennium* is the same as that of *New Wineskins,* that is, North American Roman Catholic women Religious. This is not the exclusive audience, for obviously much of the material in this work, as in its predecessor, is applicable to Religious in other cultures, to Protestant and Anglican Religious and members of ecumenical Religious communities, to male Religious, especially those of nonclerical institutes, to members of Secular Institutes and of secular or third orders connected with Religious orders, to members of Societies of Apostolic Life, and to various kinds of associates of canonical institutes. I have learned from conversations with laypeople, both Catholic and non-Catholic, that much of the material in *New Wineskins* was directly relevant to committed lay life, and I hope that that will be the case with this work as well. Indeed, it should be the case that Religious Life, rooted in and expressive of baptismal consecration and mission, would have more in common with than distinctive from Christian life in general.[2]

The choice of the specific audience is dictated by very practical considerations. First, the forms of life in some way analogous or related to Religious Life are so numerous, and each is sufficiently specific, that "ringing the changes" on everything that is said to account adequately for the variations would make the text excessively cumbersome, even if I were capable of doing it. Those living these other forms of life are much more competent than I to make the appropriate distinctions and qualifications in terms of their own life. Second, this work is a reflection on experience and even within canonical Religious Life itself, to say nothing of related forms of life, the experiences of female and male Religious, North American Religious and those in Latin America, Asia, Africa, and Europe, and those in clerical and in nonclerical institutes are irreducibly diverse. I cannot speak from experience about and therefore am not competent to analyze the experience of men or of people whose cultures I do not share. Third, the specific experience with which I propose to deal is extensive and varied enough that doing it justice will more than fill the pages of three volumes of reasonable length. Finally, I am taking something of a chance in attempting to include, as fully as possible, in my specifically intended readership, both the so-called apostolic and contemplative forms of women's Religious Life.[3] This will present sufficient challenge in terms of distinctions and qualifications, even though what the two forms of life have in common is much more evident today than it was in preconciliar times.

The choice to write a new book rather than to revise *New Wineskins* was dictated by two realizations. First, the essays in the earlier volume retain their validity as reflections on the experience of the two decades that followed Vatican II and therefore, at least in my judgment, should stand as they are. Second, the experience that now requires reflection is not generated by the same dynamics as was the experience of the 1960s and 1970s. Although this distinction is simplistic, I think it is indicative of something important to say that in the immediate aftermath of the Council, Religious were dealing predominantly with changes *within* Religious Life itself as Religious encountered the "world" from which they had been almost hermetically sealed for centuries, whereas in the last fifteen years the concern has been much more explicitly with the interaction *between* Religious Life and the ambient culture, both secular and ecclesial.

There is a cause and effect relationship between the two phases. As Religious congregations responded to the Council's reaffirmation of the world as the locus of salvation and reconceptualized themselves as existing not out of or separate from the world but in, with, and for the world, they began an extensive dismantling of the structural barriers between themselves and other people and between the privatized culture of preconciliar Religious Life and the surrounding culture. At first, the primary impact of this dismantling was experienced within Religious Life itself. Dress, horaria, dwellings, community life, and ministries changed. This called for revisions of constitutions, and from that followed changes in internal structures, institutional involvements, and relationships within and outside the congregation. Foundational to these observable changes, of course, was a new theology and a rapidly evolving spirituality, but it was the breakdown of the total institution that precipitated what was to follow.

The opening up of the institution interrelated Religious with American secular culture in a new and much more intimate and pervasive way. To invoke only a few pertinent examples, permanent commitment through vows could not be proposed or explained without some reference to the cultural experience of ubiquitous career mobility, familial reconfigurations, indefinitely delayed marriage, and rampant divorce. Poverty had to be seen through the prism of attitudes toward money, lifestyle, and social class in a capitalist culture and in relation to a global economy. Ministry had to take account of the categories of career and promotion, employment and compensation, insurance and retirement. In short, it was not just that ceasing to be a closed system had repercussions for the internal life of the social system we call Religious Life but that the system itself was now in pervasive interaction with its cultural environment in ways that have deeply influenced it. It is primarily this interaction between Religious Life and culture, both ecclesial and secular, that is the focus of this work, and especially of volume 1.

It has seemed to me that this task of analyzing and rethinking Religious Life could best proceed in three phases, the first a consideration of the global or general context (both cultural and ecclesial) influencing Religious Life, the second focusing specifically on the life itself through an exploration of its distinctive and constitutive relationships, and the third focusing on the influence of Religious Life on the context (again both ecclesial and cultural). In the global phase (volume 1) I want to address the larger question of "locating" or situating Religious Life in the multiple contexts that now qualify it in significant ways. It is a question of "finding" the treasure that is Religious Life. This task of "locating Religious Life" is a distinctly postmodern undertaking in the sense that there is no grand scheme or metanarrative within which all the influencing environments can be coherently related to one another and cumulatively create the single "space" or "place" of Religious Life. There was a time when we could describe the relationship between the Church and the world and within the Church the place of each form of life. This enabled us to properly place Religious Life in relation to all its significant publics and/or others: Vatican, hierarchy, local clergy, other forms of Religious Life, other congregations within one's own form, Catholic laity, other "seculars." And none of the relationships overlapped in intrinsically contradictory ways. Religious Life was subject to some, superior to others, in opposition to still others.

Today, Religious Life is situated vis-à-vis a plurality of incommensurable, overlapping, or totally unrelated realities, movements, and structures, and each of these situations may affirm, challenge, or radically call into question the self-understanding and claims of Religious concerning the meaning and significance of their life. How, for example, are Religious related to their obvious analogues in other world religions such as Buddhist or Hindu monastics or Islamic Sufis? How are Religious related to clergy or to laity within the Catholic Christian community? How are women's Religious congregations related to feminism as a cultural movement? What kind of sociological reality is a Religious congregation? What does the new cosmology and its effect on theological categories have to say to the fundamental Christocentrism of Religious Life?

This list does not exhaust the questions, but it does suggest how different they are from those we were asking in the 1960s and 1970s and how each question pertains to a sphere of reality that may have little or nothing to do with the spheres from which the other questions arise. Responding to one such question sometimes does not seem to help much in responding to another. This fragmentation and pluralism are characteristic of postmodernism, and the pertinence of these questions to Religious Life suggests how involved in the cultural context of postmodernity Religious Life is. It is not possible to put these complexes together into a single, unitary worldview. Rather, they have to be held individually and together in a pluralistic way. This engagement with the diverse universes to which Religious Life is related is the global task of this work and especially of volume 1.

Second, there are the questions that are specific to Religious Life itself but which must be asked and answered differently because of the different contexts in which Religious Life is situated today. In volume 2, therefore, I will be concerned with the relationships that constitute Religious Life as a state of life: the multiple relationships established by the commitment to Religious Life through profession; the central distinctive relationship to God in Jesus Christ that is consecrated celibacy; and the relational context in which Religious Life is lived, namely, celibate community. Struggling with questions about commitment, about the meaning of consecrated celibacy as the defining and distinguishing feature of the life, and about the varied ways in which the reality of community is embodied to form the life context of this commitment has generated an experience that is ripe for examination. This experience has been, in my opinion, predominantly life-giving and liberating, but it has also been, from some perspectives, frustrating and even traumatic. Wise people can learn from both positive and negative experience. My intention in volume 2 is to examine that experience in light of history, tradition, Scripture, theology and the social sciences, but especially in terms of the spirituality involved in responding to the vocation to "sell all," that is, to give the all of one's life to the All who is God in this particular form of life.

Third, major changes within Religious Life have resulted from the engagement over several decades with new questions in a new context. New horizons have opened; freedom and responsibility have enriched experience; mistakes have been made; what once seemed simple is now recognized as very complex; the relative importance of various aspects of Religious Life has been/is being reevaluated. The specific task of volume 3 will be to revisit these areas of concern. I will be examining the experience of the recent past, especially in the spheres of mission/ministry and personal/corporate spirituality as these shape the life of Religious themselves and through which Religious influence the ecclesial and cultural context within which they live. Religious Life is indeed a treasure hidden in the field of this history and culture, worth the price of one's life, but that price is offered not just to acquire the treasure for oneself, but also to "ransom the field" itself. Religious Life cannot be lived well today without influencing both the postconciliar Church and the postmodern cultural context in which it is located and lived. As that context has influenced, indeed transformed, Religious Life so Religious Life must influence its context. The hope and the goal of those who, unlike the rich young man in the Gospel, are willing to sell all to follow Christ in Religious Life is nothing short of the transformation of the world by the Gospel.

Needless to say, this work is not the product of one person's reflection. My heartfelt thanks are offered to several groups and individuals without whose help this work could not have been undertaken. First, my gratitude goes to the numerous Religious congregations that have invited me to reflect with them on their experience and have thus helped me to discern the real questions and to appreciate the diversity of approaches to them. I am deeply grateful to the writers and lecturers who have been discussing Religious Life over the past decade and from whom I have learned so much, especially Margaret Brennan, I.H.M.; Joan Chittister, O.S.B.; Mary Collins, O.S.B.; Barbara Fiand,

S.N.D.deN.; Constance FitzGerald, O.C.D.; Doris Gottemueller, R.S.M.; Mary Milligan, R.S.H.M.; Patricia Wittberg, S.C.; and others, including men Religious whose work on their own life has seeded my reflection.

I owe particular thanks to my own Religious congregation, the Sisters, Servants of the Immaculate Heart of Mary, whose never-failing support and appreciation of my work has made me both proud and humbly grateful to be a Religious in these challenging times. I want also to thank the Carmelite community of Baltimore for their wonderful hospitality to me on numerous occasions as I have prayed and reflected on the issues discussed in this work.

The actual task of writing would not have been possible without the combination of financial resources generously provided by the Lilly Endowment and the precious resource of time provided by a leave of absence from my home institution, the Jesuit School of Theology at Berkeley. My editors at Paulist Press, Lawrence Boadt and Donna Crilly, have been, once again, perfect collaborators. And my research assistant, Jan Richardson, alone knows how invaluable her tireless chasing down of facts and figures, meticulous attention to the details of style, careful proofreading, and truly impressive skill with the computer have been.

Finally, I want to acknowledge the specific help of a few individuals who have given generous amounts of time and energy to reading and discussing with me various parts of *Finding the Treasure*. Margaret Brennan, I.H.M., Constance FitzGerald, O.C.D., and Mary Milligan, R.S.H.M. offered their knowledge of spirituality in relation to chapters 5 and 6, on the transformation of Religious Life in the postconciliar period. Nancy Sylvester, I.H.M., and Dr. Gina Hens-Piazza helped me with chapters 9 and 10, on prophecy. Lynn Jarrel, O.S.U., and Nancy Reynolds, S.P., brought their expertise in Canon Law to bear on chapters 7 and 8, on the place of Religious in the institutional Church. Barbara Kraemer, S.S.S.F., Patricia Wittberg, S.C., Rose McDermott, S.S.J., and Mary Ann Donovan, S.C. have helped me in numerous ways with questions of history, current data on Religious Life, the development of new communities, and other matters in which they are far more competent than I. And, of course, other friends in the academy, especially the wonderful research staff at the Flora Lamson Hewlett Library of the Graduate Theological Union, have responded generously to my numerous requests for help in locating materials and interpreting data. Finally, my thanks to Bishop John Cummins of the Oakland, California diocese, whose encouragement of scholarship in general and of my own work in particular creates an atmosphere most conducive to serious work in the service of the Church.

While I have learned much from those who have helped me I have, inevitably, made the final decisions about the content of this book and bear the responsibility for what has resulted. I can only say that whatever limitations it suffers (and they are surely many) they would have been much more numerous and serious without such help. I hope my readers will profit from what they find here, challenge what is questionable, and go on to enrich the conversation about the treasure of Religious Life, hidden in the field of Church and world, for which some, in their joy at finding it, have unhesitatingly sold all.

Pentecost 1999
Berkeley, California

Abbreviations

A	*Ascent of Mount Carmel.* In *The Collected Works of Saint John of the Cross,* rev. ed., translated by Kieran Kavanaugh and Otilio Rodriguez. With revisions and introduction by Kieran Kavanaugh. Washington. D.C.: Institute of Carmelite Studies, 1991.
A.A.	*Apostolicam Actuositatem* (Decree on the Apostolate of Lay People), in Flannery, vol. 1.
CBA	Catholic Biblical Association.
CCC	*Catechism of The Catholic Church.* Collegeville, Minn.: Liturgical Press, 1994.
CCL (1917)	John A. Abbo and Jerome D. Hannon, *The Sacred Canons: A Concise Presentation of the Current Disciplinary Norms of the Church* (in paraphrase), 2 vols. St Louis: Herder, 1951.
CCL (1983)	*Code of Canon Law: Latin-English Edition,* translation prepared under the auspices of the Canon Law Society of America. Washington, D.C.: Canon Law Society of America, 1983.
CMSM	Conference of Major Superiors of Men.
CTSA	Catholic Theological Society of America.
C.U.	*Convenientes ex Universo* (Justice in the World), from the Synod of Bishops, 1971, in Flannery, vol. 2.
CWS	Classics of Western Spirituality Series. Mahwah, N.J.: Paulist Press, various dates.

Denziger — *Enchiridion Symbolorum,* edited by Heinrich Denziger. In English as *The Sources of Catholic Dogma,* translated by Roy J. Deferrari from the 30th ed. of *Enchiridion Symbolorum.* St Louis: Herder, 1957.

DN — *The Dark Night.* In *The Collected Works of Saint John of the Cross,* rev. ed., translated by Kieran Kavanaugh and Otilio Rodriguez. With revisions and introduction by Kieran Kavanaugh. Washington. D.C.: Institute of Carmelite Studies, 1991.

E.E. — *Essential Elements in Church Teaching on Religious Life,* from the Congregation for Religious and Secular Institutes. English translation in *Origins* 13 (1983): 133–42.

E.T. — *Evangelica Testificatio* (Apostolic Exhortation on the Renewal of Religious Life), Paul VI, 1971, in Flannery, vol. 1.

Flannery — Flannery, Austin P., ed. *Vatican Council II: The Conciliar and Postconciliar Documents,* 2 vols. Grand Rapids: Eerdmans, 1975 and 1984.

FORUS — Nygren, David J., and Miriam D. Ukeritis, *The Future of Religious Orders in the United States: Transformation and Commitment.* Foreword by David C. McClelland. Westport, Conn.: Praeger, 1993.

G.S. — *Gaudium et Spes* (Pastoral Constitution on the Church in the Modern World), in Flannery, vol. 1.

I.I. — *Inter Insigniores* (Declaration on the Admission of Women to the Ministerial Priesthood) of the Sacred Congregation for the Doctrine of the Faith, 1976, in Flannery, vol. 2.

LCWR   Leadership Conference of Women Religious.

L.G.   *Lumen Gentium* (Dogmatic Constitution on the Church), in Flannery, vol. 1.

N.A.   *Nostra Aetate* (Declaration on the Relation of the Church to Non-Christian Religions), in Flannery, vol. 1.

NCR   *National Catholic Reporter.*

P.C.   *Perfectae Caritatis* (Decree on the Up-to-Date Renewal of Religious Life), in Flannery, vol. 1.

P.O.   *Presbyterorum Ordinis* (The Ministry and Life of Priests), in Flannery, vol. 1.

S.C.   *Sacrosanctum Concilium* (Constitution on the Sacred Liturgy), in Flannery, vol. 1.

S.R.V.   *Sacris Religionis Vinculis* (Introduction to the Rite of Initiation to the Religious Life) of the Sacred Congregation for Divine Worship, 1970, in Flannery, vol. 2.

U.R.   *Unitatis Redintegratio* (Decree on Ecumenism), in Flannery, vol. 1.

WOC   Women's Ordination Conference.

Introduction

In preconciliar days Religious[1] themselves and their lifeform were easy to "find," both in the physical sense of recognition and location and in the theological sense of situation in relation to reality outside and inside the Church. Religious Life was a form of life in the Roman Catholic Church characterized by the lifelong profession of the evangelical counsels of poverty, chastity, and obedience according to the approved constitutions of a particular order or congregation. Religious themselves were easily located in their special domiciles (convents or monasteries) and easily recognized inside or outside their institutions by their distinctive dress (habit). Both the lifeform itself and the high visibility of the members effectively separated Religious from "the world" outside the Church and distinguished Religious from "the laity" in the Church.

Today, "finding" the phenomenon is anything but easy. First, it is difficult to "locate" Religious as individuals and second, it is difficult to "situate" Religious Life as a lifeform. The difficulty in *locating* Religious arises not only nor even primarily from the fact that, in general, they no longer wear distinctive dress nor live in special housing. It arises from the overlap between Religious and others in regard to very significant features of their life, which raises the question of the distinctive meaning or purpose of Religious Life itself. For example, we are now well aware that monasticism is not specific to Christianity. Monasticism seems to arise from the constellation of a human archetype across time, in many cultures and in both genders, which has given rise to both eremitical and cenobitical forms of monasticism in virtually all the great literate religious traditions. The question of whether there is anything specifically Christian about Religious Life or whether it is simply the Christian version of an anthropological constant is quite legitimate.

It is also the case that Religious, especially women Religious, as they have interacted with a wide variety of people who are not Catholic or even Christian, religious believers, or women, have found that they have far more in common with some of these colleagues and friends than they do with many Religious of their own congregations. For example, a Religious can find herself asking whether she experiences herself primarily as a peace activist, a theologian, a feminist, a Sister of Mercy, a doctor, an ecologist, or even a Catholic.

Furthermore, even within Christianity and specifically within Catholicism, the canonically clear-cut divisions among clergy, Religious, and laity (which were never really as clear-cut as they seemed to be in preconciliar days) have become quite fuzzy in practice if not in law. Are clerical Religious primarily clergy or primarily Religious? And what of nonclerical Religious whose primary ministries are clerical, such as pastoring parishes and serving as chaplains, and thus whose primary social location is the diocesan structure rather than their Religious community? Are nonordained Religious primarily laity or actually neither laity nor clergy? And what is to be said of laity, married or single, who participate actively and sometimes by formal commitment in the life and ministry of Religious congregations as associates, members of third orders, or by other titles? Are members of so-called noncanonical communities Religious or not, theologically if not canonically?

All of these overlappings and interactions between Religious and others raise in an acute way the question of the theological-spiritual meaning of Religious Life itself. If it claims to be a particular realization of Christian life, then there must be something *particular* about it, and it must actually *realize*, that is, incarnate and bring about, that something.

In short, there are major questions about meaning, identity, and boundaries that have arisen in the past two decades that require examination and demand some kind of (at least provisional) response if Religious themselves are to know who and what they are and if the Religious lifeforms in the Church and world are to be clear and compelling. These questions are important, not because lack of clarity makes some people feel insecure or because there is some ecclesiastical or spiritual "turf" to be guarded as exclusive property. They are important because, first, living with integrity and persevering commitment, to say nothing of joy and enthusiasm, depends upon a sense of the meaning and significance of one's life commitment. And second, healthy relationships of Religious within and beyond the Church depend in significant ways on a deeply appropriated and nondefensive identity of Religious within and among themselves. This identity is the basis for witness and participation in the ongoing human enterprise of utopia or, in Christian terms, the realization of the Reign of God in this world.

"Finding" Religious Life today is also a problem of *situating* the life in relation to a variety of realities that have only marginally touched Religious Life in the past, if indeed they touched it at all. This problem is especially acute because there is no single grid upon whose coordinates to plot the features of the life and thereby pinpoint its exact place in relation to other realities on the same grid. Each question or issue is a world in itself, and these worlds overlap without being coterminous or identical.

For example, Religious Life that is essentially an intense faith life within a particular world religion (Christianity) and that was once able to assume that all its members believed all of the dogmas and espoused all of the moral and spiritual practices of that tradition (whether or not this was actually true of any particular Religious) is caught up today in the postmodern theological whirlwind in which no tradition can remain hermetically sealed and serenely confident of its own unique validity and superiority. This is having titanic repercussions in the personal faith life of individual Religious. And how, in such circumstances, to bring a congregation together in faith without coercion is a monumental task for leaders of such groups. Religious today must situate themselves in a very shifting landscape of developing theology and spirituality.

Religious, especially women Religious, are also facing the agonizing problem of how to situate themselves in relation to the institution of Roman Catholicism. Catholicism's entrenched patriarchy and resulting antiwoman practice, which were accepted as natural and God-ordained in the past, are now perceived as intolerable by most women Religious, and the assumed control of Religious congregations by the Vatican, historically but no longer accepted as natural and self-evidently justified, has alienated many committed Religious from the institutional Church even as they remain deeply attached to their congregations. Religious must resituate themselves today in relation to both the ecclesial reality of Church as the Body of Christ and the People of God, and the ecclesiastical reality of Vatican-centered Roman Catholicism.

Feminism, a worldwide movement for the emancipation and participation of women, has deeply penetrated women's Religious Life. Feminism is not simply an inner attitude or a personal stance; it is a public commitment to an active praxis of subversion of patriarchy, liberation of women and other oppressed groups, and reconstruction of family, society, and Church as communities of equals. How is this agenda related to the evangelical agenda of preaching the Gospel? Do Religious take their direction from a patriarchal ecclesiastical organization or from an emancipatory liberation movement? Religious, especially women, must situate themselves in relation to feminism and other movements (for example, peacemaking or ecology) that may or may not have a relationship to Catholicism but that are, in any case, not identical or coterminous with it and definitely not under its control.

The purpose of volume 1 is to address this global issue of locating and situating Religious Life in the vastly expanded context in which it now finds itself, recognizing that this context is not a surrounding reality like the frame around a painting, but is more like the water in which a fish swims or the air that we breathe. The context is outside and inside. Religious Life affects and is affected by the medium, or more exactly the array of media, in which it lives.

It is crucial to recognize that the array of issues and realities that constitute the pervasive ambiance of Religious Life are not commensurate with one another. In a sense, each is a world in itself or belongs to a world to which the others do not belong. Theological pluralism, interreligious dialogue, feminism, postmodernist spirituality, ecclesiastical hierarchicalism, the mystical-prophetic vocation, and so on are not topical subpoints under a general, unifying heading. This variety of problematics determines the approach to this overarching question of "finding" Religious Life today, of locating and situating Religious and their lifeform in the postmodern context in which we find ourselves.

Postmodern thinkers have borrowed a French word that is difficult to translate to talk about how issues have to be approached in this pluralistic and fragmented world that no longer enjoys a unitary worldview, a global metanarrative into which everything somehow fits. *Bricolage* means piecemeal work, an assembling from what is at hand for the best solution to the presenting problem without trying to establish that such a solution is some kind of absolute, valid for all time, and self-evidently compelling for all who can reason. Some people have used the image of the quilt, made of whatever pieces are available but achieving beauty through the assemblage itself under the craft of the quilter. The unity of the final product and its utility result not from a preordained plan correctly followed but from the inner directedness of the one creating.

In volume 1 I am going to engage in a multidisciplinary and interdisciplinary bricolage. In ten separate but not unrelated chapters I will take up the issues evoked above, and some others that are similar, in order to describe and analyze the context and suggest a meaning for contemporary first-world Religious Life.

Part 1 attempts to locate Religious Life in its human context. In chapter 1 I will discuss Christian Religious Life as a human phenomenon, that is, an anthropological, psychological, and sociological vocation within the context of analogous phenomena in other world religions in search of both its commonality with these analogues and its Christian specificity. In chapter 2 we will turn to the sociological question of Religious Life as an organic lifeform and as an institution, and what that might suggest about appropriate boundaries and creative interactivity with the surrounding environment. Finally, chapter 3 will be devoted to the question of whether the project of Religious Life can make sense in the historical-cultural setting of millennial postmodernity.

Against the background of these considerations part 2 will be devoted to trying to locate Religious Life in its specifically Christian context as a theological, spiritual, ecclesiastical, and ecclesial reality. In chapter 4, which is foundational to all that follows, I will investigate the theological meaning of the life of consecrated celibacy as a prophetic vocation in the Church. In chapters 5 and 6, which are really two parts of one topic, I will suggest an interpretation of the experience of renewal in Religious Life since the Council as a kind of corporate spiritual "dark night" that has and is effecting a deep purification and transformation of the life itself and the people who live it. Borrowing a metaphor suggested by another commentator on Religious Life, I am suggesting that Religious Life went into the conciliar vortex as a pretty impressive dinosaur, a huge, intimidating, and seemingly indestructible ecclesiastical phenomenon, and that it is emerging, like some species of the dinosaurs of old (which are not really extinct but have evolved into birds), as a songbird, much smaller, more fragile, less controlling, but perhaps in the long run more essential to a world in which beauty is more important than raw physical power. In chapters 7 and 8, again two parts of one topic, I look at Religious Life as an ecclesiastical phenomenon in an effort to make sense of the hierarchical, canonical, and theological situation of Religious in the Church and to engage some of the thorny issues raised by the intersection of this situation with conciliar ecclesiology and contemporary experience among the People of God. Finally, in chapters 9 and 10, also two parts of one topic, I try to draw on all that has preceded to interpret the historical emergence of the form of Religious Life that most women Religious in the first world live today, namely, a form that is truly Religious and contemplative without being cloistered and ministerial without being clerical, or what I call mobile, ministerial Religious Life. In these chapters I take up the issue of charism and charisms, discuss in greater detail the prophetic spirituality arising from the charism of Religious

Life in the Church, and suggest some implications for the participation of Religious Life in particular issues with which the People of God are engaged today, such as the interreligious encounter, the dialectic between religion and spirituality, and feminism in the ecclesial context.

How each of these issues is related to the others is something that cannot be nailed down in any permanent or essentialist way. Characteristic of postmodernism is the necessity to hold a variety of separate but somehow related realities at the same time, to juggle a variety of unlike objects without dropping any of them. Nothing that can be said about these various factors will bring us to a stable situation in which Religious Life can be defined as some kind of Platonic essence whose "elements" are clearly delineated and henceforth unchangeable. Rather, I hope to facilitate insight into the variety of factors that constitute and contextualize contemporary Religious Life. Much of what I write will be contested by others whose vision is perhaps more acute than mine; and much will require revision before the ink is dry on the paper because of significant changes in contemporary life. But if the project is at all successful it will contribute some clarity about what the issues are, what is at stake in each area, what some of the deadends and some of the promising options might be, what resources are available for engagement with our reality, and why the effort toward coherence and clarity is worth the candle.

Every religious, finally, must continue to work out, day by day, in relation to the multifarious reality in which she or he finds her or himself, what the life means and how it can be lived coherently and persuasively today. There is no prefabricated game plan that merely requires to be executed. But neither are we condemned to mindless incoherence, uncritical eclecticism, or sheer dissipation. Bricolage built the medieval cathedrals, and these unsigned masterpieces, built over decades or even centuries, have a unity and a beauty that have never been surpassed. Religious life is a work in process. No one but the Spirit of God is in control. The aim of *Finding the Treasure* is not control but insight.

The issues with which this volume is concerned are complex and are often sources of deep suffering for the people whose life is under discussion. But I hope that what will emerge from the engagement of this admittedly difficult subject matter will be a sense of the meaningfulness and the ultimate significance for Church and world of this lifeform. I hope it will help those who live the life, those who are contemplating entering it, and those who relate to it from other situations to recognize in contemporary Religious Life a mysterious beauty, ever ancient and ever new, a treasure hidden in the field, which is worth the search and the price.

Part One

Locating Religious Life
in
Its Human Context

Chapter One

Religious Life as a Human Phenomenon among the World's Religions: Monastics, Virgins, Virtuosi

I. Introduction

When today's older Religious entered the convent sometime after 1900 and before Vatican II, neither they nor their formators had any real sense that Religious Life was not and had not always been the type of life into which they were being initiated in the novitiate. Religious Life, in other words, was seen as a kind of self-evident and nonproblematic essence that might take slightly different forms in apostolic congregations and contemplative orders, in Dominican and Mercy congregations, or in the United States and Africa. But there was little sense that this type of life was not only not a sui generis and relatively static Catholic reality but a cross-cultural phenomenon occurring in most of the major world religions and that the life itself, even within Catholicism, had undergone enormous transformations throughout history which were not simply a straight line development leading to the current form.

Today our contact with and heightened awareness of both other Christian denominations and non-Christian religious traditions makes us aware that our life is not as unique as it once seemed. This raises questions of identity and meaning that our forebears did not face. Furthermore, our highly developed historical consciousness has undermined any sense of Religious Life as some kind of static essence that has remained basically unchanged throughout Christian history. We are aware not only of the historical transitions that undermined some types of the life and brought new types into being but also of the ups and downs of the life itself, of its various types, and of its particular orders and congregations. This makes us conscious of the real possibilities in our own time of the transformation of current types of Religious Life, the emergence of new types, the decline or death of congregations, or even the disappearance of the life itself.[1]

I will put off the question of historical development and its implications for the identity of contemporary Religious until chapter 9. In this chapter, I want to consider Religious Life as a human phenomenon and raise the question of how this human phenomenon is specified by its realization in the Catholic Christian tradition. Locating Religious Life in this most fundamental way can help us to see, on the one hand, that the roots of this life are deep in our humanity. It is not a transient ecclesiastical epiphenomenon developed in and because of certain historical conditions that no longer obtain. On the other hand, it can help us realize that even though this type of life itself is not an exclusively Christian (much less Catholic) phenomenon, its Catholic realization is unique and distinctive in very important respects. Both of these realizations—of the profoundly human basis of the life (what Catholic Religious share with others) and of its Catholic Christian uniqueness (what makes it distinct)—will provide resources for our project of "locating" the life, that is, of constructing a sense of identity that is more in touch with contemporary sensibilities.

Although Religious Life is being studied today by historians, feminists, organizational theorists, and others who are beginning to realize that this life has been the context for a unique and original development of female experience and the source of remarkable cultural contributions, both of which have been virtually ignored in the recounting of Western history, I am going to limit myself to three areas of research that can illuminate the human roots of the vocation, namely, cross-cultural anthropology, psychology, and sociology.

II. The Anthropological Archetype: The Monk

Anthropology, the discipline that studies the human as socially and culturally situated, makes it clear that across cultures and throughout history virtually every literate religious tradition has given rise to a monastic form of life analogous to Christian Religious Life.[2] The recluses who lived in the temples of Sarapis around the Mediterranean basin in pre-Christian antiquity, the Alexandrian schools of philosophy in the second and third centuries, the Greek Pythagoreans, the Orphic communities in ancient Greece, Italy, Africa, and Gaul, and the Celtic Druids,[3] all exhibited features of monastic life.[4] Among the Jews, the Essenes who lived in the area of the Dead Sea in the two centuries before the Common Era, the Therapeutae whose life Philo described, the Nazirites, and the Rechabites lived ascetical community lives that would today be recognized as monastic.[5] In the East, the religion of Jainism gave rise to what is probably the oldest known form of monasticism, dating back to 1500 B.C.E. in its solitary form and to the sixth century B.C.E. in its cenobitic form.[6] Hinduism gave rise to Brahmanic monasticism, and Buddhist monasticism spread throughout India, Japan, Korea, China, Sri Lanka, and Tibet.[7] Islam also has its form of monasticism in Sufism.[8] In short, Christian monasticism is actually not only not sui generis; it is a fairly late version of a very ancient and widespread religious phenomenon. The roots of this phenomenon seem to lie deep in human nature itself.

The Christian discovery of and openness toward monasticism in non-Christian traditions in the second half of the twentieth century is largely due to the postconciliar interest in interreligious dialogue. Early in these exchanges the discussants discovered that fruitful dialogue among religions is most likely to occur when the area of exchange is spirituality, that is, the lived experience of the religion, rather than dogma, church order, or institutional structure. Not surprisingly, it was usually not the ecclesiastical officials, that is, the clergy or even the professional theologians, who were most competent in these dialogues, but rather the most intense practitioners of the spirituality who, in most cases, were the monastics.[9] Monasticism, surprisingly similar in the great religions of the world, is an institutionalized, full-time living of the characteristic spirituality of the religion and thus provides a point of articulation and encounter among the world's great spiritualities. Thomas Merton, the Cistercian monk who has been recognized as one of the most significant spiritual figures of the twentieth century, died while participating in such an interreligious meeting of monastics, Aide Inter-Monastères, in Bangkok in 1968. That group continues to meet, bringing together monastics from East and West to explore the meaning and significance of monastic life not only for the religions in which it exists but for the world itself.[10]

In November of 1980 the North American Board for East-West Dialogue, which was the American subcommission of Aide Inter-Monastères entrusted by the Vatican Secretariat for Non-Christians with a leading role in the dialogue between Christianity and the great religions of the East, held a symposium on "The Monk as Universal Archetype."[11] At the outset of the symposium Raimundo Panikkar, a theologian of religions renowned for his work in interreligious dialogue, gave a lengthy presentation that provided the basic material for the discussions. He made an important distinction between the "monk as archetype" and the "archetype of the monk."[12] The topic Panikkar discussed was not the monk *as* archetype, that is, the monk as a paradigm or ideal of human life, but rather the archetypal character *of* monasticism. Panikkar maintained that the "monk archetype" is a universal pattern or psychic paradigm of spirituality that informs the struggle toward full humanity of all serious human seekers, whether or not they become monastics in the formal institutional sense, and it is not specific to or limited within any particular religion or religious tradition. This implies that monastic life in its restricted institutional sense (including its Christian form) is rooted in a much more universal human tendency.

Panikkar pointed out a striking polarity intrinsic to this monastic archetype, namely, that when the archetype gives rise to a specific form of institutionalized monasticism, that life appears in its cultural or ecclesiastical setting as something difficult, special, and unusual, and at the same time as something to which everyone is called. It is this polarity that probably explains why, on the one hand, Catholicism has always defended the legitimacy of a special lifeform in the Church distinct from that of the Christian layperson, and Protestantism, on the other hand, has repudiated that lifeform as a threat to the universality and equality of the call to Christian holiness.[13] There is a sense in which Religious Life is both special and ordinary, the calling of a few and the realization of a call that is somehow universal.

Interestingly enough, Panikkar, in his penetrating analysis of monasticism as a human archetype, deliberately eschewed any discussion of the particularly religious dimension of monasticism. He concentrated instead on its philosophical-anthropological character. His purpose was to expose and analyze the dimensions and the dynamics of the ultimate human quest, whether or not that quest takes a religious shape, or, in other words, is specifically theocentric. The monastic impulse, he maintained, is at one and the same time the aspiration toward simplicity and the integration of complexity. It is here that he located the specificity of the monastic archetype as an anthropological constant. This archetype constellates and focuses the dynamics of any person who is consciously seeking the fullness of humanity in his or her one and only human life. In other words, Panikkar was considering monasticism as the archetype of human spirituality rather than as an institutional lifeform of particular religious traditions.[14]

Analyzing or even reporting Panikkar's fascinating development of this thesis and the discussion it provoked is beyond the scope of this chapter, but I mention it here because it raises to visibility an important feature of our topic, namely, that monasticism is not an accidental, esoteric, or insignificant development within certain religious traditions such as Catholicism. While some people espouse monasticism as a religious lifeform and devote themselves to it in a full-time way that excludes and/or relativizes every other aspect and dimension of life, it is actually something that is alive in the depths of every spiritually sensitive person, whether or not they are religiously affiliated in the institutional sense of the term. Just as the parental archetype functions in all healthy, generative adults whether or not they actually produce or raise children, so the monastic archetype functions in all spiritually healthy persons, focusing their deepest aspirations toward the fullness of life and calling for some concrete organization of those aspirations toward integrity and transcendence. The actual monastic, in any tradition, is the person who makes an exclusive life work of cultivating and realizing that universal archetype and in doing so makes it historically visible within a particular religiocultural tradition.

As universal and archetypal, then, monasticism can be tentatively defined or described as a unifying quest for the fullest possible realization of the true self in relation to reality conceived as a whole or as transcendent.[15] In different religious traditions this self-realization is variously understood as liberation, salvation, redemption, integration, perfection, or simplification. When this archetype is realized in the monastic life as a concrete lifeform it can be defined, cross-culturally, as a "religious institution[s], ritual, and belief system[s] whose agents, members, or participants attempt to practice religious works that are above and beyond those required by the religious teachings of their society or of exceptional individual religious and spiritual leaders in their society, i.e., those who have interpreted radically the tenets that apply to all believers or to the whole society."[16] It is also characteristic of institutional monastic life that its adherents attempt to do this on a full-time basis to the exclusion of anything that is not directly related to the monastic project. It is this choice to go beyond what is required by undertaking a full-time and exclusive quest for the transcendent that makes the monastic project a visible lifeform within the tradition.

Catholic Religious in active congregations, especially women, in the years since Vatican II have vigorously insisted that their lifeform is not monastic. This insistence arises from the fact that during most of their history they have been impeded in their life and ministry by the imposition of restrictions drawn from the lifestyle of enclosed orders, such as cloister, an horarium structured for the choral recitation of the Divine Office, culturally inappropriate dress, and impediments to acquiring necessary professional preparation for their ministries. Conciliar renewal has involved divesting apostolic Religious Life of these restrictive features.

However, I would suggest that Catholic Religious Life, no matter what form it takes, eremetical or cenobitic, contemplative or ministerial, stable or mobile, is in fact, in its inner reality, monastic. Religious Life is the Catholic historical realization of the monastic archetype. In other words, there is an important distinction between *monastic life* as the realization in a concrete historical lifeform of the monastic archetype and the *monastic lifestyle* of enclosed orders. Much of the monastic lifestyle is inappropriate for ministerial congregations, but monasticism as archetype is the paradigm of all Religious Life. This is the basis of the analogy between Catholic Religious Life and the parallel forms of life in other religious traditions and grounds the enlightening comparison among them.

The similarities across time and culture among monastic lifeforms is striking. The most universal and defining characteristic is perhaps the easiest to identify and the most difficult to define or describe. It is that which suggests the very name "monastic," namely, the "aloneness" of the Religious. The monastic is one who "goes apart" in some sense. This does not necessarily, or even usually, mean that the monastic is a hermit, although that seems to be the oldest form of the life. The cenobitic or community form of the life is far more common, and the life of wandering asceticism is still widely practiced in Asian monasticism. The aloneness or apartness of the monastic means that the she or he, either singly or with others, creates an alternative lifeform to that of the religious society at large and does so in function of a single, lone, unique objective. This usually involves a distinctive social status possessing an inveterate tendency (one recognized by Luther as particularly dangerous in the Christian community) toward elitism. But whether Religious are admired or despised in their respective traditions, their lifeform is distinctive. Celibacy, not usually undertaken as a lifetime commitment in most traditions, is very frequently a constitutive element of this distinctiveness and, as we will see, has a special role in Catholic Religious Life where it is undertaken as permanent.

Across cultures monastic life begins with the personal decision of the aspiring monastic to embrace the life. This personally discerned vocation is usually tested by the elders of the institution who, if they accept the novice, usually initiate him or her into the life by allowing or requiring the neophyte to profess some kind of perpetual or temporary vows and to don the special dress or insignia of the order. Life within the order virtually always demands a commitment to voluntary poverty, which in some traditions is extreme, involving daily begging for sustenance, and in others is a moderate form of simplicity of life within often well-endowed monastic settlements. (It is interesting that historically the acquisition of wealth by the individual or by the community has almost always led to a decline in the lifeform and has necessitated a call for reform if the community was to survive.) The life also demands some form of submission by the members to the authority structure of the monastic community. Sometimes this takes the form of a rigorous and intimate master-disciple relationship, and sometimes it is the submission of all to the officials of the order and/or its codified legislation and customs.

Life in the monastic community, and even the life of the hermit, is virtually always regulated by a fixed schedule or horarium whose purpose is to create an orderly and disciplined lifestyle conducive to the practices intrinsic to the life. These practices are fairly common across cultures and religious traditions: asceticism in the form of silence and solitude, fasting, restriction of sleep, and exposure to the elements; meditation and chanting; confession of and public penances for infractions of the rules; study of the sacred texts of the tradition; work for the common good. Very often the monastic community becomes a center of learning and of transmission of the culture, both sacred and profane.[17]

One of the major distinctions among the monasticisms of different cultures arises from the relation of the monastic life-form to the surrounding culture. Basically, there seem to be three patterns of such relationship. In some cases an entire religious group attempts to live a radical version of its faith and becomes, in effect, a monastery or religious order. The Shakers are a good example of a monastic experiment of this type that was very successful during its lifetime and lasted longer than most such experiments.[18] Cults and sects of various kinds are similar, and often disastrous, attempts. In one sense, this version of the monastic life, the radical utopian community, is atypical and usually short-lived. For one thing, if the group espouses celibacy, as the Shakers did, it becomes totally dependent for its continuance on conversions from the outside social system with which it seldom has close or even friendly relations rather than, as in more typical situations, recruiting members from its own surrounding religious culture. Also, when an entire tradition attempts to live a radical form of its faith, it often must create and maintain, by totalitarian authority structures, indoctrination, and coercion, a level of collective belief and behavior that amounts to fanaticism, that cannot be sustained over the long haul, and that sometimes leads to bizarre and dangerous conclusions. Jim Jones's People's Temple and the Heaven's Gate experiments, both of which ended in mass suicide, were particularly shocking examples of this phenomenon. Monasticism is, like art, a particular and specialized vocation, and it is probably not meant to supplant ordinary life within a religious tradition.

A second type of relationship between the monastic life and the surrounding culture is particularly characteristic of Buddhism in its various cultural forms. Buddhism is an essentially monastic religion in that final liberation or salvation is not generally believed to be possible for anyone except the monastic. While the life of the householder is legitimate and honorable, it is insufficient for the attainment of release from the cycle of reincarnation. Finally, in some life, the Buddhist must become a monk if the karmic cycle is to be transcended. In this system the monastic is the true and perfect practitioner of the tradition, and the laity constitute a support system for the monastic life. The vast numbers of monks and nuns in the Buddhist tradition, which includes both those who live as monastics until death and those who spend some time in monastic life and then depart to take up lay life, is explained by this understanding of monastic life as the only fully adequate form of Buddhism.

The third type of relationship, and that which is characteristic of Christian Religious Life, is that of a small specialized group within a tradition that regards lay life as normative. The consistent challenge to Religious Life as a specialized form of life within the larger religious tradition is to make actual practice accord with theory. Although lay life is, in theory, normative and a fully salvific form of Christian life, the Religious Life is actually regarded by many Catholics, including some Religious themselves, as the superior way to serve God. The presentation in much preconciliar (and sadly, some postconciliar) Church teaching of Religious Life as the "way of perfection," as a "closer following of Jesus," or as a more undistracted and single-minded form of discipleship[19] has reinforced this view of Religious Life as superior and fostered the elitism that has distorted Religious Life itself and its relationship with the larger tradition. Since Vatican II Religious congregations, especially nonclerical orders, have been struggling to define themselves in nonelitist terms and to reintegrate Religious Life into the larger believing community without loss of identity and focus.

Recognition of Catholic Religious Life as a particular realization of the anthropological constant of monasticism puts us in position to draw some conclusions about the life. First, this anthropological universality should provide some reassurance that Religious Life, despite the enormous challenges it currently faces, is not going to disappear from the Catholic landscape. Although some orders or congregations and even some particular types of the life may disappear, the life itself will survive or be reinvented, because the human archetype that gives rise to this lifeform in virtually all religious traditions will remain active in Catholicism.

Second, Religious should not hesitate to recognize and proclaim their lifeform as monastic even if this is not the preferred terminology in most settings. Monasticism as the single-minded concern with the God-quest, institutionalized in a distinct lifeform, is at the heart of Religious Life no matter what type of Religious Life the particular order or congregation embraces. The lifestyle elements of cloistered Religious Life[20] are not what makes the life monastic. In their eagerness to reappropriate and legitimize the apostolic character of their life, some ministerial Religious have become very hesitant to forthrightly acknowledge their deepest vocational motivation, the single-minded and exclusive devotion to the quest for holiness. Whatever motivated most Religious to undertake the life, and few would not admit to very mixed motives at the time of entrance, they would find it very difficult to sustain Religious Life today if the absorption in the God-quest were not the fundamental motivating factor in their lives.[21]

Third, and most important for our purpose in this section of locating Catholic Religious Life in the broader context of the human spiritual quest common to all the world religions, it is very important to be clear about the specific differences that distinguish Catholic Religious Life from monasticism in other religious traditions. Three such distinctions are particularly important.

The first and most basic specific difference between Catholic Religious Life and forms of monasticism in other religious traditions is the focus of Catholic Religious Life on the PERSON OF JESUS, who is believed to be not merely an historical personage upon whose memory to model one's life but living and interactively present in the life of the believer. This living relationship with the resurrected Christ is the basis and only truly adequate explanation for the most consistent and characteristic feature of Catholic Religious Life, namely, the *lifelong commitment to consecrated celibacy*. From its inception in the life of the consecrated virgins of the first century through all its permutations up to the present, Christian Religious Life has always involved perpetual profession of religiously motivated celibacy.

There are basically three motivations for celibacy as a practice within monasticism. Most characteristic of non-Christian forms is the ascetic motivation, which focuses on achieving control of the most imperious bodily urges and the pacification of passions. Closely related to the ascetic motivation is that of removing from one's daily life the burdens and responsibilities of family life, which distract one from ascetical practice, interfere with the monastic horarium, and restrict one's freedom to travel for purposes of begging, pilgrimage, teaching, or seeking greater solitude. While both of these motivations have, at times, been offered in support of Christian celibacy, neither of them has been fully convincing even in times past. Today, in a climate of renewed appreciation of sexuality, marriage, and family, they are even more evidently deficient within the Christian context. And it is interesting to note that neither perpetual commitment to monastic life nor to lifelong celibacy has been a common feature of non-Christian monastic life, in which celibacy is a means to an end, as is the monastic life itself.

For Catholic Religious the only fully adequate motivation for lifelong consecrated celibacy is the relationship of the Religious to Jesus Christ.[22] This relationship is experienced as a total affective involvement that is incompatible with an analogous marital relationship with another human being, and in its psychological-spiritual exclusivity is self-evidently and necessarily permanent, as is the relationship between spouses. This experience, which is at the heart of the vocation to Catholic Religious Life, implies no negative judgment on human sexuality or pejorative comparison with marriage. It is a personal response to a personal call that is specific but neither superior nor normative. Although there are undoubtedly many people who have entered Catholic Religious congregations for other reasons, often excellent in themselves, none of these reasons seems capable of fully justifying and sustaining, in the face of competing affective possibilities, the lifelong commitment to consecrated celibacy.[23] When celibacy is freely chosen, not as a means to an end but as the expression of a particular relationship with Jesus Christ, it is clearly distinguishable from the ascetical celibacy of non-Christian monasticism.

Faith in and commitment to Jesus Christ also involves a specifically Christian *conception of salvation* that leads to monastic beliefs and practices that are quite different from those of non-Christian monastics. Catholic Religious Life is not aimed at liberation from physical or bodily life in history. Christian faith in Jesus involves the conviction that the one who believes in him has eternal life here and now and that whatever follows human death is not substantially different from the life of grace. In other words, for the Christian believer, and therefore for the Christian Religious, grace and glory are substantively continuous. Consequently, although there have certainly been periods in Christian history in which life in this world has been denigrated in favor of a celestial afterlife, this is a theological aberration that leads to practical distortions. The authentic Christian conviction of the continuity between grace and glory and the goodness of creation, including one's own bodily person, relativizes and refocuses the ascetical element in Religious Life, which is not aimed at releasing one from the conditions of time but attuning one to the present experience of eternal life in Christ.

The second characteristic feature of Religious Life that distinguishes it from its non-Christian analogues is its situation within the ECCLESIAL SETTING of Catholicism. The fact that Religious Life is not an alternative to but a form of Catholicism has several consequences. First, despite the fact that elitism has tainted both the theory and practice of Catholic Religious Life throughout most of its history, any claim by Religious to superiority in the believing community is actually theologically unjustified. This is definitely not true of non-Christian monasticism, which has always been understood as either the only fully authentic and genuine form of spirituality in relation to a less perfect lay life or as an elite form of spirituality in relation to an ordinary form. Theologically, in the Christian tradition, there is no substantial distinction in the life of grace, that is, in participation in the life of

Christ, among the baptized. The only real distinction arises from the intensity of the person's love of God. Sanctity, not state of life, is the only qualitatively significant distinction of one believer from another. Religious Life is a minority position within the larger community which is normatively lay, and its only justification is a personal vocation not to preeminence in the community but to a particular relationship with Jesus Christ, which is *distinctive without being superior.*

Second, the situation of Catholic Religious Life within the ecclesial community places it in a relationship of *mutual and equal complementarity with the other consecrated state of Christian life, matrimony.* If the mystery of the Resurrection, which renders Jesus personally present to the believer, exercises a particularly powerful influence in the vocation to Religious Life, the mystery of the Incarnation, which grounds the positive evaluation of the flesh and of history, exercises a determining influence in the vocation to matrimony. Marriage, in the Christian community, is not a surrender to the inferior desires of human nature but a sacramental participation in the mystery of the union between Christ and the Church (cf. Eph 5:32). Consequently, unlike non-Christian monasticism, in which celibacy is characteristically undertaken as a superior ascetical practice, the consecrated celibacy of the Christian Religious is an accentuated witness to certain aspects of the Christian Mystery while the sexually expressed unity of baptized spouses is the accentuated witness to other aspects. The Church needs both forms of witness and they need each other.

Finally, because of the situation of Catholic Religious Life within the ecclesial community, it is essentially and always *a form of Gospel life.* The Gospel, as Vatican II reminded Religious, is the ultimate norm of all Christian life and therefore of Religious Life.[24] Consequently, all of the elements of classical monastic life are relativized for the Christian Religious. The spiritual mentor, whether superior, formator, or spiritual director, never really takes the place of Christ; the Rule never supersedes the Gospel; the rhythm of life is always governed by the liturgical cycles of the Church's year. In other words, Catholic Religious Life is first of all and substantively Christian life itself.

The particularity of Religious Life as a lifeform, although it makes the life distinctive, can never legitimately separate it from the larger community, elevate its members above their fellow Christians, or create a style of life that is not centered on and governed by the Gospel. In this respect it differs significantly from non-Christian forms of monastic life, which either set the standards for the larger community or become a substantive alternative to the mainstream religious life of the community.

A third cluster of specific characteristics of Catholic Religious Life concerns its RELATIONSHIP WITH THE WORLD. Although there has been a long history of world denial in Christianity in general and a fortiori in Religious Life, hatred of creation and focus on an otherworldly realm is not theologically justified within the Judaeo-Christian religious tradition. As Vatican II clearly proclaimed, the reality, the goodness, and the destiny of God's creation grounds a legitimate and committed secularity (not to be equated with secularism) on the part of the believer.[25] Consequently, Catholic Religious, unlike their non-Christian monastic counterparts, cannot construe or construct their life as an escape from this world.

The understanding of *mission and ministry* as intrinsic to Religious Life, even to enclosed contemplative life, flows directly from the Christian theology of this world as the locus and material of the Reign of God. Religious Life does involve a certain type of "going apart," the creation of an alternative lifeform in relation not only to the ecclesial community as a whole but to secular life. However, the Gospel itself offers a very nuanced and pluriform interpretation of the "world" as a theological category. All Christians, including Religious, must affirm the goodness and finality of the world, which God so loved as to give the only Son (cf. Jn 3:16), and be actively involved in furthering the mission of Jesus to the world. In this respect, Christian Religious Life differs markedly from many non-Christian forms of monasticism.

The positive evaluation of material creation, including the world and the body, also involves a *relativization of the ascetical ideal* by Catholic Religious. Christian asceticism is not a commitment to the total subjugation, much less the dissolution, of the body. Nor can it be a commitment to a Pelagian project of achieving salvation through self-mortification and/or a Gnostic escape from the world and history. Asceticism in the Christian tradition, and therefore in Religious Life, is essentially a means of integration of body and spirit in a harmonious, fully human personhood.[26] This does not preclude the adoption by Religious of a more focused and strenuous, even more demanding, program of asceticism than that required by the normal discipline of the Church. But that program must remain in the service of integration, not destruction, must not be proposed as normative in the ecclesial community, and must not be made the basis of some claim to moral or spiritual superiority. Holiness, not asceticism, is the only title to nobility in the Christian scheme of things.

III. The Psychological Archetype: The Virgin

As already stated, the lifelong commitment to consecrated celibacy is the most distinctive characteristic feature of Catholic Religious Life. Consecrated celibacy arises from and expresses a particular relationship to Jesus Christ and thus must be clarified primarily in terms of theology and spirituality. However, as the anthropological category of the monastic archetype that can help clarify, both by way of similarity and by way of contrast, the Christian form of monastic life as monastic in relation to analogous phenomena in other religious traditions and as specifically Christian in contrast to such phenomena, so the psychological archetype of the virgin can throw some light, again by way of similarity and contrast, on the celibacy that is characteristic of Religious Life. Attention to the human substrate of the spiritual and religious characteristics of Religious Life emphasizes the rootedness of this form of life in basic human experience, while clarifying how the life transcends and transforms these natural dynamics.

It has been noted by psychologists and teachers that little girls and adolescents, including some who are neither Catholic nor Christian, often express a desire to "be a nun" when they grow up. When such an aspiration arises in a child whose religious tradition offers no such vocational possibility, we have to recognize that *nun* in this case does not designate a concrete historical phenomenon but an archetypal pattern. It is this archetype and its relationship to the reality of consecrated celibacy, both as lived by real Religious and as a corporate lifeform, that I want to investigate.

Peter Brown, the consummate historian of early Christianity, in his study of sexual renunciation in the early Church, has shown that the practice of celibacy by Christians in the first centuries was much more than a personal ascetical or mystical practice.[27] Rather, it was a withdrawal of the person from the social economy of the state. The reproductive capacities of the citizen, upon which the future of the city depended, were part of the social, economic, and political capital of the society rather than the purely private possession of the individual. It was the civic duty of young men and women to marry and to reproduce. Women in particular derived their primary social identity and value from their bearing of children. Consequently, for early Christian women and men to refuse to marry was not considered a private religious decision but a challenge to social order. Specifically, it was a reservation of one's sexuality, and therefore of one's person and posterity, from the all-encompassing demands of the social order. Virginity constituted a redefinition of selfhood and personhood, one that established a certain heretofore unheard of autonomy of the individual in relation to family and society. The category of autonomy is the point of connection between the historical development of Christian consecrated celibacy and the psychological archetype of the virgin that we will now explore.

The notion of the psychological archetype was developed by C. G. Jung.[28] According to Jung an archetype is a pattern of instinctual behavior in the collective unconscious of the human race. Because the collective unconscious is universal rather than specific to one race, people, or religion, these archetypes are found everywhere. They come to expression in myths and fairy tales whose structures are remarkably similar among peoples from all areas and eras, although the stories are conditioned by the images, beliefs, and cultures of the specific societies. "As preexistent patterns, they influence how we behave and how we react to others."[29] Experiences in the personal life of an individual can constellate the archetype as actual emotions and behaviors unique to the person but similar to those of others under the influence of the same archetype. For example, the birth of her child might activate the mother archetype in a woman, who will then mother in ways consonant with her own culture and personality. Or, a very unhealthy activation of the mother archetype sometimes occurs when a woman encounters a needy and immature man.

Esther Harding, one of the earliest and most respected women Jungian analysts, wrote a book on the "feminine principle" in which she explored, among other archetypes and dynamics, the "virgin goddess" archetype. She supplied the description that has been taken up by later theorists:

> ...the woman who is virgin, one-in-herself, does what she does—not because of any desire to please, not to be liked, or to be approved, even by herself; not because of any desire to gain power over another, to catch his interest or love, but because what she does is true. Her actions may, indeed, be unconventional. She may have to say no, when it would be easier, as well as more adapted, conventionally speaking, to say yes. But as virgin she is not influenced by the considerations that make the nonvirgin woman, whether married or not, trim her sails and adapt herself to expediency. I say whether married or not, for in using this term *virgin* in its psychological connotation, it refers not to external circumstances but to an inner attitude. A woman who has a psychological attitude to life which makes her dependent on what other people think, which makes her do and say things she really does not approve, is no virgin in this meaning of the term. She is not one-in-herself but acts always as female counterpart or syzygy to some male. This "male" may be an actual man...or it may be some quite abstract *idea*....[which is] the manifestation[s] of the male within her, her own animus, and she is related to this psychological male in much the same way as many married women are related to their husbands.[30]

This description contains a number of important ideas for what follows. First, the virgin archetype has more to do with the inner autonomy of the person with respect to outside influences and forces than to physical intactness.[31] Second, the psychological virgin archetype often puts the person in whom it is realized in conflict with the "conventional" or the accepted in her or his surroundings. Third, the archetype is not strictly limited in its realization to either women or those who have never had sexual intercourse. Because the notion of being inviolate, unpenetrated, "one-in-oneself" is so well symbolized by the physical intactness of the woman who has never been entered sexually by a man, the female physical virgin is the natural picture of this archetype, but men can also realize it and so can widows, women in a healthy marriage, or the divorced who have transcended the negativity of their marital experience. Fourth, the "male" influence that violates the virgin archetype is not necessarily a real man or even the influence of a real man. It is unhealthy heteronomous influence that moves the person to think or act against her or his own integrity. Harding is discussing women's experience and perceptively notes that the negative influence that makes women act contrary to their own integrity comes most often from men, either real males in their environment or the "internalized" male voice or animus that undermines women's autonomy.

Jean Shinoda Bolen, a contemporary American Jungian analyst, took up Jung's theory of the archetype and Harding's description of the virgin archetype but developed their theories beyond the stereotype-prone animus/anima dichotomy of Jung within which Harding operated.[32] Bolen, following Jung's insight that the archetypes of the unconscious appear in the myths of various peoples, looked at the Greek Olympian story as an enlightening Western myth in which the archetypes are personified. She studied the genealogies, personae, and "histories" of the seven primary goddesses of the classical Greek pantheon as a sevenfold typology of the feminine archetype. Three of these goddesses (Artemis, Athena, and Hestia) present variations on the virgin archetype; three (Hera, Demeter, and Persephone) manifest the vulnerable or primarily affiliative archetype; and one (Aphrodite), goddess of love and beauty, offers a transformational archetype.

The great advance of Bolen's theory is that it offers at least seven very diverse archetypal patterns of genuine femininity, including several that are characterized by what were previously thought of as "masculine" traits only available to women through their recessive "animus." It is especially the virgin goddesses as archetypal who offer ideals of genuinely feminine courage, wisdom, intelligence, focus, originality, ingenuity, physical prowess, creativity, competitiveness, sisterliness and egalitarian relationships. In her theory the virgin archetype is differentiated and complex. I want to summarize her presentation in order to examine how the virgin archetype in its variety can help illuminate the human substrate of the phenomenon of consecrated celibacy, especially as lived by women Religious.

In the schema Bolen develops, Artemis, goddess of the hunt and of the moon, is the personification "of an independent feminine spirit. The archetype she represents enables a woman to seek her own goals on terrain of her own choosing."[33] Artemis was a favorite daughter of Zeus who offered to grant her whatever she asked. Artemis asked for a silver bow and arrow, a pack of hounds to aid her in her hunting, nymphs to accompany her in her exploits, a short tunic so that she could run free, mountains and wilderness as her special place to roam, and eternal chastity. Thus the Artemis archetype is realized in women who are highly attractive to but remain independent of men, prize their freedom and autonomy, can take care of themselves, are close to nature and animals, are egalitarian and helpful in their relationships with women, and seek their own goals (which may or may not be prized by others or approved by society) in realms of their own choosing.

Like all the archetypes, the Artemis archetype has its negativities. Artemis can be contemptuous of weakness and vulnerability in others, aloof and "cool" in relationships, emotionally inaccessible, merciless when angered or offended. In short, the Artemis woman needs to develop her relationality, openness to others, and capacity for bondedness.

Athena, who sprang full-grown from the head of the father-god Zeus, was stunningly beautiful, appearing in full golden armor as the goddess of wisdom, war, and crafts. She was the superb strategist who made the Greeks successful in their wars and the skilled craftsperson who made them productive in peace. She was eminently practical, efficient, focused, logical, unmoved by overwhelming emotion.

Her major difference from Artemis is that Athena is male-identified. She is preeminently her father's daughter. She gravitates toward men who are important, powerful, and authoritative, and she identifies with the patriarchal social order, which works well for her because she is equal to or better than any man. She avoids entanglement with men but she works well with them as colleague, companion, and confidante. Women, who are generally "inferior" to her as they are to men, are much less interesting to her, and she will oppose any attempt by women to upset the patriarchal order. Athena is the woman who has never felt oppressed by men and who is complimented by being told she thinks or operates "like a man." She is mature, pragmatic, self-contained, moderate, realistic rather than idealistic, diplomatic, and interested in important matters, which she almost always handles very well.

Athena's negative traits, like most people's, are the obverse of her virtues. She lives in her head, never letting herself get out of control, never surrendering to passion. Thus she tends to be alienated from the wealth of emotional power that she rarely lets surface. Athena can have a "Medusa" effect on people, devitalizing their experience, being insensitive to their deepest concerns, and impervious to moral and spiritual matters that are not relevant to her projects. She can, like the Medusa on her shield, turn people to stone. Athena is capable of intimidating and even terrorizing those over whom she has authority, especially if they are less competent than she is. Athena can also be so goal-fixated that the end comes to justify the means and she can find it hard to put global concerns or commitment to ideals ahead of her personal projects or objectives.

Hestia is the goddess of the hearth and home, the inward-focused natural contemplative among the virgin goddesses.

She is retiring and largely invisible, represented less as a persona than as the fire in the hearth. Although not usually seen, she has a warm, energizing, peaceful and centering effect on others, who feel welcomed and affirmed in her presence. Hestia is not concerned with goals or projects outside herself. She is occupied with her inner agenda and with making the house a home, bringing loved ones together, and facilitating relationships among them.

Hestia's negative features are less violent or destructive than those of Artemis or Athena. Her main problem is a lack of initiative and ambition. Her creativity, which is very real in her own domain, does not produce in the world of war, work, or thought. In fact, producing at all can be a problem for the Hestia woman who can happily spend hours arranging the flowers, folding the clothes, preparing the festive meal, receiving her guests, and reflecting on what concerns her. There is little time, energy, or motivation left for getting anything done in the "worldly" sphere. Hestia's major problem is her anonymity, her tendency to self-effacement and avoidance of assertion. She is not likely to resist domination, her own or anyone else's, and thus can let herself be taken for granted, doing all the work without being recognized for it or taken into account in the decision making about it. She does not get involved in issues of justice or right and will compromise on nonpersonal matters for the sake of peace. She does not easily see a connection between her own integrity, which she prizes above all, and the struggle for justice in the world around her sanctuary.

In the foregoing descriptions we see three versions of the virgin (or nun) archetype, which are patterns realized in innumerable ways in many real women who may or may not be actually celibate. Bolen suggests that women in whom a particular psychological archetype is strong will tend to seek a life situation in which their natural inclinations can be realized. Thus, for example, the woman in whom the Hera (wife) archetype is strong will seek marriage (or union with a powerful man) even above children, and the Demeter (mother archetype) woman is more concerned with children than with a spouse. Women in whom the virgin goddess archetype is strong are less concerned with marriage and family and more likely to seek their personal fulfillment in goal-oriented achievement and contemplative pursuits. They may be politicians or scientists, outdoorswomen or athletes, educators or researchers, hermits or contemplatives, poets or artists, administrators or builders. They may or may not marry and have children, but their life does not revolve exclusively around either. And a lifeform, such as Religious Life, which is corporately dedicated to the types of pursuits characteristic of the virgin archetypes is likely to be particularly attractive.

Religious Life, I would suggest, is a natural environment for women in whom the virgin archetypes are predominant. The life was probably doubly attractive in the period before women's emancipation made career choices other than marriage and motherhood generally available. In other words, it may not be the case that every Religious, or even most of them, gave up marriage and children as the ultimate sacrifice in order to follow a "higher and more difficult calling." It is more likely the case that Religious Life offered many women the possibility of psychological development and fulfillment of their deepest human longings that domestic life did not. In other words, there may well be a deep psychological "fit" between many women and celibacy.[34] This does not negate the very real sacrifice involved in the choice to live the call to celibacy with integrity and fidelity over a lifetime, any more than marriage to one man, which precludes further "playing the field," is devoid of sacrifice. But it does mean that the inner autonomy of the virgin archetype may be the ideal pattern of psychological maturity of some women, and when it is combined, in a particular woman, with a deep love of Christ and the desire to promote the reign of God, it can supply the natural human foundation of a vocation to consecrated celibacy.

This hypothesis is borne out, I think, by one of the findings of the 1993 Nygren and Ukeritis study of Religious in the U.S. The researchers found that not only did women Religious report "greater fidelity to the vow of chastity than did men," but also that "[m]ore specifically, both brothers and priests reported that chastity was the most difficult and least meaningful of the three vows. Sisters, on the other hand, rated chastity as least difficult and most meaningful. Sisters consistently rated obedience more difficult than [did] brothers or priests."[35] If the foregoing description of the effect of the virgin archetype in women is actually true for the majority of women Religious, it could account, on the natural level, for both the fact that women Religious found celibacy highly meaningful and relatively nonstressful and that they were usually faithful to their commitment to it. And it would also tend to explain why obedience, by contrast, was more onerous to women whose natural psychological endowment is a high level of personal autonomy and resistance to heteronomous control. Finally, it suggests that the meaning of celibacy for women and men (both groups taken in general, because there are variations in both) may be much more diverse than we have tended to think. The fact is that, until very recently, male writers working out of male experience have supplied most of the theological and ascetical theory on Religious Life and especially on celibacy. It may be time to develop a spirituality of consecrated celibacy for women on the basis of female experience of the meaning of sexuality.

The hypothesis that many if not most women who are attracted to Religious Life and find it a satisfying environment for their personal development have some strong virgin archetype influence in their psychological structure may also help explain certain obvious features, both positive and negative, of female Religious Life as an historical institution. First, Religious women as a group have been outstanding examples of high female achievement in spheres not historically considered appropriate for women. They have founded, administered, and staffed major institutions of education, health, and social service, often succeeding against nearly insuperable financial, personnel, and ecclesiastical obstacles.[36] Their history, which is attracting a great deal of attention from feminist scholars as the untold story of the most daring and accomplished cohort of women in American history and perhaps in Western history generally, is filled with women of outstanding intelligence, focus, courage, strength, determination, heroic self-sacrifice, personal discipline, and strategic cunning.[37] The self-reliance and skill of Artemis, the practical power of Athena, and the contemplative centering of Hestia have been corporate features of Religious Life as an institutional form.

Second, the history of Religious Life has been a saga of struggle over the issue of cloister. The male authorities of the Church have, since the beginning, attempted to enclose women Religious, to keep them out of the public sphere, to control their autonomy and contain their initiative, even while using their services with both appreciation and trepidation. Women Religious have both acquiesced in this effort and resisted it.[38] The acquiescing has usually been because and to the extent that women saw cloister as a validation and protection of their contemplative solitude and life of prayer. Often it has been an acceptance of an onerous restriction as the price of peace. In this acquiescence we see the Hestia archetype in full flower. However, women Religious have also, again from the beginning, resisted cloister precisely because it both subjugated them and impeded their ministerial projects. The resistance to heteronomous control and the felt need for action in service of a great cause are traits of Artemis and Athena. The struggle over cloister may be the clearest expression of the ambiguities of the virgin archetype when it is a compelling psychological feature of real women who have come together in a powerful social institution that incarnates corporately that archetype.

Finally, the ambivalence of male, especially clerical, response to women Religious, both as individuals and as communities, may have more to do with the powerful corporate institutionalization of the virgin archetype than with the reasons usually adduced for the tension. Men have much less psychological leverage in relation to virgin archetype women than in relation to affiliative archetype women. Even Athena, although she is male-identified, is never submissive to men. None of the virgin archetypes is "daddy's little girl," convinced that "father knows best," a "damsel in distress," a "sleeping beauty waiting to be kissed," or ready to "stand by her man" to her own disadvantage. The autonomy, competence, and inner-directedness of these women can fascinate, intimidate, humiliate, devitalize, challenge, and terrorize men, especially those whose own masculinity is insecure. Men often admire such women, envy them, and fear them simultaneously. A male professional or businessman can be simultaneously totally dependent upon his Athena-type administrative assistant and deeply resentful of his dependence on her. When a man enrages an Artemis woman he does not encounter the impotent emotional frustration of the "little woman" but a cool and deadly force he may not survive. And Hestia, who is so plainly unimpressed by and uninterested in his manly exploits, can undermine the male ego in devastating ways. Looked at through the prism of archetypal psychology, the historical need of a male hierarchy to swathe women in identity-suppressing veils and habits and to enclose them permanently in cloisters is less mystifying, as is the fear of feminist nuns on the part of many contemporary churchmen and their summary removal of competent women Religious from positions of pastoral influence. If Religious Life is the corporate institutionalization of the virgin archetype, the ambivalence toward it of a hierarchy composed entirely of men who are resolute in their opposition to including women in the ecclesiastical power structure is readily understandable.

However, if women in Religious Life have embodied, both individually and institutionally, the positive power of the virgin archetype, they have also manifested its negative characteristics. Many Religious themselves have testified to their suffering, in preconciliar days, under Athena-type superiors. These achievement-obsessed women drove themselves and everyone under their sway with a relentless perfectionism that delighted higher superiors with its institutional effectiveness and terrorized their subordinates. Such a woman could be ruthlessly demanding of children and employees. Whether she was admired for being "better than any man" at running a tight ship on mission or dreaded as "worse than any man" in dominating her subjects, she was certainly more feared than loved and the title "mother" was sometimes a cruel irony.

The cool autonomy of the woman Religious overly identified with the Artemis archetype can make her emotionally unresponsive, nonrelational in community, and uninvolved with her students, patients, clients, and colleagues. At worst it can lead to narcissistic self-absorption in her own projects that drain her best energy away from shared life and ministry. Self-sufficient in the extreme, such a woman may choose to live alone not for healthy solitude or because of ministerial necessity but to avoid interdependence and community accountability.

Placid Hestia-type women, especially if they enter large, active orders, can easily become the invisible nonparticipants who contribute nothing significant to community life or ministry. They can see themselves as misunderstood "contemplatives" who are above such mundane affairs as political struggles in or outside the congregation. They avoid meetings and committees, cannot be bothered with financial accountability, and refuse to acknowledge responsibility for the larger enterprise. Congregational commitments to justice, ecological responsibility, solidarity with the oppressed, or corporate stands on issues of the day do not interest them. They may make a life's work out of caring for their room or apartment and spend most of their time reading, writing poetry, or sitting in front of the television.

Congregations as well as individuals can manifest the negative traits of the virgin archetypes. An unhealthy status stratification ruled in some congregations in which an Athena woman who could handle the high school boys was valued more than the maternal primary teacher, or the self-sufficient Artemis became a superior or supervisor at a young age and remained in positions of power for decades while the gifts of less assertive women were never fostered or affirmed. A certain corporate arrogance and sense of entitlement certainly characterized many preconciliar Religious congregations. And the secrecy, closed lifestyle, and cultivated nonrelationality of many congregations might have had more to do with corporate psychology than with the Gospel. Perhaps one of the reasons that the decrease in social power resulting from declining numbers, rising median age, and decreased financial resources, as well as the surrender of various status symbols, has been so traumatic for some congregations is the threat these diminishments represent to the archetypal corporate self-image of autonomy and power.

Both of the archetypes we have examined so far suggest that there is a natural, human substrate for central features of Religious Life. The anthropological monastic archetype of single-minded absorption in the quest for life-integrating transcendence suggests a human basis for the absorption in the God-quest that is at the heart of Religious Life. And the psychological virgin archetype of autonomous, creative, and contemplative psychological solitariness suggests a natural "fit" between women in whom this archetype is strong and the consecrated celibacy that is central to Religious Life, as well as a corporate psychology that accounts better for the development of Religious congregations than the domestic models proposed by Church authority. However, just as our examination of the anthropological archetype of the monastic needed to be qualified in terms of the Gospel if it was to be relevant to Religious Life, so our exploration of the psychological archetype of the virgin needs to be qualified if it is to be helpful for understanding this lifeform.

First, it is crucial to recognize that, as Bolen explains, it is hardly likely that anyone is completely ruled by or identified with a single archetype. At different times and in various circumstances different archetypes become active.[39] The three forms of the virgin archetype probably mutually influence the woman whose personality is primarily influenced by that archetype. But she may well be influenced also by the affiliative archetypes: the capacity for the faithful love of Hera, the maternal warmth of Demeter, and the receptivity of Persephone, as well as the transformative sexual energy of Aphrodite. The virgin archetype might not even be dominant in a given Religious. Thus, it is more the lifeform itself that seems to incarnate the virgin archetype and thus to attract women in whom that archetype in one or other of its forms is dominant and to foster the emergence of the traits of that archetype in other women who enter and in whom it might be naturally recessive.

Second, as was said at the beginning of this section, the active presence of the virgin archetype in the psyche of a woman does not necessarily lead to entrance into Religious Life or to faithful celibate chastity. It would be a serious distortion to try to reduce the mystery of the vocation to consecrated celibacy to a psychological predisposition or the mystery of fidelity to psychological determinism.

Third, what makes consecrated celibacy as a lifelong commitment in Religious Life capable of fulfilling the affective potentiality of a mature woman is the presence in her life of Jesus Christ loved beyond herself and all other things. Religious Life founded on any other premise, no matter how psychologically coherent and professionally effective, would make little sense spiritually. This means that the virgin archetype, when realized in Religious Life, involves the transcendence of psychological solitude itself in a relationship which both consolidates a woman's "one-in-herself" integrity and fulfills her capacity for life-giving love and spiritual generativity.

Finally, Religious Life is first and finally life according to the Gospel under the influence of the Spirit of God. The theological and moral virtues, not the power of psychological archetypes, give both impetus and shape to the enterprise of self and world transformation that is integral to Religious Life.

Of course, one may not be at all attracted to the "personae" of the Greek goddesses as a psychological typology and hermeneutic of celibate experience. One might not even think that Jung's archetypal psychology is a valid model of the human psyche. No particular psychological theory is essential for understanding the mystery of grace in the human spirit. However, some theory of human structure and functioning, that is, some theological anthropology involving some understanding of the human subject as such, seems essential for a realistic exploration of the dynamics of spirituality,[40] and Jung's theory, expanded by Bolen, seems to offer some resources. In any case, it does seem clear from ordinary experience that people are different, that they have predominant traits that structure their responses to situations and relationships, and that there is a variety of "types" of people who seem to share some traits in common.

What I have tried to suggest in this section on the virgin archetype is that there are certain psychological traits that seem to predispose a woman for the celibate life and that make the "fit" between her personality and the Religious life-form more natural and thus her ability to persevere in the life more likely. Under the term *virgin archetype* I am clustering those traits that could be summarized as a certain "one-in-herselfness," which inclines her to find, structure, and develop her identity less in terms of who she is related to (as daughter, wife, or mother) and more in terms of who she is in herself. The virgin archetype's three "personae" suggest that this integrity involves a heightened personal autonomy, focus, and commitment to personally chosen goals (Artemis), a capacity to find psychological fulfillment in commitment and achievement in the sphere of work (Athena), and the ability to find in aloneness a deep and nourishing solitude of the spirit (Hestia). When these traits are present in some combination in a Catholic woman, a genuine encounter with Jesus may well raise the question of vocation to Religious Life, and there is a good chance that she will find the life, itself a kind of corporate institutionalization of the virgin archetype, congenial.

IV. The Sociological Ideal Type:
The Religious Virtuoso

A third discipline from which we can draw some enlightenment, again by way of similarity and difference, is sociology. Patricia Wittberg, a Sister of Charity who is a sociologist, has written several books and articles applying sociological theory to contemporary Religious Life in the United States in an effort to describe, analyze, and suggest remedies for what she perceives as the current crisis of Religious Life on the brink of extinction.[41] One of the categories to which she appeals, that of the "religious virtuoso," is intriguing because of the light it throws on the empirical structure and dynamics of Religious Life as institution. Like the anthropological and psychological categories already discussed, this sociological category can seem deceptively adequate to the reality of Religious vocation and must be carefully qualified if it is to be truly illuminating.

The "religious virtuoso" as an "ideal type" is a category developed by Max Weber (1864–1920), one of the founding figures in the field of sociology.[42] He observed that in virtually all cultures there seem to be people who want to go beyond the religious requirements of their societies and who thus become "experts" in religion or spirituality and serve a social function as models or embodiments of the religious and spiritual ideals of the society as well as functioning in some situations as the organizers or facilitators of religious practice, teachers of religious doctrine, or skilled practitioners of spirituality. Wittberg follows Weber in admitting that the elitist resonances of the term *virtuoso* are problematic in the Christian context and she, with Weber, repudiates them. However, for our purposes, these resonances and their implications cannot be simply disclaimed. They must be dealt with if this sociological category is to make a positive contribution to our understanding of the human substrate of the phenomenon of Religious Life.

The category raises up, first, a sociological fact that cannot be denied, namely, that Religious Life is somehow distinct from lay Catholic life lived in the married or single state. It is also an undeniable fact that this distinction, almost from the beginning, has been interpreted within a dichotomous hierarchical dualism as superiority to the lay state. This interpretation is theologically faulty, was rejected by Vatican II,[43] and must be energetically repudiated. Wittberg contends that, from a sociological point of view, the collapse (however necessary and legitimate it might be) of this ideology of superiority removed the major motivation for espousing Religious Life and thus contributed powerfully to the demise of the institution, which she sees occurring.[44] The dualistic thinking, deeply ingrained in the Western mind, which can understand distinction or specificity only in terms of superiority and inferiority, is a formidable obstacle to developing a sound theory of Religious Life that both delineates it sufficiently to be motivating and avoids doing so at the cost of denigrating other forms of Christian life. In mining the sociological category of "religious virtuosity" for resources in this task I want to be very careful not to exacerbate the problem. Thus, a first contribution that I want to take from the category of virtuoso is the notion of "distinction" or "specificity" or "recognizable difference," purified of dualistic implications of superiority.

Second, a virtuoso is someone who is gifted in a particular field, has developed the gift to a superlative degree, and for these two reasons is superior to others both in and outside the field. Mozart had a prodigious musical talent that he honed from childhood, and he has few peers even in the world of music. Tiger Woods is a supremely talented athlete who has developed his golfing prowess to the point of being perhaps the best who has ever played the game. Einstein in science, Georgia O'Keefe in painting, Emily Dickinson in literature, and Bill Gates in technology would be recognized as virtuosi in their respective fields. People like Teresa of Avila; Black Elk; Gandhi; Martin Luther King, Jr.; Chuang Tzu; Mohammed; and Abraham Heschel are analogous figures in the realm of religion and spirituality. While some Religious (the ones we call saints, whether canonized or not) are religious virtuosi in this sense, no one would argue that all Religious are in this category or that there are no religious/spiritual virtuosi outside Religious Life. What, then, does the category offer that is usable for our project of "locating" Religious Life in relation to other lifeforms?

It is important to begin by distinguishing between the individual Religious, who may or may not become a "virtuoso" in the sense described above, and Religious Life as a lifeform, which clearly exists to foster such virtuosity in all its members. Anyone who enters Religious Life (or more importantly perseveres in the life) for the right reasons can be said to possess "religious talent or ability," that is, the capacity for and commitment to a quest for God that, as Wittberg says, goes well beyond the "church on Sunday" level.[45] Of course, many people possessed of this talent for religion/spirituality do not enter Religious Life, but it makes no sense at all to enter Religious Life if one is not primarily concerned with the God-quest. Unlike marriage or even an ecclesiastical career, Religious Life

can appeal to no other legitimate intrinsic motivation. Wittberg points out that in the course of history there have been a
plethora of other motivations for entering Religious Life, such
as social status and personal power, as well as all kinds of social
pressures and encouragements to do so.[46] While this is
undoubtedly true, no such motive has ever been considered
adequate or even appropriate as grounding for the life.

Anyone who lives Religious Life faithfully and well over a
lifetime will excel in the religious quest, that is, will become
holy, whether or not this is the kind of holiness that the
Church canonizes or the heroic but unspectacular holiness of
the anonymous saint. Again, many people who become genuinely holy in their lifetimes, including some who are canonized and many who are not, do not enter Religious Life. But,
once again, Religious Life is distinguished by the fact that it
has no other legitimating finality except holiness, personal
union with God. A married couple who spent fifty years
together and did not achieve deep interpersonal union, whatever else they might have accomplished, would be failures in
their state of life, in matrimony *as such,* even if they did not
divorce. Similarly, the Religious who fails to attain genuine
personal holiness is not just missing the point of all Christian
life, whatever other good they might do, but failing in their
particular state of life, in Religious Life *as such,* even if they
remain in the life until death.

So, a second gleaning from the category of virtuosity is that
Religious as individuals have no monopoly on "religious talent" or on its development in holiness. Thus, they are not necessarily, as individuals, superior in holiness to anyone else, nor
is their lifeform intrinsically superior as a path to holiness. But
their lifeform is one that has no other justifying finality except
holiness and no other adequate or valid purpose for existing
except to foster the quest for holiness. It is this institutionalization of the "naked" or "exclusive" concern with the God-quest
that is part of the specificity of the lifeform.

The category of virtuosity, then, actually becomes enlightening primarily in talking of the specificity or distinctiveness,
not the superiority, of the lifeform, and in talking about the

lifeform itself rather than in talking about individual Religious. Applied to individual Christians the term *virtuoso* applies to some Religious and to some who are not in that state of life. However, Religious Life as a lifeform is a social phenomenon whose central and defining purpose and objective is the facilitation of the God-quest to the exclusion of any other primary life commitment. It is the exclusion of other primary commitments as the way to God that distinguishes the lifeform as such. Religious do not seek God primarily through exclusive relationship with one or several other human beings (family), through leadership in the institutional Church (clergy), or through profession or career (even undertaken as ministry). As Religious they are involved full-time, primarily, and in a very real sense exclusively in the God-quest. By *exclusively* I do not mean that they do not do anything else but that *nothing else* defines the shape or scope or depth or timing of the religious quest. On the contrary, the religious quest determines what else they do and when and how and to what extent they do it. This does not necessarily mean that they are better at it, that is, holier, but it does define their life as "religious" the way "married" or "clergy" or "artist" or "athlete" or "intellectual" defines people whose life, including their way to God, is structured in terms of upholding one of these commitments as primary.

If all this is true, I would suggest that the category of "virtuoso" is so fraught with ambiguity that we need to take what is useful from the category, that is, the two points in the preceding paragraphs (namely, the sociological distinctiveness of the life and the exclusive concern with the religious/spiritual dimension of life as the only legitimate foundation and finality) and find another term to express what it implies about Religious Life. We are trying to develop an understanding of the distinction or specificity of the lifeform that does not imply exclusive access to the reality of Christian holiness nor intrinsic superiority in relation to it.

By way of example, the successful graduates in a liberal arts class are all committed to and accomplished in the sphere of "education" or, ideally, wisdom. All have earned the same degree and are considered educated. But some have specialized, or attained wisdom, in art, others in science, others in technology, and so on. None of these specializations is intrinsically superior nor is it better to be educated as a musician than as a scientist. The specializations, the particular path to wisdom and the shape of one's education, arise from personal calling. One is not better educated—more a virtuoso—in virtue of the specialization chosen but in virtue of how competent one has become in the field chosen.

In the sphere of Christianity, the analogue to education or wisdom is holiness. All who become saints, with capital or lowercase "s," are holy. Some have attained holiness through marriage, others through single life, others as clerics, others as Religious, or even through some succession or combination of these. Religious in other words do not have exclusive access to holiness nor, necessarily, superiority in relation to it. What specifies their life, their "specialization," is their exclusive life-commitment to religion itself. Like the person who shapes her or his life around art, or sports, or scientific research, or family (even while also participating in some or all of the other spheres) and who may or may not be better than others in the chosen sphere, the Religious is a specialist in the God-quest in the sense of having structured her life around it in a total and exclusive way. Religious Life, then, as a lifeform, is specific and distinct in its concentration on the religious quest as absolutely determinative of all else but not superior to other ways of seeking God and holiness. The lifeform exists to facilitate and support Religious who, as individuals, specialize in this specific arena but who are not necessarily superior to those who specialize in other arenas.

All this being said, it is natural to expect that, other things being equal, someone who specializes in art will know more about it than someone who specializes in science and that a married person will know more about the development of sexual intimacy than a celibate. Likewise, it is not unreasonable to expect that people who specialize in the religious quest will have a certain competence in this area, if only because they continually read about it, study it, undergo continuous formation in it, share life with others who are similarly involved, and spend their lives dealing with others specifically in terms of the religious dimension of human life. If we keep in mind that, just as many doctors have egregious health habits, many married people are interpersonally underdeveloped, and many parents are abusive, so many Religious are not proficient in spirituality, it nevertheless makes sense to look to Religious for particular competence in the areas of prayer, discernment, and so on. Furthermore, just as a midwife might be better than a gynecologist with an M.D., a social worker may be better with children than a parent, and a friend might be a better confidante than a spouse, so many who are not Religious in the institutional sense are superior to many Religious in the sphere of spirituality.

The issue, in short, is not competition for pride of place. It is cooperation among the many and varied charisms in the Church. Part of the problem is that until very recently the Catholic community has assigned all expertise in ministry to its clergy and all expertise in holiness to Religious. This monopoly excluded laity from both spheres. As laypeople have responded to the conciliar call to mission and holiness, they have found themselves, often enough, involved in spiritual turf wars, which are not just unseemly among the People of God but truly pernicious. In the effort to undo this mischief we need to avoid creating another form of mischief, the inability to recognize specific vocations and gifts, in ourselves or in others, and to develop these gifts for the sake of the whole. It has been observed, correctly, that if everything is ministry then nothing is ministry. And if everything is Religious Life, nothing is.

V. Summary and Conclusions

The argument of this chapter is that Religious Life as a lifeform and the vocation to undertake it are phenomena deeply rooted in our humanity. The mysterious interaction between God who calls and attracts and the person who hears and responds is not thereby reduced to the purely natural. Nevertheless, it is not an unnatural or irrational phenomenon, and its human roots can be examined. Doing so can help us see Religious Life and the vocation to it as related to wider human experiences even as it remains distinct and specific, both within the Church and beyond it.

I have proposed that Catholic Religious Life is a realization of the anthropological archetype of the monastic, which is operative in all the world's great religions and moves the person toward the exclusive quest of the transcendent; of the psychological archetype of the virgin, which seems operative especially in women and which produces in many a certain relational autonomy and a satisfying capacity for self-determination in work and life; and of the sociological ideal type of the religious virtuoso, which appears as a combination of giftedness for and specialization in a particular arena of endeavor, namely, the God-quest.

We have seen that the specifically Christian character of Religious Life modifies each of the types in significant ways. The Christian monastic's quest of the "one thing necessary" is christocentric, and this gives rise to the specifically Christian monastic commitment through perpetual consecrated celibacy expressing that relationship, while the situation of Religious Life in the Church community modifies the practices of monasticism. This same christocentrism affects the functioning in the Christian Religious of the virginal archetype by focusing the autonomous affectivity of the Religious on Christ and on her capacity for satisfying work in a self-determined domain on the fostering of the Reign of God that Jesus preached, that is, in ministry. And finally, the Christian religious virtuoso who does indeed specialize in spirituality does not find her identity or raison d'être in a claim of spiritual superiority to other Christians.

All three types have in common a life-unifying, an integrating dynamic. When operating together in shaping the spirituality of the Catholic Religious, that dynamic is focused in the relationship with Christ that is central to the Christian God-quest. If this analysis is faithful to the reality of the Religious lifeform, it amounts to a claim that Religious Life is *religious,* not primarily in the institutional sense but in the sense of a tradition-shaped, coherent spirituality, and that it is a *life,* not an organization or a workforce or a platonic essence of some kind. Because this spirituality is Christian, it necessarily involves community and ministry but neither of them, or both together, suffices to explain or justify the life. And because it is a life it generates a lifeform that is organic and integrated, not a collection of customs, practices, activities, or even relationships. It is this theory of Religious Life that will undergird all that follows.

Chapter Two
Religious Life as an Organic Lifeform: Getting It Together

I. Introduction

Just as increasing contact with the world's great religious traditions raises the question of the meaning of Religious Life as a human phenomenon, so interchange with a wide spectrum of contemporary spiritual seekers is raising a question about the sociological character of the life. Specifically, a whole complex of questions arising within and outside Religious Life about sociological boundaries and group identity invites Religious to examine their life from yet another perspective in the attempt to "locate" the life within the continually shifting social patterns of contemporary religious and spiritual aspirations.

The question that people inside and outside the Church, including many Religious themselves, are asking is whether, at this critical point in the history of the earth, humanity, and the Church, such a seemingly insular form of life makes any sense at all. Are we not being urgently called to form community across the traditional boundaries of race, gender, marital status, sexual orientation, ethnicity, nationality, religious tradition or lack thereof, occupation, or lifestyle rather than to emphasize or institutionalize such relatively (from a cosmic perspective) unimportant distinctions?[1] Is not the only important distinction between people who seek peace and justice on a worldwide scale and those who do not? Is it not more important, indeed imperative, to come together around what we have in common, namely, our commitment to saving the earth, transforming society, and creating a future for the planet and the race, than to insist on ultimately insignificant differences in religious beliefs or lifestyle choices?

These questions are at the base of a complex of problems that have come to be referred to generically among Religious as "the membership issue" (which will serve as a convenient label for this area of discourse), even though there is much at stake in this discussion besides membership in the strict sense of the word. Wrapped up in the membership issue are questions about the validity of the form of life itself and especially of celibacy as a defining characteristic of the life, inclusivity (vs. exclusiveness) and egalitarianism (vs. elitism) as religious values, the future of Religious Life itself as apparently fewer people feel called to vowed membership, the continued ministerial effectiveness of congregations whose membership is declining numerically and aging dramatically, the challenge to risk new forms of Religious Life as did founders in the past, the real purpose of the life and whether this purpose is specific to Religious, and so on. In this chapter I will attempt to map the contours of the membership issue and to clarify the questions before suggesting a theory of Religious Life as a lifeform in the Church and what that might imply in regard to the questions raised.

II. Mapping the Contours of the Issue

The immediate point at which the membership issue is raised for many congregations is the request, made with increasing frequency and insistence, by laypeople to associate or affiliate with the congregation. These laypeople do not want to "enter" Religious Life in the traditional sense of the word. They are usually quite clear about not wishing to leave their present life situation, including marriage or other relationships, profession or job, home or geographical location. They do not wish to make a perpetual or irrevocable commitment to the congregation in terms either of complete financial disclosure and interdependence or in terms of ministerial discernment and corporate decision making in regard to their own lives. In other words, they want to associate with the congregation or some of its members in certain respects or in regard to certain aspects of the community's life, such as ministry or prayer, but they are not seeking to make the community of the present or the future the defining context of their lives.

Often these people seek to participate in some benefits of community membership, such as spiritual formation or educational opportunities, and they wish to contribute to the community on a free-will basis financial assistance, ministerial time and energy, and their specific professional expertise and experience. They often, although not always, want to experience in some limited and self-defined way the solidarity of community life itself. In some cases, they wish to participate actively in the government of the congregation by exercising active and/or a passive voice.

The desire to participate actively in congregational government as voting members of local communities and provincial or general assemblies and chapters, and to be eligible for election to office as well as the desire to participate in decisions concerning leadership, finances, and property has raised the specific issue that is so acute at the moment, namely, the issue of actual membership. Associates or affiliates by definition as well as by Canon Law[2] are not members of the congregation. They are not bound to it by life commitment, have not contributed their entire financial resources to it, are not accountable to its leadership, are not subject to its legislation, and are not liable for its debts or the stances it publicly assumes. However, once the issues of voting, election, binding decision making in financial matters and in other internal affairs of the congregation are raised, the issue becomes one of membership in the strict sense of the term. And this raises the issue of sociological boundaries and corporate identity, which lead into the theological question of the nature and meaning of Religious Life itself.

Many Religious congregations have responded to requests for affiliation by initiating programs for laypeople whom they may call "affiliates," "associates," "volunteers," or sometimes "co-members" or "lay members." In some respects these programs are the successors of third orders, secular orders, sodalities, confraternities, and associations of the faithful which, in the history of the Church, have been associated with Religious orders. However, the differences between the contemporary "associates" (a term I will use for the laypeople under discussion here, regardless of what a particular congregation calls them) and members of historical third orders and their analogues are as significant as are the similarities.

First, contemporary associates do not join preexisting organizations (e.g., a sodality or confraternity) founded specifically for laity by the congregation, nor do they tend to come together themselves into such organizations. Rather, they tend to relate individually, directly or through some member(s), to the congregation itself. Second, while the congregation may have a Religious acting as an official liaison with associates, this person is not regarded by associates as a "quasi-superior," as were moderators or chaplains of third orders or sodalities. Third, contemporary associates do not see themselves as living a form of the charism adapted to their lay state and thus participating in the spirituality or ministry of the members of the congregation who live the charism in its fullness. They see themselves as participating in the spirituality, life, and mission of the congregation on their own terms and according to their own life situations, just as the members participate according to their vowed commitment. Fourth, guidelines for associates of a particular congregation tend to be not a "rule of life" guiding the associates' practice, but stipulations regarding the associates' relation to the congregation, for example, in regard to length of commitment, financial arrangements, voting, or participation in congregational processes. In other words, the phenomenon under discussion is a new development in the history of Religious Life and cannot be adequately engaged in terms of categories derived from the past.

While many associates are not at all interested in full membership, with its attendant rights and responsibilities, some associates in various congregations, supported usually by some members, are asking for full membership, realizing clearly that, since they do not want to undertake many of the current conditions of membership, they are, in effect, asking for a redefinition of membership as intrinsically pluralistic. The question that is being raised is whether or not a Religious congregation can or wants to sustain several forms of full and coequal membership, such as members with vows and those without vows, members who make permanent commitment in the congregation and those who make temporary commitment, members who participate in the full range of congregational life and those whose participation is limited to specific areas of interest to them or that are compatible with their other life commitments, members who are single and others who are married, members who are celibate and others who are involved in sexually active relationships (whether hetero- or homosexual), members of both sexes, members who are Catholic Christians and others who believe and/or practice differently, members who are believers and others who are not. In short, could a congregation not expand its understanding of membership to include as full and coequal members, sharing identity, rights, and privileges, all those who share some specified value orientation such as active commitment to personal and social transformation in justice and peace or who espouse the particular charism of the congregation, for instance, charity, mercy, or empowerment of the materially disadvantaged?

The attitudes of members of congregations toward the phenomenon of lay associates in their midst and especially the possibility of redefining membership to include as full members those who are now associates tend to be sharply divided. Some Religious, probably a minority at this point, enthusiastically support the movement, and others, also probably a minority, emotionally oppose it. Most members, especially congregational leaders, are suspended on the horns of a dilemma. They favor in principle inclusive attitudes toward membership and positive attitudes toward change and development in Religious Life, are committed to sharing fully whatever the community has that can enrich the lives of other people, and welcome a renewed supply of personal, financial, and experiential resources for their congregations. But they have serious hesitations about the actual phenomenon that is developing because there seem to be some real contradictions involved in the notion of pluralism of forms of membership.

Religious who favor pluralism of forms of membership are convinced that while this will certainly change the congregation, this change will be in continuity with the development of Religious Life in the past. New forms of Religious Life have arisen at several points in the history of the Church, and what is now being proposed—a single congregation with a plurality of types of membership—would be such a new form. Consequently, it would not destroy Religious Life but integrate it more fully into the emerging global agenda by fostering the breakdown of artificial boundaries and promoting the common commitment of like-minded people to a transformed future.

Three sets of motivations seem to underlie the enthusiastic conviction of such Religious that the time has come to incorporate fully into the congregation as members with equal rights and privileges although with differing responsibilities those associates who want full membership. A first set of motivations is *affective and apostolic.* Members of a congregation may have close personal ties with associates who desire full membership. In some cases the associates are former Religious who left the congregation because they did not feel called to certain of its basic commitments, such as Catholic identity, celibacy, or total financial interdependence, but have remained close to the community through their ties with the members or their continued participation in the mission. In other cases the associates are laypeople who have become colleagues in ministry or are family members or close personal friends of some members of the congregation. These Religious have a strong interest in creating institutional structures within their congregation that will allow these particular associates to be full and equal members, as they would like to be, without obliging them to undertake commitments and responsibilities to which they do not feel called. Personal experience with these associates has convinced the Religious of the validity of their call to participate in the congregation's charism, of their commitment to what is most basic and important in the congregation's mission, and of the important contribution the associates make to the congregation and its members. Full membership for associates seems to offer nothing but mutual enrichment, while denying such membership seems exclusive, elitist, and narrow-mindedly legalistic and evidences a fear of the new which can only, in the end, condemn the congregation to stagnation or extinction.

A second set of motivations centers on *concern for the future of the congregation* and/or Religious Life. Some Religious are convinced that their congregations cannot survive unless there is, in the near future, a significant influx of new and younger members. The one or two people, often women in middle age, who are now entering each year seem totally inadequate as a personnel base for the future. They see little evidence that large numbers of young women are going to begin to seek vowed membership, but there are evidently fairly large numbers of people, women and men, who would become members if this did not involve such things as permanent commitment, celibacy, and the other obligations of present membership.

A third set of motivations is more complicated and delicate. Some Religious experience their own vocations much more in terms of what is now called association, and they would like to have the option of *redefining their own membership* and participation without having to leave the congregation to which, in many cases, they are deeply, affectively attached. For example, some Religious would like to marry, or be involved in a recognized and accepted homosexual relationship, or own property in their own name, or be bound by temporary rather than perpetual vows, or be independent in the choice and pursuit of a profession or career that has no necessary relationship to the corporate mission of the congregation. For some Religious their alienation from the institutional Church has become so profound that self-identification as Catholic is no longer possible, even though their affiliation with their community remains intact. Expanding the available types of membership in the congregation would allow these people to renegotiate their relationship to the congregation and thus to follow their true desires regarding commitment and/or lifestyle without loss of membership in the congregation in which they may have spent far too many years to be able peacefully to contemplate severance at this point.

In considering the opposite position, namely, that of those Religious who have serious reservations about the possibility of plural types of membership, I will not take up the agenda of those whose primary motive for objecting is panic at the thought of change, a subconscious conviction that the recognition of other types of membership would undermine the validity and/or superiority of their own form of commitment, or a fear that resources expended on such new members would be diverted from their own support and care now or in their later years. Congregations and their leaders have to deal compassionately with these types of fears, which are quite real, but they cannot be the basis for decisions about the present or future of the congregation.

The real hesitation, which must be taken seriously, about a pluralistic redefinition of membership arises from a feeling and/or a conviction that there is some intrinsic contradiction involved in the attempt to combine full membership with a nonespousal of certain basic coordinates and dimensions of the Religious lifeform. In other words, there is a feeling on the part of some members and leaders of congregations that such pluralism of types of membership would involve a dissolution of the boundaries necessary for the continued existence and identity of Religious Life and of the congregation. If such is the case the result of such redefinition would be not an evolution of Religious Life or the emergence of a new form of the life but its demise. The real question is whether this is the case or not.

It must be recognized, however, that straightforward discussion of this question is very difficult if not nearly impossible in some congregations at the present time because of the "systematically distorted communication"[3] generated by the invocation of such "red-flag" terms as "inclusiveness," "change," "creative risk," and "the challenge of the future." No one who considers herself a genuinely postconciliar Religious, especially if she is in a position of leadership and therefore charged with the mission of articulating and promoting a vision for the future in her congregation, wants to be even suspected of being exclusive or elitist, of resisting change, or of jeopardizing the future of the congregation through resistance to what might be emerging as life-giving innovation even if it is filled with risk. In my opinion, failure to address a serious question because examining the issues honestly might make one appear less forward-looking than one might wish is to yield to a dangerous form of intimidation. The issues under consideration bear directly on the future of Religious Life and avoiding them is not really an option.

Finally, although in one sense this is a sociological question, a question about the boundaries necessary for the identity and functioning of a corporate entity and how that entity interrelates with its environment, it cannot be reduced to an exclusively secular or academic analysis. As I have attempted to show in the preceding chapter, Religious Life, while certainly a human endeavor and thus susceptible to anthropological and psychological as well as sociological analyses, is a specifically Christian theological reality, and therefore whatever is said about its corporate identity and mission must take account of the action of the Spirit and the response of faith. The attempt to treat Religious Life and congregations in purely sociological terms—according to organizational, community, or social movement theories—while very helpful in illuminating the dynamics of the life in the context of its social, political, and economic environment, filters out the essential spiritual dynamics which, in the last analysis, determine the life.[4] In what follows I will attempt to bring both sociological and theological reflection together to bear on the issue of Religious Life as a lifeform in the Church.

III. Clarifying Issues of Similarity and Difference

In the post-Tridentine period Religious Life was a "totalitarian" form of life, not in the sense that it was oppressive or dictatorial (although in some instances it was), but in the sense that it was a completely separate enterprise that absorbed the entire life of its members so that they did not have meaningful contacts, projects, or interests outside the institutional life of the congregation.[5] One result of this insularity of the lifeform was that Religious had little sense of having anything in common with other people, movements, or lifeforms, even within the Church and certainly beyond it.

In the post-Vatican II period the contacts between Religious and others, within and outside Catholicism, have dramatically broadened and deepened. Religious have realized that they have a great deal in common with others not only as human beings but in regard to the most important aspects of Religious Life itself: faith, prayer, community, commitment to protecting the environment and transforming society, and even in respect to their own congregational charisms of truth, charity, mercy, or solidarity with the poor which are certainly not the private preserve of any one congregation.

This newly discovered commonality has led to a sense of unity and solidarity with all kinds of people and movements within and beyond the institutional Church and raised, in an entirely new way, the question of the distinctiveness of Religious Life. The question has become, "Should Religious create and sustain a lifeform that does not include within itself, at least potentially, all those with whom Religious have important commonalities?" Or, to put the question more sharply, "Is not Religious Life as it is presently conceived a way of creating, sacralizing, and perpetuating divisive boundaries between people who have every reason to recognize, celebrate, and promote their shared vision and values?"

This question cannot be engaged without making some important distinctions among kinds and degrees of commonality. Although a human being shares important commonalities with every living creature on the planet, clear decision making often requires us to make real distinctions between plants and animals, between other animals and humans, and even among humans. In other words, there is a variety of ways of being alike and different and this fact has implications for concrete choices.

A. Identity

Religious recognize their identity, that is, their complete unity and unreserved solidarity with all humanity. Thus Religious, like all creatures, share fully in the earth community, that is, in the planetary organism that we are coming to recognize as not only our environment but as that to which we belong rather than that which belongs to us. Religious also share fully and without reservation in the human family itself in which the planetary community achieves self-consciousness and which therefore has a particular responsibility for the well-being and future of the earth. Finally, Religious recognize their special solidarity with that part of the human family that is actively concerned with and committed to "the good," that is, to love, justice, peace, truth, beauty, and the promotion of these values in themselves and throughout creation. As we noted in chapter 1, Raimundo Panikkar and others have recognized this type of consciousness as the expression of the "monk archetype," that is, the universal human aspiration toward transcendence, the movement toward the "Center," the spiritual quest for depth and meaning, the search for union with and realization of ultimate value.[6] This archetypal aspiration is active in many people, some of whom are formal participants in institutional religion but many of whom are not. Often Religious find themselves more in tune with such spiritual seekers, including those who do not know anything about or have even rejected Christianity, than with some Catholics, including some other Religious and Church officials, whose pedestrian approach to spirituality seems unrelated to the urgent issues of our time.

B. Analogy

Analogy is a kind of relationship in which similarity in certain respects is combined with important differences in other respects. Such analogy exists between some Catholic Religious and some individual participants in other Christian communions as well as in other religious traditions. Recently, for example, some Religious have discovered deep commonalities between their own spirituality and that of some Native Americans. The ecumenical dialogue has brought together Catholic Religious and non-Catholics in a variety of shared justice enterprises, common experiences of prayer and worship, and retreats of various kinds. In many traditions there are communities composed of spiritually (and sometimes religiously) committed seekers whose lifeforms closely resemble Catholic Religious Life in certain important respects. Such lifeforms, as we saw in chapter 1, exist in Islam, Buddhism, Hinduism, Jainism, and Judaism. Such forms also exist in ecumenical and/or nondenominational communities of nonviolent resistance, houses of hospitality, and the like. There is not a complete overlap among any of these lifeforms and Catholic Religious Life but what they have in common is deep and real, and dialogue between Religious and members of such communities, as well as shared involvement in prayer and service, has proven extremely fruitful.[7]

C. Common Elements of Faith and/or Lifestyle

Besides the more global similarities of identity and analogy that Religious have discovered between their own commitments and those of others, there are also elements in the faith and/or lifestyle of Religious that they share with others who live, in general, very differently. For example, many people have developed or are interested in developing a personal practice of prayer or meditation. Others are seeking a vital liturgical community. Religious sometimes discover that people who have no interest in Religious Life as such are deeply attracted to the characteristic spirituality or charism of the congregation, such as Carmelite mysticism, or Ignatian contemplation in action, or Franciscan poverty and creationism, or Benedictine integration of prayer and work. Other people are vitally concerned with forming intentional community that may or may not have a religious or even spiritual focus. Still others share engagement in a particular form of social analysis and praxis, such as feminism, pacifism, community organizing, education, or providing housing, health care, or social services to the underprivileged. There are people attracted to voluntary, ecologically motivated simplicity of life, to a celibate lifestyle, to a rule-governed personal spiritual practice, to spiritual direction, to regular community review of life and discernment, or any of several other elements that are part of many Religious communities' lifestyles.

The discovery by Religious of what they have in common, either globally in terms of identity or analogy, or partially in terms of particular lifestyle elements, with other individuals and groups is basic to the question facing many communities today as some of these people seek association of one kind or another with the congregation that can lead to the question of full membership. It seems that what these seekers share with Religious is far more important than what they may not share, especially since what these laypeople do not share is not rejected by them in principle or in practice. In fact, often there is great respect and admiration for those aspects of Religious Life, such as permanent commitment or consecrated celibacy, in which the person seeking association is not interested. They are not asking the Religious congregation to abandon these aspects but simply not to make them obligatory for everyone. In other words, there is no attack on anything the community values but simply a request for a more flexible understanding of belonging and therefore a more pluralistic definition of membership.

The situation so far described raises three questions, one of which is fundamental and two of which must be addressed in terms of the answer given to the basic one. The fundamental question concerns the very nature of Religious Life. Depending on how one answers that question, the issue of inclusiveness and the question of numbers of entrants and the implications of this for the future of Religious Life and the mission of a congregation can be faced.

IV. The Fundamental Issue: Religious Life as a Lifeform

The thesis I am proposing in what follows is that Religious Life is a *lifeform*. In selecting this organic model for understanding Religious Life I am not denying the appropriateness or usefulness of other sociological categories such as intentional community or theories of social movements or organizations, which are helpful in analyzing some aspects of the life as a sociological reality. Rather, I am trying to suggest a holistic model that will enable us to see the internal structure and dynamics of the life as simultaneously sociological, theological, and spiritual. In arguing that Religious Life is a lifeform I am proposing that it is better understood as an organic rather than as a mechanical or ontological phenomenon. My suspicion is that the unrecognized but operative model underlying the discussion of the membership issue thus far has been an organizational one that is either mechanistic (aggregational) or implicitly Platonic (essentialist).

A. Meaning of Lifeform

1. What a lifeform is not: First, a lifeform, and therefore the organic entities that embody it, is *not an organization with entrance requirements*. While there is an important sense in which a Religious congregation is an organization (a topic to be taken up in chapter 7 and again in volume 2), it is much more than that, and its organizational aspects are in service of its more intrinsic features. The Religious community, in other words, is not really analogous to a health club that anyone may join who can afford the fees and is willing to obey the house rules or even a business enterprise that people join or leave in terms of mutual benefit.

An organization such as a health club should have only those entrance requirements that are strictly necessary to promote its purposes, and these can and should be changed when they unduly restrict membership or the members' use and enjoyment of the facilities. Furthermore, rules apply only to the areas of club activity in which a member chooses to participate. Pool rules affect only those who choose to swim and court rules only those who play tennis or handball. New facilities or activities can be added and others removed without destroying the organization, provided they are financially feasible and not contrary to the basic purpose of the club. Members can join or resign at their discretion without affecting other members, and there is no problem with having various kinds of members, for example, charter members, lifetime members, annual members, off-prime-time members, and drop-ins. Some individual members may have a great deal in common either personally, such as being married to each other, or within the purposes and functions of the club, such as being mates on the tennis team, while others may participate in nothing except the anonymous early morning lap swim and never even get to know any other members. Some members will devote a good deal of time to participation in club business and affairs, and others may choose not even to read the by-laws when they join, and there is no negative implication in the latter behavior provided it does not lead to infraction of the rules. Some officers may be full-time employees of the club while others serve for a brief time to represent the special interest of particular members. In other words, the model that underlies an organization is basically mechanistic and aggregational. The entity is composed of elements that are removable, replaceable, interchangeable, and that can be combined in various ways. None of this is true, as we will see shortly, of an organic lifeform.

Second, a lifeform, such as a Religious congregation, contrary to what is sometimes implied in Vatican documents,[8] *is not a Platonic essence* composed of "essential elements" that is realized in substantially identical but accidentally different ways in different historical situations. Although this model is more integrated than the organizational one, it fails to take account of the profoundly evolutionary character of Religious Life that is evident from any study of the history of this lifeform in the Church. It tends to suggest that ideally no real change will occur while attempting to disguise genuine development as minor modifications implicit from the beginning.

2. What a lifeform is: A lifeform is an organic reality constituted by the simultaneous presence and interaction of a number of coordinates that generate the organism with its
particular dimensions. I am choosing the words *coordinates*
and *dimensions* rather than *elements* in order to emphasize the
constitutive, simultaneous, interactive, and interpenetrating
character of these features. *Elements* suggests self-enclosed
realities that can be added to or subtracted from a whole without necessarily internally affecting other elements or the
whole. A pile of stones remains a pile of stones until the next-
to-last stone is removed and even after it ceases to be a pile,
each stone remains a stone. Even when "elements" are considered essential to a composite reality, for instance, a subject
and a predicate in the constitution of a sentence, each retains
its independent reality affecting the other element extrinsi-
cally. In an organic reality, such as a plant or animal, no "part"
can be affected without internally affecting other parts as well
as the whole. In other words, an organic entity does not have
"parts" in the mechanistic sense of the word. All of the entity
is the entity even though in different ways.[9]

The coordinates of a lifeform characterize the organism as
a whole. For example, age, bodiliness, rationality, or location
in time and place (dimensions) characterize the whole of the
human entity even though the person cannot be reduced to
any of them. I do not say that my body is so old or so tall but
rather that I am this age and this tall. But I would never agree
that age or height are my ultimate or defining characteristics,
that is, that I can be reduced to or equated with either.

The coordinates of an organic entity can be realized differently and can evolve (e.g., one can be overweight at a certain
point in time and can gain or lose weight in healthy or unhealthy
ways), but unless they continue to characterize the entity, one is
dealing with much more than accidental or superficial change.
Height and weight can change but one is always "so tall" and
weighs "so much." Rationality can increase or decline but if it
disappears in permanent coma, we speak of the person being in
a "vegetative state," which is a recognition of such a qualitative

change that the very understanding of personhood is affected and consequently so are decisions about medical treatment.

Coordinates of an organic entity function in intimate interaction among themselves. Whether a person is overweight depends partially on how tall she is, how old she is, what culture she lives in, and affects her self-image, her relationships with others, even her choice of clothes. Location in place and time profoundly affect one's relationships, one's opportunities, and one's health. One's health affects employment, friendships, spiritual practice, and achievements. One's achievements affect one's salary, self-image, relationships, future opportunities, and so on. In short, the difference between "elements," whether considered essential (in a Platonic sense) or aggregational (in a mechanistic or organizational sense) on the one hand, and coordinates of an organic entity on the other, is highly significant.

B. The Coordinates and Dimensions of Catholic Religious Life as a Lifeform

Let us begin with an attempt to describe the lifeform we call Religious Life in its contemporary realization. If the theory that Religious Life is best understood organically, as a lifeform, is correct, there will be a recognizable continuity between the present phenomenon that I am describing and this lifeform as it has existed throughout its history. At the same time there will be striking, even startling, differences between earlier realizations of the form and the current one. And it will be easy to imagine even more striking differences in the future, even though the fundamental continuity will be part of any imaginative construction.

The reader who is a Religious or well acquainted with the life will have to introduce numerous qualifications as we go along because of the diversity among Religious congregations, but if the project of description is successful she will recognize the description as generally accurate. It is crucial to realize that what follows is not a prescription of what Religious Life *must* be but a description of what it *has been and currently is* because the question this chapter is engaging is whether certain theoretically possible developments are compatible with the lifeform. This does not settle the question of whether the lifeform can be or should be changed into something else, which is a subsequent question, but whether certain changes could occur without changing it into something else.

1. Catholic Christian faith: A first constitutive coordinate of Catholic Religious Life as a lifeform is Christian faith in its Catholic incarnation. Catholic Christian faith is monotheistic, trinitarian, and christocentric. It involves visible and communal ecclesiality, including some kind of recognition of the Petrine ministry, the normativity of Scripture in the revelational process, and sacramental life. Obviously, all of these characteristics of Catholic Christian faith are in a state of radical reevaluation in our time, both in their theological understanding and in their practical sociological realization. But that does not abolish or suspend their intrinsic and constitutive role in the Catholic realization of Christian faith. Furthermore, Religious, especially women Religious, are in a state of serious tension on many fronts with the Church as institution. However, Catholic identity, no matter how it is currently being understood and practiced, has been and remains constitutive of Religious Life.

2. Perpetual commitment in consecrated celibacy: A second constitutive coordinate of Religious Life is perpetual commitment in consecrated celibacy. Although this coordinate can be and historically has been realized in a variety of ways, for example, in eremitical life, double male-female monasteries and/or orders, single-sex communities, communities open or not open to homosexual members, communities open or not to formerly married people, it has always been constitutive of Catholic Religious Life and has always meant religiously motivated, sexually abstinent, nonmarriage chosen in free response to a personal vocation individually discerned. Again, this coordinate is undergoing serious reexamination in our own time but actual Religious Life (as opposed to what might be imagined as possible in theory) cannot be described without it.[10]

3. Community: A third constitutive coordinate of the Religious Life being considered in this book—namely, cenobitic (i.e., communitarian as opposed to eremitical or solitary), ministerial, or contemplative life[11]—is lifelong commitment in a particular, selfsame, and recognizable community. By particular I mean that Religious do not simply enter Religious Life in general. They make profession in a particular order or congregation and remain in that same congregation for life unless they transfer formally and permanently to another congregation to which they then belong while ceasing to belong to the original one. The community is selfsame in the sense that it continues in its identity even as its membership changes through new entrants and deaths or departures, through changes in its government and leadership, through revisions of its constitutions, or modifications of its lifestyle or ministry. It is recognizable in that it has boundaries of some kind by which members are distinguished from nonmembers. People who were not members enter and others who were members leave, and entering and leaving change the status of the person in relation to the community.

This community coordinate involves at least three implications that, despite profound and dramatic changes over the history of cenobitic Religious Life, remain constitutive of the lifeform. The first is complete and unreserved *economic interdependence* of the members, which involves the permanent and total commitment of all personal economic resources to the shared life, full financial disclosure, and complete financial accountability. Obviously, the enormous variety of ways in which this economic interdependence has been legislated and lived is beyond recounting in a brief space. At times it has involved obligatory dowries by those entering and permitted differences among members in lifestyle and clothing. In our own lifetime it has ranged from a system of minute permissions for every material item used by a Religious and absolute uniformity of housing, food, and clothing to fairly autonomous management by Religious of salaries, budgets, credit, and bank accounts. But total economic interdependence, usually undertaken formally by the vow of poverty, remains constitutive of the type of community involved in Catholic Religious Life.

Second, Religious community also involves the full and unreserved *participation of the members in the community's governmental structures and procedures* according to the rule or constitution of the congregation, including a determined relationship to community leaders or officers, the form of corporate discernment that the community embraces, and full personal accountability according to the norms the community establishes. Again, the evolution of this dimension of community even in the last few decades from the virtual divine-right monarchy of preconciliar communities to the egalitarian and collegial forms of contemporary women's Religious Life is dramatic. But the dimension itself, full acceptance of and involvement in the congregation's governmental structure and function, usually formalized by the vow of obedience or some analogue thereof, remains constitutive.

And finally, the community coordinate of Religious Life involves the permanent acceptance of the community itself as the primary and determining *relational context* of one's life. No matter how multiple and various the relationships a Religious maintains and/or establishes with persons and groups outside the congregation, including her own family of origin, none of these can become the ultimate determiner of her life, her decisions, her ministry, or her participation in congregational life. A Religious may live in a group composed entirely of members of her own congregation, or intercongregationally, or in a mixed community, or singly. But her community remains the personal and corporate horizon of her life, no matter how this is actualized in participation in the congregation's life. Undoubtedly, contemporary communities have evolved in very important ways in their capacity to include and validate the multiple relationships of their members and to embrace a variety of lifestyles and living situations among their members, but the primacy of the community as the ultimately determining relational context of the life of the members remains.

4. Mission and ministry: The fourth constitutive coordinate of cenobitic Religious Life as a lifeform is lifelong, full-time, ministerial involvement in the corporate mission of the congregation. This involvement, which was at one time largely understood to mean that every Religious participated in the same work(s), such as teaching or nursing in active congregations, or recitation of the Divine Office, adoration of the Blessed Sacrament, or some other form of prayer in contemplative ones, today can and does take a variety of forms for individual members and for the same member over the course of a lifetime and depending on age, health, talent, and other factors. A congregation may have members involved in a wide variety of works or professions, but these are all undertaken as ministries (not jobs) and are all related to one another as expressive of the corporate mission of the congregation. This is expressed in the expectation that the individual's ministry be discerned with congregational authorities and interpreted in terms of the congregational charism and mission. A Religious, even one who may be the only member of her congregation involved in a particular work, does not have a private occupation, career, or profession—a life work—that is unrelated to the corporate mission of the congregation. Where one member ministers the congregation is present and active, and whatever accrues to the Religious through her work, including recompense, prestige, influence, or advancement, belongs ultimately to the congregation. Members who are prevented by age or health from active work are not "retired" from the congregational mission, even though they may participate primarily or exclusively through interest, prayer, and suffering. Again, there has been startling evolution in the understanding of mission and ministry in Religious congregations over the course of history and especially within the past two decades, but the lifelong and full-time involvement of members in the corporate mission and ministry of the congregation has remained a constitutive dimension of Religious Life.

In summary, Religious Life as it has existed in the Church for nearly two thousand years has gradually evolved into a lifeform in which certain coordinates are recognized as constitutive of the life itself. They are Catholic Christian faith and practice, perpetual commitment in consecrated celibacy, poverty, obedience, community, and ministry. These are not isolated or separable elements that are added to each other to equal the whole but the coordinates that, operating simultaneously and interactively, generate the lifeform itself.

C. Evolution, Mutation, and Dissolution of Lifeforms

Organic entities, by definition, are lifeforms that undergo change, not by extrinsic addition, replacement, or removal of interchangeable parts, but by development (or decline) that involves intrinsic changes in the entity as a whole. Basically, change in organisms occurs by way of evolution, mutation, or dissolution. In what follows I am using these terms metaphorically in their common-sense understanding, not in a technically scientific biological sense. The complexities of evolutionary theory, to say nothing of the nature and function of DNA, are outside my professional competence, and since I am using the organic model as a metaphor for the phenomenon of Religious Life, the types of change that organisms undergo is also being evoked metaphorically.

1. Evolution: A lifeform evolves as its constitutive coordinates develop, that is, as they change or are reformulated in a process of mutual and reciprocal modification in response to the stimuli of the environment. For example, as the understanding by contemporary women Religious of the relationship between leaders and members changed, under the influence of changes in both the theological and cultural environment of the Church, from divine-right monarchy to egalitarian and collegial interaction, major changes occurred in the way ministries were selected. Unilateral assignment by superiors evolved toward the confirmation by leadership of mutually discerned ministry. As ministries were selected differently, changes occurred in how living situations were determined, which led to a diversification in the understanding of community life. Uniform common life shared only by members of the same congregation who lived together in a common dwelling ceased to be the only conceivable realization of community. This has led to new relationships among members of various congregations and with laypeople, which has contributed to the present reexamination of issues of membership. This process will continue and will touch other coordinates of the life. The point is that change in any coordinate or dimension of an organic lifeform implicates other coordinates. However, even though the changes in each area (e.g., leadership, ministry, community) are extensive and even radical, the coordinates remain coordinates of Religious Life.

Sometimes the evolutionary changes in response to environmental stimuli are so extensive or so profound that the lifeform bifurcates, and parallel versions of the life develop without a real change in species. For example, the history of Religious Life has seen the development of solitary and communal forms, male and female forms, monastic and mendicant and contemporary apostolic forms, as well as various combinations of these. At the time these developments took place it was not always clear that they were developments rather than abandonment of Religious Life, because a new version of the life might include something previously deemed incompatible with the lifeform (such as apostolic mobility) or might put aside something previously thought to be essential (such as cloister). In fact, the only constitutive dimensions of Religious Life that have been constant throughout its history (and in hindsight it is clear that they are the "lifeform constituting" ones) are Christian faith, perpetual commitment undertaken by public profession, consecrated celibacy, and an alternate stance toward "the world" that somehow expresses itself in relation to economics and politics. Each particular version of Religious Life has other constitutive coordinates that make it a particular version, for example, community for cenobitic Religious and ministry for apostolic congregations. In summary, evolution in this common-sense understanding takes place when an entity changes and develops significantly but does not cease to be itself, that is, does not lose its identity.

2. *Mutation:* A lifeform mutates when it changes so radically, usually by the addition or subtraction or substitution of one or more constitutive coordinates of its being, that, while something continues to exist which has some continuity with the preceding lifeform, it is no longer the same type of being.[12] It is not always easy to discern precisely the point at which the original has ceased to be itself or that something genuinely new has come into existence. But in retrospect the judgment is often quite clear. There is, for example, some continuity

between the chimpanzee and a human being (both of whom are primates), a type of continuity that we do not recognize between an earthworm and a chimpanzee. However, the discontinuity between the chimpanzee and the human being is such that we make radically different provisions for the two. Chimpanzees are not expected to observe human moral codes; killing a chimpanzee (however evil it may be) is not considered murder; chimpanzees are not taxed or drafted and cannot vote or buy property; humans and chimpanzees do not intermarry. In short, some change took place in the evolutionary process that was so radical it involved genuine discontinuity. The "mutant" is a human being who is now recognized as a different kind of being.

Some mutations are "positive" in that the subsequent lifeform is superior in some way to the original, and some mutations are "negative" or degenerative. Furthermore, some mutations leave the former lifeform in existence even as the mutant begins a parallel developmental career, while other mutations take the entire lifeform into a new kind of being. For our metaphorical purposes the important point is that not all changes are equal in their significance in relation to an organic lifeform. Some may be very dramatic but still compatible with the identity of the organism whereas others, which may be less striking to the observer, may actually inaugurate a different lifeform. When apostolic congregations abandoned cloister and choral recitation of the Divine Office in order to facilitate their ministries, the change was seen as so significant that the members of the new orders were not officially considered Religious until 1900, when it was finally recognized that the coordinates of Religious Life were fully verified in the new form and, conversely, it became clear that cloister and a particular form of prayer were not constitutive of the life as such. On the other hand, Societies of Apostolic Life which, in organization, lifestyle, and ministry closely resemble apostolic congregations, are not and do not wish to be considered Religious Institutes.

3. Dissolution or death: Dissolution of a lifeform takes place when it ceases to be not only *as* it was before (evolution) or *what* it was before (mutation) but to be at all. The dissolution of an organic entity is called death. Again, it may be very difficult to determine exactly the moment of death, and although we have agreed on certain clinical signs in an individual that indicate its occurrence such as a persistently flat brain wave, we are still not altogether certain what constitutes death that might not be entirely or exclusively a physical phenomenon. However, again in retrospect, it finally becomes clear when something organic is no longer alive. We do not say that a person has "evolved" into a corpse nor that the buried animal has "mutated" into the apple tree planted over the grave. The organic entity has ceased to be even though its physical elements or even its spiritual contributions may be taken up into another synthesis.

Not only individuals but groups can die. The Shakers, for example, are a lifeform that seems on the point of disappearing as its last few members approach death.[13] Various Religious congregations throughout Christian history have died. Even whole versions of Religious Life such as the order of widows, anchorites, and the Beguines[14] have ceased to exist. Some forms that have died seem to have been reborn at a later time, for instance, the life of consecrated virginity lived outside a Religious institute under the jurisdiction of a local bishop has been authorized by recent Church legislation and has been taken up by a number of women.[15]

The important point here is that, unlike a mechanical entity, an organic one lives and can die. Death is not just another form of evolution or mutation. Nor is death always tragic. Some lifeforms, like the Shakers, make their contribution and die with dignity. Others, like the slave-ransoming Religious orders of the Middle Ages, are appropriate for their time and die when they are no longer needed. Others die of old age when they cease to be able to attract new members. But death can also occur prematurely or violently when the members of a congregation fail to care for their shared life or when it is violated by external powers, which can be civil,[16] ecclesiastical,[17] or political.[18] Death is a real possibility for any organic entity. It is not to be inordinately feared or resisted at any cost. But insofar as we have the power to prevent it we have important choices to make.

D. The Life and Death Questions Facing Religious Life as a Lifeform

It seems to me that those living Religious Life today are faced, individually and as communities, with a group of questions related to the possibilities inherent in the organic nature of the life itself. The first set of questions concern Religious Life as it now exists, that is, as the particular *evolving lifeform* that we have lived up to and since Vatican II. Do we Religious consider Religious Life *worth* preserving, worth continuing? Do *we want* (whatever the theoretical value of the life in the abstract might be) to keep it in existence? Do we think, regardless of how much we may want to keep it alive, that it is realistically *possible to do so?* If it is possible, are we *committed* to doing so? And if the answer to all of the foregoing questions is yes, are we *imaginative and courageous enough* to foster genuinely healthy evolution of the lifeform into a real future as opposed to a half-life of self-maintenance?

The second set of questions arises around the issue of *mutation*. Do we think the time has come for Religious Life itself, or for our own congregation, or for some of our members to change their lifeform so radically that the resulting entity will be something really different from Religious Life although in some continuity with it? There are numerous forms of committed Christian life in existence today whose members have never considered themselves nor desired to be Religious. The Grail, L'Arche, Focolari, some charismatic communities, the Catholic Worker, meditation groups, communities of pacifism and nonviolent resistance, social justice communities, Basic Christian Communities inside or outside the parish structure, ecumenical communities, as well as groups or individuals such as oblates or tertiaries attached in some way to established Religious communities, and others represent forms of committed Christian community that are not Religious Life. There is no reason why a congregation could not mutate into such a lifeform or why a group of Religious or an individual

Religious could not choose to leave their congregation and join or found such an alternative even while the congregation maintains its identity.

The third set of questions concerns *dissolution*. Do we, corporately or individually, think the time has come to end the Religious lifeform as such? If we are convinced that there is no place or need in the Christian community for a lifeform that is genuinely distinct and/or distinct in the ways that the constitutive coordinates of Religious Life establish, then the time has come to dissolve this lifeform and either to found something new or to go our separate ways into new communities, relationships, and tasks.

Any of the above decisions is possible and a good case can be made and is being made for each of them. Communities grappling with the membership issue, especially in the form of associates and/or members asking for a redefinition of membership to include on a coequal basis those who do not espouse the constitutive dimensions and coordinates of Religious Life, are facing the question in an acute form. It seems to me that the clear and present danger is not that congregations will decide one way or the other but that they will not decide at all and will passively submit to having the choice simply happen by allowing constitutive dimensions of their lifeform to be abandoned, rendered meaningless, or made inoperative until they simply "wake up dead."

One vital characteristic of organic entities is self-determination. If the hard disk on one's computer begins to show signs of malfunction, one takes the computer to the service center and has the disk repaired or replaced. One does not consult the computer on the subject. But if a human being develops symptoms of distress, we do not simply begin replacing parts. The person must be a vital and ultimately the determining participant in the decisions about treatment. The person's decisions may be unwise, counterproductive, or even fatal. But regardless of the outcome, we do not make crucial, especially life-determining, decisions for others or allow others to make them for us. If Religious decide, after mature reflection and prayerful discernment, that the time has come for a new form of committed community life alongside Religious Life (mutation) or that Religious Life has outlived its viability and has no possible or desirable future (dissolution), then the indicated course of action should be undertaken courageously. But Religious congregations, in my opinion, should not allow themselves to be intimidated or forced into mutation or dissolution by outside forces calling for or demanding their transformation into something that others who are not living the life see as preferable or even as necessary.

V. The First Dependent Issue: Inclusiveness

The most sensitive aspect of the membership issue is "inclusiveness." Those who favor the redefinition of membership make the case for this change largely in terms of inclusiveness, and those who have serious reservations about it hesitate to voice them because they do not want even to appear, much less actually to be, noninclusive. The sensitivity of Religious around the topic of inclusiveness is historically understandable, theoretically well-founded in feminist ideology and praxis, and theologically valid. But this sensitivity also has the capacity to tyrannize that is characteristic of unexamined, emotionally freighted presuppositions. Addressing the question of the identity and boundaries of Religious Life as a life-form requires careful examination of the issue of inclusivity.

A. Source of Sensitivity About Inclusiveness

Historically women have been excluded by dominant males from participation in virtually every sphere of society and every arena of action that involved power, decision making, status, or influence. Whatever the reasons given publicly, the real reason for women's exclusion has been gender. Perhaps the most egregious and painful such experience for committed Catholic women has been their exclusion from ordained ministry, with its attendant symbolism and reality of sacramental inferiority and dependence. Thus, women Religious know firsthand the suffering of exclusion, especially the particularly degrading humiliation of being excluded on the basis of one's very person-hood, of that which makes one oneself. It is more than under-standable that women do not want to be the agents of exclusion in relation to others. The suppression of choir/extern distinc-tions within communities as well as the active efforts in many Religious congregations to facilitate membership for women of color, older women, poor or uneducated women, previously married women, and celibate lesbian women testifies to the commitment to removing artificial barriers.

A second historical factor in the sensitivity around the issue of inclusiveness is the guilt and lingering regret many Reli-gious feel about the very real exclusiveness and elitism that characterized preconciliar Religious Life. The official theol-ogy of Religious Life defined it as a "state of perfection" that was intrinsically superior to marriage, and this theology gener-ated an ethos of separation based on a veritable "holiness code,"[19] which marked the person of Religious with sacred clothes, reserved special places for them in the Christian litur-gical assembly, cloistered their dwellings, conferred special titles of nobility, and demanded special behaviors by others in regard to them. Religious who have responded to the conciliar challenge to renew their lives according to the Gospel have disavowed this kind of elitism in theory and in practice, and it is very understandable that they do not want to establish a new version of it by excluding people from membership through insistence on unnecessary requirements.

As feminist consciousness has increasingly come to charac-terize renewed Religious congregations the feminist values of equality, mutuality, and inclusivity have been espoused as self-evidently desirable in all relationships both within and outside the congregation. Any form of exclusion seems somehow to betray the feminist commitment to the construction of a world and society in which the dichotomous hierarchical dualisms of patriarchy have no place. Thus, even the appearance of divid-ing the Christian community into Religious who define and control membership and non-Religious who, if they wish to belong, must conform to requirements they did not help to formulate, is repugnant.

The sensitivity of Religious to the accusation of exclusivity rests finally on the Gospel itself. The more scholars of the social world of Jesus study his historical teaching and praxis, the clearer it becomes that one of the most original features of Jesus' life and ministry was his universal compassion expressed in a nondiscriminatory ministry and an inclusive table fellowship that broke through the purity boundaries of race, religion, ethnicity, gender, economic class, physical condition, and even sinfulness.[20] Religious, contemplating this remarkable characteristic of Jesus' mission and realizing that it is in this very practice of inclusiveness by Jesus that women Christians find the Gospel legitimation of their own struggle for equality in family, society, and Church, do not want to exclude from their own community anyone who seeks to belong.

B. Inclusivity in the Gospel

Jesus' practice of compassion raised a direct challenge to the holiness or purity code that governed his society. Whereas the purity code mapped everything from household utensils and food to social relationships according to grades of closeness to or distance from the center of purity, namely, the Temple, Jesus maintained that nothing God created was intrinsically unclean (cf. Mk 7:18–19) and that no one God made and loved was outside the pale of divine acceptance (cf. Lk 19:9–10; Lk 13:15–17). Because eating with someone in Jesus' culture signified acceptance of and a sharing of life with that person, Jesus' practice of inclusive table fellowship made it clear that he accepted into his love, and therefore that God accepted, all who wished to be with him, regardless of whether they were Jew or Gentile, slave or free, well or sick, rich or poor, male or female, adult or child, sinner or law-observer.

However, Jesus also made distinctions among people in relation to the lifeform and lifestyle he established with his immediate circle of followers. These were not distinctions in love or acceptance, or in degree of discipleship, but reflected certain boundaries in regard to the itinerant, family-less lifeform Jesus developed. In Luke 8:38–39 Jesus, after healing the

Geresene demoniac who then declared a desire to follow him, told the man to return to his own people and bear witness to God's saving action in his life. The Gospel supplies no reason why Jesus did not allow the man to join the circle of his itinerant band. Perhaps it was because the man was not a Jew and Jesus saw his movement as a reform of Israel. Perhaps it was because the man was actually more likely to gain a hearing among his own people than was Jesus or his Jewish disciples. In any case, Jesus called this man to a different life of discipleship and ministry than that to which he called Peter, James, John, Mary Magdalene, Suzanna, and the others who went about in his company.

In Luke 9:57–62 and its parallel in Matthew 8:18–22, Jesus does not accept into his immediate circle of followers some people who declare their desire to join him. Jesus' words to these aspirants about the birds of the air having nests and the foxes having dens but the Son of Man having no place to lay his head suggests that these people were not attracted to the itinerant lifestyle of Jesus and therefore were not called to this form of discipleship. Another man who asked to follow Jesus wanted to return to say good-bye to his relatives, and Jesus apparently decided that he was not called to the kind of detachment from family that this new lifeform involved. The Gospel gives no indication that any of these people is excluded from Jesus' love or compassion. None of them is declared reprobate or even spiritually inferior. Indeed, the implication is that they are enthusiastic disciples of Jesus. But there were obviously certain coordinates that characterized the life of Jesus' immediate band, and those who could not or did not choose to embrace the whole of this lifestyle were not accepted into that company.

Furthermore, Jesus obviously had friends who were special to him and with whom he enjoyed a relationship that he did not extend to all in the same way. In John's Gospel the Beloved Disciple, Martha and Mary and Lazarus of Bethany, and Mary Magdalene are presented as enjoying such a special relationship to Jesus. In the Synoptics Peter, James, John, Mary Magdalene, and a few other women have a privileged relationship with him. In short, Jesus' compassion, inclusive love, and universal call to discipleship did not entail abolishing all boundaries or homogenizing all relationships. To love all does not mean to relate to all in exactly the same way.

C. The Illusory Character of the "Ideal" of Total Inclusivity

Some of the uncomfortableness of Religious with any form of distinction among people seeking membership in their congregations arises from an unexamined "ideal" of total inclusivity. Whether or not it is possible in the concrete, they would like to be able to include anyone and everyone who seeks to join without insisting on any qualifications beyond basic good will and an identification with some aspect(s) of the congregation's project. In fact, such an "ideal" is self-contradictory in theory, impossible and undesirable in practice, and psychologically unhealthy.

First, total inclusivity is a *self-contradictory* ideal. Every choice involves excluding whatever is incompatible with that which is chosen, whether the latter is a spouse, a school, a name for one's child, a movie, an outfit for an occasion, a neighborhood in which to live, a time for meditation, a car, or any other finite reality. Refusal to choose is itself a choice which also involves exclusion.

This basic law of choice is accentuated in relation to two areas that are especially pertinent to Religious Life, namely, lifeform and lifestyle. As a *lifeform* Religious Life is an organic reality and no organism can include in itself, quantitatively or qualitatively, everything that presents itself for inclusion. For example, whatever may be its objective value as an element, arsenic must be excluded from the human organism. The athlete who tries to increase size and performance beyond human limits by the use of steroids risks disease and death. Organisms have limits as to what they can include and remain healthy.

As a *lifestyle* Religious Life is analogous to an art form. Religious construct a lifestyle that, in its integration, balance, proportion, and emphasis, expresses and fosters a particular vision of the Christian life. Art involves giving form to material according to an inspired vision, and forming involves not only selection of materials but also the removal or exclusion of certain materials in order to shape that which is envisioned. The sculptor chips away part of the marble; the painter selects only certain colors and limits the size of the canvas; the musician chooses some sounds and excludes others. In a sense, excluding is as crucial to the work of art as including. Choice, in short, is intrinsic to human life and activity, and all choice necessarily involves exclusion. However, the exclusion involved in choice does not necessarily imply a negative judgment on what is excluded. It is as important as it is difficult for those who have experienced rejection to internalize this obvious realization.

Second, the "ideal" of total inclusivity is *impossible and undesirable* in practice. Even cursory reflection on everyday experience reveals the necessity and desirability of many types of exclusion. Parents must eventually exclude the growing child from their bed; most people exclude others from the bathroom when they are showering; a scholar must exclude otherwise desirable sounds such as conversation or music while trying to write; a counselor disconnects the phone, thereby excluding callers, while seeing a client; selling tickets to an event is a way of excluding those for whom there are no seats; making an appointment excludes others from that time; preteens are excluded from certain films that are quite appropriate for adults; locking one's diary in a drawer excludes others from one's personal reflections; men are excluded from feminist consciousness-raising sessions. In other words, there are numerous perfectly valid reasons, moral, social, political, and personal, for excluding people from certain places, activities, experiences, and relationships. Total inclusivity is neither possible nor desirable in ordinary life, but exclusion does not necessarily imply inferiority or rejection.

Third, and most important for our subject, total inclusivity is *psychologically unhealthy* for any personal organism. Selective exclusion is a function of establishing and maintaining boundaries, which is absolutely necessary for any organic reality if it is to maintain its own identity and establish healthy relationships with others. An organism, whether individual or social, needs to know where it ends and "the other" begins in order to experience *that* it exists and *who* it is. The blurring of boundaries leads to inappropriate merging of identities, to invasion of privacy, to projection and introjection of feelings, and in general to the inability to relate realistically and healthily to the other as other. For an organic entity the complete loss of boundaries is synonymous with death.

However, the boundaries of a mature organism are neither rigid nor impermeable. Organic boundaries are not an extrinsic construction *against* relationship but an internally generated organ *for* relationship. Such boundaries are not a wall but a "skin" that enables one to touch and be touched. Giving and receiving, interchange with systems outside the self, is a very important source of life and growth. The more mature and self-identified a person or group is, the more confident, unapologetic, and nondefensive about its boundaries it can afford to be.[21] Beginning teachers, for example, are often told "not to smile until the second semester," that is, not to relax in any way the status boundaries between teacher and student lest the latter take over. But the experienced teacher can relax with students without fear of blurring the roles. The rather artificial exterior status boundaries have been replaced with real interior role boundaries. Similarly, people who are mature in their faith can share prayer, worship, projects, and dialogue with people of other religious traditions without fear of syncretism, indifferentism, or losing their faith. An organism that is secure in its own identity neither absorbs the other into itself nor allows itself to be absorbed, even as it relates with appropriate intimacy with an increasingly rich and varied spectrum of other organisms. Once again, having boundaries that mark off the self from others does not necessarily involve any negative judgment on or rejection of the other. In fact, it is the condition of possibility for relating to an other as a true equal in mutuality and love.

If the foregoing is true, namely, that undifferentiating inclusivity is not what the Gospel enjoins, is not humanly possible, desirable, or healthy, and that exclusion does not necessarily involve or imply a negative judgment about or a rejection of that which is excluded, the question that needs to be asked is, "What kind of exclusion *is* divisive of the community, morally wrong, or contrary to the Gospel?" When are boundaries undesirable or even illegitimate?

The criteria are simple to express but difficult to apply. Boundaries that are unjust, unloving, or unnecessary (which is not the same as being unwelcome to someone) should be abolished. Boundaries are *unjust* when irrelevant or artificial criteria, especially those over which people have no control, such as their physical characteristics, are used to exclude people from places, roles, activities, or relations in which they have a natural right to participate. To exclude people from voting in their own country on the basis of skin color, to exclude adult Catholics from ordained ministry on the basis of gender, to exclude a person from access to transportation or a restaurant because they must use a wheelchair is to establish unjust boundaries. However, it is not unjust to exclude a child from voting or a Hindu from the Catholic priesthood, or someone who insists on smoking from a bus or a restaurant.

Boundaries are *unloving* when they exclude people from our compassion or unnecessarily bar them from communication and active help in need. No one, no matter how evil their behavior, can really be excluded from the compassionate love of a follower of Jesus. Ideally, we must try to maintain communication even with our enemies and remain open to assisting them in any way we can. However, loving another does not necessarily mean doing or allowing them to do whatever they demand. Discernment is necessary and often very difficult, especially when someone asks something of us that seems to be within our means or power to grant but that we have good reason to refuse.

The parents who send the crying child to bed because they judge he needs the sleep, the minister who refuses an after-hours appointment at the end of a difficult day, the community that decides it is not prudent to sign a particular petition supporting something that is clearly a just cause, or the person who decides not to share intimate personal information with someone who is earnestly seeking her friendship because she judges that kind of friendship with this particular person inappropriate are all making difficult and even painful boundary decisions. What all of these decisions have in common is that the person affected by them feels excluded. He or she may feel angry, hurt, rejected, wronged, or even abused. This does not necessarily mean that the decision was unloving nor that it should be revised. In the last analysis only the person making the decision, the person who must determine and maintain the boundaries, can apply the criterion of loving compassion.[22]

Finally, there are boundaries that are simply *unnecessary* and serve no purpose except that of emphasizing superiority or promoting dominance. Jesus frequently admonished his disciples against establishing status boundaries in the faith community through religious titles, sacred clothes, or special places in the assembly (cf., e.g., Mt 23:1–12). However, it is not the case that all distinctions among people and groups denote or promote superiority or dominance. Children, for example, even when they have become adults, usually do not call their parents by their first names but use special titles of respectful affection. A faculty lounge that is off-limits to students is not necessarily an assertion of privilege or exclusiveness. Choir robes or vestments at worship are not necessarily status symbols. But the ubiquitous competitiveness and dominance in our society and Church make us rightly very suspicious of any distinctions that are not evidently necessary and useful.

D. Conclusion

All of the foregoing considerations are pertinent to the struggle over inclusiveness in regard to membership in Religious congregations. In the past, for reasons that were historically understandable but can no longer be countenanced, congregations were exclusive in antifeminist (if not inhuman) and anti-Gospel ways. Within communities there were unnecessary and oppressive distinctions between superiors and subjects. There were class distinctions between choir Religious and lay sisters or externs. Some entrance requirements were objectively unjust, for example, that one be legitimately born or that there be no known alcoholism, criminality, or mental illness in the family of the applicant. Some criteria were unloving as well as unjust, such as prejudice against applicants of color, unnecessary and elitist academic requirements, or even the refusal of people because they were physically unattractive. Certainly Religious congregations erected unnecessary status boundaries in terms of titles, clothing, housing, communication and the like.

The renewal of Religious Life after Vatican II involved willing, but often painful, demolition of all those boundaries that had no intrinsic relationship to the lifeform but which divided communities internally and from the rest of the Church and the world. Because these boundaries had been so effective in defining Religious identity, their surrender led to serious identity confusion and even loss during the last two or three decades. This has made it difficult for many Religious to locate themselves in the Church and has made some Religious diffident about presenting their life as a possibility to others.

As Religious gradually regain a sense of identity, founded no longer on artificial and superficial status boundaries or rigid distinctions unrelated to the Gospel but on a reappropriating of the meaning of their own specific (not superior) vocation in the Church, they need to clarify their real and necessary boundaries in terms of the constitutive dimensions and coordinates of their lifeform. The purpose of such boundary clarification is not to exclude but to establish and maintain identity. No one is excluded from Religious Life who wants and is able to live the life. Those who freely choose not to embrace the lifeform are, because of their own choices, excluded from membership. However, this involves no judgment that they are inferior, no rejection, no refusal of love, no unjust denial of rights. It simply specifies the kind of relationship the community has with those who are not participants in its lifeform. This kind of distinction and relationship is what healthy boundaries enable between diverse organisms. Some of these laypeople will be simply friends and/or benefactors of the congregation. Others will be lay associates of one kind or another. A plurality of types of relationship is possible, desirable, and healthy. But total merging, boundary loss, identity confusion are neither healthy nor desirable even though they may be desired by some people.

VI. The Second Dependent Issue: Numbers and the Future

The concern of some Religious with the membership issue centers less on inclusivity than on the issue of numbers. The number of people entering most Religious congregations has declined dramatically in the last two decades while the median age has risen into the sixties and seventies.[23] It appears that such congregations are dying and that unless they can drastically increase the number of younger people entering in the very near future they will be extinct within another decade.[24] Since a relatively large number of laypeople who have no desire to undertake the lifeform as a whole would like to be members on other terms, it seems only prudent to accept as members those who are available. In other words, diversification of membership seems to be one of the signs of the times in regard to Religious Life.

An alternate conclusion might be that the situation invites us to reexamine the issue of numbers in relation to the future of Religious Life. One of the striking features of contemporary Religious Life is the fact that despite the apparent signs of impending death constituted by small numbers of entrants, rising median age, and increasing financial strain, most renewed Religious congregations of women continue to exhibit impressive signs of vitality. Creativity, commitment, generosity, strong leadership, healthy diversification and transfer of training, inclusivity, partnering, vision, an effective preference for mission over maintenance, life-giving ministerial choices, and hope continue to mark these congregations.[25] This also is a sign of the times. The coexistence of these seemingly contradictory signs calls for a second look at what is afoot.

A. The Fixation on Numbers in Ministerial Congregations

For at least three historical reasons most ministerial Religious congregations share a conviction, which may be quite unfounded, that large annual groups of entrants are a sine qua non of health and survival for the congregation. *Large* is a relative term, usually determined by the size of the congregation in the years when it was at its peak in numbers and institutions (often the 1950s and 1960s). A congregation that has never had more than five hundred members may consider an entrance class of twenty to be appropriately large, whereas a congregation whose highest number was two thousand may envision an entrance class of sixty or seventy as minimally normal. In either case, an annual entrance "class" of one or two people seems totally inadequate, and leaders of the congregation may wonder whether it is even legitimate to incorporate these people who have no peers in formation or community and will have no contemporaries in the years ahead as they assume leadership and financial responsibility in the congregation.

One reason large numbers of entrants seem an obvious requirement for continued corporate health and life is that most ministerial congregations were, at least in some sense of the word, "founded for" some work such as teaching or nursing.[26] Historically, the community initiated and staffed the institutions through which it carried on these ministries. Thus, although there is no particular work that is actually essential to Religious Life as such or to any congregation as a Religious institute, the perception persists that ministry as such (whatever concrete form it takes) requires a large group of Religious as workers. And, in fact, in order to fulfill the ministry that helped call many congregations into being, such as meeting the social, health, educational, and faith formation needs of large groups of immigrants in nineteenth-century United States or victims of the revolution's destruction of the infrastructure in eighteenth-century France, large numbers were absolutely necessary.[27]

Second, one of the main differences between ministerial Religious Life and monastic life is its economic foundation.

Whereas monastic life is a stabile, economically self-sufficient lifeform, ministerial Religious, because so much of their time and energy was devoted to the ministry carried on "outside" the community setting itself, had to depend on payment for their services as the primary source of subsistence. In the early days of Religious Life in the new world "payment" was minimal and life was often bare subsistence. Donations from the parish, fees from students who were better off, tuition from music or art lessons, payment from patients who could afford to pay, special "collections for the sisters," benefactions from wealthy friends, and the like were combined with an extremely frugal lifestyle, donated services from doctors and workers, and payment in kind from grateful beneficiaries of the community's services to keep the congregation financially solvent or to bail it out when debts mounted.

Gradually, congregations established themselves on sounder financial footing, developed investment policies, professionally trained their personnel, and upgraded their institutions to the point of being able to turn the latter into financially stable works. A major factor in the establishment of congregations as fiscally sound enterprises was the absolutely common life of the members, which could be maintained at a very restrained level of consumption, and the contribution of all members' salaries to the common fund. Large numbers of young sisters replenished the work force in the institutions, making it unnecessary to employ many other workers at full salary. There was, in short, a self-evident connection between financial security and large numbers of young Religious working in the congregation's own institutions. They were the key to ongoing economic well-being. The decline in numbers of young Religious, which makes it nonfeasible for congregations even to maintain their own institutions at precisely the time when large numbers of retirees are making major financial demands on the congregation, seems ultimately fatal from an economic point of view.

A third reason the decline in numbers of entrants seems to presage imminent death in ministerial congregations is that a formation tradition developed in the years of large numbers, that congregations have continued to regard as normal and healthy, although it has become impossible to maintain. This creates the impression that formation is not only being done badly but that there is no real way to improve it. Formation of ministerial Religious was basically done in "classes" or "bands," that is, in large, almost school-like groups. Novices were taught both academic and professional subjects that prepared them for ministry and the rudiments of Religious Life and spirituality in classroom settings. They worked together in large groups in kitchens and gardens and workrooms. They recreated together in isolation from the professed community and developed both a social context and an esprit de corps that they carried into adult Religious Life. Novices and young professed learned who they were as Religious and as members of the congregation as much or more from this group experience as they did from their formation directors, with whom they often enough had a cohort-based, superior-subject relationship that was somewhat analogous to the ambivalence if not antagonism of adolescents toward their parents. Given this experience it is difficult for many adult Religious to imagine how an adequate or even healthy formation can occur in the absence of a fairly large group, all of whose members share the formation experience.

All of these factors, which have a certain self-evidence as nonnegotiable indicators of health and well-being in ministerial congregations, need to be reexamined in light of the experience of the past twenty-five years.

B. Numbers and Religious Life

At the time when most Religious congregations peaked numerically, ecclesial and sociological factors converged to encourage many young people to enter Religious Life who would not consider that option today. In the Church Religious Life was regarded and presented as the highest calling to which a woman could aspire. It was a life of perfection, intrinsically superior to marriage and more pleasing to God than any other choice a woman could make. Furthermore, in the 1950s the postwar redomestication of women was in full flower. The "real woman" did not work outside the home, and if she was Catholic there was great motivation for her to have numerous children and to remain in the home fulltime to care for them until the last one was independent. The only other possibility was the single life, "spinsterhood," presented implicitly and explicitly as a fate no woman would choose because it certified her inadequacy as a woman. Consequently, a young Catholic woman who really wanted a higher education, a profession, some measure of autonomy in relation to what she might perceive as a fairly stifling domestic life and/or male supremacy in a patriarchal marriage had only one readily available path to such a life, namely, entering the convent.

Without doubt many young women entered the convent from a combination of motives that were not clear to themselves or to their formation personnel, who often were not prepared with either an adequate theology of Religious Life or a sophisticated psychological framework within which to discern a genuine vocation to Religious Life. Although genuine spiritual motivation undoubtedly played some, and probably a major, role in the choice to enter the convent, many young women entered Religious Life in part because they were spiritually idealistic, were romantically attracted to the mysterious and elite life represented by the convent, desired to do something extraordinary for God, wanted to teach or nurse or do social work, were attracted to the professionally active, mature, and often genuinely holy sisters they knew, wanted something they perceived as other or more challenging than the lives of their mothers, wanted to see themselves and be seen by others as "special" in a world where women were rarely more than support systems for men and caretakers of children, wanted to prolong the life of comradeship with young women their own age or the mentor relationships they had with their teachers, and so on.

In fact, it is highly unlikely that very large numbers of people are actually, or ever were, called to Religious Life. A lifelong commitment to consecrated celibacy, which is at the heart of the vocation to Religious Life, is not the "normal" path to Christian holiness. In retrospect, we can probably affirm that many of the young women who flocked into our congregations in the 1940s, '50s, and early '60s were not really called to Religious Life as such. At most they felt called to be Sisters of Mercy or Dominicans in the sense that they were attracted to the community and its work without understanding the specificity of Religious Life which was realized in that community. The result was a falsely inflated image of what a healthy Religious congregation looks like, namely, a large group of women whose ranks are incessantly augmented by the annual or even semiannual influx of dozens of young recruits. Even given the high attrition rate during the postulancy and novitiate, profession classes in large orders often numbered thirty or forty members or more. And the theology of Religious vocation at that time as well as attitudes toward life commitment in the Catholic community at large made leaving Religious Life after final profession so difficult that many persevered long after they knew they were not called to the life.

If it is true that relatively few people are actually called to the fairly unusual vocation that is Religious Life, it must be the case that Religious communities do not actually need very large numbers of members. It is instructive to note that many contemplative communities that have been in existence for hundreds of years have never had more than a couple dozen members. They have welcomed one or two candidates every year or so, and some have stayed. But they have never had bulging novitiates or been unduly concerned about a year in which no one entered or no one stayed. This is no doubt due to the fact that these communities are not pressured by the felt need for workers, either to staff institutions or to earn money. They are basically about the business of being Religious, and numbers, beyond what is necessary for a healthy community life, has not been seen as a major issue. Unlike contemplative communities, however, apostolic congregations understand ministry as intrinsic to their vocation, but I question whether that fact necessarily implies or justifies the anxiety about numbers that leads ministerial Religious to equate reduced numbers with imminent death. If ministerial communities could reexamine the relationship between their identity as Religious communities on the one hand and their ministries and finances on the other, they might discover that the felt need for numbers is, at best, exaggerated.

Furthermore, small contemplative communities have always formed their members either individually or in small novitiates of two or three. While the challenge of formation is quite different in a ministerial community and includes professional preparation that requires more than a novitiate of one or two can provide, the comparison does suggest that formation for Religious Life itself does not necessarily require a group setting comparable to an incoming college freshman class. Perhaps the goals and objectives of Religious formation need to be re-examined and distinguished from professional preparation, which may need to be undertaken in another context.

In short, I am suggesting that as far as Religious Life itself is concerned numbers are a relatively insignificant factor. As long as there are some people entering who are truly called to Religious Life, who interiorize the charism of the community, and who persevere, the future of the congregation as a locus of Religious Life is quite secure. Religious Life itself has no need of large numbers. In fact, large numbers may well mean that the life is poorly understood and inadequately presented. Religious Life *needs* only as many people as are called to it because it does not exist to produce some specific product.

C. Numbers and Ministry

The problem with the foregoing, of course, is that it seems to sidestep the issue of ministry, which is, after all, intrinsic to ministerial Religious Life. In part 4 B above, I suggested that ministry is the fourth coordinate of ministerial Religious Life and therefore maintaining the resources, both personal and financial, for the exercise of ministry according to the charism of the institute is crucial to the identity of the congregation. Ministry is not, in other words, an optional occupation of the congregation if it happens to be in a position to offer such. Obviously, a congregation cannot carry on its ministry if it has no ministers. In other words, aside from the issue of Religious Life as a personal vocation to live the Gospel in a particular way, there is the issue of works, which is not only the source of a community's livelihood but also the way in which it lives its call to participate in the transformation of this world according to the Gospel. We need, then, to attend to the second issue, namely, work as ministry.

It seems to me very important for Religious to appropriate and internalize the fact that Religious Life is not an ecclesiastical job corps, a source of cheap labor for the projects of the hierarchy. Most American Religious congregations, no matter how they started out, were soon "possessed" by local bishops who regarded the sisters as a readily available and inexpensive diocesan resource. Even as congregations became pontifical and thus were no longer, strictly speaking, under the local bishop, they continued to deploy their personnel in response to episcopal or clerical requests for teachers or missionaries or nurses or even domestics in seminaries and priests' residences. There is no need to pass judgment on this approach to ministry, which made a certain kind of sense in an immigrant Church and in a society in which women were generally seen as support systems for male personnel and projects. Indeed, what is amazing is the extent to which courageous superiors managed to retain some autonomy for their congregations in regard to ministry. But what we need to realize today is that there is no essential reason to equate ministry with the ownership or staffing of institutions or with the carrying out by the congregation of particular works such as teaching or nursing.

Ministry is intrinsic to the vocation of Religious in apostolic congregations. And the ministry of each member is a participation in the corporate mission of the congregation. However, if the corporate mission is understood to be the embodiment of the charity of Christ, the extension of the mercy of God in the world, participation in the reconciling mission of Jesus, or some other particular formulation of the Gospel mandate rather than as a specific work such as teaching or nursing, then the possible ways of incorporating that mission in the ministry of the individual Religious are numerous. And if this is so the congregation can develop a number of forms and styles of ministry that do not require large numbers, indeed do not require any more Religious than the congregation has, because it is the

Religious who would then determine the ministry, not the ministry that would demand a certain number of Religious.

By way of example, a congregation might carry out its mission by orchestrating programs of volunteers or associates in ministry. There might be no more than one or two Religious involved in a particular ministerial enterprise, which would be staffed by others. The role of the Religious might be to facilitate the spiritual and/or professional formation and ongoing development of the staff or simply to provide the continuity for the ministry as staff members come, participate, and move on.

Another model might be the joint undertaking by several congregations of a ministry they discern as responding to an unmet need. This might be a college or hospital or homeless shelter or AIDS hospice or drug program or community organizing agency or literacy program or spiritual renewal center. It would be directed by a board or other form of administration composed by the member congregations, and it might even be partly staffed by members of the cooperating congregations. Such cooperative ventures could be a partial answer to the current dilemma of Religious congregations being unable to undertake long-term systemic ministerial commitments because they cannot assure continuity of personnel.

Another possibility, one which is being extensively used at the present time but which may be ready for evaluation and revision, is for Religious to work in ministerial projects for which the congregation does not carry any institutional responsibility, such as parishes, schools, hospitals, or other agencies run by the diocese, the state, or secular organizations. The advantage of this arrangement is the freedom of the Religious to actually minister rather than having to worry about keeping the project in existence financially or otherwise and also the relative freedom of the Religious to leave the ministry when that becomes appropriate without fear that the people served will be abandoned. However, there are disadvantages in these situations that need to be addressed. The Religious may have very little leverage in such a situation and may find herself simply "working for" a cleric or a bureaucracy whose ministerial sense or commitment may have little in common with hers or with that of the congregation. Furthermore, the experience of the past two decades is making it very clear that Religious ministering in diocesan agencies often have not only very little leverage in terms of values and decisions but are also very vulnerable to unjust treatment by clergy in diocesan structures that offer no recourse to nonclerical employees.[28]

One model being developed by a number of congregations is that of institutional sponsorship. Rather than administering or staffing an institution such as a school or hospital, the congregation, through board membership and other legal arrangements, has a major role in determining and maintaining the mission of the institution and influencing its personnel and procedures. Here one or a few Religious can exercise major ministerial influence not only on the institution and the personnel but through them on large populations and whole professions.

Religious have also discovered that by concentrating their energies on the leadership roles in a particular ministry they can facilitate the ministry of many other people and assure systemic continuity even though they are not actually staffing the institution or agency in question. A number of schools and hospitals and other agencies have a single Religious as administrator but through her the congregation plays a major ministerial role that is consonant with its mission and charism.

Some Religious are also beginning to experiment with the founding of small, freelance enterprises in which a number of individual Religious, from the same or diverse congregations, come together to address some particular unmet need they have discerned. Often they work with laypeople who share the vision. But the projects are alternatives to the large institutional approach and allow for greater flexibility and creativity in regard to the ministry while allowing the Religious to experience a corporate identity and solidarity in ministry which they find extremely strengthening. It might be that this type of companionship in ministry will function psychologically for some younger Religious analogously to the way large entrance classes functioned for earlier generations, that is, creating an esprit de corps and a shared history of adventures that bond the participants across generations.

These suggestions do not exhaust the possibilities, but they should suffice to suggest that a number of unexamined presuppositions underlie the conviction that large numbers of members are essential to effective congregational ministry and have unnecessarily demoralized congregations that have small numbers of highly committed and effective members. There is no need for a congregation to own and operate institutions or to staff every ministry in which it participates. In fact, this may be counterproductive in many cases. A congregation does not need, for effective ministry, any more members than it has. The important thing is that every member be fully involved according to her ability and gifts in the corporate mission of the congregation and that the congregation maximize its ministerial influence by its creativity in discernment and deployment.

D. Numbers and Finances

While the foregoing may be true about the work of Religious considered as ministry, it leaves untouched the issue of the work of Religious as a source of income for the congregation, which also suggests the need for large numbers in the congregation if it is to survive. Not only have Religious in ministerial congregations historically supported themselves through remuneration for their apostolic work, which creates an unexamined presupposition that this is the only possible approach for the future, but the economic situation of Religious congregations has been immeasurably complicated in the last couple of decades by the serious disproportion, for the first time, between earners and nonearners in the congregation. In the past fewer people lived to very old age, and medical procedures for the very elderly were less numerous, expensive, and available. At the same time, the number of younger members working full time outnumbered the elderly and the infirm, which meant that the congregation had both personnel and financial resources to care for its elderly. Today congregations have neither resource available, and the only solution appears to be a dramatic increase in numbers of younger members, which is highly unlikely to occur.

While this shifting proportion between the old and the young is not peculiar to Religious congregations and is presenting challenges for American society as a whole, it is definitely complicating the issue of numbers in Religious congregations. The tendency to define acceptable ministry for a Religious in terms of its earning potential is, in my opinion, a dangerous trend. Obviously, highly trained professionals, which many Religious are, can command high salaries if they are willing to work for the agencies and in the circumstances in which such salaries are available. But this may very well not be where the most urgent ministerial needs are. Some Religious today are finding a job on the basis of pay and then using a modern version of the "good intention" to interpret it as ministry. It is not surprising if such "ministry" soon ceases to nourish or be nourished by prayer, to provide a basis for shared faith with fellow Religious, or to make Religious Life itself continue to seem meaningful apart from work. Religious in such circumstances can easily conclude that their primary value to their congregation is their salary rather than their person or their ministry. And a class system that subtly stratifies members according to salary can become operative in fact even while it is vigorously denied in principle.

I certainly do not have any ready answer to the question of how Religious congregations can support themselves, including caring for their elderly, and actually choose their ministries in terms of what needs to be done rather than in terms of salary. However, time itself may be part of the answer. The fact that far fewer people are entering Religious communities means that eventually, in the not-too-distant future, there will not be large numbers of Religious retiring, and the relationship between retired and earners will begin to come into better balance. This obviously cannot be the entire solution. Religious congregations have to find ways, as many are already doing very effectively, to obtain funds that make them less completely dependent on salaries. Raising money may be one of the areas in which we need Religious who are specialists.

Congregations with overseas missions, especially men's orders, have long relied on direct mail solicitation and other fund-raising techniques to support their ministries. Such enterprises, along with careful investment, obtaining grants, enlisting ongoing support from lay patrons, various kinds of support from associates and affiliates, and other creative methods of generating financial resources may well have to supplement and even begin to replace salaries as a major source of support for ministerial Religious. This is not a collapse into irresponsibility, into not being able to "pay our own way" in a financially competitive society. It is a recognition that what we choose to do, serve human needs, is intrinsically valuable and worth support but that we live in a society which does not reward altruistic activity financially. Making the system work for us and through us for the least of Jesus' sisters and brothers will take ingenuity and the prudence of the serpent, but it is not an unworthy or reckless project.

The point of the foregoing is that the presupposition that major if not total support for the congregation must come from the salaries received by active members for the work they perform as ministry needs to be called into question. It has a great deal to do with the anxiety over numbers of members and is capable of seriously distorting the approach of Religious to ministry. Money should not drive the ministerial or the membership concerns of a Religious community. Once this is accepted, creativity and imagination can be mobilized to make it unnecessary. But until it is clearly recognized that allowing finances to determine our understanding of our life and ministry is not a life-giving option, we will continue to see small numbers as a death knell when, in fact, large numbers may have very little if anything to do with the viability of a congregation.

VII. Discernment

The membership issue has raised two major questions: that of boundaries and the possible redefinition of membership; that of numbers and the future of Religious Life. I have attempted to suggest ways of thinking about these two issues that resist pressures on the one hand and panic on the other. However, both issues do offer a challenge to Religious to discern carefully the road ahead. I would suggest that there are two areas of discernment which the membership issue is raising for ministerial congregations and which need to be addressed by Religious themselves.

A. Should Religious Life Continue?

The people whose lifeform is in question, namely Religious themselves, need to respond to the question of the viability of this life. Do we believe in Religious Life; do we find it life-giving for ourselves; do we think it is vital for the Church and the world; do we want to continue to live it? If the answer to these questions is no, that is, if we do not have the vital energy for the project, then we should actively end it and either enter a new lifeform that already exists or found something new for which we do have the energy and commitment. It seems to me that the ultimate tragedy would not be to arrive at the conclusion that our lifeform has served its purpose and the time has come for something new. The ultimate tragedy would be to allow something we do believe in to disappear by default because we have not exerted the necessary energy to analyze the problems and face the challenges that confront us.

If, on the other hand, the answer to these questions is yes, we need to do several things to implement that answer. First, we need to actively resist outside pressure toward mutation or dissolution (both of which would do away with the very lifeform with which others want to associate) even as we attend with energy to appropriate evolution. No living organism can afford to stagnate. The changes congregations and individuals have made since Vatican II are significant, but the process must continue. However, because Religious Life is an organic lifeform, Religious must retain the right and the responsibility of corporate self-determination. There are many people, including the Vatican, some local bishops, and some laypeople who would like to be full members but without assuming the responsibilities of the life, who are convinced that they know what it is time for in our life. It would be arrogant not to listen to their input. But in the last analysis it is those who live the life in its integrity who must decide what is genuinely future for us.

Second, we need to find ways to offer the invitation to Religious Life in a compelling way to those who are really called to join us in this life. For many years now Religious have been hesitant to promote Religious Life, to talk about it to prospective members, to invite others to consider it. This has been due in large measure to the unsettled state in most congregations. We were uncertain about the nature of the life and exactly what we were offering to others. As we become more convinced about our identity and mission, more secure about our place in the postconciliar Church, more committed to our own future, we should also become more confident about inviting others to join us. Such invitation need not be a new version of the somewhat indiscriminate "recruiting" of the 1950s. It can be a sober, realistic, but enthusiastic offering to others of something in which we really believe.

Third, it is not enough to interest others in Religious Life. Congregations need to develop effective formation programs for those who do enter in order to enable them to discern well whether or not they are called to this life and to help those who are called to truly "arrive," to appropriate the life with the clarity and conviction that will enable them to become the next generation.

Fourth, if congregations decide not to diversify forms of membership but to reach out through a variety of forms of association, they will have to help those who are now members but who have come to realize that they are not and never were called to Religious Life itself to negotiate the implications of that realization. Not all such people can or want to leave Religious Life. Many have spent virtually all their adult life in their congregation, which is now their only real relational context. They have been faithful to the obligations they undertook and intend to remain faithful to them. The increased clarity about the nature of Religious Life that is emerging from the struggles of the postconciliar years cannot be used to exile these sisters, but it also cannot be obscured or sacrificed in order to camouflage their somewhat anomalous situation. This is one of the gray areas of modern Religious Life, and it needs to be accepted and dealt with compassionately and realistically and according to the capabilities and insights of each congregation.

Fifth, Religious congregations committed to their own future will have to actively develop and promote new approaches to ministry that are not dependent on large numbers of Religious even as they tackle the problem of finding ways to finance those ministries and support the congregation that will free it to make life choices guided by theology and spirituality rather than being forced into compromises for financial reasons.

B. The Membership Issue as Invitation of the Spirit

A second area that urgently demands discernment and response is that of the insistent appeal by laypeople who do not feel called to assume the full responsibilities of membership for some form of association or participation in the life of Religious congregations. The good will, zeal, and commitment of these laypeople is enormous. If Religious congregations decide that they are *not* being called to respond to these appeals by self-dissolution, that is, by abolishing the constitutive coordinates of their lifeform or dissolving the boundaries which mark that life off from other lifeforms in the Church, they must address the question of what they *are* being called to by this phenomenon, which clearly seems to be the work of the Spirit.

Perhaps some light can be thrown on the issue by attempting to discern what has given rise to this widespread interest on the part of laypeople, mostly Catholic and mostly women, in association with women's Religious congregations. Vatican II called all Catholics to maturity in their faith. This was interpreted as active participation in the liturgy, informed engagement with Scripture, deepened personal spirituality, active commitment to the mission of the Church and involvement in its ministry, assumption of responsibility in the local ecclesial community, and evangelization of the secular order.

Many Catholics responded enthusiastically to this challenge. Unfortunately, neither the structures nor the official personnel of the institutional Church were prepared for this response. As many of the laity testify, many parishes are woefully inadequate as the context for adult faith and ministry. Furthermore, for numerous reasons that are not germane to this chapter and are not the fault of the dwindling number of committed but overworked and underresourced ordained ministers, many of the clergy are incompetent to lead a renewed People of God into the future. There is no point arguing, as is regularly done from pulpit and chancery, that the parish *should* be the center of Catholic life. Nor does it advance the situation to insist that the clergy *are* the leaders in faith and mission. Many postconciliar Catholics have given up on the parish and the clergy because they have found the former moribund and the latter inept. Furthermore, it is probably the case that the majority of these committed Catholics are women, many of whom are increasingly alienated from a resolutely patriarchal and sexist ecclesiastical institution.

It may be the case, and it is certainly perceived to be the case by many of those seeking association with Religious communities, that the most alive and lively form of postconciliar Catholic community life is that of women's Religious congregations. In these congregations committed women are struggling to develop truly egalitarian and collegial forms of government, working to build faith-founded and faith-nurturing community, experimenting with ministry in areas unaddressed by traditional structures, establishing relationships across boundaries of race, gender, denomination, religious tradition, sexual orientation, and class, taking on the social justice agenda of the turn of the century in regard to war and peace, discrimination of all kinds, ecology, and poverty, and supporting each other in the effort to renew Religious Life itself according to the Gospel and the charism of their foundations. Furthermore, these congregations are increasingly feminist in their theory and practice.

In view of the inability of the official structures and personnel to nurture and contextualize the emerging spirituality of this contingent of postconciliar Catholics seeking to put their persons and their energies into the new agenda launched by the Council, it is not at all surprising that these people have turned to Religious congregations as a point of focus. Here they can find solidarity, leadership, formation, support, example, and companionship in what is a very new venture for many of them. These laypeople, as we have seen, do not really want to *become* Religious. What they do want is to belong to something that is relatively stabile, structured, identifiable, and likely to be able to provide the setting and services necessary to pursue their spirituality and ministerial agenda.

Some of these people are seeking primarily a lively, prayerful, feminist liturgy. Others are looking primarily for help in the development of their interior life of prayer and discernment. Still others are seeking solidarity and support in justice involvement, direction of their ministerial energies, or genuine community based on faith and love. Many are seeking some combination of several of these. In short, women's Religious congregations are being seen by many postconciliar Catholics, especially women whose feminist consciousness has been raised, as an exciting and hopeful alternative to the lifeless or oppressive parishes from which they have drifted or been alienated.[29]

Not all of those seeking association with Religious communities come from situations of alienation or discouragement with parish resources. Some are simply seeking "something more" in their own spiritual life or are attracted by the particular charism or spirituality of the congregation. Others come because they have deep relationships, through ministry or family or friendship, with members of a congregation and want a more sustained experience of this solidarity. But in virtually all cases people seek association with Religious communities because they want to grow in the spiritual life and assume their full adult responsibilities in the Church for the world.

The question this seems to raise is whether Religious are being called to a new ministry in the Church, just as our forebears were called to the very new mission of offering education, health, and social services to immigrant Catholics. Perhaps Religious congregations are being called to undertake the ministry of promoting the emergence of the laity into that full adult spirituality and ministry to which the Council called them but which the institutional Church is often enough unequipped and/or unwilling to promote. Many Religious are in fact already involved in this ministry through their work in sponsored institutions, mixed ministries, and even in parishes where the Religious on the staff is directing the RCIA, facilitating the development of basic Christian communities, or coordinating lay ministries. However, it is perhaps time for us to recognize this ministry for what it is. This may be not simply a valuable by-product of our working in situations in which many of the ministers are lay or our having contact with laity through our ministries. Perhaps it is where a major ministerial effort of our congregations should be actively directed.

Religious have a great deal to offer to the ministry of promoting the emergence of the laity. We may be some of the relatively few people in the Church who, as a group, have a deep formation in well-tested traditions of spirituality. We also have a very long collective experience in community building and community life which could help lay communities to avoid some of the pitfalls that we know well from our experience. Religious congregations also have a long and varied experience in ministry that virtually no other group of women in the Church has. We have some "toeholds" in ministry that our lay partners do not yet have because they are new to the scene and often lack the collective organization and leverage necessary to influence the situation. Thus we are in a position to facilitate the entrance of laypeople into ministry, to help them avoid victimization by clerical privilege and unjust personnel policies and practices, and to offer them encouragement when they encounter the profound disappointments that ministry over the long haul inevitably involves.

As congregations located physically and socially in particular historical sites, we can offer the stability that individual laypeople often cannot offer one another simply because they must change locations or jobs or commitments as family and employment make diverse demands. Even as our own personnel move about, the congregation remains based in a particular place, and different members of the congregation can offer continuity.[30] Finally, as groups of women who have centuries-long experience running women-staffed enterprises, we probably have more actual feminist experience than any other group in the Church. We know from experience what women in solidarity can accomplish. We know well how women have been and are oppressed by the institutional Church, and we have learned much about how to survive, subvert, and eventually overcome such oppression.

While women's Religious congregations have a great deal to offer to the laypeople who are turning to us at this point in history, we face a serious challenge to actually foster the emergence of the laity as full and equal partners and not to promote a new kind of dependence. Little will be gained if dependence on the clergy is simply relocated in relation to Religious. The time is ripe, for the first time since the earliest days of the Church, for a fully mature, genuinely lay spirituality and ministry to develop. Just as it has proved to be extremely difficult for missionaries to promote genuine inculturation of the faith and the emergence of young Churches that are neither dependent on nor clones of first-world Churches, so it will be a serious challenge for Religious congregations to offer adequate support to the laity without controlling their development.

Religious do not and cannot know what genuinely adult lay spirituality in our time is or should be. None of us have ever seen such a phenomenon because what, in the past, has been called lay spirituality has been largely a deficient imitation of clerical or Religious spirituality. A truly lay spirituality must emerge from lay experience, be constructed on lay premises, develop lay leadership, and promote a kind of personal practice and ministerial involvement that is compatible with and truly transformative of lay life. If Religious congregations can meet this challenge to assist without taking over, we will not only have chosen to maintain our own form of life in the Church but we will have responded to the historical challenge brought to us by the people seeking association with us and we will have participated in what may be the most important renewal movement in the history of the Church, the emergence of a fully adult and responsible laity.

Of course, this development is not a one-way street. As associates join us in life and ministry as fully equal and genuinely lay, we will face the challenge of a stimulating and surprising new partnership. Religious will have much to learn and probably much to surrender as well as much to offer. The sociological context as well as the inner dynamics of our life as communities has been broadened and deepened, and such growth is always demanding. It would probably be easier to simply absorb this new contingent into our own lifeform than to engage it as other and different but truly equal. In my opinion this would be not only a surrender of our own lifeform but, at the very least, a failure to discern something new on the horizon.

Chapter Three
Religious Life in a Postmodern Context: Faith and Fidelity against the Grain

I. Introduction: Seven Hundred Years in Three Decades

Periodizing history is always a risky project. Obviously, there is no "objective" boundary marking off late antiquity from the Middle Ages, the Middle Ages from modernity, and modernity from postmodernity. Furthermore, we must recognize that even insofar as such periodization involves relatively valid description it is done from the standpoint not of the human race but of white, Anglo-European, economically secure, academically trained males. Women, people of color, Asians or Africans or Latin Americans, the poor, the illiterate would tell a very different story with very different temporal and cultural markers. Nevertheless, I think it is valid to use these periods for descriptive and analytical purposes in what follows because women Religious have lived in, and to a large extent according to, the world construction of those who have done the periodizing. In other words, what I will describe as ancient, medieval, modern, or postmodern has been internalized, until very recently, by women in general as "how things are," if not how they should or even have to be.

99

With this caveat, I want to focus on the extraordinary experience of women Religious in the brief thirty years since the close of Vatican II. In effect, Religious, in those three decades, made the passage from the Middle Ages to postmodernity, which took Western humanity nearly seven hundred years to accomplish. The transition through which they have passed is unprecedented in scale, scope, depth, and radicality, and the disorientation of this period can only be understood in light of that fact. At risk of great oversimplification, let me briefly describe that transition as background for what will follow on the cultural situation of Religious Life today and its institutional and spiritual ramifications.

When classical late antiquity collapsed with the Roman Empire in the late fifth century, the Church was the only institution in the Western world capable of dealing in any stabilizing way with the chaos that followed. It undertook to hold Europe, including what is now the United Kingdom, together while a new culture, integrating the "barbarian" cultures and the remains of classical antiquity, emerged in a new synthesis later called the Middle Ages. The medieval period has been divided very roughly into the early period or "Dark Ages" (from 500–1000 C.E.), the High Middle Ages or the "Golden Age" (from 1000–1300), and the Renaissance and Reformation (from 1300–1600), which formed a transition into modernity. For our purposes we can accept these labels even though the Dark Ages were hardly the barbarian morass that the term originally intended to denote. Our interest is in the High Middle Ages, which was indeed, from the standpoint of the Church, a golden age.

The Church, in a very real sense, created and ran the medieval world. The culture it nourished to maturity was a remarkable Christian synthesis of Jewish, classical pagan, and Islamic influences all in the service of "civilizing" the barbarian hordes who had overrun the Roman Empire and replacing that worldly empire with a religious one, the kingdom of God on earth, which was equated with the Roman Catholic Church. The medieval Church lived in the secular world not as an equal but as the unquestioned superior, charged and empowered by God to lead the secular order to salvation. The theological monotheism of Judaism, the philosophical and literary heritage of Greece, the political, legal, and organizational genius of Rome, and the mathematical and scientific expertise of Islam all made their distinct and irreplaceable contributions to a world construction that was unified and coherent as no other worldview since that time has been.

Without denying that the average medieval woman or man lived a short life in a world of rampant disease, incessant war, ecclesiastical and civil oppression, and often brutal poverty, it must also be said that medieval people lived in a world that made sense. Nature, equated with planet Earth, was a great chain of being running from the creator God at the pinnacle to inanimate nature at the nadir, all explicable by theology, which was articulated in the categories of Greek philosophy. The universe was one world in three tiers: heaven and its denizens (God, angels, saints), the earth and its inhabitants (mortals and those creatures over which they had dominion), and the underworld of limbo, purgatory, and hell. The first was the Church Triumphant, the second the Church Militant, and the third included the Church Suffering in Purgatory and the damned. All, excluding the last who no longer mattered, constituted the Communion of Saints, thus effectively unifying all humanity in one divine family. On earth a God-appointed hierarchy running from the pope through a clerical aristocracy of cardinals and bishops to the local clergy and the laity they governed was a pattern for the social hierarchy in the family, the civil hierarchy running from king to peasant, the academic/intellectual hierarchy of liberal and practical arts ruled by their queen, theology, and her loyal handmaid, philosophy. In short, the medieval world operated within a thoroughly unified worldview in which everyone and everything had its appointed place sanctioned by divine and/or religious authority, which had clear priority over the secular. Only one religion, Christianity, was recognized as "true," even though Judaism and Islam as well as various forms of paganism continued to exist. This was the world the Church built, owned, and operated.

It is hardly surprising that, as this universe began to unravel during the Renaissance and the Reformation, the Church raised and armed ramparts to resist at all costs the challenger that was emerging, namely, modernity. Although it was powerless to defeat the massive cultural transition that moved Europe and its dependents from the medieval to the modern world, the Church managed to wall itself off from this development by continuing to promote among its members and even legislate under threat of ecclesiastical sanctions adherence to its own theological worldview. It maintained in full force its late medieval, worldwide, and centralized governmental structure with its gowned and titled aristocrats, liveried servants and guards, star chamber judicial system, and all-male pastoral practice. Until the Second Vatican Council, the Church remained a resolutely medieval institution.

The effect of the widening gap between the secular world, which was eagerly pursuing the modern agenda, and the institutional Church, which remained firmly rooted in the medieval world, was that Catholics in general lived double lives. In the religious sphere they were obedient children in a medieval, patriarchal, clerical family; the rest of the time they were independent modern adults. The stress of this schizophrenic situation probably contributed as much by way of remote preparation to Vatican II as the theological renewal in Europe that clearly precipitated it.

Religious, especially women, unlike their lay Catholic counterparts, lived in the medieval Church world seven days a week. The congregation and local convent mirrored the strictly hierarchical, monolithic, and totalitarian ecclesiastical world in which Religious were esteemed and privileged subjects. The order's government, and the education, ministry, spirituality, daily horarium, community life, and even uniform dress of the members worked together to create and maintain a strictly unified medieval "world" within which Religious lived and which effectively protected them from any contact with the outside world that might undermine the validity of the system or subvert its cognitive coherence.

Although everyone expected that the conciliar document on the renewal of the liturgy, on divine revelation, or on the Church would be the centerpiece of the conciliar aggiornamento it was actually the pastoral constitution, *Gaudium et Spes* (The Church in the Modern World), that emerged as the most significant work of the Council. In it the Council officially recognized what the Church had tried for four hundred years years to deny, that the Middle Ages were over and modernity was not only here to stay (they thought!) but, properly understood and engaged, could even be seen as part of the divine plan. The Church finally recognized its solidarity with the human race.

But as the Council drew back the four-hundred-year-old blackout curtains and threw open the windows of the Church to the fresh air of modernity, what met its startled eyes was not the dewy freshness of a new day dawning but the twilight of a dying age. Modernity was winding down in the disillusionment of two horrendous world wars, nuclear brinkmanship by the superpowers that held the whole human race hostage, ecological degradation that threatened the very continuation of the planet, social malaise and poverty on an unprecedented scale fueled by the obscene wealth of the very few, and ethical challenges that outstripped the resources of any available system of thought.

It was probably not clear to anyone in 1965, least of all to the progressives in the Church who were exulting in the Church's emergence into modernity, that this modern age it had so recently embraced had nearly run its course. Women Religious were among the most enthusiastic and committed implementers of the Council. They hastened to fulfill the injunction in *Perfectae Caritatis* (On the Renewal of Religious Life), to modernize their institutes in fidelity to the Gospel, the charism of their founders, contemporary Church teaching, knowledge of theology and the secular sciences, and the reasonable expectations of modern society, all based on a profound spiritual renewal of the members.

Religious undertook serious study of their histories and charisms, revised their constitutions, abandoned age-old hierarchies among their members, decentralized government, provided for full participation of members in decision making, reevaluated even their most cherished ministerial commitments, accelerated the intellectual formation of their members, and undertook in-depth spiritual renewal. The changes most apparent to people, such as the abandonment of the habit and cloistered housing in favor of more normal and open interaction with those whom the Council called "the people of our time," reassumption of baptismal names in recognition that ecclesial identity was the foundation of Religious commitment, and the appearance of Religious in the public forum of civil life to promote justice and peace, which were now recognized as integral to the preaching of the Gospel, were only the visible tip of a moving iceberg.

The incredible speed and the radicality of the transition Religious made from an enclosed medieval institution to a fully modern one precipitated a virtual cataclysm in the life, perhaps the most painful evidence of which was the departure of tens of thousands of Religious. Since 1965 the number of Religious women in the United States has declined by half, the median age in many congregations has exceeded 65, and the numbers of new entrants has dropped from seven thousand a year to less than one thousand.[1]

Beginning in the 1980s an increasing number of efforts were made to analyze this disturbing situation and to suggest remedies for it. Most suggested that the negative features of contemporary first-world culture had infiltrated and undermined the original vision that gave rise to Religious Life and that this has resulted in a loss of corporate focus with consequent energy diffusion and depression among the members. Mary Jo Leddy, for example, working from the standpoint of political philosophy, attributed the malaise to a widespread surrender by religious to the decadent liberalism of the late twentieth-century American empire with its hedonistic consumerism and destructive individualism and suggested that we experiment with radical pluralism in hopes that some small communities of shared vision will emerge to take up where morally exhausted large congregations have left off.[2]

Gerald Arbuckle, in a number of writings,[3] used the theoretical framework of cultural anthropology to analyze the current malaise. He suggested that Religious congregations, following the normal life cycle of institutions, have become distanced from their founding myths and are experiencing the resulting potentially creative social chaos. The refounding activity of individual prophetic figures supported by authority and followed by the rank and file is required to actualize that potential.

Joe Holland suggested that Religious Life had run its course in the history of the Church[4] and that it is time to resituate intense Christian life in the human spheres of family and workplace rather than in the nonbiologically grounded contexts of parish and Religious Life.

Patricia Wittberg, following Helen Rose Fuchs Ebaugh, has examined the situation through the lens of the sociology of organizations and concluded that the collapse of the basic ideology of Religious Life as a superior form of Christianity and the loss of outside supporting resources have made the life sociologically nonviable.[5]

The Vatican attributed the malaise in Religious Life to what it perceived as widespread laxity or even infidelity of Religious, especially American women, in regard to the so-called "essential elements" of Religious Life and proposed as a remedy a return to many of the practices of preconciliar convent life.[6]

The underlying presupposition of these and some other analyses is that the suffering in Religious Life today is an indication that something is wrong, either morally or organizationally, with Religious and/or Religious Life. The source of the flaw is modern culture or the relation of Religious Life to that culture. It is certainly a welcome sign of increased sophistication that contemporary analysts of Religious Life are taking more seriously the influence of culture on the experience of Religious. And there is no doubt that Religious today are susceptible to the same culturally generated problems and temptations that bedevil modern society as a whole.[7] Finally, it is certainly true, as the first two chapters of this book have attempted to show, that the anthropological patterns and sociological dynamics that affect groups in general also apply to that form of community that we call Religious Life.

However, my experience with Religious has left me with a sense that these analyses, while insightful and useful at the phenomenological level, have somehow not connected with the deepest experience of most Religious. My suspicion is that the real cause of the current suffering in Religious Life, although precipitated by cultural change in society and Church, is deeper than secular or ecclesiastical culture; that it is, in the final analysis, spiritual. I also suspect that it is not due primarily to personal infidelity or corporate mistakes even though it is very much concerned with purification. In a nutshell, the thesis I want to explore is that Religious are experiencing, corporately as well as personally, something akin to or analogous to what John of the Cross called the "Dark Night," a dangerous and painful purificatory passage from a known and comfortable but somewhat immature spirituality to a radically new experience of God. This corporate spiritual experience has been precipitated by the ecclesial and cultural transitions in which late twentieth-century Religious have been involved, but its meaning cannot be reduced to these cultural factors. I will develop this thesis in detail in chapters 5 and 6.

Before developing this thesis, however, it is necessary to focus on the emerging cultural context of this experience, namely, postmodernity. Religious who thought they were embracing the modern world in the wake of Vatican II have, in fact, been plummeted into the cultural transition that is engulfing the Western world and will affect, one way or another, the whole world in the next couple of decades.

II. From Modernity to Postmodernity in Thirty Years

In order to understand the effect on Religious Life of the radical cultural transition in which we are currently involved, that is, from modernity to postmodernity, we have to appreciate the distinctly premodern character of Religious Life on the eve of Vatican II and the characteristics of postmodernity which challenge that world construction.

A. Religious Life as a Unified Spiritual Project

Religious Life developed in the Church during late antiquity, continued into and through the Middle Ages, and faced a sudden modernization in the wake of Vatican II. Different as these periods were, the Middle Ages and modernity had in common the fact that the worldview they assumed was unitary. Within such a worldview Religious Life made a certain kind of sense, even to those who might have had no use for it or even despised it, precisely because it was a unified spiritual project within a unified worldview.

In the preceding chapters I have described Religious Life as a lifeform, an integrated and integrating enterprise or spiritual project, organized around and in function of the God-quest. What distinguishes the God-quest of Religious from the equally valid spiritual projects of committed believers who do not enter Religious Life is not its intensity or authenticity so much as its exclusivity. Religious pursue this quest to the exclusion of any other primary life commitment such as that to spouse or partner and family, profession or career, art, or economic or political projects. In this sense, all Religious Life, I have suggested, is monastic, not because it involves the lifestyle elements of enclosed communities such as habit, cloister, common life, or choral recitation of the office, but because it is centered totally on what is identified as "the one thing necessary." *Monastic,* from the Greek *monos,* means "single, only, sole, or unique."

While recognizing that monastic life is not peculiar to Christianity but a form of life that seems to develop spontaneously in all literate religious cultures, I have suggested that Christian Religious Life is distinguished from its non-Christian analogues, as well as from other forms of life in the Church, by the particular relationship to Jesus Christ that seems to call some believers to a life of consecrated celibacy. The permanence of the commitment, therefore, derives precisely from the fact that it is a personal love relationship and as such is, by its nature, unconditional. Obviously, an unconditional relationship, such as marriage or Religious Life, may in fact be altered or even renounced because of changed circumstances in a person's life, but it cannot be *undertaken* as anything but total.[8] In other words, permanent profession derives from the nature of the commitment to Jesus Christ expressed in consecrated celibacy, not from Church discipline, the congregation's rule, or expediency in regard to community or ministry.[9] Permanent commitment is the undertaking of a unified life project.

Religious Life, then, is a project of life integration around the God-quest which, in the Christian tradition, involves a particular relationship with Jesus Christ expressed in lifelong consecrated celibacy. Historically, the means for pursuing this project has been the creation of an "alternate world" in which everything is directed explicitly to the God-quest while eliminating anything that would hinder it. *World* in this sense does not mean planet Earth but a particular construction of reality within which Religious live. Paul Lakeland in his excellent book on postmodernity says that the coordinates of "world" in this sense are time, space, and order.[10]

Historically, Religious have constructed a "world" that was not only distinct but actually separated from the secular order around them. This Religious world had its own *time*, its horarium, organized not by the rising and setting of the sun, the seasons of the year, and the cycles of life, but by the ongoing engagement of the Religious with God. The Divine Office organized the day and night; the liturgical celebration of the mysteries of Christ organized the year; age was computed from profession.

Space was constructed to foster the God-quest. The separate room in the family home of the first virgins, the cell of the desert hermits, the medieval monastery, the modern convent were regions sealed off from secular business and organized for silence, solitude, and prayer. Religious orders even transcended natural geographical, linguistic, and ethnic boundaries to establish Religious space in non-Christian environments.

Finally, the *order* of this alternate world was created by means of the vows of consecrated celibacy, poverty, and obedience, by which the Religious handled the three major dynamics of human life: sexuality and relationships, material goods and ownership, freedom and power. No matter how the vows were named or formulated, they dealt with these three coordinates of human life by way of renunciation: by celibacy the Religious renounced genital sexual relationships; by poverty, all private ownership of material goods; by obedience, independent exercise of the will. These renunciations were understood primarily as a self-emptying of the possessive ego disposing the person for union with God. But they were also a way of fostering the particular type of community life that was characteristic of the alternate world and eventually fostering the ministry of active Religious congregations. In other words, the vows were first unitive, second communitarian, and third ministerial.

The Rule specified in detail how this alternate time, space, and order were interrelated to structure daily life in this "world apart." One entered this alternate world by profession, which was referred to as "leaving the [secular] world." Conversely, to leave Religious Life was to "return to the world."

Developments in the twentieth century have not changed the basic meaning of Religious Life as the exclusive God-quest of people who feel called to this particular celibate form of relationship with Christ. However, this unitary project, precisely because of its unitary character, is much more countercultural, and therefore difficult to sustain and explain, in the fragmented context of postmodernity than it was in earlier times. Consequently, on the one hand, the necessity for Religious to create an alternate reality in which to live this vocation is even more urgent in the present context. On the other hand, Vatican II's espousal of solidarity with the world and its people, our contemporary realization that there is finally only one universe that we share with all creatures, and the fragmentation of postmodernity profoundly affect the way this alternate reality is understood and constructed.

B. The Changed Ecclesial and Cultural Context

The foregoing sketch of Religious Life is verified, despite numerous historical variations, in the fundamental continuity of lifeform, from the consecrated virgins of the first centuries, to the desert hermits of late antiquity, to the monastics and mendicants of the middle ages, to the ministerial Religious of modern times. In the last forty years, however, two major changes, one in the Church and one in Western culture, have raised unprecedented challenges, not just to the practices of Religious Life but to its very self-understanding as a lifeform. These changes are Vatican II's *affirmation of the Church's solidarity with the modern world* and the rapid emergence of what cultural critics are calling *postmodernity*.

The ecclesial change and its implications for Religious Life have been on the front burner of our consciousness for several decades.[11] Essentially, the Council reversed the Church's unqualified rejection of modernity, declaring its solidarity with the world and its peoples.[12] If Church and world were now understood as mutually penetrating realities, Religious Life must also be understood as in, with, and for the world. This change constituted a Copernican revolution for Religious who had, for centuries, defined themselves in terms of their opposition to the world. Although this ecclesial development is theologically extremely significant, it has probably not had as significant an existential impact on Religious as the cultural transition from modernity to postmodernity.[13]

Postmodernity is such a complex and multifarious phenomenon involving such a tangle of sensibilities, issues, and agendas that it is simply impossible to describe it, even sketchily, in a short chapter.[14] However, three aspects of postmodernity that are directly relevant to our topic are the following: first, how the postmodern worldview is related to the worldviews that preceded it; second, how postmodernity subverts prior notions of time, space, and order, resulting in widespread, multileveled fragmentation; and third, the varieties of postmodernity and where contemporary Religious might fit in the spectrum. The purpose of what follows is to "locate" contemporary Religious Life culturally in this postmodern context.

1. Postmodernity and its predecessors: Postmodernity is both a child of and a protest against modernity, which is itself a child of the Enlightenment. Modernity is the period of history from roughly the 1500s to about the 1960s (and, of course, it is still the dominant worldview even as postmodernity arrives). Like the medieval and late antique worlds that preceded it, the modern worldview is essentially unitary. The major difference between the modern worldview and the premodern worldviews was not in regard to unity but in regard to how the world's unity was organized and understood. The premodern Christian world, as already noted, was a great chain of being running from inanimate nature to God with humans situated a little below the angels and a little above the animals. This complex, hierarchically ordered universe was created and sustained by God. Thus, the human being, the knowing subject, was both the supremely important creature and ultimately subject to God. Truth consisted in bringing the mind into conformity with the "objective reality" of the universe so understood. In other words, the human being was subject, physically, spiritually, and epistemologically, to "what is," which "he" (the normative subject was always male) neither created nor controlled.

Modernity involved a 180-degree revolution in this understanding of reality. As the Renaissance motto put it, "*man* [rather than objective reality] is the measure of all things." Reality was still seen as a unity composed of creator and creatures, but now man, the critical rational (and male) subject, not God, was at the center of creation. God was still in "his" heaven but humanly relevant reality was constituted by the knowing human subject and his knowable object, including both human and non-human nature. The mind was no longer subject to reality, but reality was subject to the mind which constituted it as object of knowledge. From this anthropocentric self-understanding which so characterizes modernity come all the features of modernity of whose amazing positive potential and disastrous actual limitations we are becoming aware: prodigious scientific development on the one hand and reductive scientism on the other; recognition of human dignity and rights on the one hand and rampant anthropocentrism and individualism on the other; technological advancement and the rape of nature; medical breakthroughs and loss of respect for life itself; religious tolerance and the privatizing of religion; economic development and increasing poverty; the triumph of critical reason and the banishing of mystery from human life, and so on.

Modernity, in other words, still involved a unified view of the world. It differed from premodernity in that man, not God, was the center and principle of its unity. Whatever postmodernity means, it involves some kind of protest against this unitary modern worldview.

2. *Three features of postmodernity:* Postmodernity is primarily characterized by the loss of the unitary worldview and the resulting fragmentation of reality on every level. First, postmodernity involves a subversion of the notion of free-standing, coherent subjectivity that was so central to the unitary worldviews preceding it. The premodern subject was a free creature in relation to God who was the unifying center of the universe; the modern subject was the transcendental ego of the Enlightenment around whom the universe revolved. But the postmodern is asking who or what, if anything, we are. Are we subjects at all, much less free or central? Are we really, individually or as a species, anything more than an insignificant fleeting blip on the vast cosmic screen? The postmodern sense is one of *radical contingency,*[15] existential rootlessness, abandonment in an impersonal cosmos.

Second, postmodernity involves a subversion of "foundations," the pervasive sense that neither religion nor metaphysics nor even natural science can tell us what is really real, "at the bottom" of all reality, holding it all together as a unity. The postmodern suspects that there is no foundation, nothing stable on which to base one's thought, behavior, hopes, or convictions. Reality is just the never-ending, frenetic dance of finite, relative, momentarily connected scraps of existence that are constantly reconfiguring themselves in the cosmic breeze into whatever seems to be or functions as "reality" at the moment. Who is to say that any construction of reality, any set of beliefs or mode of behavior, has universal validity and therefore any claim on me? The postmodern lives in a world of universal and irresolvable *relativism.*

Third, postmodernity involves the subversion of metanarratives. A *metanarrative* is a master story that one believes comprehends the whole of reality and into which one's own story fits. Catholic salvation history is a metanarrative stretching from creation at the beginning of time to the parousia at its end. It purports to account for all of history and for all people who are either *us* (i.e., Catholic Christian believers), or *our* ancestors in the faith (the Jews), or those who are *not us,* either because they have fallen away (heretics, apostates, schismatics) or are pagans (believers in false religions) or nonbelievers (agnostics or atheists). The ideal, according to this metanarrative, is that everyone in the story who is not us should eventually become part of us.

We have become vividly aware in recent times that there are many metanarratives besides ours, each of which purports to account for the totality of reality but in a completely different way with a different group as the central and defining "us." In other words, each metanarrative, including ours, is limited and relative. Furthermore, any metanarrative that claims universality is also oppressive in that it makes everyone "other than us" subordinate parts of our story.

The postmodern sensibility acknowledges the irreducible "otherness" of those we had previously subsumed into our narrative. Attempting to bridge the chasm between oneself and these "others," even by means of some utopian social or political program that defines the good from our point of view, seems crassly imperialistic. The result is the postmodern sense of *alienation,* which leads many postmoderns into an apolitical and socially uninvolved self-positioning in the world. The tendency is to construct a social "cocoon," or what Bellah and his colleagues called "lifestyle enclaves"[16] in which to live one's own life as uninvolved as possible with the lives and concerns of others, especially those really different from oneself. The motto of modern tolerance, "Live and let live," has become the postmodern motto of alienation, "You do your thing and I'll do mine," meaning our realities are essentially unrelated, and I do not want to hear about yours nor have you intrude into mine.

The radical contingency, foundationless relativism, and isolated alienation characterizing the postmodern sensibility are intensified by the subversion of the world-unifying coordinates of time, space, and order that has resulted from technological development. *Time* is no longer governed, as Genesis proclaimed, by the sun that rules the day and the moon and stars that rule the night. We can have endless day, twenty-four-hour shopping or partying in daylight-bright malls or casinos. It may be midday where I am and the middle of the night for the person with whom I am talking by phone or email. *Space* is nearly erased by air travel that can take me from eighty-five-degree sunny weather in Florida to a below-zero blizzard in Montana in little more time than it takes to change clothes. And air conditioning in the former and central heating in the latter create a universal, seasonless climate that makes changing clothes largely unnecessary. The principles of *order,* what is nonnegotiable and what is relative, the relation between work and well-being, the meaning of property, community, and commitment, are all subverted by the universal commodification of reality. Everything, from food and shelter, to health and education, to entertainment and relationships, can be bought if one has a high enough limit on one's credit card. And one can find all of them in the ever-more-comprehensive shopping mall, the temple of postmodernity. Shopping is the national pastime, the preeminent occupation of the fragmented subject who moves shallowly but intently from one commodity to the next, achieving the only status worth having by incessant acquisition.[17]

The foregoing description, although inadequate to the immensely complex and variegated reality of postmodernity, is an attempt to evoke a feeling for the postmodern sensibility. Even those who strenuously resist this ethos find that it echoes in their consciousness, affects their choices and behaviors, sneaks into their prayer, and challenges their commitments. Postmodernity is in the air we breathe. By way of anticipation, it is clear that the fragmentation of postmodernity raises serious challenges for a life project of self-integration around the God-quest and the unified lifeform that this project generates, namely, Religious Life.

3. Types of postmodernity: Before addressing these challenges we need to distinguish three quite different kinds of postmodernity[18] because each has different implications for Religious Life, and the lifeform today includes people who would fit in each of these groups. A first group, whom we might call nihilistic or radically deconstructive postmoderns, have moved *beyond modernity* to embrace all of the features of postmodernity described above in their most extreme formulations. Such radical postmoderns repudiate the modern notion of stable subjectivity or character and are content to reinvent themselves endlessly in terms of new situations, making no claim that any version of the self is intrinsically better than any other as long as no one is getting hurt. There is no reason beyond the pragmatic requirements of the moment to embrace one conviction or course of action rather than another. And, since others are irreducibly different from oneself, which makes any social or political agenda by definition imperialistic and oppressive, one must grant the same right to continuous self-invention and total relativism to others. In the view of many theologians, myself included, radically deconstructive postmodernity is essentially nihilistic and fundamentally incompatible with Christianity or any other religious tradition.[19]

A second type of postmodernism Paul Lakeland labels "nostalgic." Nostalgic postmoderns have not moved beyond modernity; they simply *reject modernity* as a worldview or agenda. On the one hand, they embrace the technological and material advancements of postmodernity which they often use very competently, and on the other hand, they derive their values and social agenda from premodernity. Catholic nostalgic postmoderns feel that Vatican II sold out the Church by embracing modernity. They feel called to resist the conciliar aggiornamento in practice even while giving lip service to it in theory and to restore the medieval absolutism of the preconciliar

Church.[20] They are staunch defenders of premodern "family values" based on a literalist reading of the Bible, which teaches, they believe, that good families and societies are based on divinely established male hierarchies. Laws of Church and state based on nonnegotiable moral absolutes must be strictly enforced to ensure religious and social order. Lakeland identifies John Paul II as a typical nostalgic postmodern.[21] Closer to home, we might recognize Mother Angelica, who capably uses postmodern technology to promote a premodern form of Catholicism and Religious Life that simply denies the relevance of contemporary questions and reasserts the timeless and universal validity of medieval theology and ecclesial practice.

Finally, those whom Lakeland calls "late-moderns" I would call constructive postmoderns.[22] These people are postmodern in their realization that much of the agenda of modernity has run into a dead end. Anthropocentrism, individualism, consumerism, masculinism, materialism, scientism, progressivism and much of the rest of the modern heritage is socially, politically, and morally bankrupt. Furthermore, they instinctively *resonate with the intuitions* of postmodernity about the intrinsic relativity of reality and the questionableness of absolutes, whether these concern a supposedly unchanging and universal human nature, a revealed moral law that is impervious to changed historical circumstances and new knowledge, or an infallible teaching authority that knows the right answers about everything for everyone everywhere without having to engage the evidence.

However, unlike the radical and nostalgic postmoderns, constructive postmoderns acknowledge that modernity also birthed important values. They affirm as genuine values the modern appreciation of the dignity and inalienable rights of every human being and therefore of the equality of women, children, people of color, and members of other oppressed groups, the validation of critical reason against dogmatic authoritarianism, tolerance, freedom of conscience and religion, of inquiry and speech, the right to participate in decisions that affect one, as well as the commitment to the well-being of all people within a world order based on justice.

The commitment of modernity to these values represents progress toward fuller humanity and constitutes an unfinished agenda that cannot be simply abandoned in the name of post-modern radical deconstruction.

Constructive postmoderns not only bring forward genuine values from modernity but they also relate ambiguously to postmodernity itself. While recognizing the questionableness of premodern religious and metaphysical foundations, they continue to think that some foundations, for example, in a constantly revised consensus, may still be possible. While questioning the moral absolutism of premodernity, they want to hold that some morality that generates and is generated by character is required by our very humanity. They dare hope that recognizing the real "otherness" of others need not result in total alienation but invites us to dialogue that is genuinely open to finding together a new path toward shared life.

In short, constructive postmoderns relate ambiguously to both modernity and postmodernity, participating with a mixture of excitement and unease in its time-, space-, and order-subverting features. They see both the liberating possibilities and the nihilistic potential of postmodern deconstruction. Most of the best contemporary Catholic theologians are constructively postmodern in this sense. The increasing pluralism of theology, once an almost totally unified field of discourse, and the rapid evolution of theory even within a single school of theology or a single theologian's work attests to the creative potential of the breakdown of the medieval monolith but also to the chaotic disarray that such a breakdown necessarily involves. Chaos, however, as quantum physics is instructing us, is not necessarily a destructive situation but one brimming with creative potential.[23]

III. Implications for Religious Life

Two presuppositions seem to follow from what has been said thus far. First, given the conciliar understanding of the Church's relationship to the world, it is no longer possible to understand Religious Life as purely and simply "other worldly" or totally "anticultural." If there is a sense, and I think there is, in which Religious Life constitutes an alternative reality to and a courageous prophetic presence in the world, it cannot be by way of total separation or unqualified condemnation. It must be by way of dialogue with the surrounding culture. I will return to this topic in detail in chapter 10.

Second, as has been said, the surrounding culture is not, as Vatican II thought, that of the modern world, but of the emerging postmodern world. Within the unified worldview of modernity the integrating and unified project of Religious Life was understandable even to those who had no use for it. But the fragmentation of postmodernity makes this project, founded on a permanent commitment within a particular religious tradition, deeply countercultural. This is not merely because it espouses some values that are not popular in an individualistic and consumerist society (which was the self-understanding of Religious in the immediate postconciliar period when they were dealing with modernity) but because the very idea of such a unifying life project is barely comprehensible in the contemporary context of fragmentation.

In view of this, it is no mystery why relatively few younger people who are not frightened fugitives looking for a cultural hideout or seeking the family they never had are attracted to this life, and why those who are attracted have such a difficult time with concepts such as permanent commitment. This does not necessarily signal either the end of Religious Life nor the necessity to deconstruct it into a radically postmodern experiment in occasionality that requires nothing that the surrounding culture cannot understand. But it does demand deep reflection on the relationship between Religious Life and contemporary culture if we are to be able to make this life comprehensible to our contemporaries, our candidates, or even ourselves.

In subsequent chapters in this volume and especially in volume 2 I will be dealing with the vows, community, vocation, commitment and other constitutive features of Religious Life, and in each case we will have to draw on the foregoing understanding of the ecclesial and cultural context of contemporary

Western society in order to analyze and reenvision these realities. What is important at this point is to realize how deeply embedded Religious Life is in the turn-of-the-millennium culture. A life that managed to construct and define itself for centuries as essentially outside and independent of its surrounding culture can no longer do so and no longer wants to do so. But the situation of cultural involvement is very new for contemporary Religious. In the next three chapters I will explore some of the implications for the self-understanding of Religious as well as the spiritual crisis that this cultural involvement has precipitated.

Part Two

Locating Religious Life
in
Its Ecclesial Context

Chapter Four

Religious Life as a Theological Reality in the Church: Consecrated Celibacy and the Vocation to Prophecy

---

I. Transition and Introduction

The purpose of the chapters in part 1 was to "locate" Religious Life in the widened cultural context that has become operative since the emergence of Religious Life from its somewhat isolated and completely ecclesial preconciliar context. We began by recognizing its rootedness in the anthropological, psychological, and sociological substrate of humanity as well as its Christian specificity in relation to its analogues in other traditions. We then examined the life-and-death implications of the character of Religious Life primarily as an integrated organic lifeform rather than as an organization or an essence. As a lifeform its continued existence and vitality will be a function, to a large extent, of its successful relationship with the surrounding systems that constitute the cultural environment of postmodernity. Against the background of this resituation of contemporary Religious Life in the context of the first world at the turn of the century, we can begin to interrogate it as an ecclesial reality, that is, to inquire into the theology, spirituality, ecclesiastical situation, and charismatic contribution of this lifeform within the Church for the sake of the world in the new millennium.

In the preconciliar Church the specificity of Religious Life as a graced reality, indeed even its superiority to other forms of Christian life, was so seemingly self-evident that an exploration (as opposed to an assertion) of its theological character would have seemed superfluous. The challenge to the theological validity of the life that was raised by the Reformation was condemned by the Council of Trent,[1] but the challenge itself was never theologically engaged. Today Christians are much more aware that the fullness of the Christian life is the calling of all the faithful. This raises the question of the meaning, and the theological validity, of a specific vocation in the Church to which not all are called.

As a Christian lifeform Religious Life must be understood, first and foremost, as sharing the common Christian heritage and only then as a specific incarnation of that common heritage which is distinct and recognizable without claiming to be either separate or superior. A major contribution of Vatican II to Christian self-understanding was the affirmation, virtually two thousand years in the making, that all Christians are equally called to one and the same holiness and to participation in the Church's mission in virtue of their baptism.[2] There is no question that this recognition of the universal call to holiness and mission has challenged Religious to reexamine the meaning of their life which, for centuries, has been defined, erroneously but very really, in terms of separation from and superiority to the life of the Christian laity.

All Christians, by baptism, are incorporated into Christ and share in his identity as Son of God and his mission as prophet, priest, and king. Although all of this language needs to be shorn of its masculine exclusivity, it is the traditional language for talking about the union of being and action between Jesus and God and Jesus' mission in this world. The holiness to which all believers are called is participation in the divine filiation of Jesus, that is, union with God. The mission to which all are called is participation in Jesus' roles as herald, mediator, and promoter of the Reign of God.

Individual Christians live this identity and mission in different ways, but the differences consist more in the way they constellate, emphasize, and witness publicly to the various dimensions of this universal Christian vocation, rather than in the presence of specific elements in some Christian vocations and their absence in others. For this reason, it seems futile and counterproductive to try to work out the meaning of a particular vocation in the Church by establishing that it and it alone incarnates one or another specific feature that is found in no other vocation.[3]

The constitutive feature of Religious Life, not as Christian but as Religious, is the commitment of Religious to Jesus Christ in lifelong consecrated celibacy, just as the constitutive feature of matrimony (not as Christian but as marriage) is the commitment of the spouses to Christ through the lifelong commitment to each other in faithful sexual monogamy. Neither commitment (which is clear from the fact that they are mutually exclusive) is intrinsic to the Christian vocation as such, and many Christians live their baptismal identity and mission with heroic fidelity and integrity without making either of these commitments. But for Christians who do make such a commitment it becomes the organizational principle of their specific Christian lifeform. This commitment generates the emphases and accents that will distinguish their lifeform from others within the Church and outside it.

However, it is the lifeform itself as an integrated whole that is distinctive. The vocation cannot be defined by any one of its characteristics or by all of them arranged serially. Thus, faith, prayer, community, simplicity of life, discernment, commitment to justice, love of neighbor, chastity, hospitality, fidelity, generosity, ministerial involvement, and all the other features of committed Christian life must be integral to every form of life in the Church. None of the features intrinsic to Christian identity and life are the special province or exclusive trait of a particular state of life or lifeform. But how they are integrated will differ because of their incorporation into a particular lifeform. In what follows I will attempt to describe Religious Life theologically, highlighting what is specific to it as a lifeform and thus what Religious Life as such contributes to the life of the ecclesial community.

By way of proleptic summary, I will propose that Religious Life is a prophetic lifeform in the Church whose prophetic character is rooted in and derives from the celibate solitude that unites contemplative immediacy to God and solidarity with the marginalized of society and expresses itself in the vows that address to the world the challenge of the Reign of God.

II. Consecrated Celibacy as Constitutive Principle of Religious Life

Theologically, Religious Life is a mystery, not because it is a conundrum in a hedonistic and consumerist society or because it is an exotic spiritual subculture, but because the intimate interchange between God and a human being that elicits the free commitment of lifelong consecrated celibacy is as unfathomable as the attraction between two people that leads to marriage. Mysteries cannot be explained, only reverently explored. As Thomas Merton, who attempted repeatedly to make the Religious vocation understandable to his contemporaries, realized toward the end of his life, Religious Life requires no justification to those who embrace it and can provide no defense to those who challenge it.[4] But even the effort to clarify it for those well-disposed toward it runs into formidable obstacles.

First, Religious Life is not a Platonic essence realizing itself diversely in various historical circumstances.[5] It is a movement in the Church that has taken on a wide variety of forms throughout its nearly two-thousand-year history, and the diverse forms are integral to the life in such a way that describing Religious Life "in itself" as a quasi-essence is no more possible than describing human nature apart from any particular human beings. Consequently, describing Religious Life in the singular is virtually impossible, as is coping descriptively with its enormous variety.

Second, and flowing directly from the preceding observation, whatever anyone, myself included, says about Religious Life would probably be disavowed by some other Religious who live the life with authenticity and integrity. Any exploration of the mystery of the life is only as convincing as it is responsive to and clarifying of the lived experience of real Religious. And that experience is so diverse that every generalization is bound to be challenged from some quarter.

Third, it has become increasingly difficult, if not impossible, to explain Religious Life in terms of what Religious do in the Church. If, in the not-so-distant past, American Religious were a formidable and specialized jobs corps for ecclesiastical projects in education, health care, and social services, that is no longer the case. Not only have reductions in numbers of personnel, financial resources, and institutions rendered them a less formidable cohort, but also it is clear that there is no ministry performed by Religious that cannot be equally well performed by lay people. In other words, Religious Life, if it is significant in the Church, is so not because of what Religious do but because of what the state of life is, and the latter is much more difficult to discern than the former.

A. "Defining" Religious Life

With these caveats in mind, I begin with the quasi-definition of Religious Life as a *state of life* in the Church, entered into by *perpetual profession,* and constituted by *lifelong consecrated celibacy.*[6]

1. State of life: A state of life is a permanent, stable, and public form of life in the Church which raises to visibility in a special way some aspect or dimension of the Christian mystery that all the baptized are called to live. When Vatican II clarified that Religious Life was not an intermediate state or class between the clergy and the laity, some Religious concluded that, since they were not clergy, they were laity and therefore that Religious Life itself was not a distinct state of life in the Church. This was not the meaning intended by the Council nor is it compatible with actual experience. The fact that Religious Life is not a hierarchical state (which is really an ecclesiastical "class" rather than a state of life) in the structure of the Church does not mean it is not a state of life. Both *Lumen Gentium* (Constitution on the Church) and *Perfectae Caritatis* (Decree on Religious Life) recognize that Religious Life is a state of life distinct from both the

ordained and the lay.[7] Although the terminology of states of life
in the Church is not only ambiguous but almost hopelessly confused (a topic I will address in chapter 7), experience makes it
clear that Religious are a distinct category of persons in the
Church because of their lifeform. Neither committed Religious
who have a firm sense of personal identity nor the laity who associate with Religious experience Religious as laity in the ordinary
sense of that term. This distinct and recognizable lifeform is
what is meant here by a state of life.

As a state of life Religious Life is permanent, stable, and
public. One does not drop in and out of the life as one might
change residences or jobs or even nationalities. One does not
belong to it provisionally or temporarily or partially. Furthermore, Religious Life is not an interior disposition or private
attitude that one may or may not choose to make socially visible. It is a public, institutionalized, permanent lifeform in the
Church that one enters (or leaves) by public juridical acts.

2. Entered by profession: Profession is the act by which one
solemnly, formally, and publicly undertakes or enters Religious Life.[8] These adjectives do not have anything to do with
the elaborateness of the ceremony of profession. Rather, they
denote the fact that, first, Religious profession is not a casual
but a very deliberate act requiring mature reflection and discernment, lengthy probation and preparation, and a definitive decision (solemn). Second, entrance into Religious Life
cannot be done implicitly or by mere association with a congregation or its members or simply by virtue of long participation in some aspects of the life. It must be "done" at a
particular moment and by a particular act before which the
person is not a Religious and after which she is (formal).
Third, by the act of profession a person acquires certain rights
that others in the Church do not have and that others have an
obligation to honor, such as active and passive voice in congregational affairs. And the professed Religious undertakes certain responsibilities and obligations that others have a right to
expect her to fulfill, such as the sexual abstinence implied by
celibate chastity and the simplicity of lifestyle and nonowner-
ship implied by poverty (public).

B. Celibacy as Constitutive of Religious Life

The constitutive feature of Religious Life as a state of life, in other words, that which both organizes it as a form of life in the Church and distinguishes it from other forms, is lifelong consecrated celibacy. A section in volume 2 will be devoted to consecrated celibacy itself, which is a very complex reality, especially in relation to contemporary American culture. At this point, for the purposes of discussing the theological nature of Religious Life as a prophetic lifeform in the Church, I want to focus on one aspect of Religious Life that flows directly from consecrated celibacy and undergirds the prophetic character of the life, namely, solitude. Celibate solitude is the root of immediacy to God as a mode of Christian experience and of social marginality as a position in the world which, operating together, ground Religious Life as a prophetic lifeform in the Church.

1. Celibate solitude and contemplative immediacy to God: The deepest meaning, the raison d'être, of consecrated celibacy is the love relationship between the Religious and Christ. It is lived in the context of community, both that of the Church and usually that of a particular order or congregation. And it is oriented toward the service of one's sisters and brothers. Religious Life is not, in other words, an isolated life. Nevertheless, celibacy chosen as a public and permanent state of life establishes the Religious in an existential solitude that no bonds, however deep, of friendship, community, or solidarity in mission can mitigate.

Aloneness is, in a certain sense, the inner structure of the life of the Religious as faithful and fruitful mutuality is the inner structure of matrimony. In this sense, as discussed in chapter 1, all Religious Life is monastic. This does not imply that ministerial Religious Life involves the lifestyle elements of monastic orders such as cloister, habit, or choral recitation of the Divine Office. But all Religious Life is organized around the single-minded God-quest, the affective concentration of the whole of one's life on the "one thing necessary," which is union with God. This aloneness, if cherished, attended to, and dwelt in as the heart of one's vocation, finds its positive meaning in contemplative prayer. If it does not find its meaning there it will lead, sooner or later, to a bitter and empty isolation, to the boredom and mediocrity of the "professional" minister, or to abandonment of the life itself in search of affective fulfillment.

As incarnate spirits, born in the flesh and immersed in history, human beings characteristically seek God and work out their salvation in and through the mediation of material creation. This is the natural element of human and Christian experience. The fundamental mediation is the relationship with another human being in a permanent and fruitful union of love. Nevertheless, natural and good as this approach is, there have always been some Christians who have felt called to bypass this preeminent human mediation of the divine, and with it many other mediations that sustain and express it such as personal ownership of property, career, personal independence in the choice of lifestyle, and so on, in order to seek God with an immediacy that would be as foolhardy as Hosea's marriage if it were not experienced as a response to God's own invitation. In chapter 1 we saw that this vocation to the monastic God-quest seems to occur in all the great religions of the world.

In Christian history, from the very first days of the post-Resurrection Church, we find people who experienced this vocation: the Christians of apostolic times who chose virginity rather than participation in the sociohistorical project of procreation in and for the Empire; the men and women of late antiquity who abandoned the city for the starkness of the desert wilderness; the medieval monastics and mendicants who retreated behind monastery walls or roamed the roads of medieval Europe preaching the Gospel; the missionary Religious who set out for regions where the name of Christ had never been heard. Today, this same single-minded absorption in the quest for God draws some Christians into Religious Life, a life characterized by celibate solitude and the various renunciations that express and support it. As we have already said, the primary motivation in the Christian context for this bypassing of the most fundamental natural mediations of the God-human encounter, especially fruitful sexual intimacy with a beloved partner, is not asceticism, much less hatred of creation, but the desire for God.

This desire for God alone as the direct and immediate object of one's love is an essentially contemplative project. Here we touch the mystical core of Religious Life. By mysticism, or the mystical dimension of Religious Life, I do not mean paranormal experiences (or any particular experiences, for that matter) or unusual states of consciousness, but what Bernard McGinn calls the direct consciousness of the presence of God in its preparation, reality, and effects.[9] *Contemplation* is probably a better word than *mysticism*, at least one less liable to historical misunderstanding, to describe the constant seeking of union with God that is the purpose of Religious solitude.

There is a distinction between seeing God in all things and seeing all things in God. Both are forms of contemplation.[10] The difference lies in where one "starts." To start with creation and discern God present and at work in all things is different from starting with God as the first point of reference in which all thought and action originate. Religious Life has something to do with being drawn to the latter as one's characteristic approach to union with God. Celibate solitude incarnates that approach. The Religious, at least in desire, comes to every historical experience out of her immediate involvement with God rather than seeking and finding God primarily through her involvement with historical experience. It is the experience of having been "found" already, having been claimed and possessed in a way that relativizes all other claims upon oneself, that dominates and shapes the consciousness of the Religious no matter what the activity or sphere of engagement.

Celibate solitude and the contemplative immediacy to God it generates is also a path fraught with danger because it is, in a sense, "nonnatural." It is not unnatural or antinatural because nothing is more fundamental to our humanity than the quest for God. But because it involves a bypassing of the most fundamental natural mediations of the God-human engagement it involves risks and temptations that are well documented in the history of spirituality and especially of Religious Life: ascetical extremism, rigidity, misanthropy, false mysticism, gnosticism and esotericism, elitism, and a host of distortions in the practice of prayer.

By describing Religious Life theologically as a vocation to mystical immediacy to God I am not claiming that all Religious experience their vocation this way or that only people who do experience it this way are truly called to Religious Life. Religious Life as a lifeform presents a wide variety of features and characteristics that are attractive to people for a variety of reasons. Some people are primarily drawn to the life because it offers involvement in a worthwhile project larger than themselves. Others are attracted to religiously based community life. Some have been drawn by the desire to exercise a particular ministry. Some probably come in search of a quiet and orderly life that is relatively free of the complexities of modern life and thus conducive to spiritual practice. Certainly no one would question the validity of such motivations if they are sufficient to sustain the person's commitment to the life, especially the renunciation involved in celibacy. But just as a theological description of matrimony as a sacrament of the union between Christ and the Church (cf. Eph 5:32) and of the Christian family as an *ecclesiola* or domestic Church is not a phenomenology of all actual Christian marriages but rather an explanation of the deepest theological meaning and ideal of matrimony as a lifeform, so a description of Religious Life as an essentially contemplative vocation, a call to mystical immediacy to God that becomes ever more constant and absorbing in the course of a lifetime, is less a phenomenology of actual practice than a theological description.

Furthermore, I am not claiming that those who do experience their vocation as a call to immediacy to God actually live that mystery at "white heat" on a day-to-day basis. Obviously, such a consistently contemplative approach to life is more than a little ambiguous since the Religious, like everyone else, is constantly caught up in the everyday business of dealing with life in this world. It is as impossible for the Religious to sustain such mystical immediacy to God in full force at all times as it is for spouses to sustain the full, felt intensity of marital union at every moment as they involve themselves in parenting, work, career, and other relationships. The lives of even the greatest saints in the history of Religious Life make this abundantly clear. The disarming humility of the desert monastics who recounted their failures with wry humor in a context of continual compunction, the incessant "have mercy on me" of the hesychastic Jesus Prayer of the Eastern monks and nuns, the confessional writings of Teresa of Avila and Thomas Merton and so many others testifies to both the intense desire for direct union with God and the virtual impossibility of living such immediacy in uninterrupted intensity.

Finally, I am not suggesting that only Religious experience such a vocation to mystical immediacy to God or that all who do experience such a vocation feel called to enter Religious Life, but only that this contemplative vocation is theologically intrinsic to the life as a lifeform, regardless of how it is or is not incarnated in the life of any particular individual inside or outside Religious Life.

In short, I am not trying to describe or prescribe how the life is or must be experienced on a day-to-day basis by the real people who espouse it but to discern the theological specificity of the life, what makes it itself as a distinct form of life in the Church. Consecrated celibacy generates an existential solitude that only ultimately makes sense and becomes fruitful and fulfilling as the context and climate of an intense, exclusive search for God rooted in a sense of having been found, called, and claimed by God for such a project. It is this search, becoming ever more continuous, conscious, and constant over the course of a lifetime that I am calling "immediacy to God as a mode of Christian experience."

2. Celibate solitude and social marginality: The call to celibate solitude has always involved, existentially, the development by Religious of an alternative lifestyle in relation to the larger culture in which they lived. The meaning of this move has been understood and explained in a variety of ways, always partially determined by the Religious's perception of the surrounding culture and its relationship to Christian faith and life.

The first Religious, for example, understood their choice of virginity as a statement of independence in relationship to the

Empire viewed as the opposite, if not the implacable enemy, of the Church. By vowing virginity they stated publicly that they belonged to Christ, not to the emperor, and that their future lay with Christ in glory, not in the glorious future of the Roman Empire. The desert monastics viewed their wilderness habitat and way of life as an alternative to and a protest against an over-acculturated Constantinian Church that had become too assimilated to the "world." The medieval monastics created an alternative Christian world in the largely "barbaric" setting of postimperial Europe. And the ministerial Religious Life that developed in the modern period incarnated the Church's rejection of modernity and the "world" it was creating.

In each case, Religious Life involved the creation of a distinct life setting in which the exclusive, solitary God-quest of the Religious could be pursued in the midst of a "world" that did not share their spiritual passion. Entering Religious Life was seen as somehow "leaving the world." What that meant and involved depended on how "world" was understood. In the Gospel of John we find the three understandings of "world" that have operated in Christian theology since its inception. First, the world can be understood neutrally as the material stage upon which human history transpires, and this is a world no human, Religious or lay, can "leave" since it is our earthly habitat from which we draw our material sustenance and for which we have a responsibility (e.g., Jn 17:15). Second, the world can be understood positively as the beloved creation for whose salvation God sent the only Son, and this world is the object of prayerful and/or ministerial concern to Religious (e.g., Jn 3:16). Finally, the world can be understood negatively as the constellation of the forces of evil against the Reign of God. It is this world that Religious, historically, chose to renounce and abandon (e.g., Jn 17:14).

In only the first case is the world relatively synonymous with material creation, an environment for human beings and action. The world, in the theological sense, is primarily not a thing or a place but a reality construction that involves both a particular understanding of the purposes of human life and the creation of social structures and ordering of relationships to achieve those purposes. Although "leaving the world" usually involved an actual physical separation from one's surroundings—family, city, the secular order—it was primarily a choice to live differently. Religious Life was an alternative reality construction involving a different kind of social structure and different ways of ordering human relationships governed by a different understanding of the purposes of human life.

Historically, the alternative world of Religious Life involved a distinctive understanding of time embodied in an horarium of uninterrupted prayer and the liturgical celebration of the mysteries of Christ, a distinctive understanding of space as separated by cloister from the surrounding *saeculum* of war, commerce, procreation, and pleasure seeking, and a distinctive order of life structured by the vows lived in community according to a detailed rule of life administered by a superior who exercised sacred authority. The effect of this alternative world construction was to marginalize the Religious in relation to the surrounding culture. The fabled inquiry of the desert monk to the visitor from the city, "How fares the world?" captures this feature of the life. The monk or nun was no longer "in the world," much less "of the world."[11]

The social marginality of Religious in relation to their culture has had an interesting history. At the very beginning Religious did not separate themselves physically from the surrounding culture but lived, often in their own homes, in the midst of the Church community, which itself functioned as an alternative "world" in the midst of the larger society. The Church was distinguished from its surroundings, not by physical ghetto, but by its faith in Jesus as the Messiah and Son of God and the love of the community members for each other and even for the outsiders. Religious, in the midst of the Church, were distinguished not by cloister but by their virginal commitment and its behavioral manifestations.

However, when the monastics of the third and fourth centuries departed for the desert, they did so to distinguish themselves not only from the world, but from an overly worldly Church, and therefore they found it necessary to physically separate themselves from the larger culture, inside and outside the

Church, in the most radical way possible. They actually left the "civilized" world for the wilderness of the desert.

The extreme marginality of the desert hermits was soon mitigated by the growing preference for cenobitic life precisely because it allowed deeper integration into the sacramental, and therefore communitarian, life of the larger Church, and soon enough by the move back into the cities but within monastery enclosures. The physical separation of cloister was itself soon mitigated by the mendicant embrace of the "apostolic life" or a life of preaching, teaching, or other ministry among the people. Women monastics of this period did not have the same freedom male monastics enjoyed but, even as strictly enclosed, these women Religious saw themselves involved, through prayer and vicarious penance, in the ministry of the male mendicants.

The foundation of apostolic orders in the premodern and modern periods called for a further mitigation of the physical separation of Religious from the surrounding society. If Religious were to influence those to whom they felt called to minister, they had to be present to them as preachers, teachers, missionaries, personal or courtly advisers, healers of body and spirit. This entailed modifications in the monastic horarium and enclosure and increasing contacts between Religious and the laity. The strictures on such contacts, especially in the case of women Religious, remained stringent right up to Vatican II, but the historical pattern of gradual reintegration of Religious into the Church community and even into the surrounding nonecclesial society is fairly clear.[12] The direction of movement is away from an understanding of Religious marginality in terms of physical separation and nonparticipation toward an understanding of Religious Life as an alternative reality construction by which Religious are in the world, but not of it.

Finally, at Vatican II, the call of the whole Church to solidarity with the people of the modern world and the call of Religious to renew their life came together to undermine definitively the understanding of Religious marginality as physical separation by means of agrarian horarium, enclosed space, and medieval clothing and customs. Religious women in particular, with amazing alacrity, abandoned or abolished centuries-old customs, dress, patterns of behavior, and structures of enclosure and emerged from their mysterious convent world into the full light of modernity.

As Religious began to interact with their contemporaries in virtually every sphere, from education and work to social action and recreation, serious questions arose about what really distinguished Religious from other people. For many Religious, to say nothing of their lay counterparts, the convent subculture had been virtually synonymous with Religious Life, and when it disappeared the lifeform itself seemed to have evaporated. Many who left Religious Life in the decades after the Council did so because they could not see any point to accepting the burdens of a life that no longer seemed distinctive, much less superior.

In fact, Religious Life was not evaporating but Religious were being driven deeper into the theological and spiritual reality of their life which, for many, had never become fully explicit because the daily routine of the life and their ministerial work had carried them along. The surface distinctions of preconciliar Religious Life, real as they were, did not constitute the life theologically but made it a sociological subculture or lifestyle enclave. Religious Life, as we will see, continues to be an alternative reality construction rendering Religious marginal to their society. But it is the engaged marginality of prophecy rather than the disengagement of escape or self-protection.

III. The Coordinates of Religious Life as Prophetic Vocation

Contemplative immediacy to God and social marginality are the coordinates of Religious Life as a prophetic lifeform in the Church. My concern in this book is not with the history of Religious Life or even Religious Life within Church history, but with the interface between contemporary Religious Life and postmodern, first-world culture. Consequently, in speaking of Religious Life as prophetic, I am specifically concerned with how contemporary Religious Life addresses today's issues of social justice and the emerging culture of postmodernity. I will take up the conditions, spirituality, and arena of this prophetic vocation in chapter 10 but am here concerned with the theological character of the life.

Characteristic of late modernity has been the realization that the suffering of so many, indeed most, of the world's people is not the problem of individuals who are morally, intellectually, or socially inferior and therefore incapable of securing for themselves or undeserving of having their share of the world's goods, but the problem of societies that are structured to promote the well-being of the few by the increasing misery of the many. Prophecy today is about *social justice,* the change of structures toward the promotion of the good of all.[13]

Also characteristic of our time is the major shift in worldview from modernity to *postmodernity.* The soul-searing implications of this development for Christian faith also elicit a prophetic engagement on the part of Religious.

A. Prophecy and Social Justice: Challenging and Changing Systems

Prophecy is not primarily about foretelling the future. It is about telling what time it is, what it is time for, in the present. As Rabbi Abraham Heschel put it, the prophet's "essential task is to declare the word of God to the here and now."[14] Jesus is the prophet par excellence, the one who announced that the time is now and what it is time for is the Reign of God (cf. Mk 1:14–15). Prophecy requires three things: a clarity of vision and acuity of hearing that is a participation in God's view of humanity in history; the ability to effectively announce that vision both to the powers that oppose God's Reign and to the people who are oppressed by those powers; and the willingness to pay, even with one's life, for the ultimate triumph of God's covenantal order, the Reign of God.

1. Prophecy as participation in the divine pathos: First, the prophet has to see, to hear, human experience from God's point of view. As Heschel says, "the fundamental experience of the prophet is a fellowship with the feelings of God, *a sympathy with the divine pathos.*"[15] The immediacy to God and marginality to the social order that Religious attempt to live is directly ordered to sharing God's perception of humanity in history, to the cultivation of participation in the divine pathos.

The choice of celibate solitude is ordered to contemplation, the actualization in prayer of immediacy to God. Contemplation is the place, the locus, of the increasing coincidence of the contemplative's view with the divine view. Thomas Merton, a truly contemporary Religious who agonized over the validity of monastic solitude in a world of violence and injustice, returned again and again in his writings to the theme of contemplation as the entrance of the human person into the sphere of God. In contemplative prayer, according to Merton, we pass through the center of our own being into the very being of God, where we see ourselves and our world with a clarity, a simplicity, a truthfulness that are not available in any other way.[16] And it is this view of reality that the contemplative must bring to bear upon the social order. For the Religious, celibate solitude has as its primary purpose the fostering of contemplation. Today this involves participation in the divine perspective from which prophecy arises.

Celibate solitude also leads to the construction of the alternative lifeform that places Religious on the margins of society. Although ministerial Religious do not physically separate themselves from society as enclosed monastics, they do, through their vows, marginalize themselves in relation to the basic dynamics of contemporary culture. By renouncing marriage and thus the creation of a family whose future is of paramount concern, by renouncing personal ownership and even the pursuit of corporate wealth as well as the payment of taxes, by renouncing full and independent participation in political life and processes including political careers and military service, Religious stand back from the dynamics of society and culture.

Many people have accused Religious, as they did Merton, of failure to put their bodies where their rhetoric is, of being safely in "the wrong place" while the city burns.[17] Religious cannot protect themselves from being seen, sometimes by those whose opinion they most respect and cherish, and even at times by themselves, as "guilty bystanders." Religious, including those who are not in monasteries and thus physically marginalized, will always have to deal with the charge of relative noninvolvement in the secular order and their own inner questioning of where one really should be when the stakes are as high as they are today. Many members of ministerial Religious orders have participated personally in public social protest, engaged in organized political lobbying, provisionally held public office, gone to prison for their activism, and even given their lives in solidarity with the oppressed people they serve. But Religious Life itself, as I have tried to show, involves a certain social and political marginality by the very fact that Religious do not have the same personal stake in the ordering of secular life that their lay counterparts do. Our children, our jobs, our livelihood, our homes are not on the line in the same way. Even our participation in dangerous action for social justice is participation by choice and is supported by a corporate structure the lack of which is the very reason the oppressed can be oppressed.

Marginality, as Merton tried to explain to his contemporaries, if it is lived authentically in all its agonizing ambiguity and without any attempt at self-justification or any claims to superiority, gives the Religious a hermeneutical vantage point that is somewhat analogous to that of the poor and oppressed, those who are marginalized not by choice but by violence. To be outside the system, especially when one does not have an alternate source for the goods and services the system should make available, allows one to discern the contradictions and the violence of the system that those who participate fully in it and are its beneficiaries are less equipped to see. It is no accident that women in the Church rather than the ordained have analyzed the clerical system and are making the whole Church aware of why an ecclesiastical caste system cannot finally serve the ends of ministry. It is no accident that African Americans rather than whites, even whites who actively participated in the Civil Rights Movement, exploded the myth of the equality of the American social system. It is no accident that the poor see the collusion of big business, police power, the military, and the ecclesiastical hierarchy in a way that the members of those power groups do not see.

Religious are marginal by choice, but that marginality is in the service of prophecy, not escapism. From the edges of the system there is a view of what the system does to those who are excluded, to those who are made means to other people's ends. If contemplation fosters immediacy to God, marginality fosters immediacy to the oppressed. The Religious wants to be where the cry of the poor meets the ear of God. To feel the pathos of God is not a warm and comfortable religious experience; it is an experience of the howling wilderness driving one to protest. Marginality is not a safe haven from the complexities of modern life but freely chosen solidarity with those who are excluded against their will. Immediacy to the marginalized poor is the complement to immediacy to God in the prophetic dynamic.

The characteristic temptation for the Religious is to abandon the vocation to solitude and to throw oneself exclusively into the fray on the side of justice for the oppressed. But for Religious this is not the right choice, because God asks something different of them. No matter how extensive and intensive their involvement in the struggle for justice may be, and for many it is very extensive, their vocation is to be a consistent locus of that prophetic insight born of immediacy to God and social marginality, which are essential to the spiritual integrity of all action on behalf of justice. Religious Life is a theological and spiritual resource for the struggle, not just a source of committed workers for the cause.

2. Prophecy as proclamation: lament, vision, hope: The second requirement for prophecy is the ability to speak the vision to both the oppressor and the oppressed. To the former the prophet must speak a message of criticism and a challenge to conversion and to the latter a message of hope energizing action toward a different future. Walter Brueggemann in his challenging book, *The Prophetic Imagination,*[18] says that the first task of the prophet in speaking the vision is public lamentation. To lament is to declare, not by denunciation or condemnation but by public weeping, that everything is not all right. The guardians of the status quo, those who own, operate, and profit from the going system, want the oppressed to believe that everything is basically as it should be, that the system is designed and guaranteed by God, and that eventually all the minor problems will be remedied. The prophet says that the oppressive system is not God's plan; that God is on the side of the oppressed, of those whom the system grinds up and presses down; that the system does not have minor problems but that the system itself is a major problem.

The second task of the prophet is to recall God's promises and so, by projecting a vision of an alternative future, to engender hope. Hopelessness is a surrender to the inevitability and unchangeableness of the present arrangement. Those who control the system do so by paralyzing the imagination of the oppressed through the control of language, because what cannot be said cannot be thought or sought. The prophet is one who has a fund of language that does not come from the system. It comes from the Word of God. With this new Word of promise the prophet can seed the imagination of the oppressed with images that subvert the conviction of inevitability and divine legitimation of the system and engender hope for a different world.

Immediacy to God and social marginality are what equip the Religious for this double prophetic task of public lament and the energizing of hope. In solitude and prayer the Religious experiences the divine pathos for God's people. Sharing the divine pathos does not result in a new political program to rearrange the available pieces of the social puzzle but in a lament that will not be silenced, a howl of protest from the heart of the desert. It is the weeping of Rachel for her children who are no more (cf. Jer 31:15); it is the lament of Jesus over Jerusalem, which does not know the time of its visitation (cf. Mt 23:37–39). But contemplative immersion in God also results in a new vision not derived from the status quo but from God's promises, in new images that will energize alternative strategies, in new language for the saying of things we were not supposed to think. Amos Wilder called Jesus' discourse in parable "the language of the Kingdom," a new idiom voicing things hitherto undreamed and unleashing energy toward a new creation.[19]

Social marginality plays an especially important role in the prophetic task of announcing God's Word in the present social, political, and religious situation. While much can be done from within the system to ameliorate its worst effects, there are few people who are willing and able to cut off the institutional branch on which they are sitting, whether secular or ecclesiastical. To be on the edge, as Jesus was, gives one a certain freedom to see what is really happening in both society and Church and to say what one sees regardless of the consequences. Thomas Merton spoke often of his marginal situation, which he valued because it gave him the distance which enabled that critical balance which is something "the monk *owes to the world* [f]or the monastic life has a certain prophetic character about it." His relative marginality to, even though he was deeply involved in, the peace movement in the 1960s, enabled Merton to see the intrinsic contradiction in the self-immolation of a young Catholic Worker, Roger LaPorte, in protest of the Vietnam War, something many of those deeply involved in the activist efforts failed to see.[20] Theresa Kane, who in 1979 publicly called the Pope to listen to the voices of women oppressed in and by the Church, did something that would have been much more difficult if not impossible had she been a part of the clerical system whose ground is protected from women by the present discipline.[21]

3. Prophecy as willingness to suffer for justice's sake: The third requirement for prophecy is the willingness to suffer, even to die, for the sake of the newness one is commissioned to announce. As Brueggemann says, the prophet speaks only "at great political and existential risk."[22] Immediacy to God in contemplation and social marginality are the source of strength for those who dare to criticize the establishment, whether secular or ecclesiastical, and for those who energize the people for change. Prophets, from Moses on the far side of the Jordan to Jesus in Gethsemane, from Thomas More in the court of the king to Joan of Arc before the Inquisition, from Martin Luther King, Jr. on the balcony in Memphis to Dorothy

Day on the picket line in New York City, from Oscar Romero in the Cathedral of El Salvador to the Church women raped and murdered on a lonely El Salvador road, have testified that the willingness and the strength to lay down one's life for justice's sake comes from face-to-face encounter with the living God, who hears the cry of the poor.

Social marginality makes the prophet a natural target for establishment violence, both secular and ecclesiastical. The prophet lives on the edges of the system, not just physically but ideologically. The rules of the social order do not have a self-evident priority for the prophet, for whom the presumption is not in favor of the establishment's values but always in favor of God's justice for the oppressed. Thus, the prophet not only challenges the law but when necessary breaks it and encourages others to do the same. This is a dangerous way to live and, as Jesus remarked, the tombs of the prophets are eloquent testimony to the tension between "social order" and prophetic criticism (cf. Lk 11:45–52). In a sense, prophets court death, physical or spiritual, because their vocation is not to survive within the system but to change it.

B. Prophecy and Postmodernism: Living the Questions[23]

Celibate solitude, and the contemplative immediacy to God and social marginality it generates, can place Religious not only in a situation of engagement with the social problems of their time but also in a situation of naked engagement with the deepest religious and spiritual struggles of their world. This feature of Religious Life tends to be muted when Religious are most assimilated into the larger Church culture, as was the case in the first part of the twentieth century. Then it was the Church as institution that confronted the challenges of modernism, secularism, and scientism, and Religious were in the vanguard of this confrontation, just as they were in the vanguard of renewal when the Church, at Vatican II, embraced the modern world. In such historical contexts the prophetic character of Religious Life is primarily if not exclusively directed outward toward issues in secular society, while the interior life, supported and confirmed by ecclesial participation, can seem stable, rooted, and unproblematic. But we forget at our peril that the primary activity of the Old Testament prophets as well as that of Jesus himself was directed not at the structures of secular society but at the infidelity of the Chosen People to their covenant with God and its societal fallout in injustice and violence.

When the Church itself becomes the problem, the spiritual life takes on a particular urgency. In the third and fourth centuries many serious God-seekers saw the institutional Church so compromised by its involvement as a state religion in the Roman Empire that they felt impelled to leave the civilized world altogether and go into the desert to confront, in naked solitude, the powers of evil with which the Church seemed to have made too easy an accommodation. Today, in the midst of a restorationist papacy committed to restraining if not reversing the renewal dynamics of Vatican II, Religious who committed themselves wholeheartedly to the conciliar agenda find themselves in a confrontational situation in relation to the institutional Church. This is an agonizing position for Religious who, in the 1960s, epitomized their conciliar sense of ecclesial identity in the euphoric appropriation of St. Teresa of Avila's proud, "I am a daughter of the Church."

This situation is aggravated by two converging cultural developments that have made both "daughter" and "Church" highly problematic. The feminist movement, so intrinsic to the modernity that the Church embraced at Vatican II, quickly permeated women's Religious Life. Feminism, calling women to claim their full and equal personhood in the human race, the family, and civil society, combined with the new sense of ecclesial adulthood of all the laity fostered by the Council to make Religious who had gloried in their subordination to Church authority embodied in clerical "fathers" increasingly restive in a sacralized patriarchal system. The institution's insistence on demeaning gender-exclusive language in teaching and liturgy,[24] the massive offensive against the possibility of women's ordination,[25] violation of congregational processes and revision of constitutions[26] impelled women Religious into solidarity with their lay sisters, who were becoming increasingly aware of their oppression, especially in regard to sexual morality and family life, by an all-male hierarchy. Women Religious were increasingly unable and unwilling to see themselves as "daughters" in the patriarchal ecclesiastical "family" and increasingly uncomfortable with the heretofore self-evident equation of the Vatican bureaucracy with "Church."

The deepening struggle between women Religious and the institutional Church has been further exacerbated by the second cultural development which has undermined the theological convictions that might have provided spiritual resources for dealing with societal injustice and oppression in the Church. The emergence of postmodernity, which was discussed in the previous chapter, has raised questions that were inevitable in view of the Church's four-hundred-year Tridentine slumber. Until the late 1950s the Church's theology had remained steadfastly medieval while the Western world traversed the Renaissance, the Reformation, the scientific revolution, and the Enlightenment. Religious, with the rest of the Church, thought theology was virtually immune to historical development (despite John Cardinal Newman's celebrated treatise to the contrary). Scholastic Thomism was considered a perennial theological-philosophical system which admirably explained, "in its ultimate causes," everything pertinent to faith.[27]

The developments of the late twentieth century in the physical, social, and personality sciences, economics, and technology have created a world so radically different even from the modern world of the nineteenth and early twentieth centuries that few categories from medieval thought (e.g., substance and accidents, hypostatic union, transubstantiation, matter and form) are even intelligible much less illuminating for the ordinary believer without specialized theological training. As modernity, so brightly hopeful for human transcendence, has generated the increasingly deadly impasses of ubiquitous local wars and the threat of nuclear annihilation, a runaway global economy that is producing epidemic poverty, the social and medical ravages of the abstraction of sexuality from any moral context, ecological cosmocide, intractable racism and sexism, and the impoverishment of life by the privatizing of religion and the banishing of mystery from the horizons of human experience, a massive rethinking of the most basic assumptions about reality, knowledge, subjectivity, history, society, and value is underway. This rethinking is generating the ethos that has been dubbed "postmodernity" because of its nebulous and still unformulated character and its tensive relationship with "modernity," and the ethos is gradually spawning a nonunitary worldview within which most of the givens of Catholic theology are being seriously questioned. Theological coherence is crucial to the kind of spirituality that Religious Life involves and, increasingly, Religious have found themselves without theological resources for dealing with the emerging questions.

Religious are not alone in this theological wilderness. The "death of God" controversies in the 1950s, the liberation and process theologies arising in the 1960s, the feminist theological challenges of the 1970s, the ecological and interreligious problematics of the 1980s and 1990s have kept professional theologians struggling with a constantly lengthening agenda confronted through an epistemological and methodological kaleidoscope in which the pieces never assume the same position twice.

The laity is increasingly composed, on the one hand, of Catholics who grew up before the Council in a rote-imbibed dogmatism from which they were suddenly liberated without being supplied with workable alternative resources and, on the other hand, those who grew up in the immediate aftermath of the Council, in which they were more the subject matter of pedagogical experiments than the subjects of theological or religious formation. Long overdue but often poorly implemented change in liturgy and Church structure, sudden exhilarating ecumenical and interreligious exchange after generations of insularity and suspicion, and very mixed messages about ministerial responsibility left many Catholics feeling very much "on their own" in the sphere of religion. Cultural relativism and suspicion of all institutional authority as well as the very uncertain sound of the ecclesiastical trumpets on the one hand and the ever more dangerous and threatening societal context on the other encouraged people to turn from civic and religious engagement to seeking safety in lifestyle enclaves and privatized spirituality. Ad hoc spiritualities, often pieced together from elements borrowed from Eastern religions, decontextualized Native American practices, New Age philosophies, and therapeutic techniques did not seem to need the theological foundation or communitarian framework that traditional religion had. Generation X is a kind of incarnation of this rather rootless approach to life as a moment-by-moment invention of coping strategies that make no claims to validity beyond their aesthetic appeal and pragmatic efficacy.

Although there is, of course, much that is positive and hopeful in the present ecclesiastical and cultural situation, I am highlighting the factors that have generated the spiritual crisis of our time which Religious are living with particular acuity. I have written about this crisis at some length[28] as a kind of corporate dark-night experience analogous to that of the individual contemplative described by John of the Cross and will take it up in much greater detail in chapters 5 and 6. Therefore, I will not expand on it here. What I suggest in this analysis is that Religious have been engaged during the past thirty years in a protracted experience of "living the questions" of our time. The unraveling of the Tridentine Church's institutional, liturgical, theological, and ministerial structures within which most Religious made their life commitment and which buffered them from some of the ultimate challenges of real religious faith has brought them face to face with the spiritual questions at the heart of contemporary life.

Religious are not the only people struggling with the issues of the existence and credibility of the transcendent male deity of Christian theism, the exclusivist claims for Christ and the imperialist agenda of the Church within other religious cultures, absolutist sex-fixated morality, the male power structure that ministry and the sacraments incarnate and promote, and the ecclesiastical discipline that marginalizes, oppresses, and persecutes so many of the Church's most devoted members. But for Religious there is no relief from the existential turmoil generated by these issues. Religious Life has no raison d'être, especially now that ministerial involvement and intentional community are readily available outside Religious Life, if the foundational tenets of the faith do not hold. The ecclesial character of Christian faith, deeply threatened by current ecclesiastical practice, is intrinsic, not accidental, to Christian Religious Life. A coherent theological framework within which prayer, sacramental life, and ministry make sense in themselves and in relation to each other is crucial to the relationship with Jesus Christ that alone justifies the commitment in consecrated celibacy that is at the heart of Religious Life.

One of Thomas Merton's most important insights into his own vocation was that living the spiritual anguish of the unanswered questions and insoluble dilemmas of his historical context, both societal and ecclesiastical, was an even more important expression of the prophetic character of monastic life than direct active engagement with the social issues of his time.[29] For ministerial Religious it is probably the case that both aspects are equally important. As contemporary Benedictine Joan Chittister says, "It is a question of naming the questions. That is the function of religious life."[30] The questions Religious name are certainly the challenges they raise to the social system; but they are also, at least as importantly, the spiritual questions they face, name, and struggle with in the purifying fire of contemplative prayer. As John of the Cross, Teresa of Avila, and other contemplatives in our tradition have maintained, there is no assurance of a successful outcome when one embarks on the terrifying passage from immature faith, no matter how sincere, to the immediate engagement with God in the darkness of pure faith or contemplative union. Furthermore, no one sets out on this path on her own initiative. What I am suggesting, however, is that Religious Life, because of its character as an exclusive God-quest in celibate solitude, is a natural context for the challenge to such a journey and that it belongs not only to the interior project of Religious Life but to its prophetic character.

IV. Conclusion

In this chapter I have tried to suggest a theological location for Religious Life as a state of life in the Church based on its specific and distinctive characteristic, namely, the exclusive God-quest centered in Jesus Christ and expressed in lifelong consecrated celibacy. I have suggested that celibate solitude "places" Religious in a position of immediacy to God and social marginality that generates a prophetic engagement with their surroundings. At the turn of this century, in a first-world Western context, this engagement necessarily faces "outward" toward the massive problems of social justice that modernity has spawned and "inward" toward the excruciating spiritual crisis of faith struggling with the theological challenges of postmodernity in the context of a highly polarized Church.

The prophetic engagement of Religious flows from and is governed by the mystical or contemplative character of the life, the centrality of the God-quest. Like the prophets of the Hebrew scriptures and Jesus himself, the Religious is a person who has been claimed by God, whose life has been taken over by God to the exclusion of any other primary commitment, however legitimate and holy. Therefore, God's preferential concern for the poor and oppressed, whether they are victims of secular society or the ecclesiastical establishment itself, is the primary concern of the Religious. But like Jeremiah struggling with the God who seduced him or Hosea betrayed into a faithless marriage or Jesus tempted in the desert, agonizing in the garden, and abandoned on the cross, Religious also live in naked intensity the spiritual dark night that overtakes them at the juncture of faith, theology, and social concern. Both the constant struggle for justice and the persevering endurance of the faith struggle arise from the engagement of the Religious with God but are carried on for the sake of God's people. Prophetic action is the public face of mysticism. Contemplation is the root of public engagement.

The prophetic character of Religious Life, like that of the Old Testament prophets and Jesus himself, tends to focus even more directly on the Church itself, the faith community and its institutional realization, than on secular society. It is the task of the Church as People of God on pilgrimage in this world to be the incarnation, herald, and instrument of the Reign of God. Insofar as the Church, as community and as institution, is faithful to this identity and mission, the prophetic role of Religious is to support and foster that mission through involvement in ministry of all kinds, especially in areas or forums where it is difficult or impossible for others to go or where needs are just beginning to be discerned and institutional means are not yet developed. But insofar as the Church is unfaithful to its identity and mission, the prophetic role of Religious is to challenge and confront with the word of the Gospel the apathy, compromise, and abuse of power in the community, including and especially as it is embodied in the leadership.

Exercising this prophetic calling, especially in and toward the Church itself, is dangerous, filled with self-doubt and anxiety, and laced with interior suffering and external threat. This helps to explain the tension, to be explored later in chapters 9 and 10, between Religious Life and the ecclesiastical institution, which both needs and values the service of Religious, whether through the life of prayer or in active ministry, and also continually attempts to restrict, enclose, regulate, and control, if not domesticate, the life itself. It also helps explain why, in general, Religious who are not ordained into the institutional hierarchy have much more consistently lived the prophetic dimension of the life in relation to the institutional Church than those who have tried to combine the roles of prophet and agent of the institution.

Finally, it must be said again that the attempt to describe the theological character and location of Religious Life in the Church is not an attempt to provide a phenomenology of Religious Life as it is actually lived by all who profess it. Just as many actual lives of baptized Christians do not manifest their paschal identity and many Christian marriages do not manifest the theology of matrimony, so many actual Religious do not manifest the prophetic character of their vocation. This makes it even more urgent to properly discern and delineate the vocation, both to provide an ideal, a challenge, and a criterion for those called to the life and also to offer hermeneutical access to the life for those, in and outside of the Church, who relate to Religious in one way or another. Religious Life must not be an incoherent stumbling forward in the dark for those who live it, and it need not be an unintelligible conundrum to those who observe it. It will remain, despite all explication, a mystery, but that is the nature of relationships.

Chapter Five

Religious Life in Spiritual Transformation I: Vatican II and Renewal, an Active Dark Night?

I. Introduction

The renewal of Religious Life that was enthusiastically undertaken in the late 1960s in response to Vatican II yielded very quickly, historically speaking, to a state of crisis that has led both casual observers and serious analysts of the life to predict its imminent, indeed inevitable, demise. Even the most optimistic of its promoters can hardly be sanguine about its present or future in the face of the clear and often rehearsed signs of diminishment: rapidly declining numbers, diminishing financial resources, and loss of leverage in both Church and society. When these material factors are compounded by ecclesiastical disapproval of individual members in their ministries and of congregations in their legitimate exercise of self-determination and by intense struggles within congregations over self-understanding and identity, the picture can look bleak indeed.

Some Religious confront these distressing data with a panic that is barely held at bay by reactive rigidity. Others take refuge in a fatalistic resignation expressed in a fatigued hope that their congregation will at least die with dignity. Still others try not to think about the situation and to get on with the day-to-day business of life and ministry while secretly hoping that they will not be the ones who finally have to turn out the lights. Religious and secular analysts have suggested both reasons and remedies for the situation based on anthropological, psychological, sociological, political, organizational, and canonical considerations.

Nevertheless, as I noted in chapter 3, in the face of such indisputable cause for concern and without discounting the pertinence of analyses of the situation through the secular disciplines, my experience with Religious and their congregations makes me think that other factors, suggesting a different line of reflection, are at work among large numbers of contemporary Religious, especially women. In the past few years I have been increasingly struck by two features of contemporary Religious Life that have puzzled and intrigued me. My observations are not, and indeed cannot be, scientific because they are gleaned from experience with individual Religious, often in the context of spiritual direction or renewal work, and with Religious congregations and their leaders, usually in the context of community events such as assemblies, workshops, and reflection weekends.

II. Features of the Contemporary Experience of Religious Life

The two features of the recent experience of Religious that have precipitated my reflections are first, a paradox and second, a malaise. It seems extremely *paradoxical* that, on the one hand, Religious congregations are exhibiting all of the sociological characteristics of declining institutions and, on the other hand, they are not exhibiting the attitudes and behaviors that such decline usually precipitates.[1] Organizations predictably follow a life cycle of emergence, growth and expansion, decline, and demise, each phase characterized by typical observable traits. By any objective sociological criteria most Religious congregations are in the decline phase of the cycle and some seem close to demise. The decline phase is marked by diminishment in membership and material resources, which decreases the group's effectiveness in accomplishing its goals. American women's Religious congregations have declined from over 180,000 members in 1966 to 126,000 in the early 1990s to fewer than 90,000 at the time of this writing. Today only 1 percent of Sisters are under thirty years of age,[2] while the median age in most congregations is over sixty. Congregations that once attracted fifty or sixty postulants a year now receive one or two. The decline in financial and institutional resources of congregations is commensurate with this decline in personnel.

The typical attitudes and behaviors of declining institutions are despair, cynicism, self-interest, and protective maintenance strategies such as internal "turf battles," hardening of boundaries, restriction of resources to in-house projects, and identification with external sources of wealth and power.[3]

However, based on the widespread sampling of congregational documents by the Leadership Conference of Women Religious (LCWR) Task Force on Religious Life in 1985[4] and on the paper, "Reflections Upon the Religious Life of U.S. Women Religious" prepared by LCWR for the Fifth Inter-American Conference on Religious Life in the same year,[5] these materially declining organizations exhibit the kinds of outwardly focused attitudes and behaviors that are characteristic of expanding organizations rather than declining ones. Religious congregations, especially of women, are overwhelmingly characterized by energetic and visionary planning for the future, a willingness to risk, permeability of boundaries and increasing inclusiveness, active identification with the poor and oppressed rather than the wealthy and powerful, internal unity, a high level of personal commitment of members, and the relative absence of survival anxiety. One could interpret this paradox as expressing a denial of reality on the part of Religious. Or one could wonder, as I have heard many congregational leaders do, at the healthy attitudes and ongoing commitment, in the face of overwhelming odds, of women who are clear-eyed realists about the organizational facts.

The second feature of the experience of contemporary Religious that has captured my attention and that seems, at least on one level, to contradict the evidence of hope and commitment just mentioned is the profound *malaise*, the pervasive sense of darkness that marks the day-to-day experience of many individual Religious and even of congregations. Even as Religious go on with life and ministry with a remarkable courage and commitment, there is a darkness which is not gloom, pessimism, or self-pity. It can only be called suffering. But suffering, which is a part of every worthwhile life and has certainly always played a role in Religious Life, is not an occasional episode in the life of many Religious today. It seems to be almost a state of being, an existential dimension of everything experienced or undertaken.

In a now justly famous article Constance FitzGerald, the Carmelite specialist in John of the Cross, suggested that the category of the Dark Night of the soul from the spiritual theology of the Spanish mystic might be useful for analyzing the current cultural experience of societal impasse in the face of the overwhelming problems and suffering of late modernity and especially the suffering of women in a patriarchal and sexist Church.[6] Although she recognized that John was writing about the experience, particularly the prayer experience, of the individual contemplative, FitzGerald contended that John's description of the spiritual journey, especially of its purificatory dimension, was applicable beyond the boundaries of the author's intent.[7] Response to this article by both scholars and lay readers, religious and secular, has verified her intuition and suggested its possible application to other areas of contemporary experience.

As I have interacted with Religious around the experience of suffering in the postconciliar Church I have been struck by the similarity between what they were describing and John of the Cross's spiritual theology. As I have suggested this analogy in various contexts I have found that it resonated powerfully with many Religious whose spiritual maturity I have reason to trust. Even Religious who are unfamiliar with the writings of

John of the Cross recognize John's description, when it is explained to them, in their own experience.[8]

For some time I resisted this line of reflection not only because most of the Religious with whom I have contact are not in contemplative orders (whose members were John's primary audience),[9] but especially because I am suspicious of the tendency of many religious people, when faced with the inevitable pain caused by our own shortcomings or the systemic injustice of the institutions in which we participate, to take refuge in pious victimhood. This temptation is perhaps especially dangerous for women who have been taught to deny, absorb, or capitalize on suffering instead of doing something about it. But I have been led by several factors to reexamine the possibility that the conjunction between spirituality and culture, both ecclesiastical and secular, is the locus and perhaps the precipitating factor, though not the ultimate cause or purpose, of the current malaise in Religious Life. Such a line of analysis may prove more enlightening of the situation than purely phenomenological or social scientific explanations.

First, contrary to what has been suggested by some analysts of Religious Life, it is not my experience that the majority of Religious, especially women Religious, have sold out to the materialism of contemporary liberal culture. If anything, Religious women work harder and longer for less pay than anyone in the Church with comparable qualifications. They are more often than not too responsible for their own good, remaining in ministerial positions that are patently abusive because of their commitment to God's people. Without any coercive pressure from superiors these Religious not only make their annual retreat (sometimes at the price of vacation) but also attend summer courses, prayer workshops, days of reflection, personal development seminars, and lectures. They are voracious readers of spiritual books, seek out spiritual direction despite high costs in time, money, and travel, and eagerly undertake spiritual renewal programs. Religious are conscientious participants, often at the price of already scarce free time, in congregational tasks. In short, if my observations are at all accurate, women Religious are at least as committed as they ever were to ministry, community, and their own spiritual lives. And the fact that these dimensions of their lives are no longer either provided for or enforced by authority, much less a source of gratification, means that these Religious are acting out of personal conviction rather than routine, obligation, or self-seeking.

Second, when Religious give voice, often in the context of spiritual direction or faith sharing, to the pervasive suffering that I have observed, they tend to talk little about overwork, underpay, lack of job satisfaction and official recognition, or even clerical oppression. They talk about the inability to pray, the lost sense of God's presence, agonizing alienation from Church and sacraments, fear of loss of faith, a sense of inauthenticity or shallowness in ministry because of the theological incoherence of their own positions on issues, their inarticulateness or even paralysis in the effort to share faith in community, soul fatigue.

In short, the suffering of Religious who have survived the three decades since Vatican II does not seem to be due, in the main, to serious infidelity, either individual or corporate. And it does tend to center in their religious experience rather than in external circumstances no matter how much the latter may exacerbate it. The Dark Night, as John of the Cross describes it, is the experience of purification that comes upon the person who has, for a long time, lived the spiritual life with fidelity and courage but who remains in need of purification not from gross sins of omission or commission, not from laxity or negligence, but from the roots of sinfulness to which the conscious mind does not have access and which are, therefore, not amenable to the direct action of the will. It is the apparent similarity between the character of the suffering that seems so widespread among Religious today and the nature of the Dark Night as it is described in John of the Cross that has led me to raise the question of the spiritual character of the suffering.

Finally, there seems something significant in the fact that the Dark Night, which has always been considered the individual experience of particular people as they developed in the spiritual life, seems today to be a widespread and simultaneous experience of a whole group. That has led me to inquire into the relationship between the spiritual experience of Religious and the ecclesial and societal situation of the late twentieth-century American Catholic Church, which is the common context of this group of people. The hypothesis I want to explore, not as a theological proposition but as an heuristic device,[10] is that the ecclesiastical transition from the medieval to the modern world undertaken at Vatican II and the cultural transition of Western society from modernity to postmodernity that is currently underway have precipitated a spiritual crisis that is analogous to the Dark Night and that this analogy can throw a very helpful light on the paradox and the malaise I described above. In this chapter I will deal with the first factor, the Council and its aftermath, in relation to the active night of spirit and the passive night of sense. In the next chapter I will reflect on the second factor, the engagement of postmodernity, in relation to the passive night of spirit.[11] (See page 365.)

III. The "Dark Night" in John of the Cross

John of the Cross wrote his master works of spiritual theology as commentaries on ecstatic poems that he had composed out of his own experience of the spiritual journey. They are works of his maturity, written in hindsight after he had traversed the path they describe.[12] The two treatises which deal with the path from a worldly or sinful life to union with God are *The Ascent of Mount Carmel* (henceforth, *A*) and *The Dark Night* (henceforth, *DN*), titles that can cause confusion because, in fact, both are commentaries on one poem, "The Dark Night," and both are about phases of the experience John calls "the dark night."[13]

For our purposes it is important to understand, at least in a general way, the stages and dynamics of the spiritual life as John describes them. He proposes that the entire spiritual journey, because it is one of growth in the theological virtues of faith, hope, and love, is characterized by a darkness that is the experiential manifestation of the increasing influx of God into the human spirit, i.e., what John calls "contemplation," which is another name for union with God.[14] The brighter the light of the divine presence, the darker the experience of the one whose spiritual eyes cannot accommodate such light. However, although the entire journey is one of darkness, the various stages are quite distinct and different from one another. Furthermore, the darkness itself has a double character: it is purifying or purgative and also unitive. And this is what may prove helpful in understanding the passage Religious have been undergoing since the Council.

John divides the spiritual journey into two "nights": the active night (which he treats in *A*) and the passive night (which he treats in *DN*). And each of these phases of the journey has two aspects: a purification of the senses and a purification of the spirit. Basically, the active night of sense is the subject of *A*, Book I; the active night of spirit the subject of *A*, Books II and III. However, John intersperses material on the whole journey throughout *A*, so the reader has to be alert. The passive night of sense is dealt with in *DN*, Book I, and the passive night of spirit in *DN*, Book II. Our concern in this and the next chapter is with the experience of each of these nights. However, it is crucial to realize that these phases and aspects of the spiritual journey are not four sequential periods of time, each of which is completed before the next begins. As in the more traditional division of the spiritual life into the purgative, illuminative, and unitive "ways," all of these processes go on throughout the spiritual life with one or another predominating at a given time.

IV. The Active Night and the Experience of Contemporary Religious

The major distinction between the active and passive nights, as the terms suggest, is the relative preponderance of human and divine causality in the experience. In the active night the person herself is the primary actor, always inspired, strengthened, and enabled by God, but actively choosing what to do, when, how, and for what purposes. God's gradually increasing influence as the person progresses in the spiritual life is in inverse proportion to the activity and initiative of the person. Thus, the person is most clearly "in charge" in the active night of sense, less so in the active night of spirit, and much less so in the passive nights. This pattern is fairly clear in the recent experience of Religious who energetically undertook the renewal of their life in the wake of Vatican II and have found themselves progressively less in control of the developments that have followed, including both the fallout of the Council and the emergence of postmodernity.

A. The Active Night of Sense and Contemporary Experience

Although John of the Cross devotes fifteen detailed chapters to the first aspect of the active night, his teaching is fairly easily summarized. The purpose of the active night of sense is to turn from the self and sin to God. When this aspect has done its basic work the person has definitively chosen Christ as the center of her life and has achieved a basic personal integration, what John calls an accommodation of sense to spirit. The person is far from perfection or holiness, much less contemplative union with God, but her life is essentially well ordered. The chaotic, impulse-ridden hedonism and selfishness of the "worldly" life has given way to a disciplined, basically God-centered life characterized by relative internal freedom and ministerial fruitfulness (cf. *A* I, 13, 13). The primary means for achieving this end are, positively, meditation on and imitation of the life of Christ (*A* I, 13, 3–4) and, negatively, a consistent and generous mortification of the unruly passions of the ego which John describes in his famous "nada" verses at the end of Book I (*A* I, 13, 6–12).

Most contemporary Religious whose experience predates Vatican II will easily recognize in *A,* Book I, the life of ascetical effort and conscientious prayer that began in their formation years and continued into a demanding community and ministerial life. It was a life of generous self-denial at which they became progressively adept and in which they found genuine peace imitating Christ in seeking the will of God for the good of others. It was marked by deepening prayer, typically discursive and affective, which was the center of gravity of life and mission. Recognized signs of spiritual growth were increasing generosity, fidelity in prayer, responsibility in ministry, charity within the community, self-control, and the ability to accept hardship for the common good. It was also a life marked with the ups and downs, the failures and successes, that John describes as part of this process of detachment from self and attachment to Christ.

One of the negative aspects of preconciliar Religious Life was that it did not, institutionally, encourage Religious to move beyond this initial stage. A deep suspicion of mysticism and its supposed "singularities" translated into an overreliance on established (and controllable) spiritual means, a discouragement of individuality in the life of prayer, and a general unavailability of resources for personalized spiritual development.[15] The spoken and unspoken message was that no one should presume that she was called beyond the most ordinary (meaning rudimentary) stage of spiritual development. "Keep the Rule and the Rule will keep you" epitomized the fixation in a practice-dominated spirituality that was presumed adequate for all.

However, the Council found Religious as a cohort (there were always exceptions, both positive and negative) living something analogous to the reality of the active night of sense as their ordinary spiritual experience. It is not at all surprising, therefore, that this devout and well-trained cohort was probably more prepared than any other group in the Church *as a group* to respond with alacrity to the Council's challenge to aggiornamento. They were committed to obedience to Church authority, accustomed to strenuous effort, disciplined, responsible, and energetic. The renewal of Religious Life called for by the Council was actually very analogous to what John of the Cross describes as the challenge raised by the successful negotiation of the active night of sense, namely, the entrance into the active night of spirit.

B. The Active Night of Spirit and Contemporary Experience

The spiritual dimension of the active night involves a qualitative deepening of the process of purification and a significant growth in union with God. The person who has become a relatively integrated human being, a dependable community member, and a responsible and respected minister must now begin to detach herself from the "props," both spiritual and psychological, that motivated her in the first stage of active purification. The real purpose of this night of spirit is to strip away the "sweetness" of the spiritual life and drive the person into a naked faith in which one seeks God rather than the gifts of God; where nothing, not even the "spiritual life," competes with God for one's love.

This stripping involves an active and willing detachment, not from gross sin and inordinate passions as in the first stage, but from a much more subtle attachment to the self in and through attachment to the spiritual. It can usually only be accomplished through the actual loss of real spiritual goods to which one has become attached. The person who has experienced, over a long period of time, the purgation of the first stage of the active night, knows, deep down, that under the admirable layer of her well-ordered life there is much that is entangled, ambiguous, selfish, egotistical, out of order. She welcomes, even if she dreads it, the purification that still needs to be accomplished and begins to actively pursue it.

John of the Cross describes the person in this stage as willingly surrendering some of the spiritual posturing and self-absorbed pleasure seeking in religious activities of the first phase. She abandons the search for the extraordinary and settles into a quiet, devoted, loyal, and unpretentious participation in the ecclesial and Religious community. "Saying prayers" gives way to deepening prayer, or, as John puts it, her prayer is less centered in sense and more in spirit. From fascination with interesting insights and *ideas about* Christ she moves into ever deepening *relationship with* Christ, who is now not only the model to be imitated but the whole content of

God's self-gift (*A* II, 22). She no longer seeks extraordinary manifestations of God's favor because Jesus suffices. As she moves beyond the dutiful and fervent saying of prescribed prayers and performance of required practices, her spiritual repertoire expands and, at the same time, all means become increasingly relativized (cf. *A* II, 4–5). She is less "heroic," less concerned about how she looks to others and especially to herself, and more concerned with genuine faithfulness. She knows that the "one thing necessary" is love and other elements of the spiritual life begin to fall into place.

John describes this phase as a purification of the intellect by the darkness of a faith that no longer feeds on abundant insights, of the memory by an emptiness that demands naked hope for what is unseen, and of the will by an absence of felt devotion that demands a more generous and unselfish love. We might not be drawn to the faculty psychology of John of the Cross (with its distinctions of intellect, will, memory, and so on), but most people who have persevered in the spiritual life for some time will recognize this description of the experience. The spiritual life is deeper and more authentic, but less exciting, spectacular, or satisfying. It demands an effortful daily perseverance that is not sustained by sensible consolation. Love rather than results, fidelity rather than appearances, intimacy with Christ rather than displays of devotion, real service whether or not it is appreciated or rewarded, self-transcendence as a daily manifestation of steadfast commitment mark the life of the person in whom the active night of spirit is doing its work.

I would suggest that Vatican II precipitated something analogous to a corporate experience of the active night of spirit among Religious, especially women. Although the renewal seemed, at the outset, to be largely about external modifications such as modernization of the habit, adjustment of the horarium to contemporary timetables, democratization of community procedures, and other easily observable phenomena, in fact the renewal precipitated changes that profoundly touched the spiritual dimensions of Religious Life. If that life as we have described it in the foregoing chapters is fundamentally a project of seeking God, whatever touches that God-quest will reverberate deeply in the lives of Religious.

For most contemporary Religious the period of their Religious Life up to the 1960s was one of extraordinary stability. The organization of Religious Life seemed perfectly suited to its ends, namely, the perfection of the Religious and the salvation of souls.[16] Faith was laid out in catechism-clear propositions that no one questioned; the liturgy was rich and invariable; authority structures were clear and effective; the status of Religious in the society of the Church and their role in its apostolic work were well defined and unchallenged. Religious were the "good sisters," the professional religious elite of the Church. Nowhere perhaps was this more true than in the United States in the 1950s and 1960s. This was the period of the Sister Formation Movement, when women Religious became not only a spiritual vanguard but some of the best educated and most professionally competent women in the world.[17] Religious Life, corporately, looked much like John of the Cross's spiritually accomplished beginner in whom the active night of sense has been effective. Many people have suggested that the 1940s–1960s were the most developed and distinguished period in the history of ministerial Religious Life.

Vatican II, in the space of a few years, occasioned the dismantling of this entire well-ordered structure. Almost overnight, in historical perspective, the external overlay of Religious Life was stripped away, a stripping that Religious themselves willingly undertook in the effort to renew their life according to the Council's vision of a Church newly in, with, and for the world after centuries of self-imposed exile and animosity. Furthermore, the Council precipitated change in every other sector of the Church, clerical and lay, and these changes also had repercussions on Religious Life.

The forceful affirmation of the universal call to holiness and the positive reevaluation of marriage as a state of consecrated life in the Church called into question the assumption that consecrated celibacy was a superior state of life, a conviction that, rightly or wrongly, was integral to the self-understanding of Religious.[18] The ministerial explosion among the laity obscured the apostolate as a part of the raison d'être of Religious Life, throwing Religious back on the question of ultimate motivation not only for entering but for staying. The privileged status of Religious was symbolically surrendered by the abandonment of habit and titles, and the allure of mystery vanished with the opening up of cloistered dwellings, deepening even further the question of distinct identity.

Financial security, freedom from responsibility within the authority structure of a total institution, and escape from sexual issues in the monosexual community disappeared within a few years as congregations diversified their ministries, divested themselves of institutional holdings and property, changed their procedures for deploying personnel, and emerged from the convent as cloister into the ordinariness of neighborhood life. All the "perks" of the life such as instant identity, job security, and the assurance of institutional backing whether one was right or wrong disappeared. In short, all the unrecognized or at least unacknowledged enticements to Religious Life, what John of the Cross might have called the built-in consolations of the life, that had played some role in virtually every teenager's vocation, came out into the open and demanded honest reexamination.

Some interpreted this almost-overnight dismantling of a centuries-old lifestyle as blessed liberation. Others saw it as unmitigated disaster. But what it surely did was throw all Religious back on the question of what they were doing with their lives and why and whether they should continue. This is the characteristic question of the active night of spirit: why continue if the felt satisfactions are no longer forthcoming? If Religious Life could not be justified by ministry, provided no securities and no escapes, did not make one mysterious or special, was not a higher or more perfect form of life much less an assurance of salvation, there was only one reason for continuing, and some discovered that was not the reason for which they had entered while others concluded it was not enough of a reason to stay. As many left and few entered, Religious who stayed got in touch in a new way with the real meaning of their Religious vocation, the God-quest at the center of their hearts, which made a mysteriously exclusive and total demand upon them and to which they could only respond by the gift of their whole lives in consecrated celibacy, voluntary poverty, community, and corporate mission. Those who continued to choose Religious Life had now to choose it in purified faith, unsupported hope, and generous love, because it was largely devoid of compensatory packaging.

This stripping to essentials is exactly what the first phase of the Dark Night, the active phase, is supposed to do. It strips away the false sweetness of the spiritual life by definitively detaching the person from everything, good as well as evil, spiritual as well as material, that competes with God in one's life. As John of the Cross says, the point is not that a person be actually deprived of all good things, but that one become detached from them, that they cease to be one's motivation or reward.

However, for most people actual deprivation is necessary for detachment to be achieved, and this educative deprivation occurs through the surrender, willingly and finally, of everything that competes with the love of God by providing the satisfaction for which we yearn. There is not a clear-cut dividing line between the self-deprivations of the active night of sense and that of spirit because many of things to which one clings are both material (or sensual) and spiritual. The attachment of Religious to their institutions, for example, was often at least as deeply an attachment to their spirituality, charism, traditions, and historical identity (i.e., spiritual realities) as it was to a source of financial security. As Kieran Kavanaugh remarks, Books II and III of *A,* although ostensibly about the active night of spirit, have more to say about the night of sense than Book I.[19] And conversely, the end of Book I, especially chapter 13 on the "nada," certainly applies to the spiritual goods from which one must be detached as well as the sensual ones. The active night, though conveniently divided into a night of sense and one of spirit, is actually a single experience in which purification becomes progressively more interior and intimate as the person cooperates with the process.

Religious deprived themselves in the years following Vatican II of all of the sociological and ecclesiastical comforts of

Religious Life, a deprivation that cut much deeper into the spirit than the relatively easy material mortifications of pre-conciliar convent life. The suffering of willing surrender of identity, status, power, a sense of societal worth, self-evident rightness, approval by ecclesiastical authority, spiritual superiority, all of which were at least ambiguous values, was experienced through the irretrievable loss of some very real goods. Scores, even hundreds of lifelong companions no longer walked with us. Institutions deeply entwined with our congregations' histories and our own vocations were closed. Cherished ministries that enshrined aspects of our charisms were surrendered. Traditions and customs that nourished the corporate myth and helped sustain a coherent worldview slipped away. All of this was a stripping that left most Religious very vulnerable even as they courageously ventured forth from the safe confines of the convent into new and dangerous missions in the fields of social justice, direct pastoral ministry, and even non-Church–related services, where some of society's most needy were to be encountered.

V. The Passive Night and the Experience of Contemporary Religious

John of the Cross describes the passive phase of purification in *DN,* the first book of which is devoted to the passive night of sense and the second to the passive night of spirit. Again, the two nights are actually two aspects of one deepening experience rather than two completely distinct or chronologically successive stages. However, the distinction between sense and spirit provides a convenient framework for discussing the progressive interiorization of the purgative process as the distinction between active and passive emphasizes not the mutual exclusion of human and divine causality but the gradually increasing predominance of God's action in the process.

The distinction between the passive night of sense and that of spirit also allows John to account for the fact that the passive purification in some people is less intense or even stops short of disposing them for full union with God by explaining that the purgation in some people never seems to reach the depths of the spirit (*DN* I, 14, 4–6). The end of the passive phase of purification is St. Paul's "new self," not merely the well-ordered and integrated human being produced by the active night, but the divinized person living the theological virtues with such constancy, purity, and strength that she is prepared for and capable of mystical union.

A. The Transition from the Active to the Passive Night

John calls those who have engaged over a long period in the active night "beginners," not because they are just setting out on the path of conversion but because they are still in the initial phase of the spiritual life. But between the two phases, active and passive, there is a period of relative peace, a time in which the person is aware of being close to God, feels spiritually settled and energetic, enjoys an intense interior life, and willingly shares that life with others (*DN* I, 1, 2–3).

There seems to be an analogy between these happy "beginners," relatively free from carnal and spiritual attachments, basking in the maternal love of a generous God, and Religious in the euphoria of the years immediately after the Council. No task was too arduous, no risk too great, no meeting too long as we took up our new identity among the People of God. We poured ourselves into intensive community building, developed new prayer forms, made directed retreats, prepared beautiful liturgies, retrained for new ministries, marched for civil rights and peace, even went to jail to witness for justice. We gloried in our role of empowering the laity while bravely confronting the guardians of clerical turf. Like John's "beginners" we thought we had arrived at our true home in a renewed Church. With our lay companions in ecumenical solidarity and strengthened by a personalized spirituality that was psychologically honest and prophetically engaged, we anticipated long careers building the City of God.

B. The Passive Night of Sense

John of the Cross warns his readers, however, that the period of peace and security between the two phases of the Dark Night is relatively brief, and he devotes six chapters to a grimly detailed description of what he calls the "imperfections of beginners" (*DN* I, 2–7), namely, the deeply rooted and hydra-headed spiritual egoism that is too subtle to be recognized by the person her- or himself but which must be extirpated if the beginner is to become the "proficient."[20] These imperfections are, in a sense, the "flip side" of the very virtues acquired in the active night, for example, a secret pride in one's spiritual development and an accompanying sense of superiority toward the less advanced, a harsh impatience with one's own shortcomings which seem inexplicable in one so spiritual, a greediness for the new and the latest in spiritual and psychological growth opportunities and techniques, spiritual showing off in speech or prayer, or a bitter zeal and anger toward those one deems less enlightened or insightful, less virtuous, less committed to the right causes, less hard-working than oneself. What these imperfections have in common are their rootedness in the ego, which still controls the self (cf. *DN* I, 8, 3), and their virtuelike patina, which obscures them from the person herself if not entirely from others. John says that this spiritual immaturity survives the generous and sincere asceticism of the active night and can only finally be healed by God through the passive night (*DN* I, 7, 5).

A hard look at Religious Life in the early postconciliar period reveals a number of these traits. Religious as a group were very sure of themselves, appealing confidently to their own experience as a nonnegotiable norm of valid renewal. We were proud of our increasing humility in reclaiming our lay status, renouncing our "perks," dismantling hierarchical systems in our own congregations, and living more simply.[21] Our anger at oppressive Church officials and clergy who seemed unable or unwilling to implement the conciliar agenda, our impatience with lay resistance to change was righteous and vocal. None of these reactions was unfounded or even necessarily unjustified. Our experience had indeed been too long ignored by others as well as ourselves; we were moving in the right direction in our renewal efforts, and the resistance to conciliar renewal in high and low places was a real impediment to the good work we were actually doing. But the deep agitation and lack of peace that was often evident was probably a sign that mixed in with very real virtue and growth was a great deal of egoism that was largely invisible to us, individually or as a group.

The image John of the Cross uses for passage into the passive night of sense is that of God the mother weaning the spiritually immature "beginner" and making her walk on her own two feet (cf. *DN* I, 1, 2; I, 8, 3; I, 12, 1). He describes this process mainly in terms of what happens to a person's prayer as she becomes progressively incapable of "active" meditation and experiences an emptiness and dryness that leave her feeling distant from God and spiritually powerless. However, the experience is not limited to prayer but pervades the whole of life. The person who so recently experienced herself full of zeal and spiritual energy feels empty and distracted at prayer, lacking in energy for ministry, bored with spiritual activities. The gratifications of the spiritual life have dried up and this precipitates a crisis of fidelity (*DN* I, 8, 3).

Something analogous to this interior experience of the progressing individual seems to have happened to Religious as a group several years after the beginning of the renewal. Diminishments of all kinds, unanticipated and uncontrollable, began to take their toll. As many of the best and brightest left Religious Life declining numbers subverted ministerial effectiveness and even raised doubts about the continued existence of the congregation. Clerical colleagues and even some of the theologians (e.g., Charles Davis) and spiritual leaders (e.g., Sister Francis Borgia Rothluebber and Sister Charles Borromeo Muckenhirn) of the conciliar reform left ministry, Religious Life, or even the Church as Vatican restorationism and local oppression began to undermine the hopes generated by the Council.

New noninstitutionalized ministries undertaken with zealous enthusiasm (e.g., ministry to the homosexual community) folded for lack of resources or were shut down by frightened authorities. Religious themselves, experienced and successful in their ministries, were sometimes fired by insecure pastors who resented their competence, and they found that their congregations lacked the resources and the local hierarchy lacked the will to defend them. The Vatican, followed by local hierarchies and many clergy and laity, repudiated much of the renewal effort of Religious and demanded their return to preconciliar forms of the life.[22] Religious were unwilling and unable to meet these demands, and this resulted in recurring confrontations and ongoing low-level tensions, a kind of intraecclesial guerrilla warfare between progressives and conservatives, that undermined mutual respect and sapped energy and commitment.[23] The earlier surrender of institutional bases as well as the decline in personnel and financial assets left congregations without alternate resources for independent functioning in the face of increasing ecclesiastical pressure and their own growing societal anonymity.[24] As the papacy of John Paul II became more overtly restorationist and an unrestrained curia began a punitive campaign against any challenge to Vatican centralism, the joyful and courageous engagement of Religious and others in the renewal of the Church gave way to a grim tenacity in the face of constant harassment.[25]

All these factors, and others too familiar to need rehearsing, so undermined the confidence of Religious in their identity and their mission that many hesitated to propose Religious Life to possible candidates, thus exacerbating the decline in personnel. Many congregations found it increasingly difficult to evoke real leadership among their members as individual Religious began to carve out careers for themselves that could not be interrupted for terms in congregational leadership or formation. Those available for leadership were sometimes those least equipped for it, and incompetent administrations made some serious mistakes that were not easy to remedy. Many members, unwilling to deal with the conflicts, discouragement, and often disorganization at the center, marginalized themselves within their congregations. Often these were highly effective professional women who had been well educated in preconciliar days and who had taken advantage of the support for education in new areas in the immediate wake of the Council. They took refuge from the disarray at home by staying too busy at work for community presence or participation. The esprit de corps of many congregations hit a low ebb in the mid-1980s, and there was much talk of communities preparing well for their own demise.

John of the Cross's description of the passive night of sense can perhaps throw some light on this period from the mid-1970s through most of the '80s, marked by such darkness and suffering in so many Religious congregations. First, it was a period in which Religious had little control over the negativities they were experiencing. Opposition and oppression came from every side. Friends were no longer supportive; enemies had superior strength and influence. Resources for dealing with the problems were scarce. In many ways the greater the effort Religious made the less effect it seemed to have. At times the very efforts to mediate disputes and sustain dialogue, within and outside the community, seemed to have the opposite effect of increasing the animosity and deepening the divisions.

The pervasive experience of the passive night of sense is powerlessness. All the systems that seemed so functional in the past break down. Nothing works. John says that this is true interiorly in the person's prayer life where meditation dries up, spiritual insight ceases, hope seems dead, love feels weak and tepid. Whatever individual Religious were experiencing interiorly, the corporate prayer life of many communities certainly went through a period of breakdown. Communities struggled over Eucharist, inclusive language, innovative forms of prayer, times and places for prayer, common retreats, and even art and music. Nothing pleased most people even some of the time. Desperate for spiritual nourishment, many Religious found themselves in a virtual desert no matter where they turned or what they tried.

But the breakdown of systems was also felt in ministerial and community experience. John of the Cross talks about the paralysis of the faculties: "[God] binds the interior faculties and leaves no support in the intellect, nor satisfaction in the will, nor remembrance in the memory" (*DN* I, 9, 7). But he knows that this affects not only the effort to pray but one's interactions with others and one's attempt to fulfill one's responsibilities in work. The dryness and boredom, the sense of powerlessness, the lack of interest, the feeling of futility in everything makes all effort feel exhausting, feeble, and pointless. One is tempted to just give up, get out, find something to do that would let one feel more alive, more useful. The thirst for some kind of satisfaction and meaning becomes extreme.

John says that what is going on is a passive purgation that will finally transfer the initiative and control of life from the human ego to God. However, he alerts his readers to the real possibility that what they are experiencing is not divine education but psychological breakdown, and so he offers signs that, when they occur together, indicate that what is occurring is of God (*DN* I, 9). He does not say that the suffering is in no way due to the sinfulness, weakness, lack of psychological integration, or immaturity of the person, because, in fact, to a large extent it is. However, it is not due to deliberate evil but to the deep-seated egoism that subverts the good one does and is manifested in the ineffectiveness of one's efforts.

The signs John offers possibly indicate that what Religious experienced in the posteuphoria period after the Council, due indeed in some measure to many imperfections in Religious individually and corporately, was nonetheless primarily divine education rather than dissolution. First, the person in whom this suffering is part of the passive purgation of sense finds no satisfaction in the spiritual life, whether in prayer or in ministry, but also finds none in other sources. No matter how frustrated, discouraged, and impotent many Religious felt during these years, those who stayed continued to try to make a difference. They did not give themselves over to dissipation, luxury, or escapism. And many recount that they were as bored and fatigued in their attempts to relax and forget what was happening as they were exhausted by their struggles in prayer and ministry.

The second sign John gives is that "the memory ordinarily turns to God solicitously and with painful care, and the soul thinks it is not serving God but turning back, because it is aware of this distaste for the things of God." Anyone who accompanied Religious in spiritual direction or retreats during this dark period will recognize this sign. The near desperation with which Religious struggled to find some way back to their earlier commitment and fervor, some technique or instrument that would reassure them that they were serving God, was so often accompanied by self-castigation for shallowness and lack of zeal. But, says John of the Cross, despite their feelings of powerlessness and tepidity, these people are able to continue to dredge up the strength and energy necessary to do the work God gives them to do because they are being interiorly nourished by the beginnings of contemplation, which they do not recognize and can barely feel. Religious, individually and corporately, continued throughout this period to minister and even to venture into new and more difficult ministries. They went into the ghettos and slums, the prisons and hospitals, the soup kitchens and inner-city schools; they were on the picket lines for peace and justice; they answered the call to impoverished foreign missions; they were among the first to reach out to the victims of AIDS, alienated youth, and drug addicts; they took up the slack in parishes depleted of clerical ministers. And they continued in these ministries despite lack of recognition, appreciation, or adequate recompense, and often in the face of social derision and ecclesiastical oppression.

The third sign is the sheer inability to engage in discursive prayer, "in spite of one's efforts" (*DN* I, 9, 8). I cannot help wondering if the explosion of interest during this period in Ignatian retreats and in such techniques as centering prayer was not, to some extent, an effort to deal with this anguished powerlessness in the interior life. The Spiritual Exercises provide step-by-step instructions on how to meditate as well as the opportunity to discuss one's efforts daily with the director, evaluating the results and correcting course in the process. Centering prayer, by contrast, provides an atmosphere and a legitimation for the kind of interior "rest and quietude," the seeming "idleness," that John says is the only appropriate (or possible) behavior for the person in this state (*DN* I, 10). Interestingly enough, many Religious combined versions of these two types of prayer in their efforts to find a way forward, but very often, despite daily faithfulness to one or other or both techniques, they found themselves "unable to pray."

The presence of the three signs together, according to John, indicates that, whatever psychological undoing might be going on, the purgation of the passive night of sense is the primary cause of the experience. I suspect that many Religious who persevered through the 1970s and '80s could recognize their experience in John's description.

The purpose of this purgative suffering, says John, is to accommodate the "lower part of the soul to the spiritual part" (*DN* I, 11, 3) or, in more contemporary language, to further the integration begun in the active night, in which sense was accommodated to spirit. In those who successfully negotiate this night John says that a number of spiritual benefits occur (cf. *DN* I, 12–13). The person herself is scarcely aware of them but they are effective, and often quite evident to those observing the person. I think some of these traits began to appear among Religious, individually and corporately, toward the end of the 1980s and the dawning of the new decade, although the onslaught of the next stage of purification has been so intense that there has been little chance to recognize or appreciate them.

First, says John, these emerging "proficients" reach a new level of self-knowledge and correspondingly deepened knowledge of God. They know from experience, in a way that was "not apparent in the time of [their] prosperity" (*DN* I, 12, 2) how sinful, weak, and impotent they really are. Many Religious came to feel a certain diffidence about even using the title "Sister" or presenting themselves as Religious because it seemed to be claiming some kind of spiritual proficiency or excellence they knew they did not possess. They did not really want the conversation to turn to God or the spiritual life because they knew they had little or nothing to say. And they listened much more attentively, with genuine admiration and even envy, to their lay friends and colleagues who seemed far more spiritually alive than they themselves. This is a qualitatively different kind of humility in regard to God, oneself, and others than the professed humility of the beginner who is secretly proud of her spiritual gifts.

Second, the purifying suffering detaches one from a reliance on spiritual practices to produce fervor since, for a very long time, none of these has worked and the person can barely remember a time when they did. They are learning to live for God alone regardless of how they feel (cf. *DN* I, 13, 1). They develop a kind of continuous nostalgia for God and concern about their own infidelity, which they now know is ever ready to emerge. In short, all the spiritual imperfections that John described at the beginning of Book I are gradually being healed, not by the efforts of the suffering individual but by the action of God. All that remains is a humble desire to serve God that no longer relies on success, image, or accomplishment and is no longer deeply angered or totally discouraged by one's own or other's incapacities or sinfulness. The person is coming to a kind of autonomy in the spiritual life, an ability to walk on her own two feet, which is not proud independence or reliance on self but a freedom from reliance on anything other than God whether this be her own strength, spiritual practices that worked in the past, the authority of experts, or the approval or admiration of others. This freedom will eventually fit her for what John describes as a certain equality with Jesus as lover.

Although the closer one comes to the present the more risky is the project of interpretation, it seems that, beginning in the late 1980s or early 1990s some kind of qualitative change in the experience of Religious, individually and corporately, began to occur. The profound, justified, and almost existential anger seemed to be turning into a calmer but no less powerful determination to persevere in the struggle for a renewed Church and a just world, neither of which they now realized was going to come quickly or perhaps even in their lifetime.[26] Rather than being in a nearly continual state of shock, outrage, and trauma at the violence and chicanery in the institutional Church and the systemic injustice in society, Religious settled in for the long haul and began a second phase of renewal in their own congregations.

What seemed to be emerging after the extremely volatile and even chaotic period of the preceding couple of decades was a kind of stability that might be better described as a moving equilibrium. John of the Cross talks about a calming of the passions of joy, sorrow, hope, and fear, an interior harmony that gradually seeps up in the soul (cf. *DN* I, 13, 15). There is something quieter, purer, stronger, less melodramatic about the person, a humility that is more simple and unpretentious, a steady self-confidence that rests not on one's abilities or any kind of expectation that things will go well or even get better but on a deep trust that God is somewhere, active, in the midst of it all, even the ongoing evil and suffering.

The rapid drain of departures began to slow down and those who had decided to stay began to develop new bonds, perhaps survivor bonds. People began to have some sense that what and who was left was all they had to work with and that somehow, properly stewarded with God's help, it would be enough.[27] Religious stepped back from some of the experiments in ministry, living situations, and personal lifestyles to evaluate their experience, to reaffirm what was working and in some areas to redirect their energies.

It is hard to pinpoint any particular event or insight, much less a particular moment, that precipitated this almost imperceptible change. But leadership in some congregations began to reemerge as extraordinary women, seasoned veterans in many cases, took the reins. Numerous communities reported remarkably energizing assemblies or visionary chapters with a concomitant resurgence of esprit de corps among their members. Real contemporary Religious such as Helen Prejean, C.S.J.,[28] rather than *Come to the Stable* or *Flying Nun* stereotypes, began to appear in the media, raising the visibility of the life as a serious vocation for adults. This might be a factor in the small but visible increase in promising candidates that some congregations are experiencing as well as in the resurgence of lay assistance in the form of response to fund-raising efforts, various kinds of planned giving, and increasing formal and informal association of laypeople with Religious congregations, which they often identify as more reliable and renewed loci of spiritual resources than their parishes. Religious who had "disappeared" from community for a time began to reappear at congregational functions and reassume active roles in community affairs, bringing with them the solid professional experience and realism gained in the years of relatively independent coping with the secular environment.

A new kind of solidarity among Religious congregations seems to be emerging, partly but not entirely due to a shared experience of internal diminishment and ecclesiastical oppression. Communities have begun to cooperate with each other in regard to health care and retirement, formation and ongoing education, ministry and spirituality. Remarkably, transfers of members from one congregation to another are taking place without animosity or suspicion as people seem to have learned through the emphasis on individual development and discernment that people's personal vocations have priority over institutional agendas.[29] Congregations have begun sharing their charisms with one another, ministerial Religious finding time and space for prolonged prayer in contemplative communities and sharing educational, professional, and other types of resources with those communities. Intercongregational congresses and shared projects of various kinds have built solidarity among Religious across community lines. Communities sharing a common founder or charism have begun meeting together and in some cases reuniting or merging. Religious are finding that, in ministry, they can do together what they cannot do separately, and the competition for institutional priority and leverage so characteristic of preconciliar times seems truly a thing of the past.

Finally, there seems to be a theoretical revival occurring among Religious and within congregations that suggests a renewed confidence in the viability and vitality of the lifeform. A fairly large number of serious books, articles, and collections of essays on Religious Life has appeared after a virtual theological moratorium that lasted from the end of the euphoric postconciliar period until the late eighties. These studies are both critical analyses of the situation[30] and inspirational but realistic challenges for the present and future of the life.[31] Increasingly, Religious are acknowledging to themselves and one another that the attempt to replace theological interpretation of their life with sociological, psychological, and professional expertise has left a serious vacuum. Even the widespread and sometimes almost desperate appeal to spirituality was not an adequate substitute for an intellectually coherent, workable, personal appropriation of the mysteries of the faith. This has not evoked a return to the somewhat arid and disincarnate theology of preconciliar times but a serious and strenuous, sometimes even conflictual, encounter of postconciliar theology, the social and personality sciences, wider ministerial experience especially with the poor and marginalized, more diversified and personally appropriated spirituality, and a much expanded consciousness of the world outside of the Church and Western culture.

No doubt there could be several explanations for this quiet and subtle, but I think very real, reviving of Religious Life. But from the standpoint of spiritual development it might be analogous to what John of the Cross describes as the core of the transformation effected by the passive night of sense, namely, a qualitative deepening of the theological virtues of faith, hope, and charity.

In the passive night of sense all the external and internal props of faith are stripped away and the person is left clinging in naked commitment to God alone, who is no longer quasi-visible in the form of external success or approval or interior consolation in prayer. Believing becomes a choice for God that offers no assurance of success in this life or even of salvation in the next. The optimism based on personal and corporate resources and competence has been crushed by the impasses in dialogue, the failures and disappointments in ministry, the disillusionment with authority and institutions, the betrayal by friends and abandonment by colleagues who cannot take any more. Hope begins where optimism ends. Hope is Jesus' courageous abandonment in the midst of darkness and death on the cross, when there is no longer any possibility of escape, of vindication, of things finally turning around. Joan Chittister has quoted the saying that anger has two daughters, hope and courage. It may be that one purpose of the passive night of sense is to transform rage into courageous hope that is determined to keep putting one foot in front of the other even unto death. The only motivation for continuing the struggle in the absence of external or internal satisfaction and delight is the love of Christ that called Religious to this life and will, finally, not let them go. But in the passive night of sense it is barely felt. John of the Cross says that its presence is known in two almost imperceptible experiences: the ability, despite feelings of lassitude, weakness, and ineffectualness, to continue to do God's work; and the desire to be alone and quiet, to somehow be in God's unfelt presence without attempting to manipulate oneself or God by the techniques or methods that once worked so well. Many Religious will recognize these features in their lives, despite feelings of discouragement and fatigue. They are not in burnout and are not planning to retire early or abandon ministry. They do not really want a mindless, distracting vacation but often long only for a retreat in which there will be a minimum of words and a chance for restorative quiet.

It has not been the intent of this chapter, nor will it be of the next—in which I will juxtapose the final stage of purification, the passive night of spirit, with the experience of Religious dealing with the emergence of postmodernity—to assert that Religious have been engaged in the dark night experience described by John of the Cross. No one can really know that. Furthermore, John was talking about the personal experience of individuals, not the corporate experience of a whole social cohort. I have been trying only to suggest that there is enough analogy between what Religious have experienced in the aftermath of the Council and the purification described by John of the Cross to allow the hypothesis that the purely sociological and psychological analyses, however accurate at one level, are inadequate. The experience has been, at its deepest level, spiritual. And it has not been one of static, unrelieved, and pointless anguish but a journey that seems to have had a clear beginning and has moved toward some kind of resolution, even though it is clear that it is not over. If this is true it might help explain the paradox and the malaise noted at the beginning of this chapter, namely, the simultaneous diminishment and courageous commitment of Religious, individually and corporately, in a situation of suffering that is profound but does not seem to be destructive.

Chapter Six

Religious Life in Spiritual Transformation II: Enlightenment and Postmodernity, a Passive Dark Night?

I. Transition

In the last chapter I explored the possible analogy between the experience of corporate suffering in Religious Life during the immediate and later postconciliar periods of renewal and the active night of spirit and passive night of sense described by John of the Cross in the latter part of *The Ascent of Mount Carmel* and the first book of *The Dark Night* respectively. In this chapter I want to extend the analogy into the passive night of spirit (which John describes in the second book of *DN*) by suggesting that the emergence of postmodernity into the consciousness and experience of individual Religious and congregations has precipitated a deeper, more interior purification than that previously described, precisely because it touches more intimately the God-quest that is at the heart of Religious Life.

In the previous chapter I tried to highlight two points about John of the Cross's doctrine that are particularly important for what follows: (1) that although his descriptions tend to center on the interior life of prayer the purification he is describing is actu-

183

ally worked out in all dimensions of the person's experience, interior and exterior; (2) that the phases and stages John marks out as distinct for purposes of explanation are not separated in experience, either as chronologically successive or as bearing on only one dimension of the person at a time, for example, the senses or the spirit. Rather, "earlier" phases continue even as the purification becomes deeper and more interior. Consequently, I discussed the two phases, active night of spirit and passive night of sense, as overlapping. The self-stripping that Religious willingly undertook as part of renewal (active) precipitated losses over which they had no control (passive) in a single experience of purification that was progressively more intensive and interior even though often exteriorly caused.

In this chapter I want to suggest that there was a similar overlapping and deepening of the two passive stages of purification, namely, that of sense and that of spirit. Rather than the former ending or completing its work and being succeeded by a qualitatively different experience, it continues even while being overlaid and intensified as ongoing historical developments raise new challenges to the life and ministry of Religious.

In the previous chapter I concentrated on the "exterior" dimensions of the passive night of sense: the humbling, distressing, exhausting, demoralizing effects of loss of status, power, institutional leverage, companions, coherence of lifestyle, and the supportive communal prayer life and shared myths and symbols that had sustained community and ministry. In the first part of this chapter I will talk about the "interior" dimensions of the passive night of sense and in the second part how they are being further intensified by their extension into the realm of the spirit. My hypothesis is that the cultural transition from modernity to postmodernity has both intensified the suffering occasioned by conciliar renewal of the past decades (including both its original energy and the current Vatican restorationism) and is adding new, predominantly spiritual, dimensions to that struggle.

II. The Passive Night of Sense and the Enlightenment

As mentioned in the last chapter, the image John of the Cross uses for the transition from the active phase of the Dark Night to the passive is that of God the Mother, who weans the spiritual child and puts it down to make it learn to walk on its own. We looked at how this image might illuminate the "external" experience of Religious who found themselves devoid of many of the community and ecclesial supports that had facilitated both preconciliar Religious Life and the first stages of renewal. In the second phase of renewal Religious found themselves trying to live their vocation without much to sustain them other than faith in the God who had called them, hope against all the evidence, and a determined and largely unfelt love for Christ and his members whom they served. All of this was, to a large extent, an ecclesial experience precipitated by what was going on in the Church.

But one result of the renewal was precisely that Religious no longer lived exclusively in an ecclesial context but were interacting on a daily basis with the larger society and culture. This interaction threw Religious into the modern world, so bravely but naïvely embraced by the Council, with little or no preparation. Most Religious, who had entered the convent out of high school, had not had the chance to negotiate, intellectually or spiritually, the Enlightenment with which their peers had come to grips in college. Rather, they encountered the Enlightenment and its cultural embodiment, modernity, in the wake of Vatican II. And I would suggest that that encounter was, in many respects, analogous to the "interior" face of the experience of the passive night of sense, of being removed from the secure theological and ecclesiological framework of traditional Religious Life and being made to walk spiritually on one's own.

The characteristics of the Enlightenment are well known and need not be rehearsed in detail here. Essentially the Enlightenment signaled the end of Western humanity's "dogmatic slumber," its reliance on authority in the civil, religious, and intellectual arenas. Confidence in a universal and timeless truth guaranteed by a divinely constituted authority gave way to critical and historical consciousness. Any statement's claim to truth had to stand before the bar of reason and meet the test of scientific method and rational argument. And by extension, those claiming authority had to establish their credentials by competence and experience, not by an appeal to the grace of office. The triumph of reason led naturally to a claim to freedom of conscience, speech, religion, inquiry, and assembly no longer seen as privileges but as basic human rights. The ideal of universal egalitarianism, including the call for the emancipation of women, would follow logically from the relocation of rights in human nature rather than in the divine will executed by human authorities. The entrance of Religious into the intellectual framework of the Enlightenment and thus of modernity was bound to undermine their theological security within the medieval Thomistic synthesis in which most had been trained, whether formally or by "osmosis" within the practice of preconciliar Catholicism.

Religious Life, prior to the Council, was not only authoritarian but institutionally totalitarian.[1] Religious, both individually and corporately, felt bound to give unquestioned obedience, including intellectual assent, volitional submission, and prompt execution, to Church authority, making little distinction within the hierarchy of truths or among office-holders. However burdensome they might have found the impositions of bishops or local clergy, however oppressive Vatican legislation sometimes appeared, Religious congregations did not question their own obligation to comply. Indeed, Religious gloried in their identity as "daughters of the Church," and congregations understood themselves as intrinsically ecclesial entities, "the most precious portion of the flock of Christ," as patristic literature phrased it.[2] Historically this sense of ecclesial belonging that expressed itself primarily in submission to Church authority and in the carrying out of ecclesially established ministries provided the "world," the context and framework of meaning, for Religious as individuals and as communities. As congregations began to claim a modern right to self-determination in regard to both their internal renewal and the transformation of their ministries, tensions with ecclesiastical authorities increased.[3] The ecclesiastical structure which had been such a firm foundation for Religious Life at least since the Reformation could no longer handle the actual experience of modern Religious.

In short, it was not only the institutional and structural dimensions of Church and congregation that no longer explained and supported Religious Life but it was the theological and ecclesial coordinates which had made the life coherent that no longer held together. These coordinates were deeply intertwined with the faith convictions and the behavioral commitments of Religious.

In the context of a modern understanding of self and society, many once self-evident faith propositions were shaken to their foundations. The superiority of celibacy over sexual intimacy or even the validity of celibacy as a lifetime commitment, the divinely guaranteed authority of office-holders and the resulting presumption in favor of obedience even when authority was poorly exercised, the necessity or even the healthiness of asceticism or the sacrifice of personally developmental lifestyles or ministries for the sake of the common good as defined by someone else, the value of time-consuming daily spiritual exercises in comparison with other, often secular, growth opportunities were among the convictions and commitments that came into question. This pervasive questioning was not necessarily a regression into liberal narcissism as some have suggested but a sudden onslaught of profound doubt about the value or even the validity of much that had been accepted as unquestionably true and good in a medieval theological and ecclesial context. A genuinely modern worldview was subverting the foundations of a lifeform that had developed within and drawn its coherence from a medieval perspective.

John of the Cross says, in *DN* I, 9, 7, that in the passive night of sense God "binds the interior faculties and leaves no support in the intellect, nor satisfaction in the will, nor remembrance in the memory" of the person. It is perhaps especially what John associates with the memory that was so thoroughly subverted during this period. The memory, in John's anthropology, is the locus of the coherence of life, the feeling of "a way" that makes sense, has recognizable stages, is going toward a known and desired end. The memory stores up experiences that substantiate faith, reassure hope, and enkindle love. In times of uncertainty, stress, or temptation one can have recourse, through remembrance of all one knows and has experienced in the past, to this pool of conviction. But in the passive night of sense this synthesis unravels. One cannot put things together into a meaningful whole. Past experiences of a vibrant, coherent spiritual life or of the powerful presence and action of God seem illusory. The way disintegrates into ever-branching dead-ends. One cannot situate oneself and the way forward and the way back look the same. There is an almost desperate sense of being lost, going in circles, getting nowhere.

Many Religious, and indeed whole congregations, experienced the confusion and disorientation that the breakdown of the compelling self-evidence of the Thomistic theological-philosophical synthesis occasioned. It was often not at all clear that the members of a community shared the same, or indeed any, convictions about God, Christ, Eucharist, Church, or the ramifications of Christian faith for spirituality or ministry. Increasingly, communities looked to their common commitments to peace and justice, feminism, ecology, psychological development, or even ecumenical and interreligious dialogue rather than to Christian faith, practice, or theology as a source of shared meaning.

John of the Cross says that there are two serious temptations into which people suffering through this subversion of the natural supports of faith can fall (cf. *DN* I, 10, 2). One is to despair of ever finding the way again and just to abandon the project. The other is to redouble one's efforts to make the old systems work, an activity that actually undercuts what God is accomplishing within and retards the person's progress.

There is no doubt that some Religious yielded to the first temptation, basically giving up on Religious Life even if they did not actually leave it juridically. Whether they turned to an exclusive or even sexual relationship, lost themselves in professional commitments, or just found a way to live a satisfying single lifestyle that had little to do with Church, ministry, or the Religious community, they succumbed to the chaos.

However, the modern experience of intellectual liberty, critical thought, autonomy of conscience, and pluralism that was refreshingly new and even invigorating to most Religious led many into the second temptation, the vigorous attempt to retrieve the lost sense of coherence in the spiritual life. Unlike John's sixteenth-century contemplatives whose resources for coping with purification had to come mostly from their past, modern Religious tried to cope with the breakup of the medieval synthesis not by turning back to a theology that had ceased to make sense but by finding a new synthesis within which to understand and organize their life.

As the Thomistic theological framework in which many had been educated lost its explanatory power, new contenders appeared on the scene. Process theology, Latin American liberation theology, feminism, a vastly expanded and deepened biblical culture, Eastern mystical approaches, and a host of psychological perspectives and techniques seemed to offer possible meaningful frames of reference for a personal spirituality emancipated from much of the "religious baggage" and especially the theological absolutes of preconciliar Catholicism. The effort invested in reading, study, workshops of all kinds, and the continual, anxious recourse to directed and preached retreats and personal spiritual direction during this period attested to the strenuous involvement of most Religious in the struggle against meaninglessness and spiritual incoherence. Most did not give up on God, faith, spirituality, or ministry. They struggled to find a new way to integrate them into some kind of synthesis that made sense in a modern context.

While becoming intellectually "moderns" was probably a necessary and useful development, especially for ministerial Religious who were now dealing extensively with contemporary adults, it did not actually solve or resolve the sense of spiritual emptiness and disintegration that many Religious experienced nor did it reintegrate congregations that had lost the sense of a shared religious center of gravity. It may be that the very ineffectualness of these strenuous efforts to think our way to a coherent theology and spirituality indicates that something quite different is underway.

John of the Cross (*DN* I, 10) talks about persons suffering the aridities of the passive night of sense fatiguing and over-working themselves in the effort to generate some kind of knowledge of and affection toward God. But it is useless, says John, because at this point God is trying to free them from their dependence on ideas, thinking, deliberate affective acts, and the whole intellectual and volitional apparatus that sustained their faith at earlier stages and to introduce them into a peaceful, loving attention to God that is largely unfelt, not under their control, not generated or produced by human effort. John says that contemplation, a secret and peaceful, purely gratuitous, loving inflow of God, is replacing the strenuous activity of reaching God through one's own efforts. Certainly traditional Religious Life as a corporate enterprise, to say nothing of the lives of individual Religious, was a very determined and active practice of spiritual disciplines calculated to lead to perfection. Perhaps part of what happened as that tightly efficient spiritual project was resituated in the context of modernity was that it necessarily became much more dependent on God rather than on an unquestionably true theological synthesis that assured the right answers to all spiritual questions and a divinely guaranteed ecclesiastical authority whose guidance precluded mistakes.

III. The Passive Night of Spirit and Postmodernity

As I pointed out in chapter 3 on postmodernity, the sojourn of Religious in the modern worldview (which is, of course, still the dominant worldview of our time) was brief and turbulent. Western societies had been involved in the modern project for almost four hundred years by the time the Church decided, at Vatican II, to engage it. Religious had to somehow come to terms with the modern challenge to ecclesiastical authority of the Reformation, the critical repudiation of dogmatism of the

Enlightenment, the rationalism, dualism, and progressivism of the scientific revolution, and the swallowing of industrialism by technology in the space of a couple decades. Combined with the cataclysmic ecclesiastical changes of Vatican II, the onslaught of late modernity swamped Religious as they struggled to make sense of world, Church, Religious Life, and personal spirituality in a context almost totally alien to the medieval one in which they had been formed.

Before any new synthesis could even begin to emerge much less become common property in congregations, the cultural situation had again begun to shift dramatically. Many cultural critics are comparing the contemporary transition from modernity to postmodernity to the shift from the medieval worldview to the modern. However, in important ways, the two transitions are not comparable. Modernity as a unitary worldview replaced the medieval unitary worldview. A person basically lived in one or the other of these two worlds. Postmodernity, by contrast, is marked by the absence of a unitary worldview. It is not replacing modernity but suffusing it. Nonnihilistic or constructive postmodernity is carrying forward certain aspects of the modern agenda such as the commitment to personal liberty, equality, and cultural development while repudiating those aspects that seem bankrupt such as reductive materialism, rationalism, hierarchical dualism, environmental destructiveness, patriarchy, and mindless progressivism. The new sensibility is, in many respects, much "softer" than the hard-edged masculinist sensibility of the modern period. But for that very reason it is, if anything, even more difficult to assimilate, understand, and integrate than the modern.

If the encounter with modern thought undercut the theological and religious synthesis that made preconciliar Religious Life coherent and meaningful, postmodernity is subverting all syntheses no matter where they come from or who proposes them. In chapter 3 I discussed the three salient features of postmodernity, radical contingency arising from the subversion of subjectivity, pervasive relativism arising from antifoundationalism, and isolating alienation arising from the rejection of metanarratives. There I suggested that these features seriously challenge the project of any unified lifeform. This combination of theological and existential subversion has seriously undermined Religious Life as a lifeform. I have suggested that much that has characterized this radical shaking of foundations is analogous to what John of the Cross describes in relation to the passive night of sense in which the capacity of the person to "work" the religious system is supplanted by a surrender in faith, hope, and love to a God who will not be managed or controlled even by the most earnest and sincere efforts.

A. The Effect of Postmodernity on Religious Consciousness

In what follows I want to discuss another result of the postmodern undermining of foundations that intimately affects not the lifeform as such but the spiritual life itself in its deepest interiority, namely, the loss of the God-image. I will parallel this experience with what John of the Cross says about the passive night of spirit.

It might be suggested that the whole of the spiritual life consists in the gradual maturation of the God-image. The God of childhood imagination[4] is a transcendental anthropological figure (usually aged, male, and white for first-world people) who dwells outside us in some region beyond this world and exercises an arbitrary omnipotence that we hope (sometimes confidently and sometimes desperately) is somehow beneficent. This God is internalized as superego, often in the image of parents or clergy, and fear (often mistaken for love) governs our relationship to this "God of the gaps," who is both the court of last appeal in situations that are beyond our control and the ultimate judge before whom we must finally render an account of our lives. The process of spiritual growth is one of deconstructing this childish God-image and moving into adult relationship with the transcendently immanent Holy Mystery, who is both the ground of all being and utterly beyond our imaging, our language, our control.

John of the Cross in Book II of *DN* talks about this growth process not in terms of factors that precipitate it but in terms of the spiritual dynamics it involves. In a way this is not very helpful for the contemporary person because John's abstractness supplies little to which to compare our everyday experience. John says that the "proficients" about whom he is speaking here have been exercised for a long time in the life of prayer and virtue but that they are, nevertheless, still suffering from a deeply embedded "sinfulness" that they are completely helpless to extirpate because they simply do not have access to the roots of evil deep in their spirits.[5] Thus the necessity for a purification that is deeper and more painful than anything they have so far experienced (*DN* I, 8, 2).

The primary manifestation of this sinfulness is a kind of spiritual arrogance, a comfortable sense of having the spiritual life under control, knowing who and how God is and what it means to be a spiritual person (cf. *DN* II, 2, 3–4). Indeed, there is a certain unexpressed self-confidence that one is, at least in comparison with most other people, somewhat advanced in the project of sanctity. The root of this arrogance, says John, is that "[t]hey still think of God and speak of him [sic] as little children, and their knowledge and experience of him is like that of little children" (*DN* II, 3, 3). In other words, the God-image that governs their relationship with God is still immature.

The biographies and confessions of saints and other spiritual seekers, from Augustine to Teresa of Avila, from Thérèse of Lisieux to contemporaries like Thomas Merton and Dorothy Day, bear witness to the fact that the deconstruction of the God-image is a necessary passage in the spiritual life and that it can be precipitated by any number of factors, interior or quite exterior to the person. For many modern people it was exposure to the data of science that convinced them that the God in whom they had been taught to believe simply could not really exist. The theory of evolution undermined the idea of God as creator; physics and astronomy called into question the extraterrestrial region where God was supposed to dwell; depth psychology unmasked the neurotic quality of much religion. Having no alternative model to the one in which they had grown up, they believed that in jettisoning the other-worldly God of their childhood faith they were condemned to (or liberated into) atheism or at least agnosticism.[6]

Many Religious alive today probably missed most of this characteristically modern, early adulthood anguish. Entering the convent out of Catholic high school and doing their college work in the context of Religious Life, they did not face head-on the challenges of secular science, and whatever questions did arise were buffered by the sociology of knowledge of a totally faith-saturated environment. Whereas the modern secular university student began to feel that believing was a naïve and gullible stance in an intellectually enlightened and (therefore) nonbelieving environment, the Religious who entertained serious doubts about God felt theologically retarded or even sinful in a faith-dominated environment. This situation has changed dramatically for Religious who are participating, with their contemporaries, in the emergence of postmodernity.

The issues today are not so much secularized scientism but much more subtly undermining influences that are part of the intellectual air we breathe rather than head-on attacks on faith. Post-Newtonian "new science" creates the impression that the vast network of interconnected reality that is the cosmos has no "room" in it for a kind of personal presence like that of the God of traditional theism. Furthermore, our astronauts have been into outer space and we know there is no "place" that is qualitatively different from the kind of space we know about through science and in which such a God might be hidden.[7]

Our psychological theories are more refined than the Freudian hydraulics of the early 1900s, but we are even more convinced than was Freud that most of what religion claims for God is quite well accounted for by the incredibly complex dynamics of the human psyche.

As the classical worldview has been replaced by a thoroughgoing historicism, we have become aware of the human, and therefore limited and fallible, character of all dogma, religious or secular. Whatever revelation might mean, it cannot be thought of any longer as the direct communication by an extraterrestrial God of absolute and infallible truths. At best, all theological formulations are the efforts of time-conditioned human minds attempting to say something meaningful about ultimate reality in the context of a particular culture and, at worst, they are the control mechanisms of an ecclesiastical bureaucracy. All theology, in other words, is local theology despite the pretentions to universality and absoluteness of "perennial" systems.

Our knowledge of the other great world religions undermines our sense of possessing, or even of there being, "one true faith" to which all are called. It relativizes our convictions about a monotheistic male God, Christ as the unique and absolute savior of all, a moral absolutism based on the experience of white, European males and enforced as much by guilt and terror as by conviction. It calls into serious question the validity of mission activity aimed at undermining the religious culture of other people in favor of imperialistic claims about the truth of ours.

Feminism and other liberation movements have made us painfully aware of the collusion of the Christian religion with patriarchy and all its assorted forms of oppression. And scandals rocking the institutional Church in the form of sexual misconduct of clergy, occasional participation of Church officials in political oppression and economic fraud, increasingly repressive efforts at thought control within the Church itself, and the marginalization of "sinners" of all varieties by a self-righteous and punitive power structure make it increasingly difficult to affiliate with, much less believe in, the Church as the unique and privileged place of divine presence and revelation.

In short, the onslaught of postmodernity which is antifoundational, relativistic, and keenly aware of the limited character of all claims, whether intellectual, cultural, religious, or personal, has irremediably undermined the whole structure of religious belief and practice as it was imbibed by most Religious in their formation. The most acutely painful point of intersection between the postmodern sensibility and religious faith is the God-image. Not only the "man [father, cleric]-writ-large" anthropomorphic God of Christian childhood, but also the eternal, omniscient, omnipotent, utterly transcendent God of classical theological theism has become incredible.[8]

If it is the case that Religious Life is a unified life project organized around the God-quest, the radical deconstruction of the God-image is surely the most serious possible threat to the life itself both for the individual Religious and for congregations which are struggling with such diversity of religious belief and practice that finding common ground for mission or celebration is torturously difficult. Although some terrified individuals have suggested everything from loyalty oaths to expulsion of nonconformists, most congregational leaders know that trying to "remedy" this situation by force is futile if not counterproductive.[9] No one has freely chosen to lose her faith. The faith struggles in which Religious are involved have arisen from their honest participation in the contemporary cultural ethos of a modernity that is being rapidly saturated by postmodernity. But the God-question is so central to Religious Life that the darkness surrounding it at present is creating a crisis of major proportions.

Most Religious find direct discussion of this experience extremely difficult, both because it is frightening and even humiliating for one who had assumed that she had made some progress in the spiritual life over a lifetime of religious practice to put such interior bleakness into words, and because no one who has spent her life seeking God wants to shock or undermine the faith of anyone else, much less confirm them in their own incipient unbelief. Furthermore, even in a relatively safe environment such as spiritual direction, the person who tries to describe the experience often finds herself with nothing coherent to say. In fact, the "experience" is one of not experiencing. It is not simply that one's ideas about God are changing or even being subverted. There seems to be no God about whom to have ideas at all. God-talk seems empty, even boring. God has simply disappeared from the horizon without a trace.

The "without a trace" is the most terrifying aspect of the experience, because God's disappearance does not seem to have left the gaping hole one would expect, the kind of aching void left when a loved one dies. Everything seems to be perfectly normal, to be functioning quite well. It is as if some completely unnecessary hypothesis has been abandoned. Some people speak of a sense that divinity or spirit is manifest in everything that is, that everything is sacred, unspeakably beautiful and precious. But that numinous quality arises from the reality itself, not from some added dimension or presence called God. A personal God has become literally unthinkable, not able to be conceived at all.

B. Resources from the Mystical Tradition

John of the Cross says that the central experience of the passive night of spirit is the sense of the loss of God. "[T]he soul's greatest suffering in the trials of this night is the anguish of thinking it has lost God and been abandoned by him" (*DN* II, 13, 5). In John's pre-Enlightenment cultural context complete loss of faith in God would have been virtually unthinkable. But perhaps the contemporary version of this experience is not the feeling that an obviously existing God has abandoned or rejected one because of one's sinfulness but that perhaps there is no God at all, that all one's previous "religious experience" has been so much introjection of baseless "God-talk" and projection of neurotic needs for protection, intimacy, or even control. Certainly the contemporary experience is not unlike John's description of the soul's conviction that its spiritual life is simply over, never to return (e.g., *DN* II, 10, 9).

Perhaps reflection on John of the Cross's presentation of the passive purification of the spirit can throw some light on what might be occurring in the personal and corporate experience of Religious. First, John says that the intensity of suffering in this night is exacerbated by the fact that it cannot be explained to the person in such a way as to bring some kind of relief or comfort. John writes his treatise to console and strengthen those experiencing this darkness, but he realizes that those who are truly experiencing it will not be able to profit from what he says unless and until they have fairly well passed through the experience, at which time they will recognize it in retrospect (cf. *DN* II, 9, 9). In other words, part of the darkness is the conviction that there is no dawn.

The *reason* for the onslaught of the passive night of spirit, says John, is that even though the person has made a great deal of progress in the spiritual life, both in regard to the generous practice of virtue and deepening prayer, God is still an "object." God "exists," that is, stands out from the rest of reality as something other, a being beside (or above) other beings. In other words, God, no matter how spiritualized by the religious imagination, is still made in human image, still somehow oneself-writ-large. There is still a God-image controlling the person's experience of God. As the mystics have testified, a God who can be imaged, thought, a God who "exists" in this sense is not God.[10] It may be God's persona in the imagination of the believer, even a theologically well-developed persona. But it is a God stand-in. Finally, however it happens, whether in this life or by death itself, this human creation of "god" must go. Apparently this was true even for Jesus, whose anguished cry from the cross was "God, why have you abandoned me?" (Mk 15:34). Only when "god" is gone can pure theological faith really become totally operative. The "into your hands I commend my spirit" (Lk 23:46) is only total when the darkness is absolute.[11] Only when the mind is blanked by utter contradiction can the heart finally say, "Lord, to whom shall we go? You (alone) have the words of eternal life" (Jn 6:68).[12]

As John of the Cross says, no one willingly undertakes to enter into such darkness (cf. *DN* II, 15, 1). There is a need in the human spirit to retain some hold on the existential foundation of one's being that is so deep, so tenacious, that one simply cannot let go into the abyss of divinity. So the fingers of the spirit have to be pried loose from the edge of the existential cliff by a purgative process over which the person has no control. John describes it graphically. This night, he says,

> puts the sensory and spiritual appetites to sleep, deadens them, and deprives them of the ability to find pleasure in anything. It binds the imagination and impedes it from doing any good discursive work. It makes the memory cease, the intellect become dark and unable to understand anything, and hence it causes the will also to

become arid and constrained, and all the faculties empty
and useless. And over all this hangs a dense and burdensome cloud that afflicts the soul and keeps it withdrawn
from God. (*DN* II, 16, 1)

In other words, the person in relation to God draws a complete blank. Nothing comes up on the screen when the "on"
switch is thrown, not even a luminous background. It is not
that there is a glitch in the program; there is no program.

But the very next sentence is as surprising as it is illuminating: "As a result the soul asserts that in darkness it walks
securely." John goes on to explain that this security arises from
the fact that, being completely unable to think about or imagine God, the person is finally freed from all the projections,
all the neediness, all the factors that conspire to create the
god-idol that it had previously taken for the real God (cf. *DN*
II, 16, 2). The presence of the real God is completely hidden
from any of the person's own powers and is thus safe from distortion or manipulation. In this utter darkness the real God is
finally free to communicate directly rather than through distorting human categories or images.

The *cause* of the experience of darkness, says John, is that
God is flowing into the soul directly and the divine being,
which is infinite light in itself, is darkness for the feeble
human spirit, like the direct rays of the sun to human eyes
(*DN* II, 5, 5 and 12, 4). God, entering the soul by infused contemplation, is not being "filtered" by rational categories or
imaginative constructs and the onslaught of divinity is like
fire consuming a log of wood. This image of the passive
night of spirit is developed at length by John of the Cross
(*DN* II, 10). The "log" of the human spirit, he says, is invaded
by the fire of God, which dries it out, consumes all its impu-
rities, and eventually so possesses its very substance that it is
totally transformed into the fire itself. Only when the
process is complete, when the human spirit is so divinized
that it radiates the very light and heat of God, does the pain
of the consuming fire finally become the gentle burning love
of the living flame.

Although John's description of this experience is disconcertingly abstract, he does give several indications of how the reality of the divine action in the person *manifests* itself. First, the nostalgic "pining" for God intensifies. The person may be convinced at the intellectual level that the "God hypothesis" is baseless, but the heart continues to experience the urgent longings, the thirst for God that nothing can supplant or extinguish (cf. *DN* II, 11, 5–7). Second, the person is passively energized and even emboldened in the service of God despite the feelings of lethargy and torpor at the affective level. John says that this commitment to God's cause goes on in action even though the person feels unworthy and miserable and may even be unable to connect the continuing commitment to God at all (cf. *DN* II, 13, 6–10). In other words, the person undergoing this purification does not actually abandon God even though she feels abandoned in a godless universe. Interiorly and exteriorly the person is God-obsessed despite the deep sense of being utterly alone and the most deluded of all. She might even wish she could jettison the whole God-project and get on with a life that made sense, but the hold of God on the person is as strong as the person's hold on God is weak.

The *result* of the process, says John of the Cross, is the total transformation of the person in unitive love. The person's knowledge of God is transformed by what John calls "mystical theology" or secret wisdom, which is no longer discursive theology but an existential "knowing" of God as spouses know each other affectively, by mutual possession, in sexual union. She knows now that all human categories for thinking or talking about God are completely inadequate, however necessary or useful they may be in certain contexts, and she feels a deep reticence to talk about God or her own interior life. Indeed, she may have no experiential access to that life at all (cf. *DN* II, 17). Even trying to reflect on it seems futile.

This loving knowledge of God brings about a kind of reversal of the process of detachment that was characteristic of the active phases of the spiritual journey. From the courageous renunciation of all that is not God in the active night, through the gradual learning to see God in all things in the passive night of sense, the person finally comes to the point of seeing all things in God (cf. *DN* II, 11, 4), which is qualitatively different. In a sense, God is not seen at all but everything is so suffused with divinity that nothing is "secular" (cf. *DN* II, 11, 4). God is becoming all in all.[13]

A certain steadiness, equilibrium, unshakable commitment for the long haul takes over and the person lives in God without much concern about the "fireworks" of the spiritual life, whether they are present or absent. There is even a kind of relief in the hiddenness of God's presence, in the fact that one cannot interfere anymore and has only to go on in a kind of undramatic ordinariness because, whether God exists or not, whether one is holy or not, nothing else really matters.[14] John of the Cross attributes this to the perfecting of theological faith, hope, and love (cf. *DN* II, 19–21).

A modern historian of spirituality, Denys Turner, has contributed significantly to our understanding of what John of the Cross is talking about.[15] Turner disputes the understanding of mysticism (or contemplation in John of the Cross's terminology), at least in the Christian tradition, as an "experience," either of God's presence or of God's absence. The real God is no more psychologically "experienceable" by humans than expressible in human language. What we experience is the psychological "fallout," sometimes positively and sometimes negatively, of God's presence and action in the depths of our spirit. Turner says that what one can actually experience is simply the faithful living of the Christian life, but as that living deepens there is, at its center, a "hole," a moment of negativity, which is the reality of God. This is the mystical moment. It is not something to which we have direct experiential access, because God is not a "something" that can be the object of experience, even though God's presence is profoundly transformative and its effects in a person's life are experienced powerfully. One might say that as the moment of negativity expands, the experiential dimension of the spiritual contracts until all the "extraordinariness" of the spiritual life has been absorbed into the very ordinary, unremarkable fidelity of the truly holy person.[16]

Finally, it bears repeating that the *dynamics* of this final phase of purification are quite subtle. The phases of the experience are not, as we have said, chronologically sequential, although the onset of a deeper level of purification usually comes after the previous phase has begun to have its effect. In other words, by the time that the experience of the passive night of the spirit predominates, the earlier phases, which continue their work, have prepared the way. John says that, in fact, the earlier phases do not really attain their full efficacy until they are subsumed into the final phase (cf. *DN* II, 3, 1–2). In the corporate experience of Religious congregations much of the tumultuous suffering characteristic of the earlier periods of renewal, though it has not entirely disappeared, has become less central. There are still people leaving; ecclesiastical pressures emerge at irregular intervals; scandals occur; but the seemingly total chaos of earlier phases of renewal and the incessant nerve-wracking tension over virtually every detail of corporate life is much less salient.

John of the Cross also points out that the experience of the passive night of spirit, though predominantly painful especially at the beginning, is one that alternates between periods of agonizing suffering and periods of delightful respite during which the person enjoys "the benefit of spaciousness and freedom, experiences great sweetness of peace and loving friendship with God in a ready abundance of spiritual communication" (*DN* II, 7, 4), which reassures her that somehow things are all right. Many Religious congregations in the past few years have had remarkable corporate events in which the experience of unity and élan, clarity of purpose, courage, energy, and commitment have been overwhelming. There seems to be no tendency to romanticize these events or to pretend that the poverty of congregational means, the enormity of the ministerial challenge, and the reality of institutional oppression have disappeared, but there is a deep corporate reassurance that something is going in the right direction.

This type of alternating experience may be part of what John of the Cross describes as the "ladder experience" of the passive night of spirit (cf. *DN* II, 18). He says that in this phase there is frequent and even extreme alternation between what he calls "prosperity" and "penury" or joyful strength and exhausted weakness. This "up and down" dynamic is calculated to bring the person, finally, to a deep knowledge of self and of God that makes her relatively immune to manipulation by external forces.

John of the Cross devotes two chapters at the end of *The Dark Night* (cf. *DN* II, 19–20) to a discussion of *signs or effects* by which a person can recognize her or his progress in love even in the midst of conflict and suffering. They are much more subtle and overlapping than those he gives for other stages of the spiritual life, but they have to do with the gradual permeation of a person's life by the love of God. As the self-absorption of the ego loses its hold, Jesus, whom John calls the spouse at this point, becomes more and more central to the person's consciousness, motivation, and activity.[17] A rather remarkable feature of the corporate experience of some congregations in recent years has been the emergence, as if of an underground stream that has reached the surface, of the specifically spiritual and even christocentric concerns of members. This is not a return to preconciliar theology or piety. The influence of deep ecology, world religions, and the new science has qualitatively altered the context and content of religious consciousness. But there seems to be less hesitation to claim that God is what Religious Life is finally all about, whatever that will come to mean in a radically different cultural and ecclesial context.

IV. Significance of the Analogy for Contemporary Religious Experience

At this point we have to ask whether this sustained analogy between John of the Cross's presentation of the spiritual journey and the corporate experience of Religious since the Council is valid. First, it is obvious that the effects of ecclesial renewal and cultural postmodernity on religious consciousness is not the exclusive preserve of Religious. In a sense, everything said above about the challenge to faith, and especially the undermining of the God-image, is as pertinent to any Christian trying to live a spiritual life in the contemporary cultural context as it is to Religious. However, for people who have made the God-quest the exclusive center of their life, the stakes are particularly high.

Second, it is hardly my place to attempt to situate individual Religious in relation to the spiritual journey, and it would be plainly arrogant to claim that, as a group, Religious have reached the stage of contemplation that John of the Cross describes in *DN*. But it is not out of place to recognize that Religious as a group (granting that there are numerous individual exceptions) have been struggling for centuries to live the spiritual life with integrity and generosity, often within a restrictive understanding of what was spiritually possible for the so-called "ordinary" Religious. Consequently, it is not altogether inappropriate to see an analogy between what occurs in the life of individuals who seek God earnestly over a lifetime and this lifeform that has enshrined a similar quest over centuries.

My intuition is that just as traumatic events in the life of an individual can create a crisis that results in qualitative transformation for which the person has actually been being prepared for a long time, so the cataclysmic events through which Religious have passed in the last thirty years may have precipitated just such a transformative crisis at the corporate level. Two features of John of the Cross's understanding of contemplative spiritual development make me think that it can provide an analogue for analyzing this corporate crisis: first, he maintains that spiritual transformation takes place through the actual disintegration of previously achieved syntheses, which played an important role in spiritual growth but which finally must be surrendered if God is to become all in all; and second, he regards this disintegration as a genuine crisis that can issue either in transformation in God or in actual dissolution or abandonment of the spiritual life. In other words, it is a process that cannot take place easily or peacefully, and it does not necessarily succeed.

It seems to me that these are precisely the two features of
the situation of Religious Life at the end of the twentieth century. There is no question that the institutional and theological syntheses that grounded and structured Religious Life
through the 1960s have been irreversibly undermined by the
combination of the conciliar renewal and the engagement of
modernity. And this situation has been exacerbated by the
ethos of postmodernity, which is subverting the core of Religious Life by its assault, more devastating because less con-
frontative, on the reality of God in human life. In short, the
previously achieved syntheses that have played a significant
and positive role in Religious Life are disintegrating. And it is
not at all certain whether the outcome of this development
will be a further deepening of Religious Life or its demise.

My purpose in pursuing the possible analogy between what
John of the Cross says about the growth of the individual in
the spiritual life and the current passage of Religious Life
itself through the ecclesial and cultural crises of Vatican II,
modernity, and postmodernity, is to suggest two things. First,
the intersection of Religious Life with culture, both ecclesiastical and secular, is precipitating some kind of profound
change in the life itself. Whatever happens, it cannot stay the
same and it will not return to its preconciliar state. It may, as
many have predicted, simply die out. It may be replaced by
some other form of life more suited to the contemporary
Church and world. Or it may emerge, as one insightful
observer suggested, like the bird that apparently evolved from
the dinosaur, as a much smaller and more beautiful but less
self-important version of itself.[18]

Second, it is possible to interpret this change in a variety of
ways. Just as the experience of the Dark Night is in many
respects indistinguishable, while it is occurring, from psychological depression, so the experience of Religious Life today,
from a purely sociological point of view, is indistinguishable
from the death of an institution that has lost its social niche
and leverage. But it is also possible that what is occurring is a
spiritual passage, a deep transformation of the life itself.

A. Discerning What Is Happening

How Religious respond to what they are experiencing depends on how they interpret it. If Religious Life is dying, it should be helped to do so with dignity and should be decently buried. But if, in fact, Religious are involved in a protracted struggle in the night with an utterly mysterious God, resigning themselves to extinction is precisely the wrong move. In that case they are being called to hang on, no matter how long the struggle lasts, until they receive the blessing reserved for those who persevere, the transformation in love that John of the Cross says "makes [one] soar to God in an unknown way along the road of solitude" (*DN* II, 25, 4).

Discerning the character of the crisis is not easy. As in all discernment we must look not so much at the actual experience, which is precisely what is confusing and dark, but at the signs in the life of the person, or in this case the corporate reality of Religious Life, that give some clue to what is happening. The signs of institutional death have been repeatedly catalogued and need not be rehearsed here. But there are other signs that do not speak of death but of a new kind of life. Some were mentioned at the beginning of the last chapter.

Among the paradoxical signs that seem to point to fire smoldering in the embers is the fact that Religious congregations, despite diminishing resources from within and almost constant harassment from without, seem not at all inclined to give up on Religious Life itself or abandon their commitment to fostering the Reign of God in this world. The *Los Angeles Times* survey of Women Religious analyzed by the National Opinion Research Center at the University of Chicago found, in 1995, that almost 90 percent of Religious were satisfied with their life and, given the chance to choose it again, 95 percent would definitely or probably do so. Only 2 percent considered their leaving Religious Life as somewhat or very likely.[19] In other words, Religious as individuals are, at some deep level, joyful and peaceful despite incredible struggle and suffering.

Tom Roberts, a reporter covering the 1998 joint convention of the LCWR and CMSM for the *National Catholic*

Reporter expressed his wondering admiration at what he experienced, especially among the women. He said that, given the demographics,

> this conference should be talking about who's going to turn out the lights when the show's over. But these women, who represent about 90 percent of the nuns in the United States, appear to be charging ahead, perhaps real fools in the biblical sense, as if that tomorrow—the end of nuns as we know them—will never come.[20]

He called the conference "a small window into one of the great, ongoing stories of fidelity and prophetic witness in the Church." Corporately, Religious Life manifests the same stability, perseverance, and commitment that the individuals do.

Ongoing fidelity and energy for mission, despite personal suffering and weariness, are among the signs John of the Cross gives that what is happening in the darkness is of God. The other sign he adduces is that the person continues to yearn for God, despite the feeling that there may be no God to yearn for and that the spiritual life is some kind of fool's errand. Anyone dealing with Religious today, especially in the context of spiritual direction, knows that this longing for God is deep and pervasive, a veritable obsession of individuals and of communities. In short, there seems to be some real evidence that interpreting the present crisis in Religious Life spiritually is not simply denial or wishful thinking. I am not suggesting that we do not need to take seriously all the alarming signals[21] from sociological analysis or that a sellout to liberalism or hedonism is not a real and present danger. But there may be more to the situation.

B. Responding Faithfully

John of the Cross's purpose in writing his extended treatment of the dynamics of the spiritual journey was to encourage those suffering in the flames of purification and to teach them how to negotiate the passage successfully. We have already looked at what he had to say about the active night and the passive night of sense. But he seems to have little practical advice for those in the final phase of the passage. This is perfectly logical because the primary feature of that phase is its passivity. The person has little or no role in the work of purification at this point. She does not determine what to do or when or for how long. She undergoes whatever God does in her life. Whatever she might decide to do would actually constitute interference in the process.

Consequently, John of the Cross says that the primary "work" of the person is to walk in secret, in darkness, without trying to see or analyze or improve or otherwise meddle in God's work. What is happening is a gradual strengthening and purifying of the naked attachment to God alone that John talks about under the traditional heading of the three theological virtues of faith, hope, and charity but which he realizes are not three separate dynamics but three faces of love. All that the person can really do is just keep moving, acting from moment to moment with whatever strength is available, knowing that both the task and the strength to accomplish it come from God if they come at all and that what results is also God's. Prayer ceases to be planned and accomplished, evaluated and improved. One does what one can and gives up not only congratulating oneself on success but even bemoaning one's impotence. When periods of joy and peace are given, one accepts them with gratitude but does not cling to them, rely on them, or try to prolong them. And when the fire assails, or worse yet seems to have gone out, one suffers the burning or the cold, knowing that this too shall pass.

If John's advice can be applied at a corporate level it might indicate that the period of most intense scrutiny of congregational life, rewriting of documents, elaborate planning for the future, and so on may be, at least for the time being, not what is called for. Perhaps it is time for a more tentative and provisional, and therefore more humble and trusting, walking in the present. Certainly planning must continue and projects must be undertaken.[22] But we are probably learning that there is no plan that cannot be completely subverted by some change in Church or culture, some reduction or redirection of resources, some variation in the urgency of the objective itself.

We are learning to care and not to care, to invest ourselves without losing ourselves, to be of love most careful because the "one thing necessary" is more central to our corporate consciousness. We may, some years from now, look back on this period of renewal, purification, and transformation and identify it, as John of the Cross exclaims in the last line of *DN,* as "that glad night."

Chapter Seven

Religious Life as an Ecclesiastical Reality I: Where and with Whom?

I. Introduction

The revalorization of the baptismal identity and dignity of the laity by Vatican Council II, which placed its discussion of the Church as the People of God in *Lumen Gentium* (Dogmatic Constitution on the Church) prior to its discussion of hierarchy, was centuries overdue.[1] Its effect, the energizing of the laity to reassume their proper, baptismally based identity as members of Christ, their true destiny as those called to the fullness of Christian holiness, and their role as participants in the mission and ministry of the Church, may prove, historically, to be the single most important outcome of the Council.[2] There is no question that this emergence of the laity is transforming the Church in its daily life and functioning. However, an unanticipated and undoubtedly unintended by-product of this salutary corporate transformation has been an institutional displacement of Religious, particularly women Religious, which has resulted in a virtual identity crisis for many.

Prior to Vatican II the Church, whatever its official theology might have maintained, was a clergy-centered as well as clergy-dominated institution. When ordinary Catholics referred to "the Church" they did not mean the People of God but the hierarchy and more proximately the local authorities, that is, the bishop and his clergy. These latter *were* the Church; the laity *belonged to* the Church. Religious in this clergy-centered Church were sociologically quasi-clergy. Like the clergy they lived apart from other Catholics, wore distinguishing garb, were addressed by special titles, carried on full-time ministries to which they were assigned by ecclesiastical authorities and which guaranteed their livelihood, were essentially unaccountable to the laity they served, enjoyed sacralized (though not canonical) authority in relation to the laity, and most importantly (for reasons we will examine shortly) did not marry. Although women and nonclerical men Religious could not celebrate the sacraments (a restriction that, in the popular imagination, was due to sex rather than ecclesiastical position and which therefore made Brothers a bit of a puzzle to most Catholics) they were for all practical purposes second-class clergy rather than (even first-class) laity.

For a number of interrelated reasons this situation changed dramatically with the Council. In attempting to straighten out the theologically tangled ecclesiology that had developed since the Council of Trent, Vatican II made a number of declarations which, in coordination with one another and the eventual revision of Canon Law in 1983, created anomalous situations within which some groups of people, most notably Religious, found themselves "displaced" or even "placeless" in the official self-description of the Church. The Council declared that, despite what it had said about the equality and common priesthood of all the members of Christ, the priesthood of the ordained differed "essentially" from that of everyone else.[3] This affirmation, often repeated, of an ontological distinction based on Orders remains more an unexplainable assertion of superiority than a comprehensible theological datum.[4] But it effectively divides the Church into two nonoverlapping groups, the ordained and the nonordained. Since the Council emphatically (and correctly) insisted that Religious were not a *tertium quid*, a hierarchical class somewhere between the ordained and the nonordained, Religious had to be situated in one group or the other.[5] Those Religious who were not ordained were, by process of elimination, defined as laity at least in relation to the hierarchical structure of the Church.[6]

Given that the ordained/nonordained distinction remained the most important in theory and in practice after the Council and became even more significant as the "parochialization" of the local Church intensified,[7] clerical Religious were confirmed in their centuries-long tendency to identify themselves primarily with the ordained and Religious who were not ordained found themselves suddenly "demoted" from their quasi-clerical status in the Church and challenged to locate themselves in fact as well as in theory among the laity.

Women Religious in general greeted this new situation with theoretical approval. The Council had strongly affirmed the baptismal dignity, call to holiness, mission, and ministerial vocation of the baptized as well as the "priesthood of all believers" which most Catholics erroneously read as the "priesthood of the *laity*," since no one ever questioned that of the ordained before or after the Council. Many Religious rejoiced in their newly discovered solidarity with the "promoted" laity and saw themselves as called to participate in the emergence of the latter from their thousand-year ecclesial slumber. However, the euphoria was short-lived.

As laypeople began to participate in all of the ministries that they suddenly found open to them, at least in theory, Religious began to wonder if there was anything Religious could do that other laity could not. If the answer was no, as it correctly appeared to be, the second question was not far behind: then why be a Religious? This led necessarily to an examination of Religious Life in terms other than ministry even as the intrinsically ministerial character of Religious Life was being strongly affirmed by renewal chapters and revised constitutions. Perhaps the meaningful differences were to be found not in what Religious do but in how they live, that is, in the lifestyle of Religious. However, Religious congregations, responding on the one hand to the conciliar call to adapt their lifestyle to the changed social and cultural conditions of the twentieth century and on the other hand to their own felt call to abandon the artificial and dubiously evangelical signs of elite status that had developed in Religious Life through centuries of preferential treatment in the Church, had surrendered most of their characteristic lifestyle differentiations. They had modified and then put aside habits; they had retired archaic titles and relegated even simpler ones to formal situations; they had reassumed their baptismal names; they had abandoned agrarian horaria and begun to share in the social life of their families and associates; they had put aside medieval practices of asceticism and recognized the importance of participating in the cultural life around them; they had decloistered and thus demystified their dwellings and many, usually for reasons of ministry, were living in "ordinary" houses and apartments; many large institutions that had been corporate power-bases had been surrendered, and the ministries of Religious were now more frequently exercised in collaboration with the laity. In short, just as ministry no longer distinguished Religious from committed laity, neither did lifestyle.

This left many wondering whether there was any real point to being a Religious. Was there anything distinctive about the life, aside from certain burdensome obligations like celibacy, the surrender of one's financial independence, and the often painful struggles with community leaders over ministry and housing and with fellow members over theology and practice? In other words, were Religious simply people who created unnecessary problems for themselves in the doing of things they could do just as well and much more easily without those problems? As these questions became clearer in the 1970s and early '80s, large numbers of Religious left Religious Life. Many who left continued in or expanded their ministerial commitment and some maintained close relationships in ministry with former Religious colleagues. Those who stayed were left with the question of where Religious fit into the life of the Church now that, at least in theory, it was a Church of the laity under the leadership of the clergy.

II. Sorting Out the Terminology
of Ecclesiastical Distinctions

Although it may prove somewhat tedious to make and to maintain consciousness of seemingly endless and practically irrelevant technical distinctions, sorting out the terminology of ecclesiastical distinctions is a basic and indispensable task if Religious are to gain some clarity around the issue of their "place" in the Church as institution. And this clarity is, in my opinion, fundamental for certain very important tasks of discernment about our present and immediate future in relation not only to other people and groups in the Church but especially to our own life. The following material does not make easy or inspiring, much less engrossing, reading, but colluding in confusion about ecclesiastical identity and location is not an avoidance of the problems but an evasion of responsibility.

A basic presupposition for all that follows is the recognition that the Church as *ecclesial body*, before any distinctions are made among its members, is the People of God. The *christifideli*, that is, the baptized, are fundamentally equal participants in the life of Christ, sharing together and equally in his identity and mission as prophet, priest, and king. There is no such thing as "the priesthood of the laity." Rather, all members of the Church, clergy and laity alike, participate in the "priesthood of all believers," and all distinctions of roles and functions in the Church are secondary to and in service of this foundational baptismal unity and equality. As Augustine said, "To you I am the bishop, with you I am a Christian. The first is an office, the second a grace...."[8] Any tendency of the office to take precedence over the graced identity, much less to legitimate domination of other members of the Church by office-holders, involves basic distortion. This being said, there are three principles of organization in the Church according to which the members may be distinguished from one another. We might say that there are three ways to cut up the "*ecclesiastical* pie," and each partition places Religious somewhat differently in relation to other Christians. It must be kept in mind that we are talking about the ecclesiastical, that is, the institutional, aspect of the Church, not the ecclesial, or theological-spiritual, reality of the People of God, the Body of Christ.

A. Hierarchical or Class Organization

If the Church is looked at in terms of hierarchical organization, there are two, and only two, classes in the Church: the ordained and the nonordained. While there may be very good biblical and theological reasons to question whether this type of organization is willed by Christ, belongs to the essence of the Church, or is intrinsically unchangeable,[9] the fact is that the Church is, and has been for most of its history, a hierarchically organized institution, and the Council strongly reaffirmed that this is not a purely historical development but that "Christ the Lord set up in his Church a variety of offices" and thus constituted the Church as hierarchical.[10] It has classes, and the basis of distinction between these classes is the possession of sacred power conferred by ordination. The ordained are those who possess sacramental power to which juridical power in the institution has become attached, and the laity are those who do not. The revision of Canon Law in 1983 provided that laypeople can be appointed by the clergy to some positions that allow the exercise of jurisdiction in certain spheres, but the major distinction remains that between those whose power in the Church is rooted in the sacrament of Holy Orders and those who do not share that power.[11] When the Church is looked at in terms of its hierarchical institutionalization, nonordained Religious (and that means all women Religious) are laity, not clergy.

B. Canonical Status

A second way of cutting up the ecclesiastical pie is according to canonical or juridical categories, that is, into groups of people defined in Canon Law as having a particular configuration of rights and duties in the Church that they do not share with other groups.[12] When the Church is looked at in this way there are three rather than two groups. First, there are the clergy, who are essentially the same people as those in the upper class in the hierarchical division, namely, the ordained: bishops, priests, and deacons. Second, there are those in Institutes of Consecrated Life and Societies of Apostolic Life, that is, those whose lives involve in some combination or form lifelong commitment according to rule, sacred bonds, and community life. Third, there are the laity, who may or may not be organized in various forms of associations.

All of these divisions involve certain anomalies that make clear distinctions among people and therefore their unambiguous canonical "placement" in the institutional Church difficult in theory and sometimes confused in practice. Noting these anomalies or "poor fits" in all the canonical groupings serves to alert us to the fact that these distinctions are the only partially successful attempts of human lawmakers to order the very rich, complex, and ever-developing life phenomenon of the Church, and they ought not to be regarded as ontologically based, divinely established, or unalterable arrangements. When they are so regarded they become a procrustean bed that fossilizes the development of life in the Church. Life is almost always ahead of law, especially the categorizing functions of law.

A first anomaly appears in relation to the clergy in the form of the permanent, as opposed to transitional, diaconate. Although the permanent deacons are ordained and therefore technically clergy, they are generally married (which in the Roman Rite has traditionally been forbidden to clerics and still is to all clerics except permanent deacons), live their lives as ordinary laity except for certain assigned functions that are usually exercised on a part-time basis, and do not enjoy most of the juridical rights or carry most of the canonical duties of priests and bishops. They are, in fact if not in law, a kind of ordained laity or lay clergy.[13]

The second canonical group in the Church, those included in the 1983 revision of Canon Law under the heading of Institutes (Religious and Secular) of Consecrated Life and Societies of Apostolic Life, also presents some anomalies. What these groups have in common is some combination or some version of permanent commitment by vows, promises, or other bonds; life according to an approved rule or constitution or other document; and some kind of shared life. Religious Institutes are clearly the normative group in this category having perpetual vows, approved rule or constitutions, and stable community life. Secular Institutes modify the last element to foster their living and working "in the world," which the Code seems to understand as working in non-Church employment and/or living outside canonically approved dwellings such as convents. Societies of Apostolic Life are distinguished by the fact that they do not make the vows of Religious Life although most of them do live some form of community life and participate in Church-related (often clerical) ministries.[14]

Again, the anomalies are numerous. While many Religious do not live the "common life" form of community life that the Code clearly intends for them, many members of Secular Institutes do live such a life, which is actually not normative for them; and the latter may work in Church-related ministries, which is in some tension with the secular mission understood by Canon Law as their distinctive trait, while some Religious do not work in Church-related ministries. The "sacred bonds" of members of Societies of Apostolic Life often have the same effect in the daily life of their members as the vows have for members of Religious and Secular Institutes and require dispensation if the member wishes to leave. There is often very little to distinguish the institutional life of members of a clerical Society, for example, Maryknoll, from members of a clerical Religious Institute, such as the Redemptorists.

The most serious anomaly is indicated by the subdivisions of Canon Law itself, whose Book II, "The People of God," is divided into The Christian Faithful (Lay and Clerical); The Hierarchical Constitution of the Church (governing the clergy and their activities); and Institutes of Consecrated Life and Societies of Apostolic Life (both of which involve both lay and clerical members). In other words, while the division of the Church by class into laity and clergy is considered basic and all-inclusive, there is a very large group of people in the Church that requires a detailed set of provisions that do not flow from either their lay or clerical condition but from a third condition that is somehow different. This clearly indicates the flaw in the oversimplified assertion of some Religious that they are simply "laypeople." In the ordained-lay division they are canonically lay. But in terms of their life in the Church they are a distinct group including both lay and ordained members but with rights and responsibilities that do not derive from either condition.

The third canonical grouping is the laity. This category includes all the baptized who are not ordained (despite the anomaly of permanent deacons) or members of Institutes of Consecrated Life or Societies of Apostolic Life (even though laity may be members of such Institutes and Societies). Beyond the overlaps implied in the parentheses of the preceding sentence, another anomaly arises here because members of Third Orders, which are now usually referred to as "Secular" or "Lay" Orders, are grouped with members of "associations of the faithful" as laity in the sense of neither clerical nor Religious. Members of Secular Orders, however, often make vows or other promises, live according to a rule or constitutions, and often share some form of community life. In other words, they are as much like Religious in many ways as they are like laity in others.

Despite all these anomalies the canonical placement supplies an important datum for our reflection on the institutional "place" of Religious. Just as nonordained Religious are not clergy, so they are also not laity in this second sense of laity. Religious are a "third group" who are, precisely as Religious, neither clerical nor lay. Unfortunately, because the clergy are a superior group (namely, the ordained) in the hierarchical division, there is a tendency to regard the canonical divisions as also hierarchical: clergy at the top, Religious (and other members of "consecrated states") as second, and laity (i.e., neither of the above) at the bottom. Religious do become, in this way of looking at things, a kind of intermediate grouping between clergy and laity, the very thing the Council correctly maintained they are not. This distinction is quite important, however, because it calls into question any overly facile assimilation without remainder of Religious to laity.

C. Theological States of Life

A third way of cutting up the ecclesiastical pie is not hierarchical and, although it has some canonical ramifications, is not properly juridical but is concerned rather with theology and spirituality. It is the most significant distinction in terms of life as well as the most difficult to describe clearly and in a way that is unifying rather than divisive in the Church. And it is in this area that Religious must come to clarity about their distinctive "place" in the Church as a special (though not superior) lifeform.[15]

In terms of theology and spirituality of states of life there are two significant principles of distinction among members of the Church. First there is the distinction based on the way people or groups are related to "the world" or what we might call the intrahistorical order, yielding the traditional but today much misunderstood and highly contested distinction between "secular" and "Religious." Second, there is the distinction based on lifelong formal, solemn, and public commitments concerning one's sexually sealed relationships to other people, which yields the distinction between the state of consecrated marriage (matrimony) and the state of consecrated celibacy (Religious Life) but leaves unaddressed the theological state and spirituality of those who, for various reasons, are in neither of these two states of life.

1. Relation to the World:

a. The problem with the traditional terminology: The traditional terminology of "secular" and "Religious" is highly problematic for many people today for a number of reasons. First, the term *secular* is offensive to many because it has, for many centuries, been a morally derogatory term expressing the perceived inferiority of those members of the Church who were not members of Religious congregations.[16] This inferiority had a double source but, for most people, the two roots were synonymous. First, a secular or "worldly" person was one who, at best, was ignorant of or incompetent in the spiritual life, and at worst one who was so preoccupied with materialistic concerns that the religious or spiritual dimension of life was neglected or suppressed. Religious were warned against association with "seculars" (even their parents!) for fear of worldly contamination.

Second, and further complicating the situation, the terms *secular* and *lay* became, in the common imagination, synonymous because Religious were assimilated to the clergy and thus not considered lay. In short, *secular* was a term that connoted the juridical inferiority of the secular laity in relation to the clergy and the spiritual inferiority of secular laity in relation to Religious (whether clerical or lay). Interestingly enough, it also suggested the spiritual inferiority of the secular clergy to the ordained in Religious communities! It is therefore not surprising that the laity today, both lay Religious and lay non-Religious, find the term *secular* objectionable.

Closely related to this rejection of the term *secular* is resentment about the use of the term which is its corollary, that is, *Religious,* for vowed members of Religious Institutes, since this seems to suggest that those who are not members of such Institutes—other laypeople—are not only secular in the negative sense of worldly but actually "irreligious" or "nonreligious" in the sense of not interested in, committed to, or developed in the spiritual life. And at the same time, it suggests that insofar as the world and Christian activity in the world is affirmed (as they are by the Council), Religious are barred from participation with their fellow laity in this newly rediscovered sphere of faith and action. In other words, the terminology seems to be not only negative in its implications for those Christians who are not Religious but divisive and exclusive.

Language has a life of its own, and it is not always possible to control its development. It may be the case that, due to centuries of value-laden use and misuse, the terms *secular* and *Religious* are irredeemable. However, in the absence of any readily available synonyms that do not require long and involved perilocutions that make conversation unwieldy, it might be useful to try to clarify these terms in the hopes of rehabilitating them for current discourse or, failing that, of suggesting what should be included in whatever substitutes for them we are able to invent.

There is a helpful analogy between this discussion of terminology for states of life in the Church and the discussion in the 1970s and 1980s about the use of the term *spiritual direction* for a particular ministry in the Church. *Spiritual direction* was another traditional but badly abused term that most contemporary Christians, including those exercising that ministry, agreed was open to serious misunderstanding, since what it denotes is neither "spiritual" (if this means exclusive of the bodily, social, political, etc. dimensions of the life of faith), nor "direction" (if this means one person exercising authoritarian power in the life of another by telling the other how to believe, pray, choose, behave, etc.). However, most people involved in discourse about the subject have sufficiently clarified the term itself and the conditions of its use that they can utilize it, at least among themselves, as a convenient code word or shorthand for the ministry of one-to-one accompaniment in the life of faith without the spiritualistic or authoritarian resonances that the term might carry. Being able to continue to use the traditional term is not only convenient but it helps to maintain the historical continuity between the contemporary ministry and its predecessors in the history of the Church, and this historical connection is both grounding and enlightening as well as helpfully critical.

    b. Secular: Let us begin with the term *secular* and the problems arising from its morally pejorative connotations. The word comes from the Latin *saeculum,* meaning "of or pertaining to the world." The term *world* has a long, New Testament based, pejorative history in Christian usage. In its pejorative sense it denotes not so much material reality (which Christian theology, at least in theory, has always regarded as essentially God's good creation) nor the cosmic stage on which human history is enacted (which is the morally neutral physical environment into which the Word Incarnate, along with every other human being, entered by birth from a human mother), but rather the dynamics of human history under the influence of original sin. These dynamics give rise to a saga of personal sin that has generated a dispensation of greed, domination, lust, and so on. This dispensation of potential and actual moral evil has often been described as "worldly" in opposition to the dispensation of grace and virtue which is "spiritual" or "supernatural" or even "other-worldly."

People are born into the dispensation of systemic evil, that is, the "world," and have an inborn tendency (concupiscence) to be controlled by it and thus promote its sad contribution to the present and future of the race. Those who succumb to its power and habitually act accordingly are "worldly." Conversely, those who, living out their baptismal liberation from this world of sin and death, have been extricated from this dispensation by grace-assisted personal effort are "spiritual" or "unworldly."

"Leaving the world" was, therefore, an ascetical journey from the life of sin to life in the Spirit, which was most often (though not necessarily) assisted and signified by a social and/or geographical separation from ordinary day-to-day life in society. The earliest Christians accomplished this by their community life, which is idealistically described in the Acts of the Apostles (cf. Acts 4:32–37). As the Church became more fully inculturated into Hellenistic society and then became the official religion of the Roman Empire, some Christians felt the necessity for a more complete break with the surrounding culture. The flight of the first monastics to the desert represented such a break, a physical "leaving of the world." The building of monasteries, walled off from the surrounding countryside and its culture, and the elaboration of the separatist lifestyle of later apostolic and contemplative Religious were concrete expressions of "leaving the world" in this sense.

There is no question that this schema still operates in the religious and theological imagination of many if not most Catholics whose religious education predated Vatican II, even though they may consciously hold a very different theology of the world and history based on the Gospel-inspired secularity (not secularism) of *Gaudium et Spes* (The Church in the Modern World), expressed especially in the preface and introduction. Consequently, even though the world, according to contemporary theology and spirituality, is clearly affirmed as God's good creation, properly autonomous in relation to the ecclesiastical institution, the locus and the raw material of the coming Reign of God and therefore an appropriate sphere of the dedicated apostolic involvement of the baptized,[17] many still harbor a suspicion that full participation in the life of the world is somehow contaminating and thus that only those who in some way "leave the world" are really first-class Christians. Consequently, they may be uncomfortable with the existence in the Church of a state of life that is deliberately and distinctively "marginal" to the secular order (in the sense explored in chapter 4) and suspect that its members are thereby claiming to be or are considered to be superior to those Christians whose primary location and sphere of activity is the secular order itself. They would much prefer that either no one be referred to as "Religious" or that everyone be referred to in this way, thereby abolishing the use of the term *secular*, with its lingering pejorative connotations.[18]

In the preceding paragraphs, I have tried to establish two points regarding the term *secular*. First, *secular* and *lay* are not synonymous terms. *Lay* means nonordained and includes both most seculars (those who are not ordained, i.e., everyone but the diocesan or secular clergy) and many Religious (all non-clerical ones, i.e., Sisters and Brothers). In other words, nonordained secular Christians and nonordained Religious Christians share the lay state when the Church is looked at from the standpoint of hierarchical organization. Therefore, the terms *secular* and *Religious* do not, in and of themselves, denote class distinction as do the terms *lay* and *clerical*. They are parallel or lateral terms describing a type of characteristic stance in relationship to the secular order. The secular Christian has the primary or fundamental relationship to that order while the Religious Christian has a qualified relationship.

Second, because *world* is not a theologically pejorative term despite its long history of largely negative use, *secular* is not a pejorative term denoting inferiority in the area of spirituality or ministerial commitment. It is a positive term expressing the choice to situate one's committed Christian faith-life and mission primarily, directly, and in an unreserved or unqualified way within the sphere of this world and this time, considered as the locus and raw material of the coming Reign of God. Religious make another choice (to be discussed below) in regard to their relationship to the world. Neither choice is superior or inferior; neither is more or less conducive to holiness or committed to ministry. They are two different choices made by different Christians in response to different vocations.

To situate one's faith-life and mission firmly and resolutely in the world in no way suggests that this world or human history are the ultimate values in one's life or the furthest horizon of one's concerns. It means that the way one chooses to serve the ultimate value, God and God's Reign, is through direct and primary involvement in the realities of the *"saeculum,"* in family, economics, politics, social life, and all the other structures and dynamics of intrahistorical existence. Secular Christians, in other words, are not simply "non-Religious." That term would denote anyone not in a Religious congregation including non-Christians, atheists, or reductionistic humanists. Secular Christians are precisely seculars, and it is at least arguable that only by claiming the term *secular* in its fully positive, postconciliar sense will we begin to appropriate the theological truth that this world and its history are called not to final destruction but to transformation in the Reign of God and that the human race is called not to escape from the world but to transform it. The secular vocation in its proper and positive sense is the calling of the vast majority of the baptized, and it is this vocation that is the primary source of hope for the transformation of the world in Christ.

c. Religious: If anything, the term *Religious* is more problematic than secular. Throughout this book I have capitalized the term when I am using it to refer to vowed members of Religious Institutes or to the Institutes themselves. I have done this precisely in order to preserve the more general meaning of the word *religious,* which is an adjective describing all of the persons, objects, and activities that relate creation to the Creator or are so related. Thus all believers, members of Religious congregations, and secular Christians as well as members of other faith traditions and many who align themselves with no institutionalized faith tradition are religious people, as are their activities of worship and service, their relationships and dreams and vocations. Capitalizing the word when it refers to members of Religious congregations is analogous to capitalizing Democrat(ic) when it refers to an American political party or its members, so that in its uncapitalized form it continues to have its broader significance as a description of any government or process based on the consent of the governed. In this sense it is to be hoped that Republicans or Independents are as democratic as Democrats; many socialist governments as well as constitutional monarchies are also democratic.

Religious, then, referring to vowed members of Religious Institutes, does not imply that other Christians are "irreligious" or "nonreligious." The opposite of *religious* in its general sense is *irreligious* or *nonreligious;* the opposite of *Religious* in its particular sense as denoting a theological-spiritual state of life is *secular.* This raises two issues that must be addressed: in what sense are Religious "nonseculars" and what does this mean for their relationship with the world, given the theologically positive sense elaborated by Vatican II; why not call Religious simply "nonseculars," that is, what is the positive content of the word *Religious* and why is it appropriate (if it is) for the state of life under consideration?

A presupposition for any discussion of Religious and the "world" is that the basic Christian understanding of the world, that is, of creation, is that it is good. Coming from the hand of the Creator who affirmed it as good "in the beginning" (cf. Gn 1–2:4) and hates nothing that God has made (cf. Wis 2:13–14), marred by sin but still the object of divine care by a God who so loved the world as to send the only Son to save it (cf. Jn 3:16), and destined for ultimate transformation in the Reign of God, the world is our beloved home. Jesus prayed that his disciples would be not taken out of the world but preserved from evil (cf. Jn 17:15). To hate, despise, or reject the world is not a Christian option.

Obviously, Catholic theology and practice, especially in the modern era, has often obscured this teaching, and that is the reason why the reform inaugurated by Vatican II involved such a strong reaffirmation of the goodness and validity of the secular order and the nobility of the secular vocation. Because the Church as a whole had lost sight of this teaching about the essential goodness of the world, Religious who, especially in the Tridentine period, saw themselves as a virtual incarnation of the institutional Church also developed and lived a sharply antagonistic, separatist, and rejectionist attitude toward the world. One of the major challenges facing postconciliar Religious has been to rediscover what it means to be in and for the world in accord with their own particular vocational charism.

Although the world is essentially good, it is also marred by sin. Thus the secular order as a whole is an ambiguous reality calling for a nuanced and variegated response to its complexity. To adopt biblical language, humans must increase and multiply and fill the earth, till the soil and care for it, govern the world in wisdom, and prophetically challenge it to justice. Different people and groups in the Church adopt different aspects of this human endeavor as the particular sphere of their own contribution. Parenting, political involvement, economic enterprise, religious leadership, and social activism are some of the particular foci of Christian action in and for the world.

One particular stance toward the world, the prophetic,[19] is particularly ambiguous but crucially necessary. Thomas Merton among others has identified Religious Life as an institutional embodiment, in the midst of the Church and for the world, of the prophetic stance. We are speaking here of Religious Life as a lifeform. Obviously many Religious do not fulfill the prophetic potential of their life, and many who are not in Religious Life are prophetic in striking ways. Intrinsic to the prophetic stance of Religious Life as a lifeform (as we saw in chapter 4) is a certain "marginality" in relation to the intrahistorical dynamics and processes of both the world and the Church itself. The prophet does not "leave the world" (or the Church) in the sense of throwing it over in disgust and becoming an isolated misanthropist or ideological ecclesiastical rebel. But the prophet (and the prophetic lifeform) does move to the edges of the social system from which a certain critical perspective can be maintained. There, on the margin, the prophet cries out in lament against the injustices of systems, whether ecclesiastical or civil, evokes the memory of God's plan for creation and the Church, and energizes hope to strive toward the Reign of God. Of course, this is not all that Religious do, and they are not the only ones who do it. And often they cooperate with others in the prosecution of worthwhile intrahistorical projects and thus participate positively in the ongoing life of the world, just as secular Christians who are primarily actively involved in politics or Church governance often take prophetic stances and engage in prophetic action in relation to institutional injustice. But the fundamental and defining stance of Religious Life as a lifeform is the prophetic one, which involves a certain ongoing marginality in relation to the world that is expressed in lifestyle, ministerial choices, and so on. And Religious undertake this stance and this task in a public and permanent way by making a lifelong (paradoxically institutionalized) commitment to it. Religious Life itself is an alternative institution in relation to both ecclesiastical and civil institutions.

The marginality of Religious Life in relation to civil and ecclesiastical society has been institutionalized in many different ways throughout history. Religious have gone apart socially as consecrated virgins in the heart of the local Church and geographically by moving to the desert in protest against the decadence of the city in the Roman Empire; they have built monasteries as alternate cities wherein to live the Gospel which they felt could not be lived in the countryside and towns of medieval Europe; they constructed lifestyles that could not be assimilated to contemporary social life in order to call into question the values of the modern world. Contemporary Religious Life is challenged to find its own way to institutionalize the marginality that its prophetic character demands, and there are many experiments currently underway to discover what that way might be.

At the heart of every institutional form of prophetic marginality, however, is the essential marginality constituted by the public profession of the vows that structure Religious Life. I discussed this aspect of the prophetic vocation in some detail in chapter 4, so here it will suffice to say that the lifeform constructed by the

Religious vows and Religious community life is itself a distancing or self-marginalization in relation to the world for the purpose of prophetic witness. In this sense, Religious today, like Religious throughout history, choose to "leave the world" in a certain sense, not out of hatred or disdain, and not necessarily by some form of physical flight, but out of love in imitation of the One who laid down his life in order to give life and passed out of this world in death for the sake of the world. We are too close to the distortions of the recent past not to have to be very careful about how and where we use this expression, "leaving the world." But the misuse and even misunderstanding of the term does not negate the meaning of the reality.

Finally, it must be reiterated that Religious are not the only people called to prophecy in the Church and in the world, nor is prophecy the only activity to which Religious are called. But prophecy is a defining theological character-istic of Religious Life as a lifeform in relation to the systems of Church and society and supplies the key to an appropri-ate understanding of Religious "nonsecularity" or self-marginalization in relation to the world as well as its often problematic self-positioning within the Church, as we will see in greater detail in chapters 9 and 10. Our current strug-gle against hierarchical dualisms of all kinds makes many people fearful of acknowledging any distinctions among people or vocations lest someone be excluded or subordi-nated or some value be monopolized by a dominant power. But no meaningful conversation about mutuality in life and ministry is possible if we do not recognize that there are a variety of lifeforms in the Church, a variety of ministries, a variety of vocations. None of them absolutely excludes some realization within itself of what is characteristic of the others, but each has its specializations, and it makes sense to recognize and valorize these. Secular Christians are not "unreligious" or "irreligious," and Religious Christians are not "unworldly" or "other-worldly." While both are called to world transformation in Christ, they go about it by focusing differently and creating different lifeforms in which these diverse foci are institutionalized.

We turn now to our second question: Given the positive value assigned to the term *secular* and the basic orientation of Religious Life toward prophetic marginality in relation to both the secular and the ecclesiastical orders, why not simply call vowed members of Religious Institutes "nonseculars" thus avoiding the problems raised by the word *Religious?* In a way, the reason is the same as that for not calling seculars "non-Religious," namely, the need to say not only what the state of life is *not* but what it *is*. People, including Christians, can be nonsecular for many reasons: because they are embittered by and alienated from the world and wish to have nothing to do with it; because they are terrified by it and wish to protect themselves from it; because they cannot cope with its complexity and resign themselves to privatization; because they are not interested in anything beyond their own well-being. Religious are not simply uninvolved in the world, that is, "nonsecular." They have taken a particular stance toward the world, a self-marginalizing one, out of a specifically Gospel motivation in relation to the world.

Furthermore, the term *Religious* points to something else besides the stance of Religious toward the world. It points to the way in which Religious institutionalize that stance, namely, by organizing the whole of their lives, in an exclusive and singly focused way, around the religious dimension of human existence. The way an artist organizes life around the aesthetic, or the scholar around the life of the mind, or married people around their family, or the politician around public life, Religious organize life around the God-quest. It is not simply that they attempt to do whatever they do "in the name of the Lord Jesus," (cf. Col 3:17), to find God and honor God in all things and to do nothing incompatible with their commitment to God. This is true of all committed believers for whom God is the meaning-giving horizon of all of life. Rather, for Religious the God-quest determines directly, immediately, and primarily all the choices and elements of their life itself even in its day-to-day and hour-to-hour reality. It controls who Religious live with and where, what work they choose to do, how they handle money, their daily schedule and its activities, and every other aspect of life. This is not an intrinsically superior way to live any more than being an artist or a scholar or a politician or a parent is intrinsically superior. It is one valid way to live one's Christianity. It is not justified by intrinsic superiority but by personal vocation. But it explains why the term *Religious* might be appropriate for such people. Just as calling those who raise a child to maturity parents does not denigrate the real generativity of others such as teachers or child-care specialists (who might actually be better at child-rearing), or calling the scholar an intellectual does not impugn the intelligence of others (who might be much brighter), so calling those who structure their day-to-day life for the whole of life around the direct concern with the God-project Religious does not call into question the spirituality of others, many of whom may be holier than the professed Religious.

To summarize, then, the term *Religious* does not contrast with *lay*. By far the majority of Religious and seculars are canonically lay. *Religious* contrasts with *secular* because the primary self-situation of Religious is marginal to the intrahistorical processes and dynamics of the world. The term *Religious* itself designates the central, immediate, and primary focus of Religious on the God-quest, which determines their daily life in a direct way over the whole of a lifetime.

It may not be possible to divest *secular* of its pejorative connotations or *Religious* of its elitist ones. If anyone can find better words for what these terms denote, it would probably be welcomed by everyone. But, in my opinion, it remains important to recognize, claim, and valorize the two distinct stances of Christians in relationship to the world: that of primary and direct personal participation in the intrahistorical dynamics of the world as a primary mode of committed Christian existence and world transformation; and that of primary and direct specialization in the religious quest, with its resultant relative marginalization in relation to the world as another valid way of contributing to the transformation of the world. Both are Christian life stances. Both are necessary if the Reign of God is to come on this earth. Both can lead to the fullness of holiness. Neither is intrinsically superior or inferior. Furthermore, the distinction does not imply that secular Christians should involve themselves only in "the marketplace" or that Religious should not, nor conversely that Religious should limit themselves to inner-Church ministries from which secular Christians are barred. This is an artificial division of labor that is motivated more by an ecclesiastical control agenda than by Gospel zeal.[20]

2. *Sexually expressed relationship to others:* The second theological distinction, which does not correspond intrinsically and exactly either to the ordained/lay or to the secular/Religious distinctions, is that which is constituted by the public, formal, and solemn profession of vows governing one's relational life. People, by making such profession, enter into a "state of life" or a permanent life situation constituted by a set of stable relationships that structure the life itself in an overall way. Basically, there are two such "consecrated states" of life in the Church, that of consecrated (sacramental) marriage or matrimony and that of consecrated celibacy or Religious Life. The word *consecrated* is problematic because the fundamental consecration of all Christians is that of Baptism. Marriage vows and Religious profession are further specifications of baptismal consecration, not parallel or alternate consecrations. Nevertheless, because not all forms of marriage are matrimony and not all forms of celibacy are Religious Life it seems necessary to specify them in order to be clear.

Both matrimony and Religious Life are permanent states of life inaugurated after serious reflection and preparation by formal, public, and solemn commitments that initiate certain obligations not shared by all the faithful and for which those who profess them are publicly accountable within the ecclesial community. Furthermore, these commitments bear not exclusively but primarily upon the relational life of the individuals involved.

Those who freely enter the state of matrimony undertake a lifelong commitment, expressive of one's love of God, to faithful and fruitful loving monogamy and to the shared raising of the children that this relationship involves. Those who freely enter the state of Religious Life undertake a lifelong commitment to sexually abstinent celibacy as the outward expression of a particular type of relationship to God in Jesus and to God's people, usually in the context of a particular celibate community. While there is more to matrimony and to Religious Life than the obligations undertaken and the life embraces more than these relational dimensions, it is these commitments that "carve out" as it were these specific, recognizable, and distinct states of life in the Church.

A difficult question that faces the Christian community today concerns the committed single person who is not simply single by default (not having met the right person, etc.) and who deliberately chooses not to enter Religious Life. There are an increasing number of such people today and the Church, traditionally, has had little positive to say about such a life, about its characteristic or ideal spirituality, about the implications of such a choice for the lived sexuality of such people.[21] No doubt this is due to the fact that few people "chose" singleness in times past, or at least this was the assumption. Those who remained single did so, or at least were thought to do so, out of necessity or by default, and the condition was understood as a misfortune to be suffered courageously as a participation in the salvific suffering of Christ. This is no longer the case. But it is not at all clear how singleness, freely chosen, shapes the relational capacity and experience of the Christian in a life-giving way or what it means to channel one's affective capacity in this way. Single people will have to initiate the exploration of this subject and supply the experiential data that can lead to the elaboration of a genuine spirituality of committed singleness.[22]

A further complication in regard to theological states of life in the Church is introduced in regard to the ordained. Ordination itself does not initiate one into a state of life but into an "ordo," an ecclesiastical position, which involves the exercise of certain functions, within the ordering (hierarchical) structure of the institutional Church. However, especially in the Western Church, being ordained does insert the person into the "clergy," which is a quasi-state of life because it governs the everyday lifestyle of its members. Clergy (except permanent deacons) in the Western Church may not marry (although this is a disciplinary regulation and not equivalent to freely chosen consecrated celibacy of Religious, as I will shortly point out) and are expected to live in designated dwellings, with other clergy, on a stipend that is insufficient for economic independence. They are not free to pursue further education after seminary without permission, to choose their own work or undertake non-Church-related professions or occupations, to be absent without leave from their designated diocese, or to resign from active ordained ministry without dispensation, which may be refused, and so on. In effect, the succession of well-meaning efforts dating back at least to Augustine to reform the diocesan clergy and make them models of sanctity for the laity has consistently assimilated the clergy to the lifestyle of Religious.[23] The ordained may be expelled or released from the clerical state but they remain ordained, another indication that ordination does not initiate a state of life but a hierarchical role. Although the person who has been thus declericalized may not, except in certain emergency situations, lawfully exercise his ordained functions, if he does illegally perform such functions they are valid. In other words, *ordained* and *cleric* are not strictly equivalent terms. The clerical state, although not really comparable to the freely chosen structuring of one's relational life by matrimonial vows or Religious profession, and not intrinsically necessary for nor historically always connected with ordination, does make the life of the ordained minister a quasi–state of life. While this is intended to foster his ministry it often does not; in fact, as many of the ordained who have remained in the clergy as well as virtually all who have left it testify, it often impedes ministry. But it does introduce considerable confusion, which we will consider in the next section, in regard to Religious Life as a state of life. In short, "clergyhood" imitates a state of life but often without any experienced vocation to such a state which, by a kind of mirror-effect, suggests that those who *are* genuinely called to the Religious state of life are likewise coerced by law, which is emphatically not the case.

To summarize this section: Religious as such are, in relation to the hierarchical structure of the Church, nonordained, that is, *lay*. In terms of canonical status they are neither ordained nor lay but members of *Religious Institutes of Consecrated Life*. In theological terms they are not seculars but *Religious* living in a *state of consecrated celibacy* rather than in the state of matrimony or freely chosen singleness.

III. Sources of Confusion in the Present Situation

From all that has already been said it is obvious that there is considerable confusion in the Church about the internal constitution of the People of God, and that confusion has been exacerbated for Religious especially by developments since the Council. However, while it is possible to sort out the terminology and thus clarify the structural (hierarchical), juridical (canonical), and theological (state of life) "place" of Religious in relation to the ordained, other laypeople and clerics, and other states of life in the Church, there are other sources of confusion which defy such clarification because they arise from serious misunderstandings in the areas of theology and spirituality and from highly problematic political and social practices in the Church. Explanation will not solve these problems, but it may be able to strip them of their theological and religious disguises and by revealing them for what they are, increase the pressure to solve them.

A. Mandatory Singleness of the Secular Clergy

The disciplinary regulation in the Western Church which obliges all the ordained (except permanent deacons)[24] to remain unmarried, with the implication that they will observe the chastity appropriate to the unmarried (total sexual abstinence), is probably the single greatest source of confusion about Religious Life in the Church. I will refer to "mandatory singleness" rather than to clerical celibacy because consecrated celibacy is a charism requiring a free, religiously motivated response to a personal vocation, a response that is perceived by the respondent as a personally life-giving choice for him or her. While there are certainly ordained who are personally called to consecrated celibacy, the majority of the clergy (if personal testimony and sociological studies are to be believed) are not called to celibacy, do not freely choose it but accept it (willingly or not) as a condition for that to which they do feel called, namely, ordained ministry, and do not find it a personally life-giving commitment but an onerous burden that often robs them of energy and joy and has accounted for the resignation from active ordained ministry of many thousands of committed ordained ministers. Although strenuous efforts are made in clerical formation programs to induce spiritual motivation for the acceptance of lifelong singleness and many clerics sustain the obligation through truly heroic and spiritually motivated personal sacrifice, the charism of celibacy cannot be manufactured and the imposition of lifelong singleness does not create true celibates.[25]

1. Mandatory singleness makes the clergy "look like" Religious: The first and basic confusion caused by mandatory clerical singleness is that it makes the secular clergy "look like" Religious. To most people priests and Religious are alike primarily because neither marries. Since the ordained are forbidden to marry as a condition for ordination and the ordained class is, hierarchically, the most powerful one in the Church and therefore appears normative, most people assume that Religious also are forbidden to marry as a condition for entrance into Religious Life. This assumption often comes to expression in the question, "Do you think the Church will ever allow priests and Sisters to marry?" Implied in the question is the assumption that Religious consecrated celibacy, like clerical singleness, is a disciplinary regulation whereas, in fact, freely chosen consecrated celibacy is at the heart of the vocation to Religious Life. Religious are not celibate in order to enter the Religious Life. Rather, Religious Life is the lifeform constituted by and developed to foster the charism of consecrated celibacy, to which its members freely commit themselves in response to personal vocation.

In short, mandatory singleness of the clergy, because it is *not* essential to ordained ministry, obscures the fact that consecrated celibacy *is* essential to the vocation to Religious Life, not because it is imposed or required but because it is that to which Religious feel personally called. To those not participating in either clerical or Religious Life what is readily seen is the external fact: nonmarriage. The meaning of this condition is judged by its character in what is perceived as the normative situation, namely, clerical life. Consequently, the witness in the Church of consecrated celibacy is obscured and diluted, and the relation of Religious Life to the other consecrated state of life in the Church, namely, matrimony, is often totally suppressed.

2. Mandatory singleness makes Religious "look like" clergy: The confused assimilation of Religious to clergy has the further negative consequence of obscuring the prophetic character of Religious Life. Because many people see Religious as second-class clergy, they consider Religious to be, like the clergy, official agents of the Church as institution and expect the same type of behavior on the part of Religious toward the institution as they have a right to expect of clergy. This expectation, which is shared by those Church officials who do not understand the nature of Religious Life, domesticates Religious Life. Religious are often expected to function as a kind of second-class ecclesiastical job corps, cheap "clergy" whose calling is to fill ecclesiastical slots (especially those the clergy find onerous) which do not require ordination.

This misunderstanding of Religious Life leads to the expectation that Religious should express only official Church positions and promote undissenting conformity to such positions. The outrage of the Vatican when twenty-four Religious signed a 1984 *New York Times* statement calling for honest and open discussion of the abortion issue in the Church,[26] a truly prophetic gesture calling on the Church as a whole, not necessarily to change its teaching on abortion but simply to seek wisdom and reconciliation on a very divisive issue, was eloquent testimony to the fact that the Vatican considered the Religious, unlike the nearly one-hundred secular Catholics who signed the same statement, as obliged to adhere publicly to official policy in a way that could not effectively be demanded of the secular laity. In other words, Religious were being treated not as laity but as clergy, that is, as official agents of the institution. (Interestingly enough, the clerics, including the Religious clerics, who signed the statement promptly recanted without, apparently, the sense of compromising their personal or vocational integrity that moved the women Religious to refuse to recant.) This misunderstanding of the place of Religious in relation to the hierarchical structure of the Church blunts the charism of Religious Life as quintessentially prophetic. Prophecy, as we have already had occasion to note, has always been primarily a witness from within the People of God to the People of God and especially to its institutional embodiments rather than to secular society as such. Assimilating Religious (who are lay in relation to the hierarchical structure of the Church) to the hierarchy for purposes of control and agency subverts the prophetic vocation of Religious in the Church.[27]

Finally, the obligatory singleness of the clergy, which makes Religious look like clergy, also encourages many people to view Religious sociologically as clergy. In other words, Religious are often seen not as a prophetic minority in the Church but as part of the privileged hierarchical class. This separates Religious from their fellow laity. The secular laity thus become "the other" in relation to two special or elite categories in the Church who are seen as the male and female branches of the sociological upper class in the Church. Women Religious are viewed as second-class "female clergy" and men Religious who are not ordained, Brothers, insofar as they are seen at all, are regarded as curiously "undeveloped clergy."

B. The "Sexualization" of Distinctions in the Church

A major source of confusion about the categories of persons in the Church and the "place" of Religious within the institution arises from the "sexualization" of the whole issue, which begins with the official attitude toward sexuality expressed in the exclusion of women from ordination and the prohibition of marriage for the clergy. The clergy, therefore, are defined primarily (at least in practice if not in theory) not in terms of what they do in the Church, that is, in terms of their ordained functions within the structure of the Church. They are defined sexually, and consequently everyone else in the Church, defined by their difference from the normative higher class, are also defined sexually. Practically speaking (although this would never be admitted explicitly today), status in the Church rises in direct proportion to one's distance from the female and/or the feminine, which is closely associated with the body, sexuality, procreation, the "natural" as opposed to the spirit, intellectual creativity, and the making of "history."

The result of this displacement of distinction from function and/or state of life to sex is that the Church becomes, in effect, not a hierarchy of sacred functions nor a mutually supportive variety of states of life but a sexual power structure.[28] At the pinnacle of the structure are those who are not female and have no intimate relations with females (clerics [except permanent deacons] and other unmarried men).[29] Next in line are those who, though female, do not exercise those female functions characteristic of their intrinsically inferior status, namely, sexual ones (women Religious). Next come those who are not women but are compromised by their sexual relationship to women (married men). Further down the power ladder are those who are women and function sexually as women, that is, those totally enmeshed in femaleness (married women). Single lay women are regarded as "in suspension" until they decide to definitively renounce sexual functioning by becoming Religious, which greatly raises their status, or to definitively commit themselves to a sexually active life as married women, which places them at the bottom of the structure. In effect, single women are regarded as "loose cannons" since they cannot be defined in male-determined sexual categories and thus submitted to male-constructed codes of control.

Power in the Church is distributed sexually. The more exclusively male or distanced from the female one is, the more power and status in the Church one has. Sex is the secret, unacknowledged basis of power, and this has a devastatingly divisive effect in the Church largely because it is unacknowledged and would be denied if named. Thus the patriarchy of the Church's hierarchical structure is doubly problematic. It is patriarchal not only in terms of its pathological "father fixation" but also in a strictly sexual sense as the claim of male superiority in relation to women. Femaleness ends up being treated as intrinsically inferior, no matter how vociferously this is denied (as it has been in recent official statements). The supposedly normative maleness of Jesus and his imputed absolute preference for male leadership during his lifetime and as a permanently binding disposition for his Church, although considered questionable if not indefensible by mainstream biblical and theological scholarship,[30] and as culturally repugnant in much of the contemporary Church, as well as being pastorally dysfunctional, has been presented in recent Church documents as quasi-infallible.[31] In any case, the sexualization of power in the Church has exacerbated the already enormous confusion about roles and states of life in the Church.

C. The Confusion around the Term *Lay*

The final source of confusion in the present situation arises from the fact that the term *lay* is used in several different ways, all of which tend to be "privative" in relation to more positive terms. In one sense this is due to the linguistic fact that adjectives are usually applied to mark a difference in relation to a more general category. If most apples are red we tend to speak of "yellow apples" or "green apples," and if no color is mentioned it is assumed that the apples are red. In some cases there is no general assumption, and an adjective is needed in every case in which one wishes to be exact (e.g., black olives and green olives, since neither is "normative"). *Laity* is the most basic term for the *christifideli* (cf. Canon 204, in *CCL*). Baptism makes one a member of the Christian *laos* or people. It can cogently be asked whether any of the baptized, whatever role or state they later enter, ever really, that is, theologically, cease to be members of the laity, part of the People of God.[32] But in fact, we tend to denote the "nonnormative" (the not-red apples) by particular adjectives (ordained, Religious) thereby implicitly making the term *lay* a "remainder category" used only for those not distinguished by some particular designation.

In relation to hierarchical status we refer to the ordained, and "lay" is everyone else (although, as we have noted, most people probably do not really imagine Religious, who in this hierarchical sense are indeed lay, as lay but as quasi-clergy). In regard to canonical categories we tend to speak of clergy and Religious, and "lay" is everyone else. In relation to theological states of life we specify Religious (and the ordained are assimilated to Religious by mandatory singleness and the resultant clerical lifestyle), and "lay" tends to be equated with "secular." Furthermore, "secular" tends to be equated with "married" (either actually or potentially), which is not accurate since diocesan clergy are secular and ordained, single people are both secular and lay, and both laity and clergy can, theologically if not legally, be married.

Although most of these imaginative moves are, as I have tried to show, at least partially inaccurate and usually confusing, there is no question about their widespread occurrence. In fact, when all is said and done, "lay" in the popular imagination tends to mean not ordained and not a Religious or, quite simply, "nothing special" in the Church. Even though "lay" really denotes the fundamental dignity of all the baptized upon which all else—ordination, matrimony, or Religious profession—rests and in which they are rooted, the term tends to be "privative" in connotation. Even more devastatingly, "lay," because of its privative connotation, means disempowered or "powerless" to most people. This is not only confused and confusing but it undermines the clarity and usefulness of language for distinctions (not relations of superiority-inferiority) in the Church, which grounds genuine mutuality of functions, states, and vocations and which is potentially much more enriching than monolithic denial of all that makes different vocations in the Church meaningful.

There are obviously differences in vocation in the Church, and the differences are important. To pretend that it makes no difference whether one has chosen marriage or lifelong consecrated celibacy, that there is no real difference between retaining the right to acquire and even amass wealth and dispose of it as one sees fit and the total renunciation of that right and/or its exercise is to deny the obvious. All vocations are not the same, and the Church is richer for this fact. But unless we can break out of the patriarchal mindset into which all of us have been socialized from birth and which dictates that all differences are dualistic and hierarchical, all relations ones of superiority and inferiority, and all interactions rooted in sexually based domination and subordination, we cannot exploit these differences for mutual enrichment.

In the following chapter I will take up two clusters of effects of the confusions about distinctions within the People of God on Religious Life, specifically in terms of the identity crisis in Religious Life after the Council and issues generated by the actual place of Religious in the Church.

Chapter Eight

Religious Life as an Ecclesiastical Reality II: Who and Why?

I. Transition

The confusion not only about terminology but also about the actual ecclesiological "location" of Religious, and therefore about the relationship of Religious to other members of the Church, became acute in the immediate postconciliar period. This confusion had been masked in preconciliar times by the de facto arrangements within the sexualized power structure. In this chapter I want to explore the *identity crisis* for Religious created by the sudden resituation of their life in a Church that seemed to assign them no official "place" and *three particular issues* generated by the actual place of Religious in the postconciliar Church: their relation to the hierarchy; the question of canonical status; and the issue of ordination.

II. The Identity Crisis in Religious Life

As I stated at the outset of the previous chapter, many Religious were overwhelmed by a sense of dislocation and even "placelessness" in the postconciliar Church, which resulted in a veritable identity crisis. Many left Religious Life, which seemed to be little else than a pointless encumbering of faith and ministry by unnecessary obligations. Many who stayed pushed the identity crisis to the margins of their consciousness, but it appeared in a deep uncertainty about inviting or encouraging potential new members to embrace a lifeform that Religious themselves had trouble defining, describing, or distinguishing from other vocations in the Church.

The preconciliar distinctions in the Church may have been theologically questionable and juridically ambiguous in some respects, but in the concrete daily life of the Church relationships among its members were quite clear and the system worked well. The clergy were in charge and held all real authority and power. Religious were their assistants, sharing to a large extent in their status, to some extent (by delegation) in their authority, but not at all in their power. The laity had neither authority nor power and were those upon whom authority and power were exercised, sometimes in the form of domination but perhaps most often in the form of service.[1]

The laity were sometimes invited to assist the clergy and Religious in Church affairs, for example, by raising money, supplying goods and services, or helping with charitable works. Any exercise of the "apostolate" proper by the laity was defined as "the participation of the laity in the apostolate of the hierarchy," who alone ministered in the name of the Church.[2] Religious, in fact, exercised an apostolate proper to them by virtue of profession and as specified by their constitutions. This apostolate, not considered the "lay apostolate" but properly Religious, was established by the approbation of the congregation's constitutions and exercised under the authority of the hierarchy. Effectively, then, there were three layers of ministry: hierarchical (in virtue of ordination); Religious (in virtue of profession and constitutions); lay (by participation in the hierarchical).

A. The Reaffirmation of the Dignity and Mission of the Baptized

In the wake of the Council this functional clarity was largely obscured. The Council proclaimed the dignity and mission of all the baptized, which they enjoyed not by delegation or permission but in virtue of their baptism.[3] This was understood by almost everyone as a revalorization of the secular laity because clergy and Religious had always enjoyed both status and official ministry, clergy in virtue of ordination and Religious in virtue of profession. So, rather than being understood as the reaffirmation of the essential unity of the People of God based on the shared dignity and mission of all who are consecrated by Baptism, this affirmation was experienced as a "promotion" of the heretofore inferior and disempowered laity which, in many instances, resulted in defensiveness on the part of the clergy about their ecclesiastical "turf." Religious, especially women, tended to favor the laity in the resulting power struggles both because the conciliar theology potentially opened up new ministerial roles for women Religious themselves and because Religious saw the empowerment of the laity as an important step in the implementation of the Council's vision of a renewed and empowered People of God.

However, an unforeseen result of this affirmation of ministry as baptismal vocation, a result we are just beginning to recognize and engage, was the narrowing or "parochialization" of ministry. This development is raising serious questions about the vocation of secular laity, lay Religious, and ordained Religious. In effect, the wide range of ministries by secular laity in and to the secular order that had been encouraged and promoted (even though always subject to clerical authority) since the beginning of the modern period and the ministries of Religious in institutions and organizations run by their congregations began to be supplanted by or subsumed into the parish as the sole locus of Christian life. This monolithic view of ministry was reflected in the conciliar decree *Presbyterorum Ordinis* (The Ministry and Life of Priests).[4] Although in many respects this document represented a tremendous advance in the theology of ordained ministry, it virtually subsumed ordained Religious into the diocesan clergy.[5] Furthermore, the precipitous decline in the number of secular clergy available for parish assignment put tremendous pressure on clerical congregations to make their ordained members available for parish service. Since the life and ministry of ordained Religious is not the particular focus of this study, I will not elaborate on this situation, but the leaders of clerical communities are increasingly concerned about the drain on community life as well as the subversion of specifically Religious identity and characteristically Religious apostolates in their men who, for all intents and purposes, lead the life and exercise the ministry of diocesan clergy.

The secular laity embraced their call to ministry with wonderful enthusiasm in the wake of the Council but, perhaps because ministry had been so long defined in terms of the administration of sacraments by priests, they tended to equate ministry with parish roles and functions rather than with the evangelization of the secular order, which Vatican II singled out as the particular area of ministerial competence and responsibility of the laity.[6] They became lectors and acolytes, youth ministers and catechists, ministers of the Eucharist both at liturgy and to the sick, parish administrative officers, religious educators. Laity interested in ministry tended to channel their energy not into the transformation of the economic, political, and social orders but into quasi-clerical service in the parish, for which many undertook serious theological and pastoral education.

Meanwhile, many women Religious, for a variety of reasons sometimes discerned and chosen but often beyond their control, left their traditional congregational ministries in schools, hospitals, and social agencies administered by their congregations and took up ministries in the parish. They were the best-trained replacements for the vanishing clergy. They became parish administrators, parish religious education directors, parish "sisters" performing virtually all the ministries of the clergy except the sacramental rituals that required ordination. Sisters with degrees in canon law and administration tended to take up positions in the chancery or in other diocesan posts.

As the Nygren and Ukeritis study, *FORUS,* noted,[7] the effect of these developments on Religious has been a progressive "parochialization" (and I would add "clericalization") of lay Religious. They tend to be assimilated into the parish or diocesan structures, become accountable more directly to the clergy than to their Religious superiors, often have little time or energy for congregational affairs that compete with analogous events in the parish or diocese, and increasingly find their affective and social life centered in the parish and its families rather than in their communities.

A distressing aspect of this relocation is the powerlessness of the individual Religious in conflict situations. She usually can count on no support from the hierarchy, whose responsibility is to their clergy, and she is not protected by diocesan protocols for employment or conflict resolution, even those developed to give minimal support to lay ministers. Her own Religious superiors have no leverage in the diocesan or parochial situation, as they did have when the congregation staffed and administered institutions it had founded or which had been founded on the congregation's acceptance of responsibility for them. The Religious who runs into conflict with the pastor or in the diocesan office is institutionally powerless. In most cases she is simply dismissed without any kind of process or adjudication of claims, severance compensation, or any chance of vindication, which would protect her good name or employment record, no matter how unjust or arbitrary the dismissal.

The progressive parochialization of ministry in the wake of the Council, although it has greatly enlivened some parishes, has seriously undermined the specificity of Religious ministry in the Church and contributed to the identity confusion of Religious themselves. Many congregations are asking what corporate ministry means and how it can be fostered when there seems to be no work shared among the members. They are concerned about what community life can mean when their members' location and life is largely controlled by the availability of parochial employment within a structure that views the Religious congregation primarily if not exclusively as a source of workers rather than as an ecclesial lifeform. Individual Religious are likewise seriously challenged to define themselves in terms of their vowed life and congregational membership when, in fact, their primary locus of life, spirituality, and ministry is the diocesan or parish structure. In short, the rich cooperation between two distinct centers of life and ministry in the Church, namely, the parish and the Religious congregation, is being blurred if not extinguished by the subsuming of the latter, one member at a time, into the former.

B. The Revision of the Church's Theology of Sexuality

Another major contribution of the Council to a renewed ecclesiology was its positive reevaluation of human sexuality. Although such was undoubtedly not the intention, this revision of sexuality has undermined the very foundations of ecclesiastical organization as a sexual power structure. The Council insisted on the positive value of human sexuality, gingerly affirmed the carefully qualified equality of women, and boldly proclaimed the beauty and sacramental dignity of marriage. This not only led to marriage being presented as a true vocation equal in spiritual value to the celibate vocation (rather than as the lack of a "real vocation")[8] but it also encouraged clergy who felt called to marriage to become much more vocal in their questioning of the legitimacy and necessity of imposing singleness on all the ordained. If marriage is neither a lesser vocational choice nor an impediment to ministry, why must it be an absolute and universal condition for ordination?

Repeated official efforts to delegitimate this question have neither halted the discussion nor stemmed the tide of men resigning from the clergy to marry. The powerful social pressure in the preconciliar Church against leaving to marry rested on the conviction, shared by clergy and laity alike, that a man who left the "highest vocation" was unfaithful to a divine and privileged calling, weak in character, and unworthy of the priesthood because he was associated with (or had fallen victim to) the despised feminine. This social pressure was largely dissipated by the widespread realization that mandatory singleness was neither intrinsically necessary for the sacrament of Orders nor, in many cases, helpful to ministry. The burden of proof shifted to those who were trying to explain why the People of God should be deprived of thousands of excellent ministers for the sake of a discipline that was difficult to reconcile with the new theology of sexuality and marriage presented by the Council.

A subtle but deep confusion that had been just below the surface for centuries was also raised to visibility by the conciliar affirmations about sexuality and marriage. There has probably always been considerable confusion among male ordained Religious about the role of celibacy in their vocation. Many ordained Religious identify much more closely with their clerical status than with their Religious state of life. They entered their congregations because they felt called to be priests but also felt that a community setting was a better one for them than the diocesan structure. Some chose Religious community for ministerial reasons, others because they wanted to go to the foreign missions or to teach or to exercise some ministry other than diocesan work (an irony in view of the parochialization that is reclaiming so many of them). Some wanted to live in an all-male group, which offered more companionship than the typical rectory and more esprit de corps than the typical diocesan presbyterate. Sometimes their formation directors, because of their own lack of clarity around the issue of consecrated celibacy in Religious Life or because the congregation in fact understood itself primarily as a clerical organization rather than as a Religious community, did not bring to the surface this confusion between Religious Life within which one might be ordained and the clerical life defined by ordination. Consequently, the celibacy issue often was not adequately dealt with prior to profession. Often enough ordination rather than profession was celebrated as the definitive rite of incorporation into the Religious order. Jubilees were dated from ordination. Furthermore, in clerical congregations only the ordained are canonically "first-class" members while Brothers, that is, members whose sole and primary identity is that of Religious, are virtually always inferiors juridically, professionally, ministerially, and unfortunately socially,[9] thereby locating the real source of identity and status in the community in ordination. All these factors combine to foster a primarily clerical rather than Religious identity in many, if not most, ordained Religious.

One result of this assimilation of the identity of ordained Religious to the clergy is that many clerical Religious have understood their celibacy as the mandatory singleness of the secular clergy rather than as the consecrated celibacy intrinsic to their vocation as Religious. Deep confusions have resulted, including a sense on the part of some Religious in clerical congregations (shared with a significant percentage of the clergy generally) that the celibacy they promise does not necessarily involve sexual abstinence but only nonmarriage and nonprocreation, neither of which is an issue in homosexual or in protected and uncommitted heterosexual sex. I will attend to this problem in some detail in volume 2 in the section on consecrated celibacy as a charism. The point here is that the widespread confusion about sexuality and celibacy among male clerical Religious, who are no longer behaviorally restrained to the same degree by the official negativity toward sexuality and marriage of the preconciliar Church, has had a very damaging effect on the perception of Religious in general. The publicity surrounding the abuses in this area, which are not new but only beginning to be exposed, has tainted not only ordained ministry in the Church but all celibate vocations.

Finally, the conciliar affirmation of the sacredness of sexuality and the dignity of marriage has erased one fallacious but very powerful source of vocational identity for Religious, namely, the conviction of having chosen, or been called to, a superior form of life in the Church, the "life of perfection" or a "higher vocation."[10] Since the Council of Trent Religious Life has been defined as intrinsically superior to marriage as a state of life.[11] The specific and primary source of the superiority was consecrated celibacy "for the sake of the Kingdom." There is no doubt that this sense of superiority based on celibacy played an important role, for many, in both the choice of and perseverance in Religious Life. Thus, many in the postconciliar period began to ask, why undertake and live with the burdens and restrictions of Religious Life if it is not a better choice, spiritually, than marriage?

Combined with the reaffirmation of the dignity and mission of the laity, this undermining of the ideology of sexually based superiority has left Religious in an ambiguous ecclesiastical position. In relation to the hierarchical structure of the Church

Religious are sociologically (though not canonically) quasi-clergy but without the rights or powers of the ordained. At the same time, although actually canonically lay, they do not enjoy the rights or freedoms of the rest of the laity. They are expected, like clergy, to represent and enforce official Church policy as agents of the institution and to abstain, like clergy, from activities, such as political involvement, considered proper to lay Catholics; but, like laity, they cannot preside at sacraments, preach, or exercise the jurisdiction deriving from Orders and are subject to the same kind of clerical control in regard to ministry and sacramental life as the rest of the laity. Canonically, Religious are either clergy or laity but in the case of women Religious who are lay, they are bound by the restrictions of both and enjoy the privileges of neither.

Religious are sometimes heard to ask, "What can I do ministerially as a Religious that I could not do equally well as a (secular) layperson?" If Religious do not see and experience their baptismally rooted ministry as constitutively shaped and specified by Religious profession and the specific charism of their congregation, the answer is clearly, "nothing." And that leads easily to a desire to "find oneself" as either ordained or lay. Some Religious desire ordination in order to do integrally what they must do in truncated fashion at the present time. They reconcile and heal, counsel, prepare people for the sacraments, comfort the dying, and serve as chaplains in institutions but are always obliged to stop just short of liturgically consummating the sacramental processes they have facilitated.

Other Religious have no interest in the aspects of ministry associated with ordination but would like to be recognized as truly lay ministers, undistinguished by special responsibility or obligation from other lay ministers and entitled to the same (admittedly minimal) provisions. In other words, while some Religious want admission to the ranks of the clergy, others would like to claim full identity and solidarity with the laity. The first is not canonically possible at the present time (and, I will argue shortly, is probably not desirable even if it were possible). The second does not work, even when both laity and Religious desire it, because Religious Life as a lifeform cannot be fully assimilated to secular lay life without losing its identity. In short, if the Church was once divided into celibate and noncelibate, it is now largely divided into clergy and lay. Religious had a clear place in the first division. They do not seem to in the second.

Finally, being neither male, lay (in the state of life sense), nor secular places women Religious largely outside the sphere of new ministerial developments. Lay men can be ordained as deacons and installed as lectors and acolytes but women Religious, because they are women, cannot be. Lay men and women are being called to take up decision-making roles on parish and diocesan councils, presumably because of the secular skills and connections demanded by these positions, but in general Religious, precisely because they are not laity in this sense, are not. The secular laity are being urged to assume their roles in the secular arena, in politics, economics, and social justice activism, but Religious, because they are not seculars, are discouraged from participating in such activities or even forbidden to do so. Women Religious, in short, often find themselves relegated to taking up the slack, without the attendant power or privileges, in clerical ranks decimated by declining enlistment and accelerating resignations.

To summarize this very complex situation, which is rendered more confusing by the fact that most of the factors in it are either unrecognized or not admitted into open conversation, the preconciliar Church was, sociologically, basically a clergy-centered sexual power structure. Religious had a fairly clearly defined place in this structure. They were more like clergy than like laity in that they had more authority and power than laypeople, and this was intimately related to the fact that they were celibate. The postconciliar Church is not yet laity centered, but the tension lies now between the clerical and the lay poles, with power deriving from ordination. Religious no longer benefit sociologically from their freely chosen celibacy, and they cannot claim either clerical or lay legitimation for their ministries. But the increasing parochialization of their ministries has also obscured the real source of identity and legitimation, namely, profession and congregational charism. This situation is confusing and painful. However, it is potentially purifying and clarifying. There is an urgency now to the question of the meaning of ministry in Religious Life and of Religious Life itself in the Church that requires sustained attention. Everyone stands to benefit from the clarity and coherence that such attention can generate but no one more than Religious themselves.

III. Contemporary Issues Generated by the Placement of Religious in the Church

I want now to take up three issues, flowing from the confusion just described, which are intensely actual: the prophetic vocation of Religious Life in a hierarchical institution; the issue of canonical status of Religious Institutes; and the "theoretical" question of the ordination of women Religious. Even discussing these issues generates enormous tension. Widespread movements among laity in the Church (the institutional class to which Religious belong) for the reform of the power structure is viewed with deep suspicion and often met with outright condemnation by Church authorities. The depth of feeling in Religious communities over the issue of canonical status distorts communication on the subject. And although the issue of women's ordination has been declared definitively closed by the Vatican (which has even attempted to invest this decision with an aura of infallibility) the discussion continues unabated.[12] However, even if one considers such discussion purely theoretical speculation about an impossibility, it raises major, highly polarizing questions about the identity and mission of Religious.

A. The Prophetic Vocation of Religious in a Reforming Church

Religious have a double relationship, both prophetic and canonical, within and to the hierarchical Church, which has, historically, always involved them in a certain tension.[13] First, as an essentially prophetic vocation and state of life in the Church, Religious Life should constitute a continual call from within the Church to ongoing reform and increasing fidelity to the Gospel. The way in which any individual Religious lives out the prophetic dimension of the life requires careful discernment, both personal and communal. But there is no question that from its beginnings as a movement Religious Life itself has been a kind of "loyal opposition" in the Church as the Old Testament prophetic movement was in relation to ancient Israel's monarchy and as Jesus was in relation to the hierarchical structures of Judaism.

Fidelity to this aspect of their vocation has been one of the most difficult experiences in the life of Religious congregations for several reasons. Religious rightly see themselves as particularly committed to the Church itself by the very fact of their total involvement in the religious dimension of human life within the Christian tradition. Deep, active love of the Church is intrinsic to Religious Life. And Religious Life has always (at least in theory) been held in particular esteem by the institutional Church. This mutual love and esteem makes it very difficult to exercise a critical function. It is much easier for Religious to criticize the evils of secular society (and the official Church has always tried to focus the prophetic activity of Religious outside the Church itself) than to protest hypocrisy, injustice, and infidelity within the Church. But the fact is that prophecy is, first and foremost, a vocation in and for and to the community of faith. The primary locus and addressee of the prophets, both those in the Old Testament and Jesus himself, was the community and institution of Israel. This is the challenging tradition in which Religious Life stands.

The second factor producing tension for Religious is that because Religious, although lay in the hierarchical structure of the Church, are a specific canonical entity, the ecclesiastical institution has considerably more leverage in regard to Religious than it does in relation to other laity. Religious can be located through their congregations; their superiors can be pressured by ecclesiastical authority to discipline or even expel them; they often minister in ecclesiastical institutions, which can be enlisted against them; they are vulnerable to ecclesiastical penalties that can be life-destroying.

Both of these factors, the prophetic character of Religious Life and its special canonical situation, make the active participation of Religious in the lay agenda of the contemporary Church both vitally important and more than a little personally painful and institutionally dangerous.

In regard to its hierarchical constitution, as has been said, the Church is a class society in which power and authority are concentrated in the hands of the upper class (the clergy) while the lower class (the laity) is in a disempowered position in regard to decision making and sacramental participation. The effort to convert the Church from a sexually based power structure into a community of equal disciples, that is, to help the Church become in truth the People of God rather than a divine-right monarchy modeled on the patriarchal Roman Empire, is a matter of increasing concern and active struggle by laity (and some clergy) throughout the world. Religious, who are lay in relation to the power structure, need to claim their solidarity with the oppressed in the Church and, in virtue of their prophetic vocation in the Church, exercise leadership in the effort for reform. Such a commitment involves resisting both the domestication and parochialization of Religious by assimilating them to the clergy and the repression of individuals and congregations through intimidation.

Most Religious congregations have yet to face this issue explicitly, preferring to handle each confrontation on an individual basis and to finesse it if possible without allowing the underlying issues of equality in the Church and the right to legitimate self-determination of Religious Life itself to emerge. Often they do not see these struggles as the expression of the prophetic vocation of Religious Life in the Church. Indeed many Religious see them as symptoms of rebellion or disobedience. If Religious are to offer active support or effective leadership in the struggle for a "Church with a human face"[14] they will have to achieve maturity and claim equality in their relationship with ecclesiastical authority. This is likely to call for uncommon courage on the part of leaders and members of congregations. Nevertheless, the movement for reform in the Church, especially in regard to the recognition of the rights of its members and the decentralization of power and authority, is becoming worldwide, and Religious have a particular responsibility to participate in calling the Church to fidelity to its foundational covenantal identity as the People of God.

In the concrete there are several implications of Religious' accepting solidarity with the secular laity in the struggle for equality in the Church. The effort for reform[15] should find Religious in support of a more democratic constitution for the Church, in which the rights of laity and lower clergy, including the right of respectful dissent, are enunciated and respected, due and open process in disputes is guaranteed, just redress of grievances is assured, moral and financial accountability of Church leaders is required, and laity have an appropriate role in the appointment of Church leaders and in decision making.[16] There is constant hierarchical pressure on Religious to see themselves as aligned primarily with the hierarchy in this struggle. Neither theologically nor juridically is this the case. Like Jesus who taught both respect for ecclesiastical leaders insofar as they legitimately hold office and resistance to ecclesiastical oppression, Religious must stand with and for the disempowered in the Church (cf. Mt 23:2–5). The problem is not that Religious have failed to take this position but they often do so with a deep sense of split loyalties or even guilt. The challenge is to recognize the theological and vocational integrity of this position. (Again, the parochialization of Religious' ministries, which tends to assimilate them to the clergy, places them in a very ambivalent and ambiguous position in relation to their prophetic vocation.) Prophetic challenge arises from love of the ecclesial community, not from rebellion, pride, or disobedience. But prophets have never been welcome in their own country (cf. Mt 13:57 and parallels).

A second implication has to do with gender. In the Church as in society in general women are doubly oppressed. Women Religious, both because they are lay and because they are women, have a legitimate stake in all the issues in the Church which weigh particularly heavily on women who have no effective voice in the decisions that disproportionately affect them. Issues of sexual morality within and outside of marriage, divorce and remarriage, and optional marriage for the clergy, even though they are not personal issues for women Religious themselves, become their issues in virtue of their solidarity with women. Clerical abuse of women and children, institutional attitudes and pastoral practice in regard to spouse and child abuse in the family and society, official Church positions and action on political issues such as equal rights for women, rape laws, and abortion policies are the legitimate focus of the concern of Religious who are women (and also of men, of course). In other words, solidarity with women in the Church on issues of equality and justice for women is part of what it means to claim lay status in a hierarchical society that is structured, in many respects, by inequality and oppression based on gender.

Finally, Religious have to recognize that in some respects we have been the most favored members of the Church's lowest class. Our sociological assimilation to the lower clergy in times past has given us a certain leverage in the Church, a good deal of experience in dealing with the institutional aspects of Catholicism, and many influential contacts in high places. Furthermore, we enjoy an institutional base and corporate strength that most of the laity, male or female, do not. Consequently, we have a particular capacity and responsibility for the empowerment of our lay colleagues. It can be difficult to keep our efforts at empowerment from becoming patronizing or, worse yet, manipulative, but the disparity between the institutional power of Religious and that of much of the rest of the laity is real, and true solidarity is not served by disingenuously denying our advantage but by sharing it.

In order to claim and live genuine solidarity with the laity in the prophetic struggle for a just and egalitarian Church, Religious need to ask, corporately, some painful and difficult questions. What do we really believe about the nature of the Church of Jesus Christ, about the kind of society and community it is called to be? Who do we think should participate in setting policy in the Church and how should such policy be set and implemented? Who is called to ministry in the Church and how should that be decided, coordinated, and recognized? What is the theological and practical relevance of feminist consciousness for the members of a patriarchal, male-dominated, and resolutely sexist Church? These are not the questions of a radical fringe but the agenda of a truly prophetic Religious Life in a postconciliar Church. If Religious are to act coherently out of a shared basis of conviction about the kind of Church we are called to become, there is probably no alternative to facing these potentially incendiary issues. In regard to the hierarchical constitution of the Church, however, Religious are not only de jure but de facto lay, and it is here that Religious need to claim solidarity with all the laity in the Church. Religious Life is also canonically a specific lifeform called to prophetic engagement in the Church. Both as lay and as prophetic, Religious must refuse to allow themselves to be co-opted into the hierarchical agenda by pseudo-clerical rewards or silenced by fear and self-protection.

B. Canonical Status

As was said above, Religious constitute a canonical category of persons distinct from clergy on the one hand and laity on the other.[17] *Lumen Gentium* (Dogmatic Constitution on the Church) and Canon Law explain that Religious are people drawn from either the lay or the clerical condition who make profession of the evangelical counsels.[18] In fact, this description is rhetorically and juridically clear but, insofar as it suggests that Religious continue to be primarily characterized, ecclesially, by their clerical or lay condition, it does not really describe very well the facts of lived experience. When laypersons become Religious they enter a lifeform and undertake a lifestyle that distinguishes them in very significant ways from the secular laity. The basic differences between the Religious Life as a lifeform and secular lay life, especially that of the married, are too pronounced to be considered purely peripheral or accidental. The fact that Religious Life requires specific canonical provisions makes this clear.

Furthermore, Religious are not really "drawn from the clergy" either. Most male Religious who are ordained entered Religious congregations as lay men, became professed Religious, and several years later were ordained. With ordination many of them adopt the lifestyle, dress, titles, ministries, and living situations of the clergy. For all intents and purposes their clerical identity has existential priority over the Religious life-form. In other words, it is often the clerical condition that draws members from the laity and from Religious Life, not the other way around, and once ordained such people are no longer, in fact, lay and often remain only nominally Religious. But, in any case, the general and particular provisions in Canon Law for Religious mark the vocation off quite clearly from the secular lay vocation and should mark it off from the clerical.

Religious, therefore, constitute a canonical category, that is, a distinct group of persons in the Church for whom there are specific provisions in Canon Law, including rights and duties not shared with other categories of people. This is what is actually meant by their "canonical status." Secular laity and secular clergy as well as consecrated virgins living outside Religious institutes, hermits, and members of various associations also have canonical status in this sense. In fact, everyone in the Church has canonical status if they are Catholics in good standing. One can change canonical status, from clergy to lay, for instance, or Religious to secular, or lay to Religious, but one does not simply "lose" canonical status except by ceasing to fall under Canon Law—by ceasing to be a Catholic. However, in practice, when Religious refer to their "canonical status" they mean their approbation by the Vatican as a canonically approved Religious Institute. When they speak of losing or giving up canonical status they mean not having their constitutions approved by the Vatican and thus not being officially recognized as a Religious Institute. In other words, they mean losing the particular canonical status of Religious and becoming canonically secular laity.[19]

Official ecclesiastical approval as Religious has been an arena of struggle in virtually every era of the Church's history. Whenever a new form of Religious Life emerged (e.g., mendicant orders like the male and female Franciscans in the Middle Ages or apostolic orders like the Jesuits and the Ursulines in the post-Reformation period), there was a period of time during which the official Church refused canonical recognition to the new groups. It maintained that the new form was not truly

Religious Life because it lacked one or more essential element of the Life such as stable dwelling or choral recitation of the Office or cloister, or because it involved elements deemed incompatible with true Religious Life such as an active apostolate outside the Religious house on the part of women. Women's apostolic congregations in which the members were not under papal enclosure were not formally recognized as Religious Institutes until 1900.[20] This means that many of the orders of women now active in the United States, mostly groups founded in the nineteenth century for such apostolic purposes as teaching, nursing, and social work, did not have Religious "canonical status" for the first several decades, and in some cases for several centuries, of their existence.[21]

The originality of the current version of the issue is not a question of a group that has not yet received official approval trying to obtain it, but of the possibility of a group that has had such approval losing it either by voluntarily surrendering it or having it withdrawn by ecclesiastical authority. This became a more than theoretical issue in the late 1960s when Cardinal Francis McIntyre forced a major part of an established congregation, the Sisters, Servants of the Immaculate Heart of Mary of Los Angeles, to accept dispensation from their Religious vows (and thus loss of canonical status as Religious) because he did not agree with their adaptations following Vatican II.

After the mandated renewal chapters that followed Vatican II most congregations revised their constitutions. When these documents were sent to the Vatican for approval many congregations found themselves forced, under penalty of nonapproval, to change significant portions of their new documents in ways that falsified their actual lived experience or to write into their constitutions provisions that did not reflect their experience or common convictions and which they knew could not be implemented. The alternative to accepting these distortions appeared to be the loss of canonical approval as a Religious Institute, a sanction so severe and so potentially divisive that virtually no congregations have been willing to risk it.

Discussion of the issue of canonical status tends to be avoided, indeed suppressed, in most congregations because of the tremendous anxiety that it generates. At times there seems to be an almost "taboo" fear that if the question is even raised the community will be polarized to the point of destruction. Nevertheless, not discussing an important issue that might well necessitate a real decision in the not-too-distant future is dangerous. Good decisions are seldom made in the midst of crisis. Not knowing what the range of consensus is among their members makes a congregation vulnerable to the "surprise attack" technique sometimes used to catch individuals and groups in no-win situations by suddenly confronting them with two equally unacceptable alternatives as the only possibilities, demanding an immediate choice, and then claiming that the choice was freely made and that the individual or group is bound by the resulting bad decision.[22] Without doubt, there are major real advantages to canonical approbation. There are also distinct liabilities involved in maintaining it. Open discussion of both can help congregations overcome irrational fear as well as reckless temerity.

Canonical status as Religious gives a congregation a certain recognizable identity in the institutional Church, which can be very useful in ministry.[23] It constitutes a kind of ecclesiastical "licensing" which is helpful to the members and also to local Church personnel and the people to whom the members minister. Canonical approbation also creates a certain commonness of structure and operation among Religious Institutes that facilitates organization among Institutes and collective action as well as mutual exchange and cooperation. The Leadership Conference of Women Religious, for example, can make use of such common structures, processes, and assumptions to enable congregations to work together on a wide variety of projects. Canonical status, regulated by Canon Law and other Church documents, fosters smoother juridical handling of some intraecclesial relations, for example, between a congregation and the local Ordinary in relation to property or ministry or between leaders of diverse congregations in regard to the transfer of members. Canonical regulation also provides certain protections for members against intracommunity abuses of authority and creates an external court of appeal should one become necessary. Canonical status, by establishing Religious in a publicly recognized position in the Church, demands accountability of the congregation and its members for the faithful and responsible living of professed life in the Church, and this is an important support for fidelity. The official relationship with the institutional Church helps keep Religious aware of their rootedness in their ecclesial identity and can provide a salutary critical challenge as a prophetic group negotiates new spiritual and ministerial territory.

While this list of advantages is not necessarily exhaustive it should suffice to make the point that canonical status is not a mere institutional decoration nor something to be lightly foregone. However, two points need to be made. First, canonical approbation, while necessary for a congregation to be called a Religious Institute in the official and canonical sense of the word, is not necessary for Religious Life in its theological and spiritual sense to exist. As just mentioned, many communities lived Religious Life fully and integrally for decades or even centuries without canonical approbation, and neither their members, the Church authorities with whom they worked, nor the people they served had any doubt whatever that they were bona fide Religious.[24] There are some "noncanonical" communities today that have never sought Vatican approbation and have no intention of doing so until relations between Religious and the Vatican are more mutual and egalitarian or certain canonical requirements are abrogated (such as the ban on male-female communities). They are stable, effective communities attracting new members and serving the Church well.[25] Theologically, they are Religious even though canonically they are not.

In other words, the fear of some Religious that loss of canonical status would deprive them of their identity as "women of the Church" and as true Religious is not necessarily well founded. Approval by the Vatican does not constitute Religious Life; it recognizes what exists and incorporates it into the Church's institutional organization.[26] The refusal of the Vatican to recognize a community may be unfortunate but it is not necessarily tragic. Just as the institutional authorities of the Church have condemned brilliant scientists and theologians, locked up important books, burned saints at the stake, imprisoned mystics, excommunicated founders, and suppressed orders (many later rehabilitated because of the manifest error and injustice involved in the condemnations), so that authority may just as mistakenly refuse canonical approbation to a prophetic community that is living Religious Life with courage and integrity today. Part of spiritual (and psychological) maturity is the ability to do what is right without approval from authority and even despite its condemnation if that becomes necessary, even though no one in their right mind would seek to precipitate such a situation.

Second, if an individual or group is so attached to or dependent on anything—financial security, reputation, property, particular institutions or ministries, official approbation, or even life itself—that they cannot consider surrendering it under any circumstances or for any reason, that individual or group has sold its soul. It is a hostage to the power that controls the nonnegotiable possession and can be made to do anything, however contrary to its truth and integrity, in order to preserve that possession. This was horrendously verified by the acquiescence of most of the state Church in Germany during the Nazi period. If a Religious congregation cannot contemplate surrendering its canonical status, even if the alternative is loss of corporate integrity, it has already lost its integrity. Neither as individuals nor as groups, especially in view of the prophetic vocation of Religious Life in the Church, can congregations afford to allow themselves to be held hostage to nonnegotiable possessions no matter how valuable they may be. In this we must follow Jesus, who refused to surrender his mission from God to either the ecclesiastical or the civil authorities who tried to control him. But we must also realistically recognize the price he paid for this fidelity.

The disadvantages of canonical status are also becoming clearer to those who dare consider the possibility of its loss. Serious interference in and even suspension of the legitimate right to self-determination of a congregation is not a purely theoretical danger. Interference in the ministries that congregations have chosen after serious corporate discernment, forced distortion of constitutions, suppression of the prophetic witness of individual Religious and whole communities, the co-opting of Religious to serve institutional agendas that are not appropriate to the congregation's corporately discerned call, intimidation and even forced expulsion of members who have acted with the full knowledge and approval of legitimate community authority and according to the charism of their congregation are some of the abuses of power that have been visited on Religious congregations not only in the past but in recent history. They are all based on an appeal to the submission to ecclesiastical authority demanded of canonical institutes.

Such abuses are not integral to, or necessarily consequent upon, canonical status, but it is canonical status that opens the community to them. However, the question some Religious congregations are beginning to raise is whether the price of canonical approbation, at least at this moment in history, is too high; whether Religious are becoming "kept women" in a patriarchal and paternalistic household that shows no real signs of developing toward equality and mutuality. No one denies the seriousness of the question. It has been compared to that asked by many battered women for whom leaving the abusive relationship means risking poverty and degradation for themselves and their children, while staying involves a continuation of the abuse, perhaps even death. And like many such women who really love the man they married who is somewhere inside the batterer, Religious love the real Church, which they continue to hope will someday emerge from its patriarchal incarnation as a true community of equal disciples.

A further consideration is that loss of canonical status as Religious, besides entailing the loss of the advantages discussed above, could also have serious financial implications for a congregation since the property of a Religious congregation is, legally, ecclesiastical property. In a legal contest over property, in the United States, a conflict between Church law and civil law would almost certainly be resolved in favor of the former. It would also mean that the external structural supports for the theological state of life would have to be assumed by the community itself, and this would put an enormous burden on the interior commitment and will to union of the group. On the other hand, retaining canonical status at the price of loss of legitimate self-determination and fidelity to congregational identity and corporate experience could destroy Religious Life as a theological and spiritual reality and replace it with a juridical shell housing an intimidated and dependent ecclesiastical job corps.

No one I know of wants this issue to become real and immediate for their own congregation. But some calm discussion of the two sides of the issue, not as advocacy for either but in terms of what each involves, can help both to "desensitize" members to irrational terror and to decide how far they are willing to go to preserve a very desirable but finally not all-important feature of their present ecclesiastical situation. Every congregation confronted with this issue will have to take into account all the particular factors that determine its own situation such as resources, personnel, ministries, timing, unity, and so on. Certainly no one can decide for or can legitimately judge the decision of a group other than its own. We can all hope that the ultimate decision will not be forced upon us, that some path to mutuality between women's Religious congregations and ecclesiastical authorities can be found or made. But I continue to believe that simply denying the question is a dangerous choice. There is great strength in achieving the interior freedom to do what has to be done, even if what we most dread never actually confronts us. Fear makes us ultimately vulnerable to domination while interior freedom makes us strong enough to face whatever needs to be faced without either temerity or cowardice.

C. Religious and Ordination

Because, as already noted, the Vatican has declared the issue of the ordination of women closed in the negative I want to be clear about what I am and am not discussing and why. First, the issue of women's ordination has been a topic of lively discussion and considerable activism for the past thirty years. Most mainline Catholic theologians have come to think that it is theologically possible and pastorally desirable in at least some cultural settings, and their arguments are in the public forum even if they are now forbidden to repeat or promote them. Furthermore, acceptance of the ordination of women has attained a majority position among virtually every category of the faithful in many countries, including North America.[27] This decades-long development has raised issues for women Religious related to but well beyond ordination itself, which remain to be addressed even if the ordination of women never occurs.

Second, it is an historical fact that many Vatican positions held just as strongly and taught just as authoritatively as the prohibition of women's ordination have been reversed (in both directions) in succeeding papal reigns.[28] Since the majority of currently active Religious will surely outlive the current pope and curia it is entirely possible that this issue will again become a matter of active concern for Religious congregations even if no one were discussing it in the interim (which, of course, is not the case). As with the issue of canonical status, discussion of the issue before it becomes critical is highly preferable to ignoring it until decisions must be made in emergency situations that militate against calm discernment.

In what follows I am not discussing the possibility of ordaining women but the purely hypothetical question of whether, if ordination of women were possible (which is officially denied), it would be desirable for individual Religious or their congregations for some women Religious to be ordained. If this question had always been purely hypothetical it would not have raised the issues I want to discuss; but since it has been a very real question for three decades it has brought to the surface issues that remain important even in the context of repression of the ordination question itself. It is also important to state clearly that if, as I will argue, the ordination of women Religious is not desirable it does not follow that the ordination of other women, if such ever became a possibility, is not desirable nor that women Religious should not, in such a case, stand in solidarity with women seeking ordained ministry.

1. Why the question of ordination became important for women Religious and the effects of that development: Women Religious prior to the Council seldom raised the question of ordination in regard to themselves or other women because it was a fore-gone conclusion that it was simply not and never would be a possibility. However, the conciliar developments in the areas of ecclesiology and ministry, especially in regard to the equal-ity of women in the Church, combined with developments in feminist thought and practice inside and outside the ecclesias-tical sphere to make the question very actual among women Religious who were early and persistent participants in the Women's Ordination Conference.[29] Furthermore, women Religious were not only involved in many ministries which, if exercised by men, would surely have implied ordination, but also the theological and professional training of these women would have made them ideal candidates for it.

Increasingly, as the numbers of ordained ministers declined drastically in the 1960s and 1970s and women Religious took up much of the slack in parochial ministry, ordination of these women seemed to some not only desirable but actually neces-sary if the Church was to continue to be a eucharistic and min-istering community. Religious within their own congregations began to experience the dearth of acceptable ordained minis-ters for the nurture of their own community life as a severe hardship and to see the ordination of some of their own mem-bers as a possible solution.

It can hardly be doubted that feminism as it was deeply inte-riorized by many Religious led to an analysis of the refusal to ordain qualified women who experienced themselves called to such ministry as a matter of injustice. Whether or not individ-ual Religious desired ordination for themselves they felt per-sonally the oppression and marginalization of women that exclusion from full and equal participation in the sacramental life of the Church and its attendant exclusion from many areas of jurisdiction represented and effected.

Gradually, as they struggled for ministerial equality of women and reappropriated the intrinsically ministerial charac-ter of their vocation as apostolic rather than cloistered Reli-gious,[30] some came to realize that there was an unaddressed, if not repressed, question at the very origin of their own choice of Religious Life. If ordination had been open to these women at the time they entered they would have chosen it, either in combination with or instead of Religious Life. As it was, Religious Life represented for them the "poor person's version" of official ministry, as close as a woman could get to the altar. The impossibility of ordination kept them from addressing, in their vocational discernment, whether Religious Life itself, which has no intrinsic relationship to ordained ministry, was really their call or was simply, in their case, a substitute for the unattainable.

In fact, only 2 percent of the respondents to the 1994 *Los Angeles Times* survey of nuns said that, if ordination were possible, they would definitely seek it for themselves, and only 15 percent of so-called liberal and 5 percent of so-called conservative Religious would probably or definitely seek it.[31] This is a very small contingent. Nevertheless, if ordination were possible it could pose agonizing problems for congregations because ordaining any of its members, as we will see below, would fundamentally change the character of the congregation, thereby affecting the life of every member and not just that of those ordained. But refusing ordination to those who feel, and perhaps always felt, called to ordained ministry and who entered and stayed in order to come as close to that calling as possible could place such Religious in the dilemma of following their vocation to ordination at the cost of leaving the community in which they have made their home for decades or remaining in the community at the cost of not following their true calling that has finally become possible. The truly radical, and often agonizing, choice of some Religious who have left their communities to be ordained in other denominations makes clear how acute this dilemma can be. It is precisely because such a hypothetical dilemma could someday become a reality that Religious need to reflect on it while it is still hypothetical.

But even as hypothetical the issue has important practical ramifications. For some Religious the coming to the surface of the fact that their true vocation is and always has been to ordained ministry rather than to Religious Life has precipitated a vocational crisis. It is far too facile to say that in such a case the woman should simply leave. Years of participation in a community has forged relationships that cannot be simply changed or abrogated on the basis of logic, and the investment of these women in the development of their congregations and its ministries is often intense. On the other hand, especially in the area of celibacy, continuing to honor obligations that one finally realizes do not flow integrally from one's deepest vocation can become extremely burdensome. I have no solution for this dilemma, but it may be of some help to those for whom the issue is personal and real to have it at least recognized and named so that it can be discussed in a context of respect and compassion.

This situation should also alert formation personnel and major superiors responsible for the admission of candidates to the necessity to address the ordination issue directly and in depth before entrance and during the process toward profession. It is now possible to raise explicitly the question of whether a potential candidate feels called to Religious Life (including its ministerial dimension) or simply to ministry, ordained or lay. If she feels called not to Religious Life as such but to ministry, ordained or not, her best option at the moment is probably lay ministry, which leaves her free of the obligations of Religious Life (to which she does not feel called) and also open to ordination (should it ever become a possibility) without facing the dilemma described in the last paragraph. Furthermore, the possibility of nonvowed association with a Religious community can, today, offer a woman the advantage of those elements of Religious Life that she truly desires, such as community in mission and ministry, opportunities in the area of spirituality, and meaningful liturgical life without obliging her to aspects of the Life to which she does not feel called, such as celibacy, complete economic interdependence, or communal discernment of life and ministry.

2. *The case against the ordination of women Religious:* At the height of optimism about the opening of ordination to women many Religious saw the ordination of some members of their congregation as a natural and desirable development. Many are now taking a second look at this assumption, and in my opinion, rightly so. The split in the Women's Ordination

Conference over whether any women should seek ordination given what some perceive as the fundamentally dysfunctional character of the present clerical system[32] is not my topic here. I would raise the questions I am raising here even if the present theology of ordination were much more adequate and the present clerical culture much healthier. The question has to do with the compatibility of ordained ministry and Religious Life and the desirability of combining them.

Women Religious are in an enviable position in regard to this question because, since no women Religious have ever been ordained,[33] women's Religious Life represents a kind of "pure case." Most clerical Religious embraced the two vocations together in a context in which the combination so affected both vocations that any sorting out of the issues was at the time, and probably remains, extremely difficult. And those trying to discuss it theoretically today have invested their lives in the combination, which makes a radical questioning difficult though not impossible.[34] Brothers, who have chosen to be Religious rather than ordained, are deeply affected by the continual need to justify, at least to others if not to themselves, what seems to be their choice not to "go all the way" to ordination, which is open to them as men.[35] The Brothers' vocation has never been well understood in the Church, which strongly suggests that women's Religious Life has been understood (erroneously) by many as "the closest women could come" to ordination.[36]

In what follows I will raise four points that I think strongly suggest that women Religious should not go the clerical route, even if it were open to them. This discussion is theoretical in regard to ordination itself since this discussion, according to the Vatican, is closed. But the realizations that the discussion can engender about the nature of Religious Life itself are not at all hypothetical or insignificant.

First, ordination introduces into Religious Life a fundamental tension, if not contradiction, between an intrinsically hierarchical vocation and a prophetic one. While there is not, or at least should not be, an intrinsic contradiction between the institutional and charismatic dimensions of the Church itself, it may well be that one person, one congregation, or one life-form can hardly live both integrally when each of the two must embody and even implement aspects of the Church's life that are often in actual conflict with the other. It is the basic task of the ordained to serve and preserve the Church as institution, to present its present teaching and implement its current policy in obedience to its actual office holders, for the sake of the community and in the service of its members. This is a very important role and ministry in the Church. It need not, indeed must not, mean subservience to oppressive authority or ruthless preference of institution over persons. But it is an institutional ministry within an essentially hierarchical structure of authority and power.

Religious Life, as Vatican II reminded the Church, does not belong to the hierarchical structure of the Church. It is not an institutional vocation but a prophetic one. I discussed the constitutively prophetic character of the vocation in chapter 4 and will discuss it in greater detail in chapter 10. But let us recall that prophecy involves solidarity with the poor and oppressed, reading from that marginalized perspective the signs of the time, and lovingly but courageously speaking truth to power in the cause of liberation for holiness. The primary, although not exclusive, addressee of prophecy is the Church itself, including and even especially its institutional embodiment.

Prophecy has always been primarily a championing of the rights of the oppressed and marginalized. As institution the Church itself is a society of "haves" and "have nots," of people in power and those devoid of power, of those whose voices control the agenda and those whose voices are silenced. The agents of the institution necessarily belong to the class of the "haves" (which need not and should not mean that they do not identify with the "have nots"), and it can be difficult if not impossible for them to stand fully with the poor of the Church. Indeed, given that their ministry is to all in the Church, it may be that they should not do so because the resulting unavoidable conflict may undermine their ministry of unity. We have seen this repeatedly in the postconciliar period when committed pastors have tried to open ministry officially reserved to the ordained to laity in general or women in particular, to go beyond ecumenical attitudes to more inclusive sacramental hospitality to non-Catholics, or to express sacramentally the compassion of the Gospel toward institutionally marginalized people such as the divorced and remarried or sexually committed homosexuals.[37] As they have struggled to include and empower the marginalized they have alienated the "loyal members" sincerely convinced that only in obedience to current Church teaching and practice can the Gospel be lived and preached. While all members of the Church are called to promote the unity of the body it is not the vocation of Religious (even though it may well be of the ordained) to do so by insuring or enforcing institutional conformity, and it may well be that in some situations it is their prophetic duty to raise questions, suggest alternatives, and stand in solidarity with the outcast as the Church struggles toward a deeper unity than what now seems possible.

Reading the signs of the time, especially from the institutional margins, involves an intuitive vision not simply of what is already established but of what the Reign of God calls for, what it is time for, even when that involves the subversion of the institutional status quo. Just as the Church as institution requires agents who will preserve and implement the current arrangements for the good of the people, so the Church as People of God needs to be called beyond what is currently understood into the desert journey that leads toward the Reign of God. The "desert," in senses metaphorical and literal, is the natural habitat of Religious whose investment in the Reign of God is not equated with or reducible to investment in the institution.

Prophecy also involves the very dangerous necessity of speaking the truth in situations of repression or denial within the institution. Again, it may not be possible or desirable for the person charged with the pastoral care of the parish congregation as a whole and its relation to the wider institutional Church to explicitly and publicly take on official persons or positions with which he might seriously disagree in private. But one way that the development of doctrine and the evolution of moral practice is fostered in the Church is through the respectful, reasoned, but unflinching dissent of those not charged with the care of the community as a whole but with contemplative living of the questions and the expression of prophetic insight.

None of the above is meant to suggest that the ordained are not called to soul-searching integrity in the performance of their ministry. Nor, even less, does it suggest that Religious are or should be the only prophetic voices in the Church or that they should be in a continuous state of confrontation with Church authority. But Religious Life itself as a corporate entity in the Church which is not an agent of the institutional aspect of the Church has a particular capacity to communally discuss and discern, to study and probe, to respectfully but persistently confront, to experiment with alternatives in the relative security from rashness that is supplied by a community of criticism, and even to courageously accept the painful consequences of being "ahead of one's time" in pushing forward issues that have not yet matured. Furthermore, as Thomas Merton so well saw, especially toward the end of his life, the essentially contemplative character of Religious Life makes it a vocation to live the questions of our time in their deepest ambiguity and urgency on a kind of "full-time basis" that is not alleviated or relativized by other primary commitments to family or profession. Only out of such contemplative participation in the depth dimensions of the questions confronting our world and Church can responses emerge that are genuinely prophetic.

Ordained Religious, especially those (increasingly numerous) who are involved full time in parochial ministry which integrates them almost completely into the diocesan structures and procedures, often experience the effective muffling of the prophetic dimension of their Religious vocation for their own sake and that of the communities they lead. Some compensate by turning that dimension exclusively toward the problems of secular society and avoiding engagement with any intra-ecclesial issues that could bring canonical sanctions. The ordained Religious who is willing to go to jail to protest nuclear proliferation may, however regretfully, use sexist official liturgical texts and refuse the sacraments to "sinners" to avoid ecclesiastical "trouble," but such dichotomizing opens his prophetic witness in the secular order to question from the standpoint of the oppressed in the Church. Clerical congregations face the continual possibility of such sanctions as suspension of faculties of their members, often essential to the ministries they have undertaken, if they challenge local or higher institutional authority.

The question I raise here is whether women Religious, either as individuals called to participate in the prophetic vocation of Religious Life, or congregations which incarnate that vocation in the Church, should willingly precipitate these tensions between institutional and prophetic ministry in their own lives. At the very least they need to look closely at the experience of clerical congregations and the long history of subversion of the prophetic for the sake of survival in the clerical structure before following that path. There may not be an intrinsic theological incompatibility between the two vocations, but there is a serious question about whether, in practice, a particular individual or congregation in the present moment of Church history can live both of them integrally at the same time.

Second, history also clearly witnesses to the effect on Religious community of the class structure introduced by the ordination of some members. Although strenuous and admirable efforts have been made since the Council by male clerical orders to dismantle the class structure in which ordained members are "first class" and other professed are "second class," it remains the case that ordination is the principle of class in the Church and therefore in clerical Religious congregations.[38] It is enlightening to realize that while the Council strongly encouraged women Religious to abolish class distinctions among their members,[39] the attempt of men in clerical orders to effect a similar equalization between ordained and lay members has met with strong resistance.[40] This expresses well the ideological conflict in the Church that maintains that there is no real inequality among the baptized, whether secular or Religious, but that there is some kind of intrinsic and ontological superiority associated with ordination, and it must not be obscured by role reversals in authority or power. In practice, even in clerical orders that have taken an official stand in favor of equality (even if the Vatican does not allow it to be implemented), it is still difficult for many male Religious to accept the idea that a lay Religious could exercise authority over an ordained, regardless of whether the former is holier, better educated, more psychologically well developed, more pastorally sensitive, or more gifted in leadership, which are the real qualifications for leadership in a Religious congregation. And the Vatican definitely prefers both that there be ordained members in male orders and that they be in the positions of authority.

Although there is enough ambiguity in Canon Law about what exactly makes a clerical Institute clerical[41] and a recognition that some Institutes are genuinely "mixed" (admitting ordained and lay members as equals)[42] that a traditionally nonclerical institute such as a women's congregation might be able to avoid being designated clerical even if some of its members were ordained, it is not at all certain that it would be able to retain its nonclerical status. The Vatican has a vested interest, for reasons of control, in Religious Institutes being clerical, and there is no necessity that a majority of the members be ordained for the Institute itself to be declared clerical.

In a clerical Institute there is no question about the preeminence of the ordained over the nonordained. In recent years some clerical Institutes have obtained the right to vote for their nonordained members and even the privilege, with appropriate indults of exception, for them to serve as local superiors, councilors, or vicars. But the fact of class distinction within an order or congregation in which some members are ordained is undeniable, and in the present state of the theology of ordination it is hardly conceivable that such a group could maintain the equality of its membership. The fact that only certain members of the community would always lead it in liturgy and would be the only lawful liturgical preachers, regardless of their gifts, would in itself create a two-tiered worshiping community, which could well be more divisive than the present situation of sacramental dependence on nonmembers.

It could be argued that if no one in the community is concerned, positively or negatively, with power, honor, status, or privilege, it would seem immaterial if some members have an ascribed ontological and practical sacramental priority over others. But I would argue that such is not the case for Religious. The point is not whether some people would *feel* superior, exercise power over others, or dominate the processes and projects of the congregation, nor that others would *feel* inferior, oppressed, or powerless. The point is that the Religious community is, by vocation, called to witness in a special way within the Church to the kind of community life the earliest followers of Jesus felt called to by their faith in him. The ideal expressed in Acts 4:32–35, of a community in which there are no distinctions based on wealth or status, has always been the particular and explicit community ideal of Religious Life. It is, of course, the ideal of the entire Church, but it is largely muted in the ordinary parish or diocesan structure by the ordained-lay dichotomy. And it cannot be witnessed to with the same clarity in a community composed of adults and children, such as the family. Religious Life, realized in an intergenerational community of biologically unrelated adults who freely hold all things in common, constitutes a particularly vivid witness to this aspect of baptismal identity. Religious Life is, quintessentially, a discipleship of equals prophetically calling the entire Church to its true identity in Christ.

In short, evangelical equality in community is intrinsic to the prophetic vocation of Religious. In the present state of the theology of ordination it is virtually impossible in fact, if not also in theory, for such egalitarian discipleship to exist in a congregation in which some members, even a small minority, are ordained. This is due both to the ascribed ontological superiority of the ordained and to the assimilation of the ordained to the diocesan hierarchical structure, however minimally, which flows from ordination itself. For this reason it seems imperative that any congregation considering the clerical option (if such ever became an issue) realize clearly the aspect of their witness that they would thereby compromise as well as the practical effects of inequality on their community life and mission.

A third cluster of considerations concerns the effect of ordained membership on the relationship of the congregation to Church authority at both the diocesan and the universal level. In the course of history relations between Religious and hierarchical authority have often been strained. The privilege of "exemption" that allows congregations and orders of pontifical right to enjoy not only legitimate autonomy in regard to their internal life but a certain trans-diocesan type of ministry has often rankled ordinaries who perceived Religious as "competing" with diocesan ministries or for vocations and/or who resented the ownership or even independent use of material resources, especially if derived from the local laity, by Religious in their dioceses.

While ecclesiastical authorities have a legitimate concern with the integration of the ministries of Religious into the diocesan structure, they have often made this the basis of interference in the internal affairs of communities. It is difficult to establish that anything done by Religious has absolutely no relationship to their ministry, whether that be their recruitment and acceptance of candidates, their appearance, their behavior in public places, their relationships among themselves or with others, or their policies and procedures in their own institutions. American Church history is rife with examples of both heroic resistance by Religious to episcopal control of their life and ministry and of debilitating submission for the sake of survival.[43] The struggles, of course, have not been entirely one-sided but in general the power has been on the side of ecclesiastical authority.

Ordination integrates Religious into the diocesan structure by an even more explicit and effective canonical title. Clerical orders can testify to the built-in tension involved in the dual relationship of the ordained member to the authority and community structures of the Religious order on the one hand and to the diocesan authority and presbyteral structure on the other.[44] This is especially the case if the order accepts parishes or stable diocesan responsibilities (as opposed to "supply" work). This tension tends to be handled by simply allowing the ordained to be assimilated to whatever degree seems necessary or desirable to him into the diocesan presbyteral structure with a corresponding suspension of whatever aspects of community life are incompatible with that assimilation. Many ordained Religious are, in effect, diocesan ordained ministers with congregational letters after their names.

There is no question that an ordained Religious is more vulnerable to ecclesiastical discipline if he deviates in any way from official Church policy or practice, whether local or universal, than the lay Religious.[45] The ordained falls under both the Congregation for Institutes of Consecrated Life and the Congregation for the Clergy. And sanctions that can be leveled against the ordained, from which their superiors really cannot protect them, including suspension of faculties to preach or preside sacramentally, administrative leave from pastoral responsibilities, refusal of assignment to ordained ministry in the diocese, and even laicization, are so frightening to those whose ministerial and even personal identity is constituted by ordination that few will risk it. The authorities in clerical congregations and orders are under considerable pressure to see that their members do not attract such disciplinary attention since it can precipitate the closure of their missions, for example, university chaplaincies or innovative parishes, and the expulsion of the order from a diocese in which they may have important historical involvements.

Finally, the formation of Religious who are to be ordained is largely structured by the provisions for the formation of diocesan clergy.[46] This not only consumes much of the time available for Religious formation of candidates but involves them in a formation that may have little relevance to the ministries they will actually exercise, for example, university teaching or administration, work in publication, or in foreign missions. It also creates a major divide along lines of superiority and inferiority, during formation itself, between candidates who will be ordained and those who will not. If only a small percentage of the candidates are headed for ordination it may well require them to be formed almost exclusively with diocesan candidates and outside the context of their own order.

In short, ordination is not simply a licensing of Religious to administer certain sacraments. It is the integration of Religious into the hierarchical structure of the Church in a way that profoundly affects formation and identity. It involves the whole congregation, and not only the ordained members, in relationships with the hierarchy that exacerbate already existing tensions and create new ones. And it modifies in very important ways the ministerial character of the congregation. The mission of Religious and the ministries in which it is expressed flow from profession and the charism of the order.[47] The mission and ministry of the ordained derive from the ordo into which they are incorporated. While theoretically there should be no real conflict between such a double source, in fact there very often is, and it is rare enough that the priority falls to the Religious source. Again, congregations that might consider the ordination of some of their members as a resource for their own inner life or as a ministerial enhancement for members involved in pastoral roles would be well advised to consider the implications for the congregation as a whole and for the individual members of such a choice. If, in the present situation in which women Religious cannot be ordained, congregations are seeing their members who are involved in quasi-clerical parochial ministries disempowered and isolated, alienated from community, and largely removed from congregational accountability, they have some data for imagining the effects of ordination, which would solidify the situation on a canonical basis.

·Finally, I would raise a consideration that does not directly affect Religious but that relates to the prophetic role of Religious Life in the Church and may have some implications for the ministries of women Religious. Although theologians have been dealing for half a century with the need to thoroughly rethink ministry in the Church and to revise the clerical structure, there has been no appreciable move to do so within the institution. As long as there was an adequate supply of males who were willing to remain celibate there was no compelling pressure to deal with the very real problems in the theology, structure, and practice of ministry.

However, as the number of ordained has declined to a point of crisis, there is mounting pressure to reassess such requirements as male gender, mandatory singleness, and the absolute connection between sacraments and the physical presence of an ordained minister as opposed to deputation of ministers for particular functions. As women, especially women Religious, have moved into parochial ministries and taken up the slack caused by the declining number of ordained, they have actually, even if unwittingly, helped excuse the authorities from addressing the problems.

First, as women perform virtually all the ministries in parishes except the sacramental ones, they help create the impression that somehow the essential ministerial needs of the Church are being met, which enables many bishops to continue to deny the problem of declining numbers of ordained. Second, the ordained, because they are thought to be essential for the Eucharist and the Eucharist is essential to Christian life, have not always responded by an increased sense of partnership with the laity in ministry but often enough by an increased sense, on the one hand, of personal power (as possessors of a scarce resource)[48] and, on the other, of a need to retain absolute control over the shrinking area of ministry reserved to them. Rather than precipitating renewal from within, the situation is creating "circuit rider" sacramentalists who are less rather than more collaborative.

It may be that the best contribution women Religious could make to hastening the reform of ministry in the Church is not becoming part of the clergy, either actually by ordination if that were possible or effectively by serving as quasi-clerics in the parochial situation, but ceasing to fill in for the clergy so that the problem becomes obvious and undeniable. It is axiomatic that people (and by extension institutions) immersed in destructive patterns seldom act for healing until they feel too much pain to continue in denial.

As I have already suggested, there are a number of good reasons for women Religious and their congregations to reevaluate the rapid parochialization of their ministries. With very few exceptions women's congregations were not founded to do parish or diocesan work, nor is such work in continuity with the charism of nonclerical Religious Life. Parish ministerial involvement inserts Religious into diocesan structures in ways that are difficult to reconcile with the autonomy and exemption characteristic of nondiocesan Institutes. It alienates Religious from the authority structures and often the community life of their own congregations and subordinates them to clerical authority in ways never intended, and often resisted at great cost, by their founders. In effect, many women Religious in parochial ministries are caught up in exactly the same dysfunctional dynamics and dilemmas that ordained Religious are, but without any of the clerical compensations or canonical protections that the men enjoy.

However, I am here suggesting that there is a further consideration. Are women Religious, in taking up parochial ministries, engaged in a kind of ecclesiastical codependency in which they cover up, often by absorbing significant ministerial and personal abuse, the ecclesiastical problem of declining numbers of ordained and thereby allow the authorities to put off indefinitely the examination and reform of ministry that is desperately needed in the Church? And is this compatible with the vocation to prophecy of Religious Life itself? The motive for such involvement is admirable: service of the people who would otherwise be spiritually "orphaned" by the demise of the clerical system. But the question that must be asked is whether, in the long run, the present collaboration of women in the disguising of the real problems will be more harmful than the short-run suffering that will make the demand for reform undeniable.

IV. Conclusions

The purpose of these last two chapters has been to address the confusion around the "ecclesiastical location" of Religious in the Church that has been precipitated by the otherwise very positive theological developments of Vatican II in regard to vocations and states of life in the Church. In the last chapter I attempted to delineate the "place" of Religious in relation to hierarchical structure, canonical status, and theological identity; to analyze the sources of confusion in the mandatory singleness of the clergy, in the historical sexualization of power relations in the Church, and in the privative connotations of the term *lay*.

In this chapter we have looked at the effects of this confusion about "place" on the identity of Religious and on particular issues faced by Religious, specifically in regard to their prophetic vocation, their canonical status, and the ordination issue.

Hopefully, attending closely to these admittedly technical distinctions, details, and developments will allow Religious to reclaim and reaffirm their specific and distinctive role in the Church as a prophetic lifeform and to work out critical issues in light of that identity rather than being pushed and pulled by circumstances and emergencies into internally contradictory decisions. Greater clarity about identity and mission should not only strengthen the sense of vocation of those already living this life but equip Religious to present their vocation to prospective members with clarity and precision. If the meaning of Religious Life once seemed clear to all simply because of distinctive dress and enclosed housing, it must now be made clear theologically and spiritually if it is to attract those actually called to this Life.

Chapter Nine

Religious Life as Charism I:
Many-Leveled Gift in Many Forms

I. Transition and Introduction

In these final two chapters I will attempt, against the background of all that has been said so far about the repositioning of Religious Life in the wake of the Council, to propose a redefined "location" of this life in the contemporary Church and cultural setting. In this chapter I will first trace within the rich and extremely complex history of Religious Life, specifically that of women, a strand of development that has given rise to the particular form of the life which is characteristic of so-called "apostolic congregations of simple vows." In describing the charism of this life I will distinguish it from and relate it to the other strand which has been called "contemplative life." Part of the argument will be that this terminology is not only not very helpful today even as pure description but that it suggests dichotomies that are truly dysfunctional. I will try to suggest more useful language that both preserves the important distinctions and highlights the real connections between these two strands of the same cord. By way of anticipation I will be trying to establish that the form of Religious Life which most U.S. women Religious live today expresses a genuine charism: the charism of Religious Life that is truly *Religious but not enclosed* and that is truly *ministerial but not clerical* (i.e., ordained).

In the next chapter I will take up the issue of prophetic ministry as the defining characteristic of this charism, inquire into the specific way that this charism is being called to function in the present cultural-ecclesial context, and discuss the spirituality of this form of Religious Life. By way of anticipation, my thesis will be that the Gospel work of liberation, especially in its ecofeminist incarnation, is the specific expression of this charism in the first-world ecclesial and cultural contexts; that the primary location and object of this work is the Church itself, which must become the sign, herald, and servant of this liberation in the world; that a prophetic spirituality that is simultaneously contemplative and active is the heart of this charismatic ministry in and to the Church for the sake of the world.

II. The Category of "Charism" in Relation to Religious Life

One of the most ambiguous contributions of the Council to the renewal of Religious Life was its evocation of the theological category of "charism" in relation to the life.[1] The primary context for the evocation of this category was the effort to recognize the distinctiveness (virtually repressed by the revision of Canon Law in 1917 and the revisions of constitutions which followed it)[2] of various Religious families in the Church and to validate appeal to that distinctiveness in the process of renewal of congregations and orders. This important and invigorating emphasis led not only to deep reflection on the founding inspiration and unique identity of various groups but also to considerable confusion, and even disillusionment in some quarters. The category itself was not theologically precise, and its use in the conciliar documents did little to clarify its meaning. However, it has potential for helping to establish the "place" of Religious in the Church.

A charism is a grace given for the sake not only of the recipient but also and primarily for the upbuilding of the Church.[3] In the New Testament graces such as preaching, speaking in and interpretation of tongues, healing, administration, and teaching are seen as gifts given to individuals for the sake of the community.[4] Questions raised by the conciliar use of the category to talk about the particular character or spirituality or ministerial option of congregations included whether a charism is necessarily individual or could be given to a whole group and whether a person who received a charism as an individual gift could communicate it to others (as opposed to exercising it for the good of others). In fact, the simultaneous empowering of the whole Jerusalem community of disciples by the Spirit on Pentecost suggests that there might be such a thing as a "group charism," at least in the sense that an identical grace is received by several people at the same time and in the same place for the same purpose.[5] But given that the only source of grace is the Holy Spirit it seems dubious that a person or group so graced could communicate such grace to another. Actually, the theology of charism is not a particularly developed category, and I am going to suggest that that may be a blessing. It leaves some scope for investing the term with appropriate and usable meaning compatible with its fundamental meaning of "grace given to an individual [or to a group?] for the Church."

Because grace or gift involves a personal experience of invisible power, claims to such a charism require, as the author of 1 John 4:1 says of "spirits," to be "discerned," or judged, in terms of reality and validity. It is entirely possible that someone could be absolutely convinced of God's injunction to her or him to do something that is not only not needed in the Church but is positively harmful. The history of heresy, cults, and false prophecy makes this clear. But the need for discernment raises the question of who is qualified and called to do that discernment. The Church has usually claimed that when it comes to Religious Life only the hierarchy is so qualified, and the Council and subsequent documents repeated this claim.[6] However, as we will see, this straightforward claim to virtually unilateral validation and control of the charism is questionable both historically and theologically.[7] Without doubt the institutional Church is part of the discernment process and may be the only agency qualified to give definitive public approbation, but it may be unduly simplistic to say nothing of counterintuitive to imply that the primary task of discernment rests with authorities outside the communities who live the life and those that are directly affected by its life and ministry.

I would like to propose that the notion of charism might be used, analogously, in at least four interrelated ways or at four levels in relation to Religious Life. First, and most fundamentally, Religious Life itself is a charism, a gift to the Church. The Council, as already noted, explicitly recognized this fact and history certainly confirms it in myriad ways. The importance of affirming that Religious Life is a gift of God to the Church lies in the implication that it was not invented, either by its adherents or by the hierarchy.[8] Although, as I tried to show in the first chapter, most religious or spiritual traditions have monastic analogues of Catholic Religious Life and that this suggests that such "religious specialization" is a deeply human, that is, anthropological, psychological, and sociological as well as spiritual impulse, Christian faith regards Religious Life as ultimately divine in origin. It has always been viewed as a response to a vocation from God, no matter how this vocation is mediated by human experience.

Furthermore, if Religious Life was not invented by its adherents it is no less theologically independent in its origin of the Church as hierarchical institution. Starting with St. Paul (cf. 1 Cor 7:21), the Church has always maintained that Christian life and holiness do not require the "life of the counsels"[9] and has condemned as heresy any attempt to insist that the life of consecrated celibacy was necessary for salvation. Whatever role the institution might play in authenticating the call of Christians to Religious Life, the institution did not invent that life, cannot impose it, and must not impede it. To do so is to interfere with the free action of the Holy Spirit in the Church.

A second way in which, or level on which, the category of charism might be applied is that of basic forms or types of Religious Life. This is the level that will be my primary concern in this chapter. Throughout Christian history the basic charism of Religious Life, that is, the call to perpetual self-gift to Christ in consecrated celibacy for the sake of the Reign of

God, has been specified in a variety of ways by domestic virgins, hermits, cenobites, monastics, mendicants, missionaries and so on. These forms of life, despite their deep identity in the shared charism of Religious Life itself, are very diverse. Just as the basic calling of the Christian can be shaped by charismatic specification in the life of the apostle, teacher, administrator, healer, and so on, it would seem that forms of Religious Life might, at least analogously, be regarded as charismatically distinguished. In speaking, in what follows, of "contemplative" and "apostolic" forms I am going to suggest that the form of Religious Life that most North American women Religious live today is such a charismatic reality.

This will imply that there is and should be, among apostolic Religious congregations, more in common than has been historically recognized. The contemporary experience of similarity among Religious from various communities is not due to a loss or dissolution of identity but to a reappropriation of a shared charism. And this should have implications for shared life and ministry that may go beyond what has so far been envisioned.

A further implication of a recognition of the charismatic character of the form of life itself is that its evolution and diversification cannot be suppressed for the sake of legal clarity or institutional efficiency. I will evoke the history of this form of Religious Life to make the point that the effort to suppress it in order to fit all women Religious into a single canonical category, that of cloistered contemplative, has repeatedly failed.[10] The action of the Spirit has brought to maturity in our own time a form of Religious Life that emerged in the first centuries of the Church and reappeared with regularity throughout the Church's history but was not officially recognized until 1900.[11]

A third level at which the category of charism might function is the one with which the Council was especially concerned, namely, that of the particular order or congregation. In attempting to validate the distinctive character of various groups the Council suggested that they return to the "charism of their founder" (cf. *Perfectae Caritatis* [Renewal of Religious Life], 2, followed by *Evangelica Testificatio* [Apostolic Exhortation on the

Renewal of Religious Life], 11). But in what, exactly, did that charism consist or how was it manifest? What did such a return entail? Was the charism of the founder precisely the grace "to found," that is, to call a group into existence and stabilize it sufficiently for it to survive? Was it the particular insight into the Gospel that gave rise to a distinct spirituality now characteristic of all the members? Was it a call to exercise a particular type of ministry such as teaching, nursing, or preaching the Gospel in cross-cultural contexts? All of these interpretations have been proposed and investigated.

As all Religious know, a great deal of time and energy has been expended on the attempt to rediscover and reinvigorate the "charism of the founder." In many respects the effort has been at least as divisive and disheartening as unifying. What was a group to do whose founder was ecclesiastically condemned (e.g., the Presentation Sisters), or which could not really identify a single dominant personality in its founding group (e.g., the Servites or the Carmelites), or if it had no founder other than the bishop or parish priest who needed Sisters for his frontier school and had little or no understanding of Religious Life itself?[12] What should it do if the work for which it seemed to have been founded was no longer needed (e.g., ransoming captives of pirates), or is seen today as theologically invalid (e.g., the conversion of the Jews), or as culturally questionable (e.g., waiting on priests), or as institutionally impossible (e.g., running hospitals under certain economic or political conditions)? Most threatening of all, what if there does not appear to be a distinctive spirituality characteristic of the founder or of the founding period? Many groups founded in the eighteenth and nineteenth centuries shared very similar spiritualities of Marian or Eucharistic piety and apostolic zeal characteristic of the European societies in which or from which they emerged.[13]

Recently, some writers on Religious Life, both theologians and historians, have advanced the hypothesis that the "charism" of the particular order (rather than of the founder) is what is significant for the identity and life of the community.[14] In other words, it is not so much a full-blown vision at the moment of initiation that has worked itself out over the history of the group but it is the ongoing "deep narrative" developed throughout the community's history with its attendant myths and symbols, outstanding events and persons, struggles and triumphs, projects and challenges, that the group has been developing from its origins to the present that has become the inner heritage of each member down through the years, giving them a shared identity. It may be the case, as it surely is for the Franciscans or the Benedictines, that there was an outstanding spiritual personality at the origin of the movement. Francis and Clare, Benedict, Ignatius, Teresa of Avila, and others were indeed founders of such stature that they left their distinctive mark on the spirituality and commitments of the groups they helped generate. But many other groups began much more ambiguously and tentatively, and it was the working out, together, of what they felt called to, what they desired, what they were capable of, that generated the constitutive narrative and ongoing history of the community. I am persuaded that such collective and seemingly nonspectacular charisms are no less authentic, valid, and powerful than the more illustrious individual charisms of the Benedicts or the Teresas. Groups that cannot look back to a famous Rule or volumes of founders' writings on the spiritual life are not necessarily any less rich in identity and history than those that can. The locus of identity is different but not necessarily inferior. The Church has always claimed that the measure of greatness is not publicity or recognition, nor even theological or literary productivity, but effective charity. The vital question is not, "Who founded us?" but "Who have we become by the grace of God?"

Finally, the category of charism can be applied at the level that is, theologically, most certain, namely, that of the individual called to Religious Life. The recognition of one's vocation to the life is, in fact, the discernment of a charism, a gift of God for the sake of the Church. This charismatic understanding of personal vocation to Religious Life has a number of implications. First, vocation is an ecclesial grace. One does not become a Religious because this type of life fits one's personality, allows one to share life with people of the same sex or

sensibilities or commitments, or opens opportunities otherwise unavailable. Living the mystery of Christian identity in
this specialized way, especially in view of the ecclesiastical dysfunctionality of the Church today, requires clear-eyed commitment to something much larger than oneself. Second, as a
charism Religious vocation requires corporate discernment
and not simply the conviction of the individual that she or he
is so called. Third, a Religious congregation that accepts an
individual because it discerns in her or him the charism of
Religious Life is committing itself to allow that individual
charism, which is necessarily distinctive and original, to be
incorporated into the congregation and to change the totality.
Like the birth of a child into a family, the entrance of a new
member into the congregation will change everything. It does
not destroy the identity of the congregation; but it will modify
it. And the attempt to so tailor the individual to the community that no ripples are felt as a result of the incorporation of
the new member is a quenching of the Spirit and thus of the
newness of life that is offered by every new entrant.

III. Historical Emergence of the Ministerial Prophetic Charism

It is not the purpose of this section (nor is it within the
scope of this chapter or my competence) to recount the history of Religious Life or even that of women's Religious congregations.[15] Rather, I want to follow the strand of the
emergence of one particular form of Religious Life, that of
institutes once called "apostolic congregations of simple
vows."[16] I want to show that this form of Religious Life has a
very long history and a very particular identity that has special
relevance for our own historical and cultural setting at the
turn of the millennium. This bears directly on the issue of who
we are and what we should be doing in this time and place. In
other words, the questions of cultural-ecclesial location and
identity of active Religious Life that have been the fundamental concern of this whole volume is now coming to a point.

A. Sketching the History

The charismatic form of Religious Life I will be discussing is primarily that of women Religious. Prior to the founding of the Brothers of the Christian Schools by Jean-Baptiste de La Salle (1651–1719), no completely nonclerical, nonmonastic (that is, actively apostolic lay) orders of men existed. Brothers, prior to this, were either choir monks or laybrothers supporting choir monks through (mostly menial) labor.[17] By the time Brothers as a distinct category of active Religious emerged in the seventeenth century, the form of life was already in existence among women and had been for centuries. Consequently, while much of what I will say is applicable to contemporary Brothers' congregations I will have in view primarily women Religious.

The history of apostolically active women's Religious congregations, despite the hundreds of thousands of women involved, had been largely ignored in histories of Religious Life until quite recently when feminist historians discovered the treasure trove of women's history embedded in the archives of such orders.[18] A number of Religious congregations have recently undertaken contemporary histories of their own life, which will do much to redress the situation of historical neglect of this important phenomenon. This neglect is not surprising since history in general has been considered the story of men with an occasional extraordinary woman (usually fulfilling a "male" role such as monarch) appearing by way of exception. Thus, most histories of Religious Life have begun with the exodus of men from the cities of the late Roman Empire to take up the hermit life in the desert and have continued with the organization of male ascetics into cenobitic forms of the life. The subsequent history of monasticism has tended to be told in terms of the great male monasteries and their reforms in the Early Middle Ages.[19] The powerful movement of the *vita apostolica* in the High Middle Ages has been seen primarily as a movement of male mendicants such as Franciscans, Dominicans, and Carmelites (with some cloistered female branches). And the full emergence of apostolic Religious orders was exemplified in the story of the Jesuits and other clerical institutes. It is not until the final stage, the foundation of the apostolic congregations of simple vows, that women are sometimes presented as major players.[20]

This presentation of the history of Religious Life has created at least two erroneous and unfortunate impressions. First, it creates the impression that the development of Religious Life was relatively straightforward. One monolithic form of the life (e.g., desert asceticism) was dominant for a certain period of time until it was succeeded by another (e.g., monasticism) which achieved ascendency usually without completely replacing or suppressing its predecessor. Second, women Religious appear in such treatments as imitators, appendages, or mirrors of male forms of life, which were adapted for them by the men. In fact, the flourishing of Religious Life has been much more luxuriant, multiform, and mixed and women much more the initiators of their own lives than this presentation suggests.

This picture is, of course, being rapidly revised as feminist historians, both male and female, have begun to unearth the buried story of women. We now know that the earliest form of Religious Life in the Church, consecrated virginity, often lived within the domestic context and local Church setting rather than in common dwellings in the first two centuries, was primarily a female movement. Both the theology and the symbology of the life were primarily feminine, whence the nuptial understanding of the life that has perdured, in healthy and unhealthy forms, throughout the centuries. Women were also among the ascetics who fled to the desert in the wake of the Constantinian establishment of the Church, though asceticism has rarely been the primary characteristic of women's Religious Life.[21] Women's monasteries, some in conjunction with male monasteries (women sometimes heading double monasteries of men and women) but some independent, flourished in the so-called "Dark Ages," which was the high point of monastic development. Women were at least as enthusiastic as men in embracing the *vita apostolica* in the High Middle Ages and many found a way, through celibate Third Orders and other forms of organization, to avoid complete cloister.

Women were also the primary figures in the Beguine movement,[22] which was a form of active life very similar to that of today's Religious, and in the anchorite movement, which was a form of eremetical contemplative life. When missionaries followed the European explorers into the "new world missions" of North America, many women Religious were among the evangelizers who forsook European safety and civilization for life on the frontier.[23] In the wake of the French revolution women Religious took up the care of the sick and wounded, the feeding and clothing of the impoverished in urban and rural settings, the protection and education of orphans, and the rescue of the abused women and other victims of social chaos. The nineteenth century saw the foundation of hundreds of congregations of Religious in the United States alone to care for the waves of immigrant Catholics.[24]

In short, what is emerging from this revision of history is the realization that, first, women's Religious Life was not simply a dependent outgrowth or an imitation of male movements but has often been a quite distinctive form of the life developed by and for women; second, that women Religious have usually outnumbered male Religious; and third, that there have been noncloistered, apostolic forms of women's Religious Life throughout history even when (as we will see shortly) such forms had not been officially recognized or approved by institutional Church authority. In other words, female, nonclerical, noncloistered Religious Life is a distinct and powerful historical phenomenon in its own right and not only deserves to be studied as and for itself but also needs to be appropriated by contemporary women Religious if they are to properly understand and appreciate their own life and charism.

Furthermore, a more thorough and inclusive examination of the history of Religious Life is making it clear that not only did Religious Life not develop in a straight line, with one form of the life following and virtually supplanting the preceding one, but also that the seemingly clear-cut and absolute distinctions among types of Religious Life that Canon Law has traditionally presented does not reflect the history of the movement in which such forms were often overlapping and intermingled. Hermits, even in the desert, sometimes came together in loose communities even while having separate cells or private rooms in a larger dwelling. Monasteries varied from small local ones to large feudal quasi-cities to great double monasteries of men and women, which were virtual alternative churches within the local church.

In the Middle Ages the *vita apostolica* movement gave rise not only to preaching mendicants like the Franciscans and Dominicans but also to their strictly enclosed Second Orders, the nuns, who lived much the same spirituality but in a monastic form of life. It also gave rise to Third Orders of men and women. The Third Orders were often composed of women who were not in a position to enter Religious Life (because they were married or had other family obligations) or did not want to be cloistered because they felt called to apostolic service but who desired to live Religious Life as fully as they could. Some of these Third Order women who were free to live a celibate life took a habit, made vows, and lived together according to a Rule, becoming the Third Order Regulars (of whom most noncloistered Franciscan, Dominican, and Carmelite Sisters today are the descendants), as distinct from Third Order Seculars who did not make public vows or live community life but embraced a Rule that embodied the spirituality of the Religious family. The Beguines, who were part of the "apostolic life" movement, were neither enclosed nor mendicants but much closer to what later became apostolic Religious Life of simple vows. Some Beguines lived in large groups that were more like monasteries, and others lived in individual dwellings in proximity to one another, sharing some elements of life in common. Anchoresses of the same period undertook an eremetical life, but while some anchoresses were strictly enclosed and had virtually no contact with anyone except those who supplied their physical and spiritual needs, others exercised from within their cells vigorous ministries to disciples and clients in many walks of life.

Similar complexity marks the evolution of women's Religious Life in the early modern period up to 1800. Despite the decree of the Fourth Lateran Council (1215) that no new orders were to be founded and the 1298 bull of Boniface VIII, *Periculoso* (later confirmed by the Council of Trent in 1563 and by subsequent legislation), which decreed that all women Religious were to observe papal enclosure in perpetuity, all manner of experiments and foundations were undertaken by women who felt called to consecrated life and to ministry to their neighbors. Patricia Ranft in her brief history of premodern European Religious Life of women[25] sketches the astonishingly varied and inventive strategies by which women in Spain, France, the Lowlands, Italy, and the British Isles managed to found and live Religious Life outside the cloister in the service of their neighbors. In some cases they made private rather than public vows, or did not wear a habit, or did not live together in the same house, or adopted some combination of these tactics. They virtually always chose consecrated celibacy, usually guaranteed by some kind of promise or vow, and usually managed to maintain community life through a common Rule, obedience to a superior, or other devices. They called themselves Oblates, Ladies of Charity, Third Orders, Confraternities or whatever they could get away with, and some eschewed any such self-designation lest they become objects of ecclesiastical "concern"; but in their own self-understanding they virtually always saw themselves as Religious in the theological sense. The official Church did not recognize them as such, but the people they served did. To this variegated group belong the Grey Sisters, the Ursulines and the Visitandines (both of the latter later cloistered by Church authority), the Institute of the Blessed Virgin Mary (Presentation), and most notably the Daughters of Charity of St. Vincent de Paul and Louise de Marillac.[26] The Daughters were the first group to successfully avoid cloister while living a life of consecration and ministry. Prior to the revision of the *Code of Canon Law* in 1983 they were considered a pious association and are now classed as a Society of Apostolic Life.

There was also, especially among women, not only a great deal of overlapping and combining of types of life but also of spiritualities within groups and among groups. This was due to women changing monasteries or orders, or having a succession of spiritual directors from different men's orders, or being involved at different times in their lives in more contemplative or more ministerial pursuits. For example, the powerful thirteenth-century German monastery of Helfta, which produced the two great Gertrudes and the two great Mechtildes, was originally Cistercian, but was deeply influenced by the Dominicans through Gertrude of Hackeborn, and finally by Beguine spirituality through Mechtilde of Magdeburg. This powerful combination of spiritualities—contemplative, intellectual, and ministerial—made Helfta the monastic glory of the High Middle Ages and a center of the flowering of mysticism for which that century is famous.[27]

In summary, throughout the period from the 1200s to the 1600s Church legislation resolutely restricted recognition of women's communities as Religious to cloistered orders. And throughout this period women continued to find ways to circumvent cloister for purposes of ministry while living the theological reality of Religious Life. Repeated attempts to found public Religious congregations devoted to ministry were made but in virtually every case foundered on the shoals of ecclesiastical repression, whether disappearing or being enclosed or finding a way to continue the ministry at the sacrifice of institutional recognition as Religious.

But, as Ranft so well describes, a gradual evolution in public perception of these official "non-Religious" was occurring as the Church in Europe became more and more dependent on the ministry of these women.

> Canon law, inheritance and feudal law, and the social status of women aside, society in general finally realized that these women were providing an irreplaceable service. They had become so indispensable to society that all other factors faded in comparison.[28]

Bishops granted recognition under various titles in order to maintain the ministry of the women and states gradually extended to them the kinds of exemptions and privileges accorded Religious, thus ironically nudging ecclesiastical attitudes to catch up with civil law. This development was earliest and strongest in France, but the rest of Europe followed suit and "before the end of the seventeenth century literally hundreds of active religious communities had been established throughout the continent."[29] Rome kept its counsel until 1900, but the development continued.

A major breakthrough occurred with the transplantation of Religious Life to the New World, first in Canada and immediately after in what would become the United States. In the late 1600s Marguerite Bourgeoys founded her "secular sisters" (later the Congregation of Notre Dame) in French Canada to minister among the Indians and the French settlers. Like Francis de Sales, who intended the Visitandines to be contemplatives without cloister, she fully intended her Sisters to be both Religious and noncloistered. Because of her deep desire to have them be and live as vowed Religious she opened the group, against her intention, to the imposition of some elements of cloister.[30] The Ursulines, who had been founded in Italy as noncloistered educators but had eventually submitted to cloister to avoid suppression, came to Louisiana in 1727 and undertook a ministry of education that led to their gradual emergence from strict cloister and adaptation to the demands of the frontier.[31] This would be the pattern of many groups of Religious arriving from the continent who discovered the incompatibility between the ministry they came to offer and the restrictions of European-style enclosed Religious Life. Many of these groups gradually became autonomous, in effect refounding their orders as fully ministerial Religious in the New World.

But the major development was certainly the foundation, beginning in the 1800s, of literally hundreds of communities of women Religious[32] who would not be canonically recognized as such until 1900 but who were truly Religious in their own self-understanding as well as in the eyes of local ecclesiastical officials and the people they served.[33] These orders eventually numbered hundreds of thousands of women.[34] They built the parochial school system that educated generations of young Catholics in the faith and prepared them for mainstream American life. They built a Catholic hospital system and founded social services for people of all faiths.[35] The network of over 150 Catholic women's colleges, which they founded, built, and staffed, was a major factor in the expansion of higher education among women.[36] And in the process they became the best educated and most professionally experienced and accomplished cohort of women in the Church's history.[37] However, what Ranft says of the women Religious of early modern Europe is equally true of American Religious:

> While religious life did indeed offer women alternatives to marriage, an education, independence, and so forth, I know of no primary source where women explicitly state any of those reasons as why they pursued religious life. In every instance they tell us their reason was religiously motivated. They wanted to become saints. They wanted to become one with Christ....[38]

Any perusal of the documents of Religious congregations in the New World would bear out this observation. The quest for God and the love of Christ was the motivation for the choice of Religious Life as well as the reason for the choice of ministry outside the cloister.

In revisiting a few high points of this history I want to emphasize that throughout this history women attempted again and again to create and live a form of Religious Life that the whole patriarchal history of the West, both societal and ecclesiastical, conspired to suppress and, if unable to abolish it, at least to contain and control it. The fact is that finally, on the American frontier, this movement, which can be traced back to the first Christian century, found the cultural and ecclesial context that allowed it to establish itself in broad daylight, gain ecclesiastical recognition, and flower into the most numerous form of the Life in modern times.

B. Drawing Some Conclusions

My point in describing, however sketchily, the historical complexity of the development of women's Religious Life is to lay the groundwork for examining anew the form of Religious Life (and in the following chapter the spirituality) that is embodied in most apostolic communities today. Several traits emerge from this sketch. First, the impulse to service of the neighbor as a direct and necessary expression of their quest for God and love of Christ, as intrinsic to their Religious vocation, has been present among women Religious from the earliest days of the Church. The institutional Church has often not recognized this "mixed" life as truly Religious in the case of women.[39] But the persistence of this form of life despite all efforts to restrict or even suppress it bears witness to its charismatic character, to the fact that it is a work of the Spirit, a gift to the Church.

Second, the recognition that ministry is intrinsic to this vocation[40] does not reduce the charism of ministerial Religious Life to a simple "response to a perceived social need" as some, including some Religious, have suggested when they have not succeeded in finding some highly original spirituality at the origin of a particular institute. Many people, including women, throughout history have responded from religious or humanitarian motives to the needs of the suffering without becoming Religious. The total commitment to Christ in lifelong consecrated celibacy lived in community and mission cannot be explained by and is not required by a desire to meet a need, however urgent that need might be. Rather, total commitment to Christ entails an equally wholehearted commitment to his members in need. Ministry for Religious is neither simply the overflow of love of God nor a substitute for it. It is its expression, its body in this world. The second commandment is as important as the first and for ministerial Religious the embodiment of love of God is active service of the neighbor.

Third, it is not surprising nor should it be disturbing that most ministerial congregations resemble each other in many respects. They share a charism that gives rise to a form of Religious Life which is indeed similar across congregational boundaries in its fundamental characteristics, even as it is embodied in a variety of distinct congregations. Just as all Religious are bound together by the charism of Religious Life itself, so ministerial congregations should see their similarity to each other in their shared apostolic charism as more fundamental than their differences. The competition and mutual disdain among orders that was fostered in the past as congregations competed for members and institutional leverage was not just unseemly. It reflected a basic misunderstanding of the charismatic basis of their shared ministerial identity. Today members of various congregations increasingly come together in shared ministries, common formation programs, and even in community living, bearing witness to the common charism of the life that makes them more alike than different. And this is to be celebrated rather than feared. Just as a family does not lose its identity but enhances it by sharing life and activity with other families, the Religious congregation does not diffuse its own charismatic identity by participating with other congregations in life and ministry.

Fourth, because the charism of ministerial Religious Life has a history almost as long as that of the Church and has been resourced by numerous spiritualities—both *generic* such as desert or urban, and *special* such as Benedictine or Redemptorist, both *devotional* and *theological* such as Marian or Eucharistic, and even *national* and *ethnic* such as American, French, or Celtic—it should not surprise or dismay Religious communities to discover that their spirituality is a braid of influences rather than a single, totally distinct product of the unitary vision of a single founder or foundress. What is unique is which strands they have chosen or inherited and how they have braided them together. Some communities have felt that they had to either discover (or invent) a single founding spirituality that all members should or must embody or else resign themselves to being charismatically ungrounded with a purely utilitarian self-understanding in terms of their traditional work. The history of ministerial Religious Life suggests that the rich and enriching intermingling of spiritualities has been characteristic of this form of the life from the beginning. The question is how to maximize this wealth, not how to suppress, supplant, or deny it.

Fifth, clarity about the charism of ministerial Religious Life should foster better understanding and appropriate sharing between contemplative and ministerial Religious, both as individuals and as communities. This is a point that will be developed more fully in the next section.

Finally, identifying the charism of ministerial Religious Life itself as a second level of charismatic identity should help Religious in such orders to situate their congregations more precisely. The first level, as has been said, is the charism of Religious Life itself, which is shared among all orders, contemplative or active, male or female, enclosed or noncloistered, diocesan or pontifical, lay or clerical. A second level is that of the ministerial form of the life, which we have been discussing and which is distinct from its contemplative analogue on the same level. The third level is that of the particular Religious family, the deep narrative of the community, which includes its own particular history and traditions, its myths and symbols, leaders and saints, struggles and triumphs, and spirituality, which give it its own unique identity among other congregations with which it shares the charism of ministerial Religious Life. And the fourth level is that of the individual members who bring into the community their particular gift, which both enriches and challenges the congregation as it continues to evolve its own deep narrative.

There is, it seems to me, no pressing need for a community to define the third level of charism with such precision and explicitness that it is marked off absolutely from every other congregation (a project on which an undue amount of energy was expended in the immediate wake of the Council). Just as most families could not say exactly how being a Smith is different from being a Johnson, both the Smiths and the Johnsons know to which family each person belongs and that belonging has historical, ethnic, affective, economic, hereditary, religious and myriad other aspects and features that individually and in concert both define family identity and defy total explication. Even in cases where members of diverse families intermarry, or have more in common, or are affectively closer than each is to her or his own family, identity perdures. It can happen that a member of a Religious congregation discovers that she is more at home spiritually and otherwise in a different congregation and eventually transfers. But that very fact makes it clear that each congregation is quite distinct no matter how much they are alike.

IV. Distinguishing the Ministerial Charism from the Monastic Charism

In this section I want to take up an issue that is at the base of a number of misunderstandings and tensions for individual Religious, new members, and congregations and that is difficult to formulate clearly, much less address adequately. It is the contrast and relationship expressed in such dichotomies as apostolic versus contemplative, ministerial versus monastic, active versus enclosed.[41] On the one hand, since the Council, all Religious have become more aware of their shared "first-level" charism, Religious Life itself, and of the dysfunctionality of odious comparisons and competition over who belongs to the "higher" or the "more effective" version of the life. On the other hand, all Religious have come to a deepening realization of the constitutive centrality of both prayer and ministry to Religious Life as such, which makes exclusivist claims to one or the other seem restrictive and even offensive. Nevertheless, there is obviously a real, lived, experiential difference in lifestyle and spirituality between an Order like the Benedictines or Carmelites on the one hand and the Mercies or St. Josephs on the other. The question is, what is the difference and what is its significance for self-understanding, spiritual development, and mutual relationships?

The confusion about similarities and distinctions was heightened by certain developments that followed the Council. Many monastic Religious, especially those bound by papal cloister, began to question the value, and even the healthiness, of the absolute isolation from other Christians (including even Religious of their own tradition), from educational and ecclesial resources and opportunities, and even from cultural and recreational enrichment that total enclosure entailed. Meanwhile, apostolic Religious who had struggled to combine a common life, agrarian horarium, recitation of the office, obligatory devotions, and *Lectio Divina* within the convent, with a much more than forty-hour-a-week ministerial life outside the convent, heaved a sigh of relief as they jettisoned or relativized the burdens of the so-called "monastic lifestyle," which they now saw as not intrinsic to their form of Religious Life. Both monastic and apostolic women Religious, growing in feminist consciousness, came to see the influence of patriarchal control agendas in the unnecessary and often counterproductive (to say nothing of unhealthy) restrictions and burdens of their respective lifestyles, and as they assumed greater autonomy they worked to humanize and feminize their lives.

Inevitably, this movement from within different environments toward similar goals brought the two types of life into closer contact and mutual influence, which raised questions about the distinctiveness of their "second-level" charisms, that is, the charism of the particular form of Religious Life they were living. Of course, it also brought increasing mutual respect and a realization that the two types of Religious Life could enrich each other in important ways. Enclosed communities could profit from the formal theological, psychological, humanistic, and other types of education active Religious had acquired; the latter could find in monastic environments the peace and solitude, liturgical participation, and spiritual companionship often difficult to find in increasingly hectic ministerial lives. And Religious from both traditions made friends, found intellectual and spiritual partners, and developed common projects with their counterparts in the other form of life.

Nevertheless, it is to the advantage of both forms of life to become more explicit and articulate about the specificity and distinctiveness of their own charismatic form of the life, not only for increased self-understanding but especially in order to help prospective new members discern their calling. In the following paragraphs I will make some theological observations as well as some suggestions about vocabulary. Since no one person can grasp the whole picture and certainly no one can control the evolution of language, these suggestions may or may not be helpful. But in any case, by making a start I may be able to seed the imaginations of members of both types of life and stimulate mutually enlightening discussion.

First, I would suggest that the least helpful linguistic distinction is that between *contemplative* and *apostolic*. By *contemplative* I do not mean a type of prayer (as distinct from vocal prayer or meditation, etc.) but the full development toward union with God of the life of prayer. In this sense every Religious is called to the contemplative life, not as an accompaniment of other activities or as one feature among others, but as the very meaning and end of the life they have undertaken. A Religious Life which is not contemplative (at whatever stage of development at a given time) is a contradiction in terms and tragically pointless. By the same token, and as the Council pointed out, all the baptized are called to mission (which is the Latin form of the Greek derivative *apostolate*). If Religious profession is a radicalization and specification rather than an alternative to baptismal consecration, then all Religious, by virtue of profession, are equally called to the apostolic life. The apostolate is not an optional extracurricular activity for any Religious but belongs to the nature of the life itself.

Second, the terms *active* and *enclosed* are also more misleading than clarifying. The contrary of active is not enclosed but passive. And no one is called exclusively to activity or passivity in either the life of prayer or the exercise of the apostolate. All life, including Religious Life, is an alternation between the two in both spheres. Furthermore, *enclosed* is a very dubious description of a form of Religious Life. It might well be asked whether enclosure in the traditional sense of cloister and grille is necessary or helpful today (whatever might have been the case in earlier ages) and in any case simply "being enclosed" cannot define a life in any spiritually or theologically substantive way. At best, a condition such as enclosure might be, under some circumstances, a means to a life of prayer but it certainly cannot be the primary feature or focus of the life.

Third, *monastic* is a term that has two rather distinct meanings, one of which applies equally to both forms of Religious Life and one of which, as I will suggest below, applies more to one than to the other. As I proposed in chapter 1, all Religious Life is monastic in the theological and spiritual sense of being a single-minded quest for God to the exclusion of any other primary life commitment. The solitariness, aloneness, single-ness of focus in the quest for the "one thing necessary" marks all Religious Life as monastic in this theological sense.

If the foregoing distinctions are not particularly helpful, how should we express the obvious differences in the two basic forms of Religious Life? I would suggest that the real difference lies in the function as touchstone of discernment of one or the other of the behavioral manifestations of contemplation and apostolate. The behavioral expression of the contemplative life is *prayer,* whether individual or shared, personal or liturgical, or some combination of these. The behavioral expression of the apostolate is *ministry,* whether to others' spiritual life, such as offering spiritual direction, or to their intellectual or material needs, through teaching, health care, or social service.

In every life the central and constitutive elements receive different emphases at different stages or in various circumstances. These different emphases do not relativize or minimize the other elements; indeed they might heighten them, but they directly affect discernment. For example, a married couple with small children will emphasize child care in a way that they will not once the children are grown. The emphasis, even though it deeply marks decades of their life together, does not mean that their own relationship as spouses is less important. In fact, if that relationship is not robust and growing in depth, the strains of raising children could prove disastrous. But the fact of having children to care for will influence discernment about everything from budget allocations to choice of housing, neighborhood, and schools; from time and place of vacations to acceptance of social engagements; from community involvement to votes on taxation; and even to what is discussed at the dinner table and what television programs are watched.

In one form of Religious Life prayer, the behavioral manifestation of the contemplative life, is the touchstone of discernment for the community and its individual members most of the time. In the other form, ministry, the behavioral expression of the apostolic life, has that role. This leads to a diversity of lifestyle as pervasive and evident as is the difference between marriages with and without small children.

The effect of the emphasis on prayer is the development of the *stabile monastic lifestyle* (as opposed to the theological sense of monastic discussed in chapter 1). The emphasis on prayer as behavioral manifestation of the contemplative life demands a certain structuring of time and place. The place may be the hermit's cell, the village chapel, the woods, or the monastery; the possible schedules range from the idiorhythmic to a fairly detailed common horarium. But there is a felt need to provide for an atmosphere of silence and solitude for personal prayer and to ensure the materials and occasions of liturgical or common prayer. These needs are best met by the choice of a stabile dwelling (whether solitary or communal) and, if communal, a community that is not subject to frequent or radical restructuring through change of personnel or schedule.

The monastic lifestyle is maintained by discernment that views ministry through the filter of prayer. Thus a monastic community will probably not ordinarily undertake ministries requiring the members to be frequently absent from the house, from community activities, or from common prayer. Intellectual formation, even for ministry, is more likely to be informal and individual in the sense of not measured by outside evaluation or geared to the obtaining of degrees or professional certification. Ministries will tend to be directly related to spirituality, such as writing, offering spiritual direction, conducting retreats or prayer days, and opening monastic liturgy or prayer space to the wider community. When decisions have to be made about ministerial involvements outside the house and community or about admitting others into the house, the filter of discernment will be less the immediate need of those to whom ministry might be offered than the integrity of the life of prayer in its various dimensions. This in no way means that the apostolic love of neighbor is less important or central to the life. But it does mean that prayer has a certain weight in the discernment process, which might indicate that certain types of ministerial activity would entail modifications of the monastic lifestyle that would threaten the life as a whole. Prayer itself is a valid and valuable ministry (as the naming of St. Thérèse of Lisieux, an enclosed Carmelite, as patron of the missions clearly attests), and no individual or community can exercise all forms of ministry simultaneously.

The effect of emphasizing ministry, the behavioral manifestation of the apostolate, is the development of the *mobile ministerial lifestyle.* This life, as the historical sketch in the preceding section tried to show, has emerged from a powerful coincidence in the vocation of some people of the God-quest with effective service of the neighbor. In this experience of Religious vocation the voice of the Beloved is heard just as surely and clearly in the cry of the neighbor in need as it is heard in formal prayer. So imperative is the need to respond that these Religious feel called to grant a priority to mobility, to going where the need is discerned, even though that has always meant a relativizing and even at times an abandonment of the external structures of the monastic lifestyle.

As we have seen, the institutional authorities for nearly nineteen centuries refused to recognize this discernment as valid and denied that such a choice was compatible with Religious Life. The effect of this nonacceptance has been both positive and negative. The negative effect, of course, has been the undue amount of time and effort ministerial Religious congregations have had to expend in justifying their life and in finding ways to avoid imposed enclosure as well as the privation of civil privileges reserved to Religious in many cultures.

The positive effect, paradoxically, has been that ministerial Religious have been pressured to find ways to incorporate the community structures, common prayer, silence, solitude, and other features of the monastic lifestyle into their own ministerial form of life. I say this has been a paradoxical blessing because, while it burdened the lifestyle and impeded ministry in many ways, it also challenged ministerial Religious to affirm behaviorally as well as in theory the importance of lifestyle in maintaining a truly contemplative life. If anything, ministerial Religious, like the couple with small children in regard to their own relationship, must give more rather than less attention to the interior life if the God-quest itself is not to be undermined by the incessant demands of ministry. This requires a deep formation for a lifelong commitment to prayer that will often be threatened by the sheer magnitude of the needs of God's people. Ministerial Religious Life demands an inventive and disciplined approach to providing sufficient time and space for a deepening life of prayer as well as adequate community solidarity and support.

However, and herein lies the major difference between the mobile ministerial lifestyle and its monastic counterpart, the filter for discernment about prayer is ministry rather than the reverse. Ministerial Religious may well opt to go where there is as yet no chapel or even the opportunity for regular liturgy. They may choose to serve on the battlefield or in the slums, where silence and solitude are virtually nonexistent. They will go to Christ's members in hospitals and schools and social agencies, where the working hours rather than a monastic horarium dictate when formal prayer can take place. They will labor in settings where it is inappropriate or even dangerous to be identified as a Religious and will thus surrender the support for their vocation that comes from its recognition by others. Often their companions in work will be people who do not share their Christian faith much less their Religious commitment or community identity. Somehow, in their choice to respond to the needs of Christ in the neighbor, ministerial Religious trust that their contemplative life, their God-quest, will not only survive but thrive as it did in Jesus, who had not even time to eat in the press of his teaching and healing ministry (cf. Mk 6:31).

In discerning through the lens or filter of ministry how to live their Religious Life, ministerial Religious have made a fundamental choice for mobility rather than stability, and this is presenting the most pressing challenge around the issue of lifestyle at the present time. For most of the history of such congregations in North America a monastic type of stability of lifestyle was, with certain modifications, maintained. This was partly due to necessity, since life on the frontier could not have been sustained except in close-knit group life. It was also partly due to ecclesiastical pressure on ministerial Religious to adhere as closely as possible to the monastic lifestyle, which was regarded as normative. Thus, most Religious who entered before Vatican II have spent most of their Religious lives in convents observing the horarium and practices of the monastic lifestyle to the extent that these were compatible with ministerial involvement.

However, one very distinctive feature directly traceable to the ministerial charism did develop that caused devastating ecclesiastical struggles and, in some cases, even split some congregations but has never been completely abandoned by ministerial Religious and is only today beginning to manifest its challenging implications. That feature is that ministerial Religious do not live together in a single dwelling over a lifetime. Rather, the congregation maintains a home base, a motherhouse or provincial house or other central headquarters, from which the members are sent out in a more or less extensive radius to serve the needs that have been discerned. Many bishops, both in early modern Europe and in frontier North America, tried (sometimes successfully) to keep Religious in their diocese of foundation, allowing only local houses to be founded. But the charism of ministerial Religious Life seems always to have pressed against this restriction, drawing congregations toward the needs they perceived regardless of diocesan boundaries or ecclesiastical strictures.

In the past, however, Religious in each local house lived the same modified version of the monastic lifestyle that was lived at the motherhouse, as well as all participating in a single ministry. The most significant difference from monastic life was that the personnel in any local house changed frequently as superiors and subjects were rotated in annual reassignments. This was certainly one of the most traumatic forms of asceticism in the ministerial life. But its full significance was muted by the fact that any house to which one might be assigned was a fairly close replica of the previous abode. There was an illusion of monastic uniformity and autonomy created by the very fact that, unlike monasteries in a particular tradition, which are usually genuinely autonomous because the members enter, live, and die in the same house, no local house had a stabile community or an individual history or character or distinctive ministry. In effect, the congregation itself, or in some cases the province, was a quasi-monastery of which local houses were dependent and identical units.

One of the most challenging aspects of renewal for ministerial congregations is that this illusion has been finally dissipated and the truly mobile character of the life has become its salient lifestyle feature. It is a feature for the handling of which there has been little preparation, and discernment is proving very difficult.

The characteristic unity of ministerial congregations is corporate rather than autonomous. Whereas the monastery, with its stabile community and location, develops its own lifestyle and character into which it incorporates new members, the ministerial congregation incorporates members into the congregation itself, not into the motherhouse as a geographically based community. After initial formation members are sent out, sometimes in groups or in pairs or singly, to minister in various locations. The situations of missionaries from the same congregation may vary enormously. It may be that no two houses will be identical or even very similar in lifestyle, financial management, or type of ministry. A university professor and a family clinic nurse in the slums, a rural social worker and a lawyer may each be living singly miles from the nearest member of their own congregation. Other members may be living and sharing ministry with members of another congregation, while still others may be living in a small group of fellow members, exercising a shared ministry or a variety of ministries. The unity of the congregation and solidarity among its members has to be achieved and maintained without the mechanisms of daily shared life that once assured a high degree of uniformity of lifestyle and sense of corporate mission.

This situation, which is proving highly challenging, will be taken up in discussion of community life in the next volume, but the point here is that this challenge is intrinsic to the charism of ministerial Religious Life. Mobility in response to ministerial needs belongs to the nature of the life. And while that mobility was, for centuries, understood usually as the mobility of the congregation itself and/or its subunits, it is now being recognized as the characteristic of each Religious as well. The issues this raises are multiple. How do individual members maintain their sense of congregational identity? What kind of corporate witness can the congregation itself give? How does the congregation achieve and maintain its genuinely communitarian nature and life? How do members support one another? How is ministry and life truly corporate and not simply individual?

The issue is precisely that of "corporateness," of being one body living a single and integrated life through many distinct members whose functions are highly diverse but intimately interdependent. If, historically, the issue has been handled by an emphasis on the single and integrated life to the point of virtual uniformity of lifestyle and ministry, today it must be handled by an emphasis on unity in diversity. It may well be that in facing this challenge ministerial Religious will contribute to the problem of community in contemporary society and the Church. But claiming mobility as part of the charism of their form of life and therefore resolutely facing the challenge rather than retreating into a preconciliar lifestyle is crucial if that contribution is to have a chance of emerging. Holding firm in the midst of high levels of chaos until the creative potential emerges requires a tenacious fidelity to the contemplative heart of the life as well as to its apostolic nature.

A final point that must be stressed in relation to the charismatic distinction between monastic and ministerial Religious Life is that such distinctions are not and cannot ever be a procrustean bed that invalidates people's lives or strangles individual gifts. We have been talking about the forms of Religious Life in their general characteristics. However, in the lifetime of any particular Religious there may be much overlapping and alternation of the characteristics of her "home" situation and the features of the other lifestyle. For example, a member of a monastic community may have a much more active engagement with people outside the community through her ministries of spiritual direction and liturgical leadership than a retired member of a ministerial congregation who spends her entire day in the infirmary in contemplative prayer. A ministerial Religious living singly may have more actual silence and solitude in her home than is possible in a large monastery with a number of enterprises that require everyone's participation for the support of the monastery. The alternation between activity and passivity, ministry and prayer, engagement and withdrawal is a constant, even for those who have made a particular life choice. The point of making distinctions is the validation of the differences and the appreciation of their mutuality, not their imposition as ironclad categories.

V. Conclusion

The argument of this chapter has been made by bringing together several lines of reflection and therefore it might be helpful to make explicit the conclusion to which these reflections are intended to lead. I have been attempting to disengage from the general phenomenon of Religious Life one specific form of that life, namely, mobile ministerial Religious Life, a form that is simultaneously ministerial without being ordained and Religious without being cloistered.

The first step was to situate the charism of this form of the life at a "second level." It is both more specific than the global charism of Religious Life itself (first level) and shared among many congregations, of which each has its own charism (third level).

The second step was to trace through the history of Religious Life the existence of this charism, especially among women, in virtually every period and its gradual emergence into ecclesiastical recognition. We saw that the vocation of some women Religious, who were in the nature of the case not ordained, to a "mixed life" of contemplation and active ministry did not begin in the modern period but can be traced back to the very earliest forms of Religious Life. Despite repeated repression by ecclesiastical authority, which intended to reserve ministry to the ordained and Religious Life to the cloistered, it emerged again and again until it was finally recognized in 1900 as a valid form of Religious Life.

The third step was to describe the lifestyle generated by this particular charism in contrast to the monastic lifestyle. The basic difference is not that one is contemplative and the other apostolic, or that one is enclosed and the other active, but rather that the touchstone of discernment about lifestyle choices is, in the one case, prayer as the behavioral manifestation of contemplation and, in the other case, ministry as the behavioral manifestation of apostolate, even though contemplation and mission remain central to both. Finally, the salient lifestyle difference flowing from this distinction is, in one case stability and the resultant monastic lifestyle, and in the other case mobility and the resultant ministerial lifestyle.

The originality of the mobile ministerial form of Religious Life is twofold. First, it is truly Religious Life, which was finally recognized by papal decree, but it is a form of Religious Life that does not require or involve cloister. Second, it is essentially and intrinsically ministerial, which was fully and finally recognized by Vatican II, but that ministerial identity does not flow from ordination but from Religious profession and is therefore not specified by hierarchical agendas and functions but by the charism (third level) of the congregation itself. It remains to discuss, in the next chapter, the characteristic spirituality of this type of Religious Life.

Chapter Ten
Religious Life as Charism II: Prophets in Their Own Country

I. Introduction and Transition

This final chapter will draw on all that has been said in the preceding chapters to "locate" and describe mobile ministerial Religious Life (henceforth ministerial Religious Life or just Religious Life) in contemporary North American cultural context as a specific, charismatic lifeform and to tease out some of the implications of that description for the actual living of the life today, that is, for the spirituality of those who embrace this life.

In previous chapters I suggested that the distinguishing characteristic of Religious Life (in any of its forms) is the exclusive commitment to the God-quest that precludes any other primary life commitment, such as that to spouse and family, profession, or project. This commitment is Christian precisely because this God-quest is centered in Jesus Christ who is, therefore, the affective center of meaning for the Religious. In volume 2, in a chapter on celibacy, I will develop the thesis that what one chooses to do with one's affectivity is finally the most important, life-shaping decision a person makes. Who, what, and how one loves determines who and what one is and will become. All Christians, it is to be hoped, ultimately commit themselves to God in Christ, but they do so through the immediate primary commitments of their lives. For Religious the love of Jesus, unmediated by any other primary commitment, is the constitutive factor in life. Thus

313

celibacy, which expresses that total and unreserved self-gift to Jesus, is the distinguishing mark of Christian Religious Life.

Although the foregoing describes the charism of Religious Life as such and is therefore characteristic of all forms of the life, I suggested in the last chapter that this global charism is specified, or "funneled" toward concrete realization, by two other "levels" of charism: that of the particular form of Religious Life (stabile monastic or mobile ministerial) and that of the particular order or congregation (e.g., Benedictine or Mercy).

Here I want to recall and emphasize the central insight that gives rise to and animates the mobile ministerial form of Religious Life, namely, the coinherence of the two great commandments of love of God and love of neighbor. In Mark's gospel (12:28–31), when Jesus is asked by a scribe which is the first commandment in the Law, he replies by joining the two commandments, love of God with all one's being and love of neighbor as oneself, into one. "There is [singular] no other commandment [singular] greater than these [the two together]." Jesus' whole life consisted in identifying love of God and love of neighbor unto his final act of giving his life on the cross in loving fulfillment of God's will for the salvation of his fellow human beings.

For the Christian, then, this coinherence of the two loves is both incarnated in and patterned according to Jesus. Christian love is not simply the observance of the two great commandments but the integration of the two in a Jesus-like identification that focuses on the neighbor in need. Loving the neighbor is more than an expression or result of loving God; it *is* loving God.[1] Loving God, therefore, entails giving oneself to and for the neighbor unto death. It is a powerful insight, claiming one's whole person, into this christic coinherence of the two commandments that is the charismatic wellspring of ministerial Religious Life. The foundation of most ministerial orders originated in the interaction between this insight on the part of the founder(s) and a particular need of a particular group of people (the poor, the uneducated, the sick, the racially oppressed, etc.). The response to the perceived need was incarnated in a particular type of ministry, such as nursing or teaching. But at the heart of this charismatic response resulting in the founding of a particular order (the third-level charism) is the fundamental call to Religious Life itself (the first-level charism) lived in and through the love and direct service of the neighbor (the second-level charism). This is why the actual type of ministry of a Religious congregation might change in changed circumstances without disrupting the fundamental continuity of the charism.

In this chapter I want to explore a further implication of this general theory of ministerial Religious Life, namely, that because the call to love of neighbor as identical with love of God, which is intrinsic to ministerial Religious Life, is patterned on that of Jesus, it is, of its very nature, a prophetic vocation. I discussed in chapter 4 how the prophetic character of Religious Life arises from the conjunction of the immediate contemplative presence of the Religious to God and the social marginality that is generated by the life of the vows. In what follows I want to explore this reality in greater detail as it bears upon and finds expression in the actual day-to-day living of the Religious Life, that is, in prophetic spirituality as characteristic of this form of Religious Life. This will take us into an area of particular anxiety and suffering for contemporary Religious: their relationship to the institutional Church.

II. Prophetic Spirituality

The Christian understanding of prophecy is rooted in the Old Testament prophetic literature. Therefore, if we are to go beyond a vague, and even romantic, rhetoric of "prophetic stance" to discern the substance of this vocation and its concrete manifestation in a mature spirituality, we must turn to the best available scholarship on Old Testament prophecy.[2] Against this background Jesus appears as a prophet who not only embodied the Old Testament vocation but gave it a new interpretation. Prophetic spirituality in the contemporary situation is a full-time commitment to the prophetic praxis of Jesus.

Three misconceptions need to be exposed and abandoned at the outset. First, prophecy is not about foretelling the future, either proximate or long-term. Prophecy is about orientation toward the eschaton, about hope for the coming of the Reign of God and action to bring that about. In this sense the prophet is motivated in the present by the future, but this has nothing to do with fortune telling. Second, the biblical credential formula, "Thus says the Lord..." has led many to think that the prophets were extraordinary individuals who had some direct pipeline to God, who gave them absolutely reliable answers to contemporary problems, which they were then charged to deliver to the appropriate authorities. This is a serious misunderstanding, indeed a fundamentalist interpretation, of biblical prophecy. We will discuss at some length below what this oracular formula really indicates about the "word of the Lord" in the mouth of the prophet. Third, and analogously, in speaking of Religious Life as a prophetic vocation in the Church we are not claiming that individual Religious, by virtue of profession, are endowed with some kind of direct access to God's will that entitles them (or even obliges them) to deliver divinely sanctioned ultimata to the rest of the Church.

A. The Basic Conditions of Prophecy

It is commonplace today to speak of any visionary commitment to the betterment of the human condition as "prophetic," regardless of the source or context of the commitment. While this has a certain cogency it is actually an analogous use of a term borrowed from the literature of a particular religious tradition, the Judaeo-Christian one. I want to return to the original tradition and its literature to talk about Religious Life as prophetic. Therefore, I begin with two basic conditions for prophecy in the strict sense of the word.

1. Religious motivation: Neither the Old Testament prophets nor Jesus were secular humanitarians. They were deeply religious individuals within a particular religious community whose tradition they had internalized and whose characteristic life they faithfully lived. There is good reason to claim that they were mystics, people who experienced an immediate consciousness of and direct relationship to God. Bernard McGinn, the eminent historian of Christian mysticism, offers the following definition of mysticism:

> The mystical element within Christianity...centers on a form of immediate encounter with God whose essential purpose is to convey a loving knowledge (even a negative one) that transforms the mystic's mind and whole way of life....Thus mysticism is characterized primarily by a sense of an immediate relation to God and the transformation this effects....[3]

This mystical dimension of prophecy supplies several important notes for all that follows. First is the fact that *God,* thematically known, sought, and served (not simply implied as a nonthematized horizon of ultimacy or a vague cosmic postulate), is the source and motivation of prophetic life and mission. And for the Christian, this is specifically the God revealed in Jesus Christ. Second, there is a *noetic* aspect to mysticism. Mystical immediacy to God brings knowledge of God's will and ways which, in prophetic ministry, shapes the content of the message preached and the activity undertaken. The cry of the prophet is not just, "Repent," but is specified by what that means in one's daily life.[4] Prophetic ministry is not merely a general encouragement of benevolence, justice, or peace. It is a commitment to a particular vision of reality that claims to be that of the God of biblical revelation. This is the foundation of the special relation of the prophet to the future, to the eschaton of God's Reign. Third, mysticism is *transformative.* It changes not only the mind but the behavior of the mystic. The prophetic activity of the Old Testament prophets and of Jesus is not simply commitment to a personal vision of a better world nor an errand carried out on behalf of a higher power. It is a passionate personal involvement in the work of God in this world.

People (including Religious) sometimes ask, "Is there any real difference between the Religious and an atheist or secular humanist providing the same service to an underprivileged person or taking part in a peace rally?" The answer is yes. One difference is the religious motivation of the former, which influences what she thinks she is doing and why she is doing it. It is admirable for any human being to assist another, and Jesus himself said that such assistance he takes as done to himself even if the person has never heard of him (cf. Mt 25:31–46). But what terminates in the here-and-now good of the assisted person for the secular humanist is part of a global project of transforming this world into the Reign of God in Christ for the Religious. Prophetic ministry is essentially a religious project.

2. *Ecclesial location:* Both the Old Testament prophets and Jesus were historically, culturally, psychologically, and spiritually situated in the religious community of Israel. Isaiah, Jeremiah, and Ezekiel did not experience themselves called to prophesy to Assyria or Babylon or Egypt but to Israel. Jesus did not address his message to the Romans. He even instructed his disciples, "Do not go into pagan territory or enter a Samaritan town. Go rather to the lost sheep of the house of Israel" (Mt 10:5–6). He had to be persuaded that his vocation to preach "only to the house of Israel" might extend to Gentiles who approached him with a faith that exceeded that of the Jews (cf. the story of the Canaanite woman in Mt 15:21–28). In the time of the prophets and Jesus there was no distinction between civil society and the community of faith, no separation of Church and state. Israel was a theocracy. To be a Jew was to be involved not only in Jewish worship but also to carry on one's business as a member of the covenant community, to struggle against Israel's enemies, to raise one's children according to the Law of Moses. The vocation to prophesy to the house of Israel was a commission to a socioreligious role within the believing community as a people.

This ecclesial location was not a narrow sectarian indifference to the world around and outside of Judaism. It was a commitment to Israel's universalist vocation. As God said to the Suffering Servant who personified Israel:

It is too light a thing that you should be my servant
   to raise up the tribes of Jacob
   and to restore the survivors of Israel;
I will give you as a light to the nations,
    that my salvation may reach to the end of the earth.
      (cf. Is 49:9)

And when the child Jesus was presented in the temple the prophet Simeon applied to him this very text: Jesus was to be the bearer of "salvation which you [God] prepared in the sight of all the peoples, a light for revelation to the Gentiles" (Lk 2:31–32).

Prophecy, therefore, is an ecclesial vocation. It arises within the Church, and its primary addressee is the Church. Its task is to help purify and strengthen the Church in its vocation as herald, instrument, and servant of the Reign of God for the sake of the whole world. There are many ways to work for the transformation of the world and many utopian visions of what such a world should be. For the Christian Religious the Gospel provides the vision, and the primary means for the realization of that vision is the being and activity of the Church in the world. Prophetic ministry is devoted to fostering this vision and activity.

Many Religious, disgusted with the venality and injustice in the institutional Church, deeply discouraged by its self-serving politics, and even frightened by its harsh persecution of its own and especially of its most prophetic members, are tempted to wash their hands of the institution and find a sphere of service outside the bounds of official religion. While there is certainly a need for the evangelization of the secular sphere (a task which the Council recognized as the special, although certainly not exclusive, province of lay Christians) and there is no clear-cut dividing line between Church and secular society which overlap and intermingle at every level, it is not the specific and direct vocation of Religious as Religious to work for the transformation of the world as business executives or political leaders. In my view the flight of Religious from the Church as primary context of ministry into religious anonymity within the secular sphere is not only shortsighted; it is, even if unintentionally, a failure in regard to the prophetic vocation that Religious Life entails. To persevere in the community of faith, to minister as a prophet in and to the Church, is to follow in the footsteps of Jeremiah and Jesus, who continued to call Israel to fidelity to the Covenant, not only for its own sake but for the salvation of the world, and who were finally martyred by their coreligionists. There are many ways to serve one's fellow human beings, many possible motivations for such service, and many spheres that require evangelization. One of the most difficult and dangerous and ultimately most crucial is the prophetic ministry in and to the Church, which calls it to covenant fidelity in the preaching of the Gospel. To say that Religious Life is a prophetic vocation is to claim that its proper sphere of ministry is the Church itself, the People of God who form the Body of Christ and the institution that should be in service of that People and its mission to the world.

B. The Spirituality of the Prophetic Vocation

The literary form of oracle in which much Old Testament prophecy is cast has led to two misunderstandings about prophecy in ancient Israel. First, it led to a misunderstanding of biblical inspiration in general and prophetic inspiration in particular as verbal dictation. This misunderstanding is not our primary concern here, although it continues its dysfunctional career in biblical fundamentalism. Second, it has led to a misconception of the prophetic vocation as the call of one person (the prophet) to listen to God (speaking directly to the prophet) and then report God's concerns, threats, or commands to the people and/or their leaders. Rectifying this misunderstanding is crucial if we are to grasp the nature and functioning of the prophetic vocation in the Church, especially as it characterizes the spirituality of Religious Life.

1. Prophecy as a three-way mediation: The prophet does not simply speak for God, delivering divine oracles unavailable to others. The prophet speaks for God *to* the people and/or their leaders but also *for* the people to God and to the leaders. In fact, the prophet actually mediates a three-way conversation involving God, the people/leaders, and the culture. Moses was Israel's greatest and prototypical prophet, and his activity provides the pattern of the vocation in the biblical tradition. In Exodus 32:7–35 we have a critical exchange between God, Moses, and Aaron-and-the-people that illustrates this three-way conversation. God, having just given Moses the tablets of the covenant on Sinai, says to Moses, "Go down at once! *Your people,* whom *you* brought up out of the land of Egypt, have acted perversely" (emphasis here and below is mine) in casting the golden calf and worshiping it. God is about to consume the people and transfer the divine promise of a future to Moses and his descendants. But Moses replies, "O Lord, why does your wrath burn hot against *your people,* whom *you* brought out of the land of Egypt...?" Moses goes on to argue that if God consumes the people the Egyptians (the surrounding culture) will be able to say that God is faithless, which, incidentally, will confirm the suspicion of the people themselves which led them to revolt in the first place. Moses challenges God to "Remember Abraham, Isaac, and Israel, your servants, how you swore to them by your own self" that they would become a great nation and inherit a land. And the exchange ends, "And the Lord changed his mind about the disaster that he planned to bring on *his* [i.e., God's] people."

Moses and God are arguing over whose people the Israelites really are, based on who saved them from slavery and whose promise and fidelity they depend on for their identity and destiny. And Moses wins! The people are God's, not Moses'. God brought them out of Egypt, and therefore God is responsible for them. Moses has first spoken *for the people to God.* Only afterward does he go down from the mountain and *speak for God to the people,* expressing the divine fury in a sentence of death for three thousand of the unfaithful Israelites and pulverizing the golden calf. But the next day he reascends the mountain and prays to God, "Ah, this people has indeed committed a grave sin in making a god of gold for themselves! If you would only forgive their sin! If you will not, then strike me out of the book that you have written" (Ex 32:31–33). Moses' identification with the people makes him ready to surrender his own relation with God if God will not reestablish God's relation to the people!

Interesting in this story is the role of Aaron, the leader of the people, whom Moses holds responsible for yielding to the idolatrous project of the people. "What did this people ever do to you that you should *lead them* into so grave a sin?" Aaron tries to wiggle out of his responsibility by claiming that the people pressured him and he had no choice, but Moses is not taken in. He holds Aaron accountable for not fulfilling his role of leadership, for letting "the people run wild" in their surrender to cultural paganism, because this amounted to leading them astray. Here Moses speaks for both God and the people to the leader of the people.

In this episode we see the basic structure and functioning of prophecy in ancient Israel. The prophet is a point of interaction and mediation between God and the people, between the people and their leaders, between God's people and the surrounding culture. The prophet is a "place" of interaction among the forces that together move history forward, either according to God's plan or against it.

The same pattern is visible in the life and mission of Jesus the prophet. Jesus does speak *for God,* indeed *as* God, to the people. His authority, therefore, exceeds that of the scribes (cf. Mt 7:29) who serve the Law in its institutional embodiment. He does not hesitate, on his own authority, to radicalize the demands even of Torah: "You have heard that it was said to your ancestors...but I say to you..." (cf. Mt 5). But Jesus also speaks to God *for the people,* pouring out his own lifeblood "on behalf of many for the forgiveness of sins" (Mt 26:28). Most of the controversies of Jesus' public life arise over Jesus' extending to sinners and outcasts the compassion and forgiveness of God against the oppressive righteousness of the religious leaders, both those who collaborated with the pagan authorities to the detriment of Israel's traditions[5] and those who made those traditions themselves an intolerable burden in the name of God.[6] The perennial temptation of organized religion is to sell out the spiritual legacy of the tradition for secular gain (money, power, safety) and to oppress the people in "the name of God" for purposes of power and control within the institution. The prophet continuously confronts and challenges the religious institution and its authorities on both these points.

The prophet, then, is not an aloof figure, secure in his or her superior knowledge of the divine will and fidelity to the divine law. The prophet is a person deeply involved in the life and struggles of the people, even to the point of accepted estrangement or abandonment by God if that is the only way to maintain solidarity with the people. What makes the prophets different from their coreligionists is not a separate status that exempts them from the tensions, ambiguities, and sufferings of their historical time and culture but the fact that they engage in this historical and cultural struggle from a position of absolute religious commitment that will not be deflected by or to any personal agenda of political power, personal safety, economic gain, or even legitimate affective or spiritual satisfaction. It is the total commitment of the prophet to the divine agenda on the one hand and to the salvation of the people on the other, out of conviction that these are one and the same, that casts their involvement in their historical-cultural milieu in a different light, even from that of well-motivated political savior figures.

2. Contemplation, solidarity, and participant marginality: Living at the intersection—of God's plan of salvation, a real historical people, and contemporary culture—makes serious demands on the prophet. Only a life of ever deepening and faithful *contemplation* can keep the prophet attuned to the divine pathos, to the dream of a suffering God for humanity and the earth. Thomas Merton, challenged repeatedly by his contemporaries to come out of his monastery and put his body on the line in opposition to racism and war, came to an ultimate insight into the role of contemplation in prophetic witness. While not all prophets are called to withdraw from the public fray into an enclosed monastery, the validity of this way of participating in the struggle for justice is a clear statement about the essentially contemplative core of all prophetic action. Moses face to face with God in the tent of meeting, Jeremiah struggling with God in his "confessions," Hosea crying out to God in the anguish of unrequited love, Jesus in his midnight vigils with the one he called "Abba" were prophets returning again and again to the source of their vocation, their intimate union with God. It was there, in contemplative communion with God, that they learned to participate in God's passion and patience. There Moses learned what it would cost to educate a stiff-necked, murmuring people to covenant fidelity; Jeremiah learned that success may not mean winning the argument against foreign alliances but being faithful, like God, to a people that had brought about its own ruin; Hosea learned that God's fidelity does not respond to ours but vice versa; and Jesus learned that rooting up the weeds could destroy the wheat as well and that this meant giving Judas the wherewithal to destroy him. Religious Life as a prophetic vocation is first and foremost a call to contemplative intimacy with God.

But if contemplation attunes the prophet to God, living in one's own historical-cultural situation in unbuffered *solidarity* with one's fellows in Church and world attunes the prophet to the people. Often enough in history Religious Life has been construed as a safe enclave of the unperturbed righteous. Secure in the enclosure of convent or monastery, Religious could construct a life that was admittedly austere but largely protected from the material uncertainties, the political struggles, the moral ambiguities, and especially the spiritual chaos of their time.

Increasingly, the dismantling of Religious Life as total institution has reinserted Religious into the cultural milieu of contemporary society. Genuine solidarity with the people of our time, "especially those who are poor or afflicted in any way"[7] (as Vatican II described the vocation of the Church), is not simply a matter of imitating the lifestyle of the materially poor. It is a matter of entering deeply into the dynamics of our culture, in which so many people are victimized in a staggering variety of ways, from material destitution to political oppression, from religious persecution to discrimination because of race, gender, age, or sexual orientation, from devastation by foreign and domestic war to ruin by "natural" disasters precipitated by ecologically ruinous policies.

As Religious have entered into less structured and controlled relationships with others in their families and places of ministry, among friends and strangers, they have also been caught up in previously unimagined ways in the moral and spiritual dilemmas and struggles of our moment in history. If there was a time not too long ago when it was self-evident that Religious held, sincerely and without question, all the official positions of the Vatican on such issues as birth control, abortion, euthanasia, capital punishment, war, mandatory clerical singleness, the ordination of women, the validity of cultural imperialism in the service of evangelization, the inferiority of other religious traditions, the absolute necessity of clerical mediation for access to God, and other issues, that time is certainly past. Religious know how real people are affected by these issues and how much more complex they are than simple absolutes, no matter who formulates or articulates them, would suggest. The intertwining tentacles of economic, political, social, religious, and sexual structures and dynamics make even the simplest choice—how to vote, what statement to endorse, what cause to contribute to, what assistance to accept, where to place scarce personnel, which project to foster—complicated enough to induce paralysis, if not despair. And these conundrums confront not only the individual Religious but the congregation that must take some kind of corporate position when a public action or statement is called for.

Undoubtedly, the most agonizing result of unbuffered participation in the culture of our own time is the spiritual crises this has precipitated. Religious no longer live in an enclosed world where everyone believes (or at least claims to believe or behaves as if they did believe) identically about God, Christ, Church and sacraments, faith, resurrection and eternal life, or even about the nature or validity of Religious Life itself. The fragmentation and relativism of postmodernity is not an external factor that tangentially reaches Religious but a *zeitgeist* in which they participate on the same footing with other believers and nonbelievers. It is the cultural air we breathe and, like our smog-filled atmosphere, it is both essential and dangerous.

Some Religious feel that this total immersion in material and institutional chaos, in moral and spiritual crisis, is an aberration in Religious Life fomented by infidelity and worldliness. Religious, according to such people, should be beacons of clarity in the surrounding cultural gloom. They, if anyone, should know right from wrong and truth from error. They should be the voice of God in the midst of widespread immorality and spineless relativism.

But an attentive reading of the prophets and the Gospels suggests otherwise. Solidarity with the people of one's own time is not a matter of extending charity with a gloved hand to people who are pitiable precisely because they are so unlike oneself, so poor and ignorant, so God-deprived. Solidarity, as Jesus made clear, is a matter of sharing deeply in the experience of one's fellow human beings, especially those of one's own religious household, not as an extrinsic gesture of benevolence by a safe outsider, but because the experience is inescapably one's own. Jesus knew the oppression of his fellow Galileans by the religious establishment because it was after him too. He knew how seductive temptations of the flesh and to power and prestige could be because he was tempted. He knew the danger of speaking out for freedom of conscience in a situation of political repression because it could (and eventually did) lead to his own arrest and execution for disturbing the peace of both synagogue and state. Jesus was no different in this regard than Moses, who felt the people's doubt as his own when the desert journey was too long and the resources too short, who was disappointed in God and even desperate at times when survival, to say nothing of safety, seemed threatened. The prophetic vocation would be reasonably easy if one always saw clearly the God who is utterly faithful and knew that the outcome had to be finally successful. It is Jesus screaming into the darkness, "My God, my God, why have you abandoned me?" who tells us what prophetic solidarity finally entails.

Prophetic solidarity with the people of our time expresses itself as a generous and resolute *living of the questions:* of alienation, doubt, oppression, incoherence, meaninglessness, hopelessness, and danger on every side. Religious are not sent as cheerful televangelists from the realm of light with the "right" answers for a people immersed in darkness. They are sent to participate humbly and fragilely in the darkness, to experience it as their own, but without losing heart. The difference is that their participation is anchored, not in the optimism of one who knows the outcome will finally be triumphant, but in an unshakable hope in the God who saves.[8] However long the struggle (and it may well outlast one's own life), however deep the darkness, however violent the engagement, the Religious continues to cling, like Jacob, to a God who is often invisible but who alone can offer the blessing we crave. This perseverance and fidelity are not based on an expectation of solutions or victory but on a naked faith and love born of contemplative intimacy with God in prayer.

Immediacy to God in contemplation and solidarity with the people in struggle takes place in a cultural context that is historically particular. Every form of Religious Life is called to be prophetic in a situation that cannot be generalized to or deduced from some archetypal and abstract context. American Religious at the turn of the twenty-first century, even in a context of galloping globalization, cannot be equated with African Religious in a rural village or Asian Religious in a Hindu culture. Solidarity with the people among whom one lives involves one in a specific cultural setting with its specific issues. We will look at some of the issues of the North American context shortly.

However, as was said in chapter 4, the relation of the Religious to culture is one of voluntary *marginality* rather than total absorption. By not undertaking one's species role as reproducer of the race, by not participating in a capitalist economy by the acquisition or use of wealth for personal purposes, by not exercising political power for individual goals, the Religious situates herself at the edges of the systems that make the culture function. From this marginal position Religious share in the "hermeneutical advantage of the poor," the vision of the sociocultural system from the standpoint of those who are not primary beneficiaries of that system but often its victims. The marginality forced on the poor and defenseless is voluntarily chosen by Religious. Having renounced the gain that full cultural participation offers, Religious have less to lose from radical change and thus greater freedom in prophetic announcement that everything is not all right, that the time of God's visitation is near, that the promises of the past are still to be fulfilled, and that God's preferential option for the poor will not finally be frustrated.

This marginality was, in times past, sometimes distorted into virtual absence from or ignoring of the cultural situation. Religious did not live in normal homes or wear ordinary clothes or follow a daily schedule that encouraged contact with those outside the congregation; they did not have to get jobs or handle money or travel in cattle-car airplanes or on congested freeways; they did not have to deal with aging parents or suddenly tumultuous relationships with people of the other sex. Even after the Council, there was a tendency of Religious toward a rhetoric of antagonistic nonparticipation or absolute "counterculturalism" that seemed to suggest that Religious could, or should, or did live in some kind of cultural vacuum unaffected by the greed, ambition, or ethnocentricity of the surrounding society.

Experience, however, has tended to mute if not silence this rather self-righteous rhetoric. Religious are just as tempted to materialism and even luxury as their contemporaries. They want to live in safe neighborhoods and comfortable homes and to hold respectable and well-paid jobs that may not be open to immigrants or people of color. Going to the bank or grocery store, to the theater or the restaurant, filling the gas tank or exercising at the health club, shopping for clothes or paying the credit card bill suffice to remind Religious that, inescapably, they are much more immersed in their culture than they want to be but, in any case, hardly "countercultural" in any pure and absolute way.

The ambiguity of the relation of Religious to culture, both ecclesial and secular, especially since the dismantling of the total institution, is an area of murkiness and anxiety. There is a sense in which consecrated celibacy, voluntary and total economic interdependence, and corporate life in community and mission establishes a radical marginality of the Religious in relation to the values and dynamics of secular culture, especially in a capitalist society, and even in relation to the ecclesiastical culture, which is often very much "of this world" in its values and procedures. But there is also a sense in which anyone who lives in and participates in such a society is continually integrated into its dynamics and solicited by its values. In other words, the Religious is involved less in absolute and unambiguous counterculturalism, in either Church or civil society, than in a participant marginality that expresses itself at various times and in various ways (and not always with absolute consistency) in selective participation, cultural criticism, critical activism, and strategic withdrawal.

There is no way to make a once-and-for-all decision about how and when one will participate or withdraw, criticize or cooperate. Even within the same congregation, the decision of one Religious may not be that of another. One goes to jail and another avoids arrest to further the same antiwar agenda. One goes to the soup kitchen and another to the college classroom to work against poverty. One serves in a diocesan chancery and another writes articles critical of the ecclesiastical system in order to further reform in the Church. The situation of Religious in relation to culture is one of resistant immersion that is extremely ambiguous. And at the same time it is one in which the Religious refuses to simply "go with the flow." She is constantly asking, "Is this really right? Does this reflect the Gospel? Can I support this or must I protest?" And she can never assume that because the "right" people are taking a particular approach, it is the virtuous path. Thomas Merton paid dearly among his fellow peace protesters for his adamant condemnation of the self-immolation of one of the Catholic Worker activists. Whatever the young man's motives, Merton maintained, suicide was not a viable tactic. Dorothy Day's resolute total nonviolence put her at odds with very-well-meaning colleagues who were, in fundamental ways, on the right side of the issues.

Again, the example of Jesus the prophet, following in the footsteps of the Old Testament prophets, suggests that we should not expect things to be less complicated and obscure. Jesus was a Jew who went religiously to the Temple, who praised the widow for contributing her mite for its upkeep (cf. Mk 12:42–44), but who also overthrew the stalls of the Temple moneychangers (cf. Jn 2:13–22) and predicted the ruin of the Temple as divine retribution for Israel's refusal of God's visitation (cf. Lk 19:41–44). He condemned the religious authorities for their abuse of the people but told his disciples to obey those same authorities as long as they sat on the seat of Moses (cf. Mt 23:2–3). Jesus condemned the abuse of the poor by an unjust economic system but counseled nonresistance to, even cooperation with, the taxation that supported that system (cf. Mt 17:27; 22:15–22). He did not participate in the militant Jewish guerrilla movements aimed at the overthrow of the Roman oppressors, but he so threatened the political system that he was arrested on a capital charge and withstood Pilate, the Roman governor, to his face. And in all this ambiguity Jesus was not unlike Moses, Isaiah, Jeremiah, Hosea, and the other prophets who were both caught up in the complexities of their historical situations and gave voice to a vision that called that situation into question.

3. *The prophet as liminal figure:* The prophet can be said to live a spirituality of liminality, of one who is neither "in" nor "out," who is not really at home anywhere in the structures of society or Church, who neither belongs unambiguously nor leaves definitively, who operates at the thresholds where realities meet, clash, and merge. Margaret Brennan spoke of Religious Life as a prophetic lifeform standing at the threshold between present and future.[9] I have described it above as an arena of interaction between God and the People of God, between the People of God and their leaders, between Church and culture. As prophetic, Religious Life is a vocation to solidarity from a position of marginality.

In relation to *God,* the Religious does not opt for a purely contemplative existence in which to pursue her own spiritual growth. She goes into the presence of God like Moses into the meeting tent or Jesus on the cross, pleading the cause of the people, who know not what they do (cf. Lk 23:34). Like Moses she holds up the arms of prayer against the disasters that threaten from every side, and like Jesus she intercedes for the victims of the disasters that cannot be averted. The Religious stands at the threshold between God and the people, unable ever to give herself over completely to the joys of contemplative union as long as the poor are hungry and the defenseless are violated.

In relation to the *people* the Religious stands, by preference, with the poor, not only with the economically destitute but with the uncared-for sick, the racially or sexually oppressed, the greed-consumed rich, the educationally disadvantaged, with all who are in any way impoverished as human beings. But because the Religious vocation is one to prophecy and therefore not to the pursuit of institutional agendas or the protection of vested power, she also finds herself on the threshold, not only between the poor and the social systems that grind them down, but between ecclesiastical systems and the poor of the Church, who are so often victimized by the bureaucracy, the obsession with orthodoxy and conformity, the legalism and vindictiveness of an ecclesiastical power system that at its worst is not all that different from the one Jesus dealt with in first-century Judaism. When the authorities bind burdens too heavy for people to carry and refuse to lift a finger to help them (cf. Lk 11:46) or make void the law of God for the sake of human traditions (cf. Mk 7:8), it is the prophet who stands at the threshold between institutional power and the victimized.

In relation to *culture,* the Religious tries to mediate between the genuine values of a culture and its own blindnesses, between the culture of the world and the culture of the Church, between individual and society within both civil and ecclesiastical cultures. It is not the task of the cross-cultural Religious missioner, for example, to destroy the host culture in the name of a Eurocentric ecclesiastical institution, but neither can she so identify with that host culture that its historical oppression of women, genital mutilation, or caste system go unquestioned. The prophetic vocation of Religious involves them in the often acrimonious debate about whether ecclesiastical culture can be enriched and humanized by some of the values of representative government and due process, even as they struggle against the dictatorship of majority rule and the tyranny of process in a secular society that systematically silences the cries of the poor. Part of the prophetic valence of Religious community life itself is its ongoing, lived exploration of the threshold dialectic between individual and community that constantly emerges in modern society in the debates over abortion, capital punishment, taxation, the draft, child care, organ donation, and so many other issues.

Religious do not participate in all these liminal situations and struggles because they have some superior wisdom about them, divinely inspired answers they need only communicate to the unenlightened. The particular role of the prophet in these threshold situations arises from the fact that the Religious has only one loyalty, to God, and one agenda, the coming of God's Reign. Any absolute vested interest arising from family (whether of origin or foundation) nation, political party, class, gender, race, economic position, institutional leadership, or any other situation of "belonging" has been renounced in favor of a naked clinging to God for the sake of the people. The Religious is not simply a citizen of the world or a child of the universe; she lives by anticipation in the Reign of God and does not really belong, in any final or definitive sense, to any group, project, or institution.

This generates many of the seeming contradictions so often observed in the ministry of Religious. They may, for example, direct an elite school where the rich seek asylum from the underprivileged and then give scholarships to it to the very poor. They are publicly identified with the Church and yet openly challenge its leadership and policies when these are oppressive. They strategize against capital punishment while standing in solidarity with the victims of the crimes. They promote democracy but undermine its military imposition in third-world countries. They preach chastity but care for the perpetrators of sexual violence. They send their members all over the world even while needs multiply at home. They champion the local Church but refuse to restrict their personnel within its boundaries. Religious are finally not owned, even by the institutional Church. Their consistency is not in fidelity to a program or platform but to God and God's Reign.

4. *Liminality and persecution:* Because Religious Life is a prophetic vocation to liminality, Religious are, in a very real way, "strangers and pilgrims" who have here no lasting city. Participants in every struggle for justice and truth, they are not finally and definitively situated within any one of them. They go where the need manifests itself even if that means breaking long-established ties. They promote simultaneously seemingly contradictory agendas because in being "for" one group or agenda they will not destroy the adversary.

One of the very logical but extremely painful results of this liminal nonbelonging is that the prophet cannot draw, for survival or protection, on any specific constituency. Unlike the revolutionary leader whose unambiguous commitment is to one cause and against the group that opposes it, the prophet has nowhere to call home, no troops on which to rely. This was abundantly clear in the lives and ministries of the Old Testament prophets as well as Jesus. Jeremiah was not only persecuted by the king whose policies he undermined but condemned by the priests and court prophets and finally abandoned even by the people. Jesus' brief popularity with the crowds dissipated when he was marked as an enemy by religious and civil authority. Religious are the glory of the institutional Church as long as they remain enclosed and habited and quietly staff Church institutions according to institutional rules, but if they threaten centralized power they can look for little support at the local or universal level and become the target of the "loyalists" among those they have tried to serve.

Part of the agony of the prophet arises from a visceral sense that whatever persecution one might have to suffer *should* come from ungodly, worldly, or sinful structures or people. Persecution by the Church always feels wrong. There is a nagging suspicion that if one were truly advancing God's agenda the Church, at least, would be approving and supporting one's efforts. Rejection and oppression by the ecclesiastical institution is the most subversive force in the life of the Religious, the most undermining experience of the Religious congregation.

Again, we must turn to Scripture. None of the Old Testament prophets was supported by the religious establishment. Jesus was rejected by official Judaism. Part of the motivation of monastic life throughout the centuries, not only in Catholicism but in other religions as well, has been protest against not only the worldliness of secular culture but the laxity, venality, and power agendas of institutional religion and its officials. Religious Life, because of its nature as a prophetic vocation, will never be fully at home in the institution. This is much more clear today than it has been in recent history in North America, during which the virtual identification of agendas between ministerial congregations and the hierarchy in the creation and nurturing of the immigrant Church has obscured the prophetic character of Religious Life. It is also clearer in proportion to the professional competence of Religious, who are increasingly less dependent on the clergy for their theological self-understanding or their interpretation of surrounding culture and its dilemmas and therefore less susceptible to institutional indoctrination or intimidation.

Realization of the fact that Religious Life is and always will be in a liminal situation in the institution, that being "daughters of the Church" means being in solidarity with the people of God and committed to the Reign of God, not being the favorites of institutional authorities, demands both realism and the development of deep spiritual reserves. Religious have to develop not only the invincible, faith-rooted hope that sustains their commitment to the coming of the Reign of God that probably will not occur in their lifetime, but also a resolute capacity to absorb persecution and condemnation even unto death. Death may be physical, as it has been for so many contemporary Religious in Latin America, Asia, and Africa. But it may also be professional, ministerial, or personal, as it has been for health-care, political, educational, and pastoral ministers who have lost their positions and reputations to persecution from within and outside the institutional Church. The capacity to love unto the end not only the people to whom they minister but also those by whom they are persecuted is not a rhetorical skill. It is the fruit of persevering prayer, self-discipline, and total commitment to Jesus in all his members that is the charism of ministerial Religious Life.

III. Arenas of Prophetic Presence in North America at the Turn of the Century

In this section I want to take up three specific areas in which contemporary first-world Religious are involved and which illustrate well the prophetic character of the lifeform: interreligious encounter; the postmodern dialectic between religion and spirituality; and feminism in the ecclesial context.

A. Interreligious Encounter

The globalization of culture that has brought previously isolated societies into contact with each other in the second half of the twentieth century inevitably raises the question of the validity of non-Christian spiritual paths. Vatican II was not unaffected by this development. Not only did it revitalize the ecumenical discussion between Catholics and Protestants[10] and open itself to reexamining its relationship with its ancestor in faith, Judaism, and its younger monotheistic sibling, Islam, but it cautiously affirmed the importance of dialogue with the great world religions beyond the monotheistic faiths, especially Hinduism and Buddhism.[11]

Although the outreach to Protestants and to non-Christians may look like two subsets of a similar enterprise, they are essentially different. With Protestant Christianity Catholicism shares a common fifteen-centuries-long history during which all the foundational documents, both scriptural and conciliar, were written. Catholics and Protestants profess the same creed. The primary issue in ecumenical relations is that of different understandings of shared categories, for example, church order, sacraments, and ministry. Thus systematic theology, which deals with such matters and is recognized as a valid enterprise by both Catholics and Protestants, is a primary player in the conversation which can proceed with mutually understood vocabulary.

Furthermore, at least in the first world, a very valuable foundation for the dialogue had already been laid in the everyday relations between ordinary laity on both sides of the Reformation divide and even among the lower clergy in various denominations. Catholics and Protestants had intermarried and worked out ways of raising families together that did not always adhere strictly to the hegemonic requirements of the Catholic Church. Catholics and Protestants worked and studied together in a society that privileged neither. And committed members of both branches of Christianity struggled side by side in the cause of justice. In these situations Catholics had learned that they had far more in common with their Protestant relatives, friends, and colleagues than the official practice and teaching of their own Church suggested. Partly because of this deep and widespread interrelationship of ordinary Catholics with Protestants, the ecumenical encounter at the grassroots level is often considerably further advanced than it is in the official dialogue at the institutional level, where issues of power and authority combine with theological intransigence to impede progress toward reconciliation.

The interreligious encounter, however, is different in virtually every way from the ecumenical one. It involves an encounter not between separated siblings but between virtually total strangers. Even the first exploratory meetings between Catholics and non-Christians quickly made it clear that there could be no assumption of common or even analogous categories in which to root theological dialogue. Terms such as *God, Savior, Church, salvation, eternal life, soul,* or *sacrament* were often without corresponding categories in traditions that operated in a conceptual universe as foreign to Catholics as ours was to them. Systematic theology was of little use since it drew its revelatory data from a scripture and tradition not shared with its interlocutors and functioned through a philosophical grid that was meaningless, if not incomprehensible, in non-Western cultures. Very quickly, it became clear that the discipline that had to engage the interreligious problematic was foundational theology. What was needed was a theology of religions that could render coherent the seemingly opposed propositions that Jesus Christ is the unique and universal savior of the world and that spiritual traditions in which Jesus plays no part at all are or could be genuinely salvific. No fully satisfactory theology of religions has yet emerged,[12] but the recognition that such a theology is absolutely necessary if we are to get beyond branding ancient spiritual traditions pagan or atheistic on the one hand, and a crass evangelism designed to obliterate these traditions through absorption on the other.

As the theological discussions among religions either foundered on the shoals of mutual incomprehension or became exercises at such high levels of abstraction as to render them almost purely academic, a remarkable meeting of minds and hearts was taking place among the monastic practitioners of the various traditions.[13] Although not devoid of academic discussion, the encounters among the monastics tended to center in a shared practice of meditation and prayer, and exploration of commonalities in monastic discipline and lifestyle. The lectures given by monastics on either side were nonaggressive, nondefensive, and nonproselytizing expositions of the bases of contemplative practice and its results for the person and community designed to invite understanding and participation by the other as far as that seemed possible or desirable.

Outstanding participants in this cross-fertilization of religions were monastics who made the study of non-Christian traditions a primary focus of their work, such as Thomas Merton in relation to Buddhism and Taoism,[14] and others such as Bede Griffiths,[15] Pascaline Coff,[16] and Enomiya-Lassalle,[17] who actually went to Asia to study and practice under Buddhist or Hindu masters and to live in or found contemplative communities in which the scriptures and practices of these traditions were the sole or a very important feature. These moves were not "experiments," much less dilettante dabblings in the exotic. They were (and are) deep commitments to transforming spiritual experience outside one's own tradition and therefore potentially subversive of one's own faith commitments.[18] They are ventures into the liminal region between ancient non-Christian religious traditions and Christian faith and thus a natural, if dangerous, place for Religious to be.

Why have Religious, especially those living the monastic lifestyle, been the shock troops of interreligious dialogue? I would suggest that the reason lies in the nature of Religious Life as a prophetic lifeform. Religious, as I have remarked a number of times in the previous pages, are not part of the hierarchical structure of the Church. Religious are not agents of the institution. It is not their task to represent or protect the institution or to guard doctrinal purity or orthodoxy. The work of Religious is to seek God with the whole of their being and life, to pursue that quest wherever it leads, and to do so to the exclusion of any other primary life commitment or work. In this respect Religious are involved, from within the Christian tradition, with the same project that motivates monastics in other spiritual traditions in their quest for the transcendent. Religious and monastics of other traditions spontaneously recognize not only the similarity of their lifestyles but especially the analogous character of their goals and practices.

Religious involved in interreligious dialogue are not concerned with the institutional unification of Christianity and non-Christian religions. They know, if they have lived the contemplative life seriously, that God is well beyond our capacity to grasp or explain and that no institutional provisions are absolute. As Bede Griffiths came to see, absolute faith in Christ as the ultimate truth need not imply that Christianity is the one true religion or that conversion to Christianity is the only path to salvation. How to reconcile both members of this belief statement is not altogether clear at the conceptual level but it is abundantly clear at the level of experience. This zone of religious experience in which the particular and the universal come together is a liminal zone which is, in a sense, the natural habitat of the Religious as prophet. It is possible to dwell in this boundary region without compromise, confusion, or intransigence (although not without concern and a proper sense of insecurity) because the final and absolute loyalty, the only place of belonging for the Religious, is God, who is not the possession or under the control of any institution or its personnel, or encompassed within any doctrinal synthesis.

The prophetic potential of the interreligious dialogue is patent. Can there be any question, in the last analysis, that the call of the human race is to unity? As Teilhard de Chardin intuited and constructive postmodernism affirms, true unity cannot be attained by the absorption or obliteration of the other. It is already becoming apparent that the Christian and non-Christian religious traditions, if they remain true to themselves, can be mutually enriching. The Catholic Religious has something to offer to this dialogue, namely, the quintessential Christian insight, deriving from the (nonexhaustive) incarnation of the universal Wisdom of God in the human being Jesus of Nazareth, that humanity is capable of and called to divinity. Christ, human and divine, is the pattern and the goal of human being. We are made for divinization. But perhaps it is not the case that the only packaging of this profound truth is the Christian religious tradition.

Religious (and others) involved in the interreligious dialogue are also the conduit into Christianity of profound insights from the great non-Christian traditions, which have yet to deeply penetrate the Christian milieu.[19] The absolute otherness and transcendence of Ultimate Reality, the oneness of Holy Mystery, the nondualistic and yet nonmonistic relation of humans to that mystery, although affirmed in the Christian mystical tradition, have not been the powerful factor in Christian spirituality that they have been in Hinduism and Buddhism, nor have our contemplative practices and communal liturgy facilitated a deep encounter with the mystery of divine Nothingness to the same degree. Just as a Buddhist need not become a Catholic to grapple with the implications of human divinization offered in Christ, so a Christian need not become a Buddhist to enter more deeply into the mystery of the Void.

The interreligious encounter, unless it is somehow arrested (which hardly seems possible, given the commitment to it of monastics on both sides, deriving not from a political or social agenda but from a conviction about the pursuit of truth that it involves), will transform all religions in the future in a move toward nonreductionistic and pluralistic unity. This is what prophetic activity is about, telling what time it is, what it is time for. It is time for the ancient divisions and animosities among religions to be replaced by mutual respect and enrichment. Interreligious encounter and exchange is a natural sphere of being and action for Religious as primary carriers of the prophetic vocation in the Church.

B. The Dialectic between Religion and Spirituality

The prophetic vocation to "live the questions" of one's own historical-cultural situation has plunged Religious into another zone of liminality that is challenging the unanimity of mind and heart on which community is built. Increasingly, first-world seekers proclaim their interest in and commitment to spirituality but their alienation from religion. This is a multilayered declaration that in many cases is, on the one hand, poorly analyzed but, on the other hand, an expression of a deeply felt experience of alienation.[20] It may emanate from spiritual dabblers cobbling together a purely idiosyncratic "spiritual practice" that meets, at least temporarily, a felt need for attention to something beyond the daily without making any serious demands for *metanoia.* But it may also come from very serious seekers who have found organized religion such a hindrance to their deepest desire for personal growth in union with the transcendent that they have struck out on their own. If the God-quest is the defining concern of Religious Life this discussion must engage Religious not as one among many interesting topics but as a crucial issue in their own area of life specialization. Furthermore, many Religious spontaneously identify with this experience of commitment to spirituality and alienation from religion.

Any serious attempt to situate oneself in this discussion demands some clarity about what the terms *religion* and *spirituality* mean. Religion can be used on at least three levels and may well be accepted on one level and repudiated on another by the same person at the same time. At its most basic, religion is the *fundamental life stance* of the person who believes in God (or the Transcendent, however named) and assumes some realistic posture in the face of that Ultimate Reality. It involves a recognition of the total dependence of the creature on the source of being and life and gives rise to such attitudes and actions as reverent adoration, thanksgiving for being and life and all that sustains it, repentance for failure to live in that holy Presence in a worthy manner, and reliance on God for help in living and dying. In this sense, religion is at the root of any spiritual quest that is not explicitly atheistic or reductively naturalistic. However vaguely they may define the Ultimate Reality or however antagonistic toward organized religion, most people speaking of spirituality are religious in this most basic sense.

Second, religion can denote a *spiritual tradition* such as Christianity or Buddhism, usually emanating from some foundational experience of (divine) revelation (e.g., Jesus' experience of divine filiation or the Buddha's enlightenment) that has given rise to a characteristic way of understanding and living in the presence of ultimate reality. Most people are born into such a tradition remotely in their home culture and often proximately in their family of origin. Whether or not they go to church or synagogue or know much about the doctrines of Christianity or Judaism, most North Americans operate within a framework that is traditionally Judaeo-Christian. Separating oneself completely from the tradition of one's origin and/or culture is extremely difficult and requires considerable intellectual effort even for those who have chosen another tradition or deliberately rejected all traditions. In this sense, even people who claim to have rejected religion in favor of spirituality probably continue to operate to some degree within a religious tradition, if only by way of contrast. This might come to expression, for example, in an explicit modeling of one's life on Jesus, even if one no longer goes to church or checks "Catholic" on a census form. It may even express itself in the version of "God" that the resolute atheist rejects!

Third, religion can denote *a religion or institutionalized formulation* of a particular spiritual tradition. Here we are talking about Missouri Synod Lutheranism, Soto Buddhism, Roman

Catholicism, Reformed Judaism, and so on. The religious institution typically involves creed (a specific formulation of doctrine regarded as normative for knowledge or faith), code (a particular formulation of behaviorally normative ethical demands flowing from what is believed), and cult (a formalized practice of worship and devotion that embodies or flows from the credal beliefs and strengthens the believers in faith and morality). It is actually at this level that many people who claim to be committed to spirituality but alienated from religion have their problems. The problem is not with religion as a basic life stance of reverence in the face of Holy Mystery and often not even with religious tradition as a broad historical movement shaping religious consciousness. The problem is with particular religions. The question, to which we will return shortly, is why religions that would seem to be the natural and necessary concrete expressions of various religious traditions have become so problematic in our time.

Spirituality is as difficult to define as experience, and precisely because it is a particular kind of experience. Although *spirituality* was originally a specifically religious and indeed Christian term,[21] it is today used much more broadly, not only for experience that is not Christian but even for experience that is not religious in any, or at least in the second or third, meanings given above. A recognized specialist in nonreligious spirituality has defined it as

> ...the embodied task of realizing one's truest self in the context of reality apprehended as a cosmic totality. It is the quest for attaining an optimal relationship between what one truly is and everything that is; it is a quest that can be furthered by adopting appropriate spiritual practices and by participating in relevant communal rituals.[22]

In other words, it is possible to speak of spirituality without any reference to Ultimate Reality beyond the totality of what exists. Such spirituality could be (although it does not have to be) not only secular or naturalistic but even atheistic.

The spirituality of most of the people (especially those who are traditionally Christian) engaged in the "religion versus spirituality" discussion remains religious in the first sense given above. They believe in God, believe that God is concerned with this world and themselves, that belief in and union with such a God can be life-enhancing, that spirituality has an ethical dimension, and that both spiritual practice of some kind and morality are pertinent to the search for union with God. In many cases the general framework of their search is the Christian tradition in the second sense given above, even though they have disaffiliated from any particular denomination such as Lutheranism or Catholicism or at least relativized their belonging through both addition (of elements they find helpful from other denominations or traditions) and subtraction (of elements they find problematic in their denomination or tradition). A more precise definition of spirituality for such people might be "a quest for life-integration through self-transcendence toward the ultimate value one perceives"[23] with such ultimate value understood, at least in general, as the God of Judaeo-Christian revelation.

Obviously, Christianity (whether in its Catholic, Protestant, or Orthodox formulation) involves a spirituality. Indeed, spirituality is the deeper dimension of institutionalized religion without which the latter becomes a shell of routine at best and an oppressive power structure at worst. What, then, is the root of the "religion versus spirituality" dichotomy? I suggest that there are three aspects of institutional religion (the third level) that have become increasingly problematic for contemporary believers precisely because of the ecumenical and interreligious experience characteristic of postmodern globalization and the general espousal in the first world of democratic and participative principles of social organization.

First, denominational religions have, historically, been *exclusive*. This exclusivity can be cultural and geographical as was the case with the great religions of the East before migration within, into, and beyond Asia became common.[24] It can be tribal, as has been the case with Native American or African religions, whose adherents never understood or intended their beliefs to extend beyond the tribe in which religion was culturally embedded, rather than separately institutionalized.

Or it can be doctrinal and cultic as has been the case with Islam, to some extent Judaism (which is unique in this respect as in many other ways),[25] and especially Christianity and its subdivisions. As long as the exclusivity was implicit because there was little or no contact with or conversion agenda toward the others, the exclusivity posed little problem. But in the cases of Christianity and Islam, which felt called to convert the world to thematic adherence to their religious faith and practice, it became both an agenda of domination and a litmus test of acceptability. There is no need to rehearse the tragic history of Christian persecution of Jews and Muslims, cultural destruction by Christian missionaries, the internecine wars among Christian denominations, the witch hunts and inquisitions within Christian denominations, or the holy wars of Islam. Religious exclusivity has been a source of hatred and violence which many contemporary believers find so scandalous that they can no longer associate with the sources and purveyors of it.

Second, and closely related to the issue of exclusivity, religions as institutions involve a particular set not only of beliefs but of obligatory practices and prohibitions. In many cases the beliefs are open to criticism by fair-minded moderns, and the practices appear arbitrary or oppressive. Increasingly, educated people reject the control of their minds and behavior in the name of God or religion that such beliefs, practices, and prohibitions represent. Shaking free of narrow-minded dogmatic impositions and guilt-inducing obligations and prohibitions for the sake of spiritual breadth, autonomy of conscience, and psychological maturity has led many to repudiate membership in a religious denomination.

But even as institutional Christianity has modified such requirements and recognized much greater autonomy of conscience and behavior for believers, there has remained another aspect of institutional practice that many find alienating, namely, the repudiation of non-Christian practices that a Christian might find attractive and spiritually helpful. As Christians have encountered other religions and quasi-religions directly, rather than purely academically, they have experienced the power of rituals and practices from Native American sweat lodges to Zen meditation, from African drumming to feminist nature rituals, from psychotherapy and support groups to channeling and crystal rubbing. Eclecticism and syncretism, familiar to the postmodern mind in the areas of art, science, medicine, business, and education, seem natural enough in the sphere of religion, but even in the case of serious scholars who are not indifferentists or syncretists the effort to deal with the possible mutual enrichment of religions is often viewed with suspicion or even alarm by institutional authorities.[26] The simplest solution to what many see as institutional narrowness and protectionism is to disassociate themselves from official membership in denominational religion and pursue a personal spirituality, which leaves one open to whatever seems to be of value in the religious quest.

A third problematic feature of religious denominations, especially within the Christian tradition, is the clerical system. Ministers, whatever they are called in a particular tradition, who fulfill an organizational or service function in a religious group such as witnessing and recording births, marriages, and deaths, providing materials for devotional practices, or maintaining places of worship or devotion may not pose a problem. But a sacerdotal clergy that claims ontological superiority to ordinary believers and claims to exercise an absolutely necessary intermediary role between the believer and God is highly problematic for many people.[27] The egalitarian theory and practice of Western societies tends to recognize only superiority based on competence or achievement. Furthermore, it will not countenance the monopoly and control of scarce resources, whether material or spiritual, by any self-appointed agency.[28] Many find intuitively repugnant the claim by an exclusive group to control access to God. In a denomination such as Catholicism, which not only has such a clerical system but in which half the membership is barred from access to it on the basis of gender, this repugnance can easily lead to disaffiliation from the institutional religion altogether.

In short, the repudiation of religion in favor of spirituality is, for many people, actually the repudiation of denominational belonging rather than of religion as such or of religious traditions in their entirety. It arises from a rejection of the exclusivism, legalism, and clericalism that afflict many religions and that seem endemic to any institutionalized form of religion. Nondenominational spirituality, by contrast, seems to allow the person to seek God, to grow personally, and to commit oneself to the betterment of the world and society with freedom of spirit and openness to all that is good and useful, whatever its source.[29] There can be no question that many such disaffiliated seekers are admirable human beings and some may even exercise a prophetic function by cogently and articulately challenging the hypocrisy and control agenda of organized religion.[30]

This is not the place to go into the advantages, for most people, of belonging to an institutionalized community of faith or the disadvantages of a purely individual and idiosyncratic attempt to live the spiritual life. Suffice it to say that most people need both the resources of accumulated wisdom and ongoing community support to make consistent progress in the spiritual life (as opposed to feeling "spiritual") and to persevere in times of dryness and suffering. The community facilitates and orders the life of worship, which an individual cannot ritualize adequately in isolation, and maintains some consistency and coherence between belief and moral practice. Left entirely to one's own devices, most people will unnecessarily repeat many of the mistakes, some dangerous and tragic, that historical bodies have found ways to correct over the centuries. Without a community of discernment, the potential for religious and spiritual fanaticism is greatly increased.

History suggests that everywhere in the world people who are serious about the spiritual life have come together in communities of faith around revelation events that have been tested by experience and explicated by serious thought and faithful practice. They have been initiated into and educated by a tradition of spirituality well developed before they were born, strengthened by the coherence of belief and practice, carried by the community's faith when they were weak and challenged to carry others when they were strong, and gradually made responsible for the purification and handing on of that tradition. They have drawn deeply from the well of a traditional wisdom, even as they have criticized its excesses and made their own contributions to its resources.

There is no question that religions, once institutionalized, are prone to all kinds of hypocrisy, routinization, self-serving corruption of leadership, injustice toward members, clericalism, and dogmatic oppression. The same must be said of virtually all institutions, political, social, educational, or economic. The question is not whether there are any perfect religions because obviously there are not. It is whether, given the balance between what membership, including identification with and participation in a faith community (as opposed to occasional dabbling), can offer and the threats to faith and holiness of institutional corruption, one wants to remain a participant in a religious tradition in its institutionalized form.

Many Religious find themselves in a very ambiguous position at the very heart of this "religion versus spirituality" struggle. Religious are, by definition, people for whom the God-quest, that is, the concern with religion in its basic sense, is central. Furthermore, the Religious Life we are discussing in this volume is generated by and located within the Christian tradition, centered on faith in and commitment to Jesus Christ in the very radical form of perpetual consecrated celibacy lived in community and mission. Even more specifically, although there are some Protestant Religious orders, the ones we are discussing here are specifically Roman Catholic.

However, precisely because Religious are so intimately related to this particular institutional embodiment of Christianity they are more exposed on a day-to-day basis than are many Catholics to the exclusivism, legalism, and clericalism that often make participation in the life of the denomination agonizingly painful. Religious, because they are existentially absorbed in the God-quest as the primary concern of their lives, are sensitively attuned to religious and spiritual developments inside and outside the Church. It is not at all surprising, therefore, that Religious are often at the forefront of spiritual developments that are not specifically Catholic, such as the peace movement, the struggle for social justice, the ecojustice movement, ecumenism, interreligious interchange, feminism, the retreat movement, psychological and other human potential experiments. Often experiences in these areas are more spiritually nourishing and challenging than poorly conducted, clerically dominated sacramental celebrations or routine Catholic spiritual practices. And the condemnatory attitude of some Church officials toward anything that is new, not specifically Catholic, and/or not clerically controlled[31] is stultifying to people who are spiritually alive and searching.

In other words, once again, Religious occupy a liminal position. They are at once very deeply involved in institutional Catholicism and often widely and deeply involved in the experiences of spirituality beyond its denominational boundaries. There is no question that the narrow denominationalism characteristic of post-Tridentine Christianity is dying. The postmodern world, religiously, will have to be much more doctrinally flexible and more interrelated in terms of faith and practice than the polemical sectarianism of the post-Reformation period could imagine. But if Teilhard de Chardin was right that distinction, not uniformity, is the basis of genuine organic unity then the various historical communities of faith will quite possibly retain their specificity even as they cross-fertilize one another. The strength and vitality of these communities may be the very condition of possibility of such mutual enrichment. And it will probably continue to be the case that strong, self-critical communities of religious wisdom will be more able to contribute to the creation of a preferred future for the universe and the race than spiritual "lone rangers" inventing personally satisfying but idiosyncratic private spiritualities that have no past and no future.

Religious are in a unique position to offer prophetic leadership in this arena. They are not agents of the institution and thus have a *freedom* in regard to their lived spirituality that clerics or other official diocesan personnel do not. The point of identification of the prophet is not with the hierarchy but with the People of God. *Contemplation* is the direct access to God from which Religious as individuals, in the tradition of the prophets, draw both enlightenment and strength that is not subject to institutional control.[32] And Religious, because they have created strong *communities* within the larger Catholic community, have a context in which to prophetically "live the questions" in this area in a way that can perhaps lead forward through the present impasse.

Within their own Religious community members can work directly and effectively, and often without the inhibiting surveillance that those working within a parish might experience, to create a valid incarnation of Catholic Christian spirituality that minimizes the exclusivism, legalism, and clericalism that are so problematic in the Church at large. The community can provide a stabile and secure base for interaction with currents of spirituality that are not explicitly Catholic and, equally importantly, a wisdom context within which to discern what is and what is not compatible with and enriching of Christian faith. It can hold patiently the challenging discoveries while the implications emerge. Its members can support one another during times of disillusionment with and alienation from the institutional Church by being Church in integrity and truth. As a community of faith they can celebrate in the power of age-old Catholic liturgical ritual even as they develop new forms of prayer suitable for this cultural setting; they can draw on and learn from the wisdom of the Catholic mystical tradition even as they learn from the prayer traditions of other faiths; they can find strength in the history of their own congregation's cooperation with but also resistance to institutional Church authority as they both work with and criticize the present ecclesiastical structure.

I strongly suspect that one of the reasons so many people feel drawn to associate in one way or another with Religious congregations, even though they do not wish to enter as members, is that these congregations provide a form of genuinely Catholic community and spirituality that is less paranoid and punitive on the one hand and more creatively faithful and open-minded on the other than what they might find elsewhere in the Church. Here they can experience Church within the institution but not be cripplingly restricted by it. In this context, for example, receiving massage during a retreat is not likely to be considered hedonist, or an ecological celebration at the equinox pagan, or Zen meditation a threat to faith. If Religious congregations can, corporately and through their individual members, witness to the possibility of Catholic Christianity not only surviving but vigorously contributing to a new religious future for humanity, they will have fulfilled an important prophetic function. But as with all prophetic activity, it involves the painful tension of being the point of interaction and interpretation between God, the people, and the culture (both ecclesial and secular) and the ever-present danger of institutional persecution. The liminal space occupied by the prophet is never unambiguous or comfortable.

C. Feminism in the Ecclesial Context

The arena in which the prophetic power and institutional challenge of Religious Life has been most evident in the last three decades is surely the encounter between the Church and feminism. The characteristics of the prophetic vocation—its mediation of the interaction among God, Church, and culture, the specifically ecclesial location of prophetic ministry, the specific concern with justice, the persecution that such prophetic activity evokes, and the significant consequences for the whole people of God of the prophetic call to conversion—are most clearly manifest in this arena. Women Religious especially stand at the threshold where the powerful cultural phenomenon of feminism meets the Church whose leadership does not want to recognize its Gospel urgency. It is a liminal zone fraught with ambiguity, tension, and even persecution but whose potential for the Reign of God is enormous.

Religious in the North American context have, for close to two centuries, been involved almost exclusively in assisting the hierarchy and the clergy in the all-consuming task of caring for an immigrant Catholic population and then preparing those Catholics to assume their role as full and equal participants in American society. During that time Religious came to see themselves, and to be seen by others, as the service and educational arm of the institutional Church. Within the Church they were highly valued by the hierarchy as the largest segment of an indispensable corps of apostolic workers from the cities of the eastern seaboard to the vastness of the western frontier. They were admired and loved by generations of Catholics as the very embodiment of the institutional Church (which was their bulwark in an unreceptive secular society) as it touched their daily lives in parishes, classrooms, and hospitals. To those outside the Church they were the most loyal and devoted members of the Catholic Church, perhaps more readily identified with the institution than even the clergy, and they gradually compelled the admiration of their adversaries by the quality of their service to Catholics and non-Catholics alike in times of war and epidemic as well as in times of peace and prosperity.

In the years since the Council, because of a conjunction of causes, this institutional identity and especially its high social status has been seriously eroded. Catholics have come of age in American society and no longer feel the need to send their children to Catholic schools for the protection of their persons or their faith. Health and social services are as available to Catholics as to non-Catholics in public institutions, which sometimes have better facilities. The postconciliar decline in resources, both personal and financial, of Religious congregations has entailed the relinquishment of many institutions. Bishops and pastors can no longer count on a constantly renewed and readily available corps of Religious workers. No longer in habits or living together in large numbers, Religious are not as visible a Church presence in society at large. But nothing has so altered the relation of Religious to the institutional Church as the strong identification of Religious with the feminist movement. There is no question that feminism is seen by the Vatican as a major threat to the ecclesiastical status quo and the feminism of Religious as the most dangerous aspect of the movement.[33] The relation between the institutional authorities and feminist Catholics, especially women Religious, has grown increasingly tense and shows no signs of immediate improvement.

In view of what has been said about the prophetic identity of Religious Life in the Church, it is the period of overidentification with the institution and with the hierarchical agenda in the nineteenth and first half of the twentieth centuries that should be seen as anomalous rather than the present situation of tension between Religious and the institution. Nevertheless, Religious who grew up seeing themselves as the "most precious portion of the flock of Christ," as first and foremost "daughters of the Church" (both epithets understood in predominantly institutional terms), have found the present situation painful and difficult to understand or accept. Being the object of official ecclesiastical disapproval is not only uncomfortable. It undermines vocational identity and ministerial confidence. And when this is combined with an experience of patriarchal oppression and sexist discrimination it is sufficient to produce genuine alienation.

The uncomfortableness of many Religious, even those who are fully committed to the feminist agenda, in regard to feminism in their Religious congregations arises from a sense that somehow a "secular" movement or cause seems to have replaced the ecclesiastical project that defined Religious Life when they entered. In many ways feminism is creating and controlling an agenda once set and controlled by the hierarchy. And, in many cases, there is a strong intuitive sense that, on the one hand, there is something wrong with this ordering of priorities and, on the other hand, that there is something profoundly right about the feminist commitment. Furthermore, there does not seem to be any way of mediating peacefully between a passionate feminist commitment to liberation and equality and a resolute hierarchical commitment to patriarchal supremacy and domination. The two seem to be on an implacable and irreversible collision course. Nothing will make this situation anything but tense and dangerous until the grace of God and the Gospel of Christ finally prevail and that may not be within the lifetime of anyone currently involved in the struggle.

A full-scale discussion of this issue would require a book,[34] but it may be helpful to consider here several points that might help set this experience in the context of the prophetic vocation of Religious Life in the Church, that is, to present it as a "living of the questions" at the point of intersection among God, Church, and culture. Feminism did indeed originate and develop as a secular movement for the political, economic, and social equality of women in family and society.[35] In this respect it is part of a worldwide movement for liberation and equality that has matured gradually since the French and American revolutions vindicated the God-given equality and rights of all people by virtue of their humanity. It is no accident that this movement for liberation arose in countries where the Judaeo-Christian tradition flourished because the insight into the inherent dignity of the human person is based on a conviction that humans are made in the image of God. They do not receive their dignity or their rights by royal birth or permission of the powerful but from the God who created them free and equal.

Although the Church since its inception has proclaimed the Gospel of liberation it has usually understood that message to mean that the Church is a zone of liberty in relation to "the world" but that within itself the Church is an intrinsically unequal society in which the hierarchy enjoys God-given authority and power over an essentially passive and powerless laity. The freedom of the children of God is a spiritual or interior liberty that permits and even demands expression in the right of the Christian to profess and practice the faith but it has no ramifications in the social order of the Church itself. In fact, the shared agenda of maintaining control of their respective populations has led almost inevitably to collusion between a spiritually powerful ecclesiastical hierarchy and the political and military power structures in secular society.

The cooperation of the institutional Church with the Nazi regime in Germany, a terrible but logical expression of that collusion, was a wake-up call for all Christians. During the second half of the twentieth century there has been an increasing realization among both pastors and laity that the liberation of people from oppressive regimes is a demand of the Gospel and that the Church itself should be fully committed to that agenda regardless of the ramifications for Church-state relations.[36] It has been extremely difficult, however, for the institutional Church, long in league with the economic, political, and military elites in Christian countries, to begin to embrace a preferential option for the poor and powerless.

The oscillation between affirmation of this option for the poor and retrenchment from it has been playing itself out in conferences, synods, and cautionary documents, in martyrdoms and ecclesiastical condemnations around the issue of liberation theology, especially in Latin America and Asia, and is far from resolved.[37] It is no secret that a major impediment to unqualified ecclesiastical support for the liberation agenda is the implication that Church espousal of justice in society implies the practice of justice in the Church. No matter how often it is promulgated or how it is explained, an ecclesiastical system that denies full participation in the Church to some of its members and such basic human rights as freedom of speech and due process to all of them will not be accepted as just by modern people. The institutional Church is caught in a major conundrum: how to preach a Gospel of divinely willed liberation, equality, and justice in society while maintaining an institutional structure of hierarchical inequality in the Church.

In the third world, the liberation agenda in the Church focuses immediately on the Gospel-motivated struggle of the poor for life, justice, and peace. In the first world, the major incarnation of the liberation theology agenda has been religiously committed feminism. It is crucial in understanding this to realize that feminism, especially in its Christian and religious form, is not simply about women. Early in the struggle feminists came to realize that the adversary was not individual abusive men, or even systemic male power over women, but a hierarchical and dualistic system of domination and subordination, that is, patriarchy. Patriarchy's primary paradigm is the domination of women by men but it has worked itself out in the interlocking web of dominative relations in every area of life and society. Domination structures based on blood, class, race, gender, sexual orientation, age, wealth, ordination, and other titles to power are all of a piece. And the fundamental dynamic of domination extends beyond relations between individuals to military conquest, imperialism, and colonialism among nations, and even to the species domination of nonhuman creation by humans. The feminist agenda, in other words, includes the struggle against patriarchal oppression in all its forms. It is a struggle for nonviolence in every sphere of life, for ecojustice, for full participation of all people in the systems that affect them.

In the institutional Church clericalism in general and the oppression of women in particular have been analyzed by Catholic feminists as a specific incarnation of patriarchy and therefore a direct object of faith-motivated efforts for liberation. Although the symbolic flash-point of the confrontation is the ordination of women, the actual and comprehensive object of the feminist project is the dismantling of the patriarchal system of domination and subordination that structures the institutional Church and its replacement by a system of Gospel equality, justice, and love.

The feminist analysis, in other words, sees the patriarchal structure as contrary to the message of Jesus and antithetical to the Reign of God. This analysis not only poses a serious, indeed an ultimate, threat to the ecclesiastical status quo but it is so radical (in the etymological sense of "foundational" or "root") that many feminists themselves do not want to admit it or state it explicitly. Women Religious in particular, fully committed to the Gospel of Jesus Christ and the People of God who are the Church, would much rather believe that the problem is a few unenlightened or old-fashioned men, unwitting stupidity in the name of good order, or well-intentioned but bumbling ecclesiastical maneuvering. To admit that they are dealing with a deliberately constructed system that cannot be salvaged because it cannot be reconciled with the Gospel no matter how it is understood or practiced is a threat not only to the ecclesiastical status quo but a challenge to believers who must reimagine the Church if they are to live their Christian identity integrally.[38]

Throughout Church history, Religious Life and its members have been embroiled in the reform of the Church itself. This has never been a comfortable or easy task. In fact, if it were, one would have reason to question whether the reformers were not simply pursuing their own advantage under the pretext of a reform agenda. The Old Testament prophets addressing the kings and the priests of ancient Israel were calling for fidelity to the covenant rather than reliance on and pursuit of worldly power, for justice for the poor, the widows, and the orphans rather than increasing wealth for the powerful, for a religion of interior devotion and public virtue rather than elaborate and empty sacrifices. Jesus the prophet, addressing the priests, scribes, and Pharisees, that is, the leaders of the Israel of his day, was calling for compassion for the poor rather than harsh insistence on legal observance, for trust in God and fidelity to God's demands rather than collaboration with pagan power for the sake of security, for the facilitation of access to a God of love rather than restriction of such access for the augmenting of clerical power and control. Religious and others who are calling today for a just and open Church in which Baptism initiates all into a discipleship of equals participating fully in the mystery of Christ, prophet, priest, and servant leader, in which the People of God enjoy the dignity of God's adult and morally responsible children rather than being intimidated and terrorized in the name of God by imposed leadership, nonconsultative edicts, prosecution without due process, and vindictive penalties, are living out that same prophetic vocation in the cultural circumstances of the contemporary Church.

Feminism is a prophetic agenda calling for the end of "business as usual" in a patriarchal system of domination and subordination. It demands a fearless preaching of the Gospel, in season and out of season, a clear and reverent speaking of truth to power regardless of the consequences. It is a quintessentially prophetic task for Religious, as individuals and as congregations, which situates Religious in a liminal zone where the Gospel-based aspirations to freedom and the culture-legitimated agendas of domination in society and Church clash, where the cries of the poor meet the ear of God. The self-doubt and questioning, the reluctance in the face of disapproval and suffering, the fear of consequences are not an indication that the work is misguided or should be abandoned until a more favorable time. It is participation in the salvific agony of the One who asked to be freed from the cup of suffering but who did not flee from his calling to give his life as a ransom for the many.

IV. Summary and Conclusion

In this final chapter I have tried to pull together all that has been said in previous chapters about the nature of Religious Life and its location in contemporary world and Church culture. My thesis is that the charism of Religious Life in general and of mobile ministerial Religious Life in particular gives rise to a prophetic vocation and ministry in the Church. This vocation is rooted in and expressive of a spirituality that combines contemplative immediacy to God and participant marginality in relation to secular society. It is located in the intersection where God, people (both as Church and as human society), and culture meet and interact. Thus Religious Life, both in individuals and in congregations, is a liminal or threshold vocation. Its practitioners are never able to give full and unambiguous loyalty to any cause or group because they belong first and only to the God to whom they have given their lives in and through a total and exclusive commitment to Jesus Christ.

Only the Gospel, the Reign of God, can claim Religious' total devotion and ceaseless labor. The Gospel is never identified exclusively and exhaustively with any human agenda; the Reign of God is never identified with any party or nation or platform, whether of Church or of society. It is rarely crystal clear where the will of God in any matter lies. So Religious move, as the prophets always have, in a no-person's zone of passionate commitment to God and God's people and redemptive loneliness in a world of factions and blind loyalties to which they cannot surrender. They occupy a zone of insecurity and self-doubt because they cannot count on validation or approval from authority or support from their beneficiaries. They will make mistakes because they have no pipeline to the divine intention. They will be frustrated and persecuted because God promises them nothing more or different from the destiny of Jesus. They will probably not see the fruition of their labors because God's plan will not be complete as long as human history continues.

No one (at least no one in her right mind) undertakes this prophetic vocation on her own initiative. It is a response to a call, mysterious in its origin and in its manifestation. It is finally a response of love to Love, and that is more than sufficient to account for its totality and permanence, even in a world of fragmented commitments and hedged bets. Like the prophet of old the Religious says, "Here I am Lord, send me," and like the prophet Jesus coming into the world, "See Lord, I come to do your will."

Conclusion

In this brief conclusion I want to construct a metaphor using material borrowed from quantum physics[1] to summarize all that has been said in this volume about the "location" of Religious Life. It is important to remember that this is a metaphor, not a photograph or videotape (much less a scientific description), because the way things are at the subatomic level of quarks and electrons is very different from the way they are at the macroscopic level of everyday reality, and scientists do not know precisely how the two levels are connected. But the way things are at the subatomic level gives us some insight into organic systems that can be very illuminating when we are trying to deal with an organic social phenomenon like Religious Life.

The "uncertainty principle" formulated by the physicist Werner Heisenberg says, in effect, that if you know where a subatomic particle like an electron is, you cannot know what it is doing, and if you know what it is doing, you cannot know where it is. This book has been an attempt to discern and articulate "where" Religious Life is, and in order to locate it I have refrained from much discussion of how the life is being (or should be) lived. That will be the topic of volume 2, when I raise the question of what the implications of the theory laid out in this volume are for such issues as vocation, perpetual commitment, vows, community, ministry, and so on. In other words, this volume has charted the "where" we will have to presume when we raise the questions of "what is going on" in the life.

Underlying the whole discussion has been a basic assumption, again enlightened by the quantum physics metaphor, that the reality of Religious Life (as scientists are increasingly telling us about the universe) is not mechanical but organic. This means that it cannot be described as if it were composed of discrete parts or elements, each of which has a particular and extrinsic relationship to other parts which, added together constitute the life. Rather, Religious Life, like the quantum world, is an intricate holistic system. Consequently, it cannot be disassembled by analysis so that a clear and unambiguous understanding of the whole can be built up from an exhaustive understanding of the parts.

As scientists tell us about the quantum world, Religious Life is "unpicturable," but that does not mean that it cannot be understood. It means that we understand it not by analysis (much less by deduction from rules) but by submitting to our experience of living it and trying to interpret that experience to arrive at what is actually the case.[2] That has led me to the attempt to situate the system itself as a whole in a plurality of contexts, both cultural and ecclesial. Each "situation" has been a placing of the whole, which looks different in one context from the way it looks in another, much like light, which can behave like a wave or like a particle but cannot be seen as both at the same time.

The organic, systemic character of Religious Life was much less apparent in preconciliar times for the simple reason that it was virtually hermetically sealed off from its environment, that is, from the other systems surrounding it. A major effect of the conciliar renewal itself and especially the renewal of Religious Life was the dismantling of the barriers that sealed the life in and the "world" out. As Religious Life began to interact in increasingly extensive and intensive ways with the systems, both cultural and ecclesial, that surrounded it, the permeability of its own boundaries made its organic character evident. The boundaries of the life were not like fences or walls that cut a material phenomenon off from its surroundings but like skin, an organ of contact and interchange, of enrichment and vulnerability, bringing together an organism and its environs without destroying its identity. The life remains a distinct reality, but it is no longer living in a world of its own and that has made all the difference.

One of the features of organic systems that quantum physics has highlighted, and that seems very enlightening in relation to Religious Life, is that they are "chaotic." This does not mean that everything is in disarray but that such systems are exquisitely sensitive to *everything* that goes on around them. Thus they can only be discussed in terms of *all* that is going on. In a quantum world the flutter of a butterfly's wing in Africa actually affects the weather in North America. Because we can never achieve an exhaustive knowledge of all the factors influencing any such system we can never know it comprehensively, never know exactly what it will do, become, or experience. However, the physicists tell us that even though the system is "chaotic" in that it is unpredictable because of the vast and various influences affecting it, and thus it never does the same thing twice, the randomness at the microscopic level is in dialectical relationship with a principle of order, the effect of what is called "the strange attractor," which establishes a pattern of possibilities within which the system acts to maintain its identity. So, at the macroscopic level the behavior of the system is coherent and comprehensible. Our own persons seem to exhibit this dialectic of randomness (an incredible and noncatalogable array of influences) and order (our consistent self-sameness in the midst of continuous change) under the influence of our self-organizing identity.

An implication of this chaotic character of nevertheless orderly phenomena, as the physicist-priest John Polkinghorne explains, is that quantum systems are "open" (like clouds) rather than "closed" (like clocks). They do not have only a temporal future in the sense that something predictable will happen tomorrow that will follow necessarily from what is happening today (i.e., if you wind the clock it will run for the amount of time fixed by its mechanism) but a genuinely indeterminate future or destiny (one never knows what a child will turn out to be but it will not be a daisy). We cannot decide that such a system is now fully constituted and no further change can occur. (Canon Law has often attempted to fix Religious Life into a pattern that will remain permanently stable and, of course, historically this has never really worked.) Rather, such systems develop, and in very unpredictable but orderly ways, the way a cloud changes shape and function without ceasing to be a cloud.

Polkinghorne says that this random/order character is due to the fact that such systems are subject to not one but two kinds of causality. One kind with which we are very familiar he calls "bottom up causality." When an energy event impacts a system, for instance, when a volcanic eruption impacts the weather, there is a rearrangement of parts, the kind of change that classical physics can measure and describe in mechanical terms. But there is also "top down causality" in which the entire system, as a whole, is affected by the inflow or influence of pattern formation, or "information." The resulting modification is unpredictable, random. This kind of change cannot be handled by mechanical physics and, therefore, cannot be known in advance or controlled.[3]

I have been trying throughout this book to suggest that Religious Life is an organic system that is genuinely open. In this sense it is "chaotic," unpredictable. It is influenced not only by major energy events like the call to renewal by the Council (bottom up causality) but also by myriad types of information input (top down causality), such as the encounter with post-modernity, changes in the theology of Church, diversity of experience of its members, historical developments in the late twentieth century, and so on. The renewal event produced some highly visible and measurable effects on particular aspects of the life such as clothing, dwelling places, ministries. But the information input has affected the whole of the life or the life as a whole in highly unpredictable ways that cannot be fully calculated, described, or controlled.

Nevertheless, this does not mean that the life has lost its identity or that it can or will develop in a totally random fashion and in all possible directions. Margaret Wheatley, an organizational specialist who has applied quantum physics ideas to the theory and practice of management, has a very enlightening chapter,

"Chaos and the Strange Attractor of Meaning," in her now famous book on change and development in business and educational organizations.[4] She raises the question of what holds together and moves forward creatively a highly "chaotic" organization that is being bombarded from every side with transformative information. She says that suppressing the input or restricting the possibility on the part of the organization's members of interacting with it condemns the organization to stagnation. She evokes the idea of the strange attractor, the force that somehow keeps all the unpredictable behavior of the system within a coherent moving pattern so that it does not simply disintegrate into meaningless randomness. Wheatley believes that the strange attractor in the life of individuals is *meaning*. Even when the projects in which a person is involved are disorganized or the environment dysfunctional, a person who has found or finds meaning in her life can still be creative in what she is doing. In systems, or organizations, the analogue of meaning is the principle of self-identity. She says,

> A self-organizing system has the freedom to grow and evolve, guided only by one rule: It must remain consistent with itself and its past. The presence of this guiding rule allows for both creativity and boundaries, for evolution and coherence, for determinism and free will.[5]

Throughout this book I have been trying to discern and describe not the external shape or possible developments of Religious Life but the principle of self-identity which, if recognized and honored, can allow for unpredictable creativity of unimaginable variety and depth and yet maintain the boundaries necessary for continuity and coherence, that is, for life. These boundaries maintain the specificity and distinctiveness of the lifeform even as the interrelationships with surrounding systems become more varied and intense. What is the "strange attractor" of Religious Life which pulls all the variety and energy into unity, maintains the moving equilibrium of the system which is never standing still and rarely does the same thing twice, which is situated in multiple contexts in each of which it looks different, but which is recognizable as Religious

Life to both its members and the members of other systems with which it interacts? I have tried to suggest that it is the exclusive, lifelong God-quest centered in a particular kind of love of Jesus which calls some people to a life of consecrated celibacy lived in community and mission. The meaning of the life which provides the principle of self-identity, the strange attractor, is the love of Jesus in the unique form of total and irrevocable self-gift to the exclusion of any other primary relationship, life project, or cause. At the heart of the life is Jesus Christ, yesterday, today, and the same forever, calling and claiming some people in this unique and finally unexplainable way. For those who have experienced this call and claim, the particular experience of Jesus Christ that is Religious Life is indeed a treasure hidden in the field of history, culture, and Church, a treasure that is worth everything, even life itself.

Appendix

(John of the Cross's Spiritual Theology and
Transformation of Religious Life)

The Active Dark Night (Chapter 5)

John of the Cross	Events & Experience	Spiritual Fruit
Active Dark Night of Sense *Ascent of Mt. Carmel,* Book I	Pre-Vatican II formation of Religious in ascetical community, and ministerial life	John's "accommodation of sense to spirit" or basic personal integration
Active Dark Night of Spirit *Ascent of Mt. Carmel,* Books II and III	First stages of renewal: the willing surrender of many of the props and "perks" of Religious Life	John's purification of intellect through faith without insight; memory through hope for the unseen; love through lacking in felt devotion

Transition
(End of Chapter 5 and Beginning of Chapter 6)

A period of satisfaction, energy, effectiveness that characterized the first
decade after the Council

The Passive Dark Night (Chapter 6)

Passive Dark Night of Sense *The Dark Night,* Book I	"External" diminishments of the 2d and 3rd post-conciliar decades —loss of personnel & resources & institutions —loss of status & power —loss of community esprit de corps "Internal" diminishments caused by delayed passage through the Enlightenment with resultant loss of theological structures of meaning	Deeper, more humble, less satisfaction-driven fidelity, courage, and selflessness in prayer and ministry
Passive Dark Night of Spirit *The Dark Night,* Book II	Purification through "loss" of the God-image in the encounter with postmodernity	Emergence of genuinely theological faith, hope, charity

Notes

PREFACE

1. Sandra M. Schneiders, *New Wineskins: Re-Imagining Religious Life Today* (New York/Mahwah, N.J.: Paulist Press, 1986).

2. Throughout the book, unless the context clearly stipulates otherwise, I will use *lay* to refer to baptized Catholics who are not ordained or vowed members of Religious Institutes. This is not a pejorative designation, as I will explain at length in chapter 7, but a recognition of the fact that Religious have rights and obligations under Church law that other members of the laity (in the sense of the nonordained) do not. That means that they constitute a canonical category distinct in some ways from other nonclerics. *Laity* is, at least potentially, a positive term whereas *non-Religious* is a privative term and open to more negative connotations than *laity*.

3. In chapter 9 I will discuss the problematic character of these traditional designations, try to discern the real differences and relationships between the two forms of Religious Life, and make some suggestions about more appropriate terminology.

INTRODUCTION

1. Throughout the text I will capitalize words which have a common use as well as a specific one when I am using the specific meaning, e.g., *Religious* will be capitalized when it refers to a person living in the specific state of Religious Life, whereas *religious* as an adjective referring to concern with the transcendent dimension of life or *religious life* meaning the conduct of one concerned with the transcendent will not be capitalized. Words such as *congregation, community, institute, order, rule,* and *constitutions,* which are fairly clearly technical terms and whose meanings are clear from their contexts, will be capitalized only when particular contexts, e.g., Canon Law, seem to require it.

CHAPTER ONE

1. Helen Rose Fuchs Ebaugh in *Women in the Vanishing Cloister: Organizational Decline in Catholic Religious Orders in the United States* (New Brunswick, N.J.: Rutgers University Press, 1993) and Patricia Wittberg in *The Rise and Fall of Catholic Religious Orders: A Social Movement Perspective,* SUNY Series in Religion, Culture, and Society (Albany, N.Y.: State University of New York Press, 1994), both analyzing the current situation from the standpoint of sociological theory, see Religious Life in the United States as collapsing. Combining psychological and sociological analyses with theological convictions, David J. Nygren and Miriam D. Ukeritis in *The Future of Religious Orders in the United States: Transformation and Commitment* (Westport, Conn.: Praeger, 1993), henceforth, *FORUS,* both sound alarms about decline but express hope and conviction that the life has a future. Other authors such as Joan Chittister in *The Fire in These Ashes: A Spirituality of Contemporary Religious Life* (Kansas City: Sheed & Ward, 1995) are convinced of the future of the life.

2. As Agahanda Bharati points out in "Sacred Offices and Orders—Monasticism," in *The New Encyclopaedia Britannica,* 15th ed., 981, monasticism exists only in literate cultures with a written, transmitted lore. Shamanism, which has some features in common with monasticism, is somewhat analogous in nonliterate societies, but the differences are, in many respects, more significant than the similarities. The major similarity is that shamans, like monastics, respond to a personal vocation and become religious specialists within the larger community. However, because they are primarily called to serve the community as intermediaries between the community and the spirit world, they also have something in common with priests. On shamanism, see Michael Ripinsky-Naxon, *The Nature of Shamanism: Substance and Function of a Religious Metaphor* (Albany, N.Y.: State University of New York Press, 1993).

3. For discussion of Celtic Druids, see Proinsias MacCana, "Celtic Mythology," in *Library of the World's Myths and Legends* (New York: Peter Bedrick, 1985), 6–19. The Druids could be found throughout northern Europe from 400–100 B.C.E. and in Ireland until the fifth century.

4. F. Cabrol, "Monasticism," in *Encyclopaedia of Religion and Ethics,* vol. 8, edited by James Hastings (Edinburgh: T. & T. Clark, 1980), 781–82, painstakingly argues that these pagan movements, even though they involved many elements of the monastic lifestyle,

cannot be considered "precursors" of Christian monasticism. What is more interesting today is not the possible influence of these ascetical movements on Christianity but the parallelism of the developments in geographically or chronologically distant spiritual traditions.

5. See Cabrol, "Monasticism," 782, for brief (although unduly negative) descriptions of these movements.

6. For further material on Jain monasticism, see Padmanabh S. Jaini, *The Jaina Path of Purification* (Berkeley, Calif.: University of California Press, 1979), esp. chapters 1 and 8.

7. See Bharati, "Sacred Offices," 985–87 on the development of monasticism in Asia.

8. Cf. J. Spencer Trimingham, *The Sufi Orders in Islam* (Oxford: Clarendon, 1971).

9. I am using the word *monastic* rather than *monk* because English does not have a feminine form of monk (equivalent to the French feminine *moniale* in contradistinction to the masculine *moine*) although both women and men live this life. *Nun* is not a happy choice, even though it is common among Hindus and Buddhists, because it is not a generic term for women Religious among Catholics but designates members of a particular type of Religious Life, namely, cloistered contemplative life in communities of solemn vows. *Sisters,* which is a more generic term for Catholic women Religious, is not common among female monastics of other traditions, which is the topic of discussion in this section.

10. The most recent dialogue of Eastern and Western monastics was held in 1996 under the auspices of M.I.D., Monastic Interreligious Dialogue, and its proceedings are available in *The Gethsemani Encounter: A Dialogue on the Spiritual Life by Buddhist and Christian Monastics,* edited by Donald W. Mitchell and James A. Wiseman (New York: Continuum, 1998).

11. The papers delivered at this symposium were published as a book by the principal speaker, Raimundo Panikkar: *Blessed Simplicity: The Monk as Universal Archetype* (New York: Seabury, 1982).

12. Panikkar, *Blessed Simplicity,* 7–9.

13. Luther's repudiation of the vows of Religious Life occurs in the Augsburg Confession, 27 (Eng. trans. available as *The Augsburg Confession: A Confession of Faith Presented in Augsburg by Certain Princes and Cities to His Imperial Majesty Charles V in the Year 1530* [Philadelphia: Fortress, 1980]).

14. The distinction between religion and spirituality, which many of our contemporaries have escalated into a mutually exclusive dichotomy, has become the subject of considerable academic discussion in the field of spirituality. I will discuss it in chapter 10 as a particular concern of Religious Life today. An excellent resource for understanding this conversation is Peter H. Van Ness, ed., *Spirituality and the Secular Quest,* World Spirituality 22 (New York: Crossroad, 1996), especially 1–17, Van Ness's "introduction" to the subject.

15. I suspect that the monastic archetype as defined here is surfacing today in the interest in "pure," i.e., religion-less, spirituality. Many people describe themselves as on a spiritual path or quest but want nothing to do with institutionalized religion. Such people, especially young people who have become disaffected with the rigidities of their familial religion but remain personally idealistic, often find themselves drawn to monastic communities, not in order to join them but simply to "hang out" in a context of "the spiritual."

16. This is the definition proposed by Bharati, "Sacred Offices," 981.

17. A. S. Geden, "Monasticism (Buddhist)," in *Encyclopaedia of Religion and Ethics,* 798, points out that in some Buddhist countries "the entire male population passed through the monastery schools," even though most left after their education to become householders. The monastic education leavens the whole society with Buddhism. Monastic schools carried the Christian intellectual tradition through the Middle Ages up to the Reformation.

18. Shakerism was a form of Quakerism brought from England to the United States in 1774 by Mother Ann Lee. It developed rapidly in the East and Midwest, reaching its peak in membership between 1830 and 1850, at which time it had around six thousand members in numerous communities. Because it was a celibate community, it had to attract new members from the surrounding society that did not share its faith. Failure to attract new members was fatal, and the community declined rapidly after the Civil War. By 1894 its membership had declined to one thousand, and by the 1970s it was virtually extinct. In its over one hundred years of existence it was an exemplary community, leaving a legacy of fine workmanship, agricultural innovation, and stirring religious music.

19. Although Vatican II did not repeat the Council of Trent's definition of Religious Life as intrinsically "better and holier" than marriage (Denziger 1810), it does in many places speak in comparative terms about Religious Life as a freer or closer following of Jesus, e.g.,

in *P.C.*, 1, in Flannery, vol. 1. This language has continued to be used in Vatican and papal documents on Religious Life since the Council. The statement in the most recent apostolic exhortation on Religious Life of John Paul II, *Vita Consecrata* of March 25, 1996, that Religious Life has an "objective superiority" (pars. 18 and 32), which appears to be a retreat from the conciliar position, is well explained by Dennis J. Billy, "'Objective Superiority' in *Vita Consecrata,*" *Review for Religious* 55 (November/December 1996): 640–45.

An English translation of the documents of Vatican II and the postconciliar documents that explain and implement the acts of the Council is available in *Vatican Council II: The Conciliar and Postconciliar Documents,* 2 vols., edited by Austin P. Flannery (Grand Rapids: Eerdmans, 1975/1984). References to specific texts are by document title, chapter, and paragraph rather than by page number. Henceforth, notes will give only the abbreviation of the document and appropriate numbers (e.g., of chapter or paragraph), as well as the appropriate Flannery volume.

20. In chapter 9 I will argue that cloister is not essential to any form of Religious Life but an historical development whose time is probably past. The more significant distinction is not between cloistered and noncloistered, contemplative or ministerial, but rather between the stabile community and the mobile community.

21. In the volume by Carole Garibaldi Rogers, *Poverty, Chastity and Change: Lives of Contemporary American Nuns,* Twayne's Oral History Series, no. 24, edited by Donald A. Ritchie (New York: Twayne Publishers, 1996), in which Garibaldi recounts from taped interviews with over a dozen women Religious who lived through the changes of Vatican II their own expressions of their self-understanding as Religious, the God-quest motivation surfaces repeatedly among both ministerial and contemplative Religious. One might expect this from a person who entered an enclosed monastery; but repeatedly apostolic Religious recount that they were hardly aware of the characteristic ministry of their congregations when they entered. They simply wanted to love God with their whole heart and make God known and loved, whatever that involved.

22. I have developed this point at length in a recent article, "Celibacy as Charism," *The Way Supplement* 77 (Summer 1993): 13–25, and will return to it in volume 2.

23. This is part of the problem with mandatory clerical celibacy. The case for celibacy as somehow necessary for, or more conducive to, ministerial commitment and efficacy is totally unconvincing and

leads necessarily to the conclusion that matrimony is some kind of impediment to full Christian involvement. And it is clearly not possible to impose a particular type of affective relationship to Christ on a person for purposes of institutional control. Unfortunately, the imposition of celibacy on clerics who are not called to this vocation has greatly obscured the witness of freely chosen consecrated celibacy among Religious, and caused endless confusion among clerical Religious, who often tend to think of their celibacy as a clerical requirement. I will discuss this problem in greater detail in chapter 7.

24. *P.C.*, 2, a, in Flannery, vol. 1.

25. This position is presented especially in *G.S.*, e.g., in III, 36, and in *A.A.*, e.g., II, 7, both in Flannery, vol. 1.

26. Probably the most fully elaborated treatment of the role of mortification and asceticism in the Christian life is John of the Cross's classic, *The Ascent of Mount Carmel* (available in *The Collected Works of Saint John of the Cross,* revised and introduced by Kieran Kavanaugh, translated by Kieran Kavanaugh and Otilio Rodriguez [Washington, D.C.: ICS Publications, 1991]). Despite the drastic character of the renunciations he presents as absolutely essential to contemplative union with God, John constantly insists that the objective is the accommodation of sense to spirit that will integrate the person, making her or him a fitting subject for the possession of and by God.

27. Peter Brown, *The Body and Society: Men, Women and Sexual Renunciation in Early Christianity,* Lectures on the History of Religions, vol. 13 (New York: Columbia University Press, 1988). See chapter 1, "Body and City," 5–32 on this important point.

28. Jung wrote a great deal about archetypes. See, for example, "Archetypes of the Collective Unconscious," in *Collected Works of C. G. Jung,* edited by Sir Herbert Read, Michael Fordham, and Gerhard Adler, translated by R. F. C. Hull (Princeton, N.J.: Princeton University Press, 1968), vol. 9, part 1, 3–41. This essay was written in 1954. See also, "The Concept of the Collective Unconscious," *Collected Works of C. G. Jung,* vol. 9, part 1, 42–53, written in 1936.

29. Jean Shinoda Bolen, *Goddesses in Everywoman: A New Psychology of Women* (San Francisco: Harper & Row, 1984), 15.

30. M. Esther Harding, *Woman's Mysteries Ancient and Modern: A Psychological Interpretation of the Feminine Principle as Portrayed in Myth, Story, and Dreams,* new and revised ed. (New York: Pantheon, 1955), 125.

31. This is a very important point. The earliest Christian writers on virginity insisted that true virginity was essentially distinct from

physical intactness even though the latter, or at least celibate chastity consequent to the profession of virginity, was demanded as its appropriate expression. Mary was virgin because of the integrity of her faith, not because she had not had sexual intercourse. The latter was the symbol of the former. Likewise, women who were widowed (and thus not physically intact) as well as victims of rape could be regarded as virgins through a notion of virginity reclaimed.

This distinction allows for a spiritual virginity of the married woman in relation to Christ in a way analogous to the marital quality of consecrated celibates in relation to Christ. Literalizing spiritual categories into physical or quasiphysical categories leads to absurdities and distasteful exaggerations and obscures access to interior experience.

32. Bolen, *Goddesses in Everywoman.*

33. Ibid., 49.

34. Patricia Ranft in her brief but excellent study, *Women and the Religious Life in Premodern Europe* (New York: St. Martin's Press, 1996), 130–31, makes the very perceptive point that "While religious life did indeed offer women alternatives to marriage, an education, independence, and so forth, I know of no primary source where women explicitly state any of those reasons as why they pursued religious life. In every instance they tell us their reason was religiously motivated. They wanted to become saints...to become one with Christ in heaven....To attain sanctity one has to realize one's potential....A saint has to...remove all barriers...that hinder her from actualizing her full potential as a human being....The most one can be is a complete human being, and a human being—a creature—is complete only when she is united with her creator. Thus the reality behind the desire for heaven and the desire to realize one's potential are one and the same. Ancient, medieval, and early modern women became women religious because they saw this as a way of realizing their potential: a way to get to heaven. This is perhaps the greatest achievement of women religious. They used religious life to perfect their humanness." I think this captures well the point I am trying to make, that there is a natural, psychological substrate that attracts some women toward celibacy, and in the religiously motivated woman who is so attracted there is a powerful overlap between the human attraction and the spiritual motivation.

35. Nygren and Ukeritis, *FORUS,* 183.

36. Many of the articles collected in *The American Catholic Religious Life: Selected Historical Essays,* edited with an introduction by

Joseph M. White (New York: Garland, 1988) recount the remarkable achievements of women Religious in the United States, especially in the nineteenth century.

37. For a survey-type chronicling of the phenomenal growth and achievements of U.S. women's Religious congregations, see George C. Stewart, Jr., *Marvels of Charity: History of American Sisters and Nuns,* foreword by Dolores Liptak (Huntington, Ind.: Our Sunday Visitor, 1994).

38. For a good overview and summary of this history see Lynn Jarrell, "The Legal and Historical Context of Religious Life for Women," *The Jurist* 45 (1985): 419–37, which is a synopsis of her doctoral dissertation in Canon Law.

39. See Bolen, *Goddesses in Everywoman,* 10–11 and elsewhere.

40. This was the burden of Mary Ann Donovan's 1998 presidential address to the Catholic Theological Society of America: "Dancing Before the Lord: Theological Anthropology and Christian Spirituality as Graceful Partners," in *CTSA Proceedings* 53 (1998): 73–87.

41. In *Creating a Future for Religious Life: A Sociological Perspective* (New York/Mahwah, N.J.: Paulist Press, 1991), Wittberg applies the categories of intentional community, bureaucratic organization, and association to the sociological reality of Religious congregations. In *Pathways to Re-Creating Religious Communities* (New York/Mahwah, N.J.: Paulist Press, 1996), she explains the sociological categories of religious virtuosity, ideology, and social movements and applies them to strategizing for the refounding of Religious congregations. In *The Rise and Fall of Catholic Religious Orders: A Social Movement Perspective,* SUNY Series in Religion, Culture, and Society (Albany, N.Y.: State University of New York Press, 1994), she uses the same categories to analyze Religious Life as a social movement and to explain what she sees as its current demise.

42. Wittberg relies on Max Weber, *From Max Weber: Essays in Sociology,* translated and edited by H. H. Garth and C. W. Mills (New York: Oxford University Press, 1958) and Ilana Friedrich Silver, *Virtuosity, Charisma, and the Social Order* (New York: Cambridge University Press, 1995) in her development of this category.

43. Chapter 5 of *L.G.,* in Flannery, vol. 1, is entitled "The Call of the Whole Church to Holiness," and in this chapter the Council affirmed that all Christians are called "to the fullness of the Christian life and to the perfection of charity," indeed to "one and the same holiness."

44. See Wittberg, *Rise and Fall,* 233–35, in which she seems to say that once Religious affirmed the "universal call to holiness" of Vatican

II and therefore no longer saw their vocation as superior, they lost all sense that it was distinct and hence began to question whether there was any purpose for it. In commenting on *G.S.*'s affirmation of the call of all the baptized to the "the fullness of the Christian life and the perfection of charity," she says that *"In one stroke, it nullified the basic ideological foundation for eighteen centuries of Roman Catholic religious life"* (214, emphasis hers). Whether or not this statement is true sociologically, it is definitely not true theologically. If the real justification of Religious Life is superiority to other Christians, then it has no justification for existing in the Church.

45. Wittberg, *Pathways*, 19.

46. See Wittberg, *Rise and Fall*, chapter 4.

CHAPTER TWO

1. Diarmuid Ó Murchú in *Reclaiming Spirituality: A New Spiritual Framework for Today's World* (New York: Crossroad, 1998), gives a fairly accurate expression of these sentiments, and his treatment, in my opinion, makes clear some of the problems with this "boundaryless" approach to human aspirations.

2. See Canon 654: "By religious profession members assume by public vow the observance of the three evangelical counsels, are consecrated to God through the ministry of the Church, and are incorporated into the institute with rights and duties defined by law." Canon 598, #2 states: "All members must not only observe the evangelical counsels faithfully and fully, but also organize their life according to the proper law of the institute and thereby strive for the perfection of their state." See also Canon 607, #2: "A religious institute is a society in which members, according to proper law, pronounce public vows either perpetual or temporary, which are to be renewed when they have lapsed, and live a life in common as brothers and sisters." In other words, perpetual profession and life according to the Constitutions of the congregation defines membership canonically.

3. The expression "systematically distorted communication" was coined by the philosopher Jürgen Habermas within his critical theory. Although John B. Thompson criticizes Habermas's theory, he gives a good description of systematically distorted communication in *Critical Hermeneutics: A Study in the Thought of Paul Ricoeur and Jürgen Habermas* (Cambridge: Cambridge University Press, 1981), 166: "The exclusion of the relevant experience from the sphere of

public language is marked by symptomatic symbols, whose privatised significance remains inaccessible to the subjects concerned." I find the concept very useful as a description of discourse in several areas within the Church today.

4. Patricia Wittberg has made a significant contribution to our understanding of the sociology of Religious community life in *Creating a Future for Religious Life: A Sociological Perspective* (New York/Mahwah, N.J.: Paulist Press, 1991), and of Religious Life as a movement and congregations as organizations in her *The Rise and Fall of Catholic Religious Orders: A Social Movement Perspective*, SUNY Series in Religion, Culture, and Society, edited by Wade Clark Roof (Albany, N.Y.: State University of New York Press, 1994). However, the lack of application of theological and spirituality perspectives to the analysis leads, in my opinion, to a number of conclusions with which I would disagree. For example, Wittberg regards the loss of the conviction of vocational superiority among Religious as an ideological catastrophe (which it might well be from a purely sociological perspective) rather than as a spiritual and theological purification that was absolutely necessary and that can, in light of the Gospel, be seen as grace rather than disaster.

Helen Rose Fuchs Ebaugh, in *Women in the Vanishing Cloister: Organizational Decline in Catholic Religious Orders in the United States* (New Brunswick, N.J.: Rutgers University Press, 1993), analyzes Religious congregations in terms of organizational theory and concludes that "the demise of religious orders in this country seems highly likely" (174). While her sociological analysis is sobering and informative, it lacks any real reference to those factors, such as vocation, which gave rise to the lifeform and which, in the last analysis, will decide its fate.

5. Wittberg, in *Creating a Future,* 11–12, discusses Religious communities of the "intentional" type as total institutions and cites Erving Goffman's important essay on the topic, "The Characteristics of Total Institutions," in *A Sociological Reader on Complex Organizations,* edited by Amitai Etzioni and Edward Lehman (New York: Holt, Rinehart and Winston, 1980), 319–39.

6. See Raimundo Panikkar, *Blessed Simplicity: The Monk as Universal Archetype* (New York: Seabury, 1982), esp. 5–25.

7. The recent (1996) Gethsemani Encounter between Buddhists and Christian spiritual practitioners around the issues of spiritual growth and social involvement is an excellent example of the depth to which such interchange can go. For a complete text of the

exchange see *The Gethsemani Encounter: A Dialogue on the Spiritual Life by Buddhist and Christian Monastics,* edited by Donald W. Mitchell and James A. Wiseman (New York: Continuum, 1998).

8. This is the impression created by the document issued by the Vatican Congregation for Religious and Secular Institutes on June 22, 1983 (dated May 31, 1983) entitled *Essential Elements in Church Teaching on Religious Life,* henceforth abbreviated *E.E.* The English text is available in *Origins* 13: 133–42.

9. This is, of course, the basis for St. Paul's choice of the human body and St. John's choice of a living vine as metaphors for the Church.

10. See Panikkar, *Blessed Simplicity,* 113–15 and the discussion that follows on married monks. Diarmuid Ó Murchú, in *The Prophetic Horizon of Religious Life* (London: Excalibur, 1989), 150–51, also raises a very hesitant question about whether, "at some point in the future our celibate archetypal values may incorporate appropriate forms of genital intimacy." Ó Murchú, however, seems convinced that genitally abstinent celibacy has a prophetic value in our times.

11. Other forms of Religious Life such as eremitical life and the recently restored form of consecrated virginity lived outside community in which the person makes the vow of virginity in the hands of the local bishop are not being considered here, but they are valid forms of the life.

12. Probably, if this were a scientifically exact description, what I am calling "mutation" would be considered phyletic evolution resulting in speciation, while what I am calling "evolution" would be phenetic evolution or more subtle change in response to environmental stimuli. However, for my purposes, I want to stress the difference between change that leaves the identity of the organism intact and change that brings into existence a really different type of entity. Mutation, strictly speaking, is brought about by some disruption (for good or ill) of the DNA.

13. See chapter 1, note 18, for a brief description of Shakerism. In many ways Shakerism was analogous to Catholic Religious Life in regard to community, poverty, obedience, celibacy, prayer and discernment, the commitment to a life of shared work, and a commitment to equality and justice. However, an important distinction between the two forms of life is that Catholic Religious Life is a life-form within a larger faith community from which it draws its members. Shakerism was the faith community and it had to draw its

members from outside itself. Since the analogy is often pressed, it is well to be aware of this important difference.

14. It is not altogether certain whether the Beguines, a lifeform that flowered especially in the Low Countries in the Middle Ages and was revived in the seventeenth century and again after the French Revolution, were Religious or not. Their lifeform was situated somewhere midway between monastic life and lay life. They made no irrevocable vows but did make vows, including chastity, for the time they were in the community. They retained their own property but lived simply in community of some sort and recognized the authority of the superior of the community and the local hierarchy. Some remarkable women who were Beguines were Beatrice of Nazareth, Hadewijch, and Mechtild of Magdeburg. Some people are suggesting that the time has come to revive this form of life, and it would seem to be closer to what many women today are seeking than Religious Life itself. A good treatment of the Beguines is Saskia Murk-Jansen, *Brides in the Desert: The Spirituality of the Beguines,* Traditions of Christian Spirituality Series, edited by Philip Sheldrake (Maryknoll, N.Y.: Orbis, 1998).

15. Provision for hermits and consecrated virgins living autonomously is made by Canons 603 and 604 respectively and the basic requirements are given in *S.R.V.,* available in Flannery, vol. 2.

The *Rite of Consecration to a Life of Virginity* was revised in accord with a directive of Vatican II (*S.C.,* 80, Flannery, vol. 1), and the Latin text was promulgated on May 31, 1970 by the Congregation on Divine Worship and became effective on January 6, 1971. The rite may be used not only for all active and contemplative Religious in women's communities who desire it but also by women (and men) who live autonomously. In the latter case they are consecrated by the local bishop. The Rite, in English, is available from the International Commission for English in the Liturgy as *Rite of Blessing of an Abbot or an Abbess and Rite of Consecration to a Life of Virginity* (Washington, D.C., 1975).

For more information on this development, which is being lived by a number of women, see T. C. O'Brien, "Virginity, Consecration To (Rite)," *New Catholic Encyclopedia: Supplement: Change in the Church,* vol. 17 (Washington, D.C./New York: Publishers Guild, 1979), 692; also Elizabeth Rees, "Autonomous Religious Life: The Consecrated Virgin Living in the World," *The Way Supplement* 50 (Summer 1984): 122–24.

16. For example, between 1536 and 1539, eight hundred monasteries in England were "dissolved" by the civil authorities as part of the Protestant Reformation.

17. For example, the Society of Jesus was partially suppressed between 1759 and 1768 by ecclesiastical authority in Portugal, France, and Spain. In 1773 the Order was completely suppressed by Pope Clement XIV. It was later restored by Pius VII in 1814.

18. A famous example is the guillotining of the sixteen members of the Carmelite monastery in Compiègne in France in 1794.

19. For a very good explanation of what is meant by a "holiness code," the resulting social mapping into "pure" and "impure," and the type of community boundaries this creates, see Marcus J. Borg, *Meeting Jesus Again for the First Time: The Historical Jesus and the Heart of Contemporary Faith* (San Francisco: HarperSanFrancisco, 1994), 46–68.

20. Cf. ibid., 53–58.

21. An excellent exploration of this feature of healthy organic realities is offered by Margaret Wheatley in *Leadership and the New Science: Learning about Organization from an Orderly Universe* (San Francisco: Berrett-Koehler, 1992), esp. 145–47. Wheatley distinguishes between the self-enclosed boundaries of Newtonian "entities," which were presumed to be walled off from all other entities, including the observer, and the principle of "self-reference," which generates the sense of identity that enables an organism to know what is and what is not compatible with its being. She says that "as an operating principle, it [self-reference] decisively separates living organisms from machines" (146).

22. The issue of boundaries, especially in professional situations, has become critical in the wake of increasing sexual abuse scandals in ministry and the helping professions.

A very interesting exploration of the conflict between a professional maintaining boundaries and a client refusing such boundaries is the book-length personal account of Carter Heyward, *When Boundaries Betray Us: Beyond Illusions of What Is Ethical in Therapy and Life* (San Francisco: HarperSanFrancisco: 1993). Heyward demanded of her therapist a personal relationship that the therapist refused on professional grounds. Heyward wrote the book as an attack on the therapist's exclusion of her from personal friendship (which included fairly clear sexual innuendos) and a justification of her own demand for such a relationship. The reviews of the book, which ranged from enthusiastic agreement that setting boundaries in the professional/

client situation represents a patriarchal helping mode that excludes the client from intimacy and equality to firm rejection of Heyward's thesis and defense of the therapist as having both a right and a responsibility to maintain boundaries in the professional situation, illustrate well the gamut of opinions on this subject. The weight of professional opinion today seems to be on the side of restraint in relationships that are not symmetrical.

23. In 1950 there were 147,310 women Religious, and that number increased to 179,954 by 1965. From that high point the numbers declined: in 1970 there were 160,931; in 1975, 135,225; in 1980, 126,517; in 1990, 103,269. Between 1965 and 1990 there was a 43 percent drop in the number of Religious, or a decline of 76,685. The current (1999) estimate is that there are 86,000 to 87,000. Furthermore, the median age rose dramatically. In 1966, 17 percent of women Religious were over sixty-five. In 1982, 38 percent were over sixty-five. For further statistics and references, see Ebaugh, *Women in the Vanishing Cloister,* 46–51.

24. Ebaugh, in *Women in the Vanishing Cloister* (p. 6 and elsewhere), confidently predicts the imminent demise of Religious Life as an institution in the United States precisely on the basis of declining membership. While I disagree with her conclusions, her analysis, which is strictly sociological, reflects perfectly the American criteria of social viability: numbers, financial security, and sociopolitical power. A purely sociological analysis is not equipped to take into account the peculiarities of a lifeform that is not ultimately based on these premises.

25. This seeming paradox is described well by Patricia Wittberg in "Outward Orientation in Declining Organizations: Reflections on the LCWR Documents," in *Claiming Our Truth: Reflections on Identity by United States Women Religious,* edited by Nadine Foley (Washington, D.C.: LCWR, 1988), 89–105, whether or not one agrees with her conclusions.

26. In chapter 9 I will contest the theological validity of this notion, but there is, in the foundational inspiration of many ministerial congregations, a close connection between the call to Religious Life and the characteristic ministry undertaken.

27. I am grateful to Peter Fitzpatrick, C.F.X., for reminding me of this point and supplying important examples.

28. I will take up the problem of the "clericalization" and "parochialization" of the ministry of Religious in chapter 8.

29. I am not suggesting that the ecclesiastical situation I am describing, which is that reported by many people, especially women, who are seeking association with Religious communities, is good or to be promoted. Hopefully the present malaise in official Church structures and the dearth of competent personnel will begin to correct itself. And certainly there are some parishes and other communities in which committed Catholics have found their faith nourished and their ministerial commitment appreciated and respected. But until the widespread eucharistic famine and the ministerial subordination of the laity is alleviated, many people whose love of Christ and the Church will not allow them simply to leave will continue to seek a faith environment elsewhere.

30. This is an issue that congregations who have moved into collegial discernment of ministries need to address. There is a great value in being able to move on when our personal services seem no longer necessary in a particular ministry, but it may be that our congregational support of new lay ownership of ministry is needed and that community presence withdrawn prematurely will leave new growth vulnerable.

CHAPTER THREE

1. Patricia Wittberg, *The Rise and Fall of Catholic Religious Orders: A Social Movement Perspective,* SUNY Series in Religion, Culture, and Society (Albany, N.Y.: State University of New York Press, 1994), chapter 1.

2. See Mary Jo Leddy, *Reweaving Religious Life: Beyond the Liberal Model* (Mystic, Conn.: Twenty-Third Publications, 1990).

3. See, e.g., Gerald A. Arbuckle, *Out of Chaos: Refounding Religious Congregations* (New York/Mahwah, N.J.: Paulist Press, 1988).

4. See Joe Holland, "Family, Work, and Culture: A Postmodern Recovery of Holiness," *Sacred Interconnections: Postmodern Spirituality, Political Economy, and Art,* ed. David Ray Griffin (Albany, N.Y.: State University of New York Press, 1990), 103–22.

5. Patricia Wittberg, *Rise and Fall;* Helen Rose Fuchs Ebaugh, *Women in the Vanishing Cloister: Organizational Decline in Catholic Religious Orders in the United States* (New Brunswick, N.J.: Rutgers University Press, 1993).

6. See the document *E.E.* For a very good sociological analysis of preconciliar Religious community life as that of a "total institu-

tion," see Patricia Wittberg, *Creating a Future for Religious Life: A Sociological Perspective* (New York/Mahwah, N.J.: Paulist Press, 1991), 11–35.

7. For a very insightful analysis of the cultural malaise of late modernity, see Albert Borgmann, *Crossing the Postmodern Divide* (Chicago/London: University of Chicago Press, 1992), esp. 20–47. For a theological appraisal, see Douglas C. Bowman, *Beyond the Modern Mind: The Spiritual and Ethical Challenge of the Environmental Crisis* (New York: Pilgrim, 1990), esp. 7–23. For an attempt to draw out the implications for spirituality of the collapse of modernity, see David Ray Griffin, "Introduction: Postmodern Spirituality and Society," *Spirituality and Society: Postmodern Visions,* ed. David Ray Griffin (Albany, N.Y.: State University of New York Press, 1988), 1–31.

8. Although members of Congregations make temporary vows for a period of time before making perpetual profession, it has always been understood that temporary vows are not valid and should not be made unless the intention is to make perpetual profession. Temporary vows are not a holding pattern for the indecisive but a prudential provision for termination if, after living the commitment as fully as possible for a period of time (which cannot be done as a novice without vows), the person (or the community) determines that this is not the life to which she is called.

9. As we already mentioned, one of the very interesting findings of the extensive study by Nygren and Ukeritis, *FORUS,* was that women Religious (in contrast to men) "rated chastity as least difficult and most meaningful" of the three vows (183). This strongly suggests a different understanding on the part of women for whom celibacy is more concerned with a positive personal relationship than with a restriction or an obligation.

10. See Paul Lakeland, *Postmodernity: Christian Identity in a Fragmented Age,* Guides to Theological Inquiry (Minneapolis: Fortress, 1997), 2–5.

11. Numerous books and articles have appeared in the last two decades attempting to articulate and address the changed situation of Religious. Some worth consulting are Lora Ann Quiñonez and Mary Daniel Turner, *The Transformation of American Catholic Sisters,* Women in the Political Economy, edited by R. J. Steinberg (Philadelphia: Temple University Press, 1992); *Claiming Our Truth: Reflections on Identity by United States Women Religious,* edited by Nadine Foley (Washington, D.C.: Leadership Conference of Women Religious, 1988); *Religious Life: The Challenge of Tomorrow,* edited by Cassian J. Yuhaus (New York:

Paulist Press, 1994); *Living in the Meantime: Concerning the Transformation of Religious Life,* edited by Paul J. Philibert (New York: Paulist Press, 1994); Joan Chittister, *The Fire in These Ashes: A Spirituality of Contemporary Religious Life* (Kansas City: Sheed & Ward, 1995); Barbara Fiand, *Wrestling with God: Religious Life in Search of Its Soul* (New York: Crossroad, 1996).

12. See *G.S.,* 1, in Flannery, vol. 1.

13. I attempted to explore the effects of conciliar aggiornamento on Religious Life in *New Wineskins: Re-Imagining Religious Life Today* (New York/Mahwah, N.J.: Paulist Press, 1986).

14. Lakeland's book *Postmodernity* provides a very accessible introduction to the meaning of postmodernity.

15. There is a linguistic problem in trying to name this feature of postmodern sensibility. *Radical contingency* has long been used to describe the non-necessary and dependent ontological character of created being in relation to absolute self-subsistent reality, or God, especially as that ontological character is recognized and appropriated by the rational creature. That is not what the term means in the present context. It refers rather to a sense of being either "subjectless" or continuously "self-invented" in function of pragmatic or aesthetic concerns.

16. Robert N. Bellah, et. al., *Habits of the Heart: Individualism and Commitment in American Life* (Berkeley, Calif.: University of California Press, 1985).

17. Kathleen Norris, in *The Quotidian Mysteries: Laundry, Liturgy and "Women's Work,"* 1998 Madeleva Lecture in Spirituality (New York: Paulist Press, 1998), 35, remarks on the relationship between fragmentation and consumerism. Lakeland, in *Postmodernity,* 3–4, makes a similar observation about the shopping mall.

18. I am relying here on the typology of Paul Lakeland, *Postmodernity.*

19. Deconstruction as such is not necessarily nihilistic. Indeed, in many areas it is a liberating process of breaking down false certainties, absolutes, and dogmatisms. By calling it "radical" deconstruction I am intending to point not to such positive challenging of moribund essentialism but to the abandonment of all sense of coherence, value, purpose, or direction that could ground either personal or communal creative effort in favor of sheer occasionalism.

20. *Opus Dei,* the right-wing personal prelature that functions as an international arm of the ecclesiastical restoration is a major example of antimodern Catholicism.

21. Many feminists have pointed out the distinctly nostalgic character of what John Paul II intends as promotion of women. His ideal of the "eternal feminine" embodied in a universal vocation of women to motherhood (physical or spiritual) as the defining characteristic of their personhood is characteristically both antimodern and strangely out of touch with postmodern feminist sensibilities.

22. I am using *constructive* not as the opposite of *deconstructive* but to stress the essentially positive or creative impetus of this position. Constructive postmoderns in this sense are not resigned to a radically fragmented, apolitical, despairing isolation in the face of postmodern deconstruction but believe that this age, like others before it, is or can be open to human values.

23. See my article on this subject in relation to Religious Life, "Congregational Leadership and Spirituality in the Postmodern Era," *Review for Religious* 57 (January–February, 1998): 6–33.

CHAPTER FOUR

1. The condemnation of Religious profession is found in the Augsburg Confession, 27 (Eng. trans. available as *The Augsburg Confession: A Confession of Faith Presented in Augsburg by Certain Princes and Cities to His Imperial Majesty Charles V in the Year 1530* [Philadelphia: Fortress, 1980], section on "Monastic Vows," 40–47). The Council of Trent reaffirmed the superiority to marriage of the state of virginity or celibacy for the sake of the kingdom (Denziger 1810) which, in effect, both condemned Luther's position and proved that his objection was on the mark.

2. *L.G.,* 5, in Flannery, vol. 1 affirms the universal call to holiness: "It is therefore quite clear that all Christians in any state or walk of life are called to the fullness of Christian life and to the perfection of love...." It is important to note that this statement contrasts sharply with the long tradition of regarding Religious Life as a "state of perfection" in which the rest of the baptized do not share and the affirmation that the life of consecrated celibacy is intrinsically superior to marriage. This latter affirmation, actually defined by the Council of Trent, was reaffirmed by Pius XII in 1954 in the encyclical *Sacra Virginitas,* 45 (available in English translation in Claudia Carlen, *The Papal Encyclicals 1939–1958,* vol. 4 [Wilmington, N.C.: McGrath, 1981]). *P.C.,* 12, in Flannery, vol. 1 states that Religious chastity "must be esteemed an exceptional gift of grace" and that "it uniquely frees

the heart" for love of God and neighbor, but it does not repeat the claim of intrinsic superiority.

L.G., 4, in Flannery, vol. 1 asserts that "The apostolate of the laity is a sharing in the salvific mission of the Church. Through Baptism and Confirmation all are appointed to this apostolate by the Lord himself." This definition of "lay apostolate" departs from the traditional affirmation that the apostolate of the laity, largely organized as Catholic Action in the nineteenth and early twentieth centuries, is a sharing in the mission of the hierarchy. This definition was repeatedly offered by Popes Leo XIII, Pius X, Pius XI, and Pius XII (see Joseph Sasaki, *The Lay Apostolate and the Hierarchy* [Ottawa: St. Paul's University/University of Ottawa Press, 1967], 73–102, for the history of the development of this position). It is now recognized that the mission of all the baptized, ordained or lay, flows from incorporation in Christ by the sacraments of initiation.

3. Unfortunately, official ecclesiastical literature is still using such intrinsically hierarchical rhetoric for distinguishing ordained from nonordained, claiming an "essential" difference between the priesthood of the ordained and the priesthood of all believers (cf. *L.G.*, 10, in Flannery, vol. 1). No one seems able to say what such a difference would be without excluding either the ordained or the laity from the priesthood of Christ. It would be much more helpful to distinguish roles in the Church that call for different ways of exercising this priesthood.

As late as August 15, 1997, eight Vatican offices issued an instruction entitled "Some Questions Regarding Collaboration of Nonordained Faithful in Priests' Sacred Ministry" (available in *Origins* 27: 397, 399–409) to which an explanatory note was appended insisting that the document was "not taking a step backward," but this did not seem to be the impression of Bishop Reinhold Stecher of Innsbruck, Austria, who criticized the document as treating lay ministers "as at best reluctantly permitted helpers in a few exceptional situations for which, unfortunately, no other solution can be found." Most theologians and others concerned with the ministry of the laity read the document as Stecher did, as an attempt to suppress as far as possible lay ministry and defend clerical turf.

4. See, for example, Merton's *A Vow of Conversation: Journals 1964–1965*, edited and prefaced by N. B. Stone (New York: Farrar, Straus, Giroux, 1988), 142.

5. The impression that Religious Life is a collection of "essential elements" was fostered by *E.E.*, the document published by the

Congregation for Religious and Secular Institutes in May 1983. Responses to this document can be found in *Religious Life in the U.S. Church: The New Dialogue,* ed. R. J. Daly et al. (New York/Ramsey, N.J.: Paulist Press, 1984). Although the document actually refers to "elements in Church teaching" rather than elements of Religious Life, its serial treatment of requirements gave the distinct impression that it was talking about elements that must be present if the life is to qualify as canonically Religious.

6. As will be clear in subsequent material I am not suggesting that the other two vows, community life, or ministry are not integral to Religious Life and vitally important. Here I am concerned with what is common to and constitutive of all forms of the Life and which therefore distinguishes it among vocations in the Church.

7. See *L.G.,* 31, in Flannery, vol. 1: "The term 'laity' is here understood to mean all the faithful except those in Holy Orders and those who belong to a religious state approved by the Church." *P.C.,* 10, in Flannery, vol. 1: "Lay religious life, for men and for women, is a state for the profession of the evangelical counsels which is complete in itself." See Canon 207 of *CCL,* in which this distinction between hierarchical structure and states of life is clearly expressed.

8. I devoted a chapter of *New Wineskins: Re-imagining Religious Life Today* (New York/Mahwah, N.J.: Paulist Press, 1986), 45–69, to the theology of Religious profession and will not repeat that material here.

9. Bernard McGinn, *The Foundations of Mysticism: Origins to the Fifth Century,* vol. 1 of *The Presence of God: A History of Western Christian Mysticism* (New York: Crossroad, 1991), xvii–xx.

10. Ignatius of Loyola ends the *Spiritual Exercises* with his famous "contemplation for attaining divine love," the aim of which is precisely to lead the exercitant to see God in all things. (Numerous translations of the *Exercises* exist. One is the American translation by Lewis Delmage, *The Spiritual Exercises of Saint Ignatius Loyola: An American Translation from the Final Version of the Exercises, the Latin Vulgate, into Contemporary English* [New York: Joseph F. Wagner, 1968], nos. 230–37.)

11. This anecdote occurs in the account of Macarius the Great (fourth century), which can be found in English in *The Desert Christian: Sayings of the Desert Fathers, the Alphabetic Collection,* translated by Benedicta Ward (New York: Macmillan, 1975), 126.

12. See Lynn Marie Jarrell, *The Development of Legal Structures for Women Religious Between 1500 and 1900: A Study of Selected Institutes of Religious Life for Women* (Ann Arbor, Mich.: University Microfilms

International, 1985) for the story of the emergence of apostolic Religious Life for women.

13. This realization was enshrined in "Convenientes ex universo" (the statement of the 1971 Synod of Bishops on Justice in the World) in the memorable declaration that "Action on behalf of justice and participation in the transformation of the world fully appear to us as a constitutive dimension of the preaching of the Gospel, or, in other words, of the Church's mission for the redemption of the human race and its liberation from every oppressive situation." This document is available in English in Flannery, vol. 2, 695–710, citation on 696.

14. Abraham J. Heschel, *The Prophets*, vol. 1 (New York/Evanston/London: Harper & Row, 1969), 12.

15. Heschel, *The Prophets*, 26. In chapter 10, where I discuss the prophetic vocation in greater detail, I will develop the contemporary biblical insight into the complementary identification of the prophet with the people. Here my concern is with the prophetic implications of solitude and marginality.

16. See Merton's "The Inner Experience: Society and the Inner Self (II)." "The Inner Experience" is a collection of essays, from an unpublished work, which were published serially in *Cistercian Studies* 18 (1983) and 19 (1984).

17. The correspondence between Merton and the young feminist theologian, Rosemary Radford Ruether, often concerned this dilemma. See *At Home in the World: The Letters of Thomas Merton and Rosemary Radford Ruether*, edited by Mary Tardiff (Maryknoll, N.Y.: Orbis, 1995).

18. Walter Brueggemann, *The Prophetic Imagination* (Philadelphia: Fortress, 1978).

19. Amos N. Wilder, *Early Christian Rhetoric: The Language of the Gospel* (Cambridge: Harvard University Press, 1971), esp. 1–17.

20. The story of this agonizing event in the history of the peace movement and of Merton's response, intemperate in some respects but necessary to clarify the relation of means to ends even in the desperation of ultimate challenges to justice, is recounted in Michael Mott, *The Seven Mountains of Thomas Merton* (Boston: Houghton Mifflin, 1984), 427–30.

21. Kane tells the story of this now famous event in "Sister Theresa Kane," *Poverty, Chastity, and Change: Lives of Contemporary American Nuns* by Carole Garibaldi Rogers, Twayne's Oral History Series, no. 24 (New York: Twayne Publishers, 1996), 223–30.

22. Brueggemann, *The Prophetic Imagination*, 67.

23. I will take up this topic of "living the questions" in greater detail in chapter 10.

24. The Vatican has repeatedly reversed attempts by the U.S. episcopacy to introduce appropriate use of inclusive language into official documents. The most egregious example was the deliberate reintroduction into the American translation of the *CCC* of the most oppressive possible use of exclusive language. In the brief opening paragraph there are seven completely unnecessary sexist uses of male nouns and pronouns for the human person. A similar process of undermining pastoral efforts at inclusive language was applied to the revision of the liturgical texts.

25. The modern phase of the struggle between women and the hierarchy over ordination has been marked by a series of increasingly dogmatic official statements, each escalating the stakes in the discussion in an attempt to end a conversation which is clearly not going to go away. *Inter Insigniores* (Declaration on the Admission of Women to the Ministerial Priesthood, in Flannery, vol. 2), issued on Oct. 15, 1976, by the Sacred Congregation for the Doctrine of the Faith, declared that the Church could not, in fidelity to Christ, ordain women. This contradicted the considered judgment of the Vatican's own Biblical Commission, which arrived at the conclusion that such a position could not be supported by the New Testament. See the article by John Donahue, "A Tale of Two Documents," in *Women Priests: A Catholic Commentary on the Vatican Declaration,* edited by L. Swidler and A. Swidler (New York/Ramsey/Toronto: Paulist Press, 1977), 25–34, in which he describes both documents.

In May 1994 John Paul II issued an Apostolic Letter, "Ordinatio Sacerdotalis," in which he reiterated the position that the Church could not ordain women. On Nov. 28, 1995, the Congregation for the Doctrine of the Faith issued a "Responsum" to the question of whether the teaching presented in the Pope's Letter "belongs to the deposit of faith," saying that it did and that it therefore required the definitive assent of the faithful since it was founded on "the written Word of God."

Cardinal Ratzinger, on June 29, 1998, issued a commentary on John Paul II's *motu proprio,* "Tuendam Fidem," expanding the Profession of Faith in Canon Law. Ratzinger gives as an example of the second level of truths that must be held without dissent or question "the doctrine that priestly ordination is reserved only to men."

For a recent history of this issue and a careful appraisal of Ratzinger's "Responsum" by the Catholic Theological Society of

America see "Appendix A: Tradition and the Ordination of Women," edited by Judith A. Dwyer, *CTSA Proceedings* 52 (1997): 197–204.

26. During the 1980s and 1990s the Vatican refused to approve revised constitutions that did not include not only requirements of habit or other details which, in fact, the congregations in questions did not observe or intend to institute but also such serious violations of the theology of Religious Life as a definition of the vow of obedience as binding the Religious to personal obedience to the Pope in a way not required of the baptized in general. So painful were some of these impositions that some congregations actually published to their members virtual disclaimers with the approved constitutions.

27. The theology of the Church, especially as practiced by professional theologians, was never as monolithic as the Vatican bureaucracy or the clergy presented it. However, for the ordinary Catholic, including Religious, Thomism and Catholic theology were hardly distinguishable.

28. Sandra M. Schneiders, "Contemporary Religious Life: Death or Transformation?" in *Religious Life: The Challenge of Tomorrow*, edited by C. J. Yuhaus, preface by B. L. Thomas (New York/Mahwah, N.J.: Paulist Press, 1994), 9–34.

29. See, e.g., his reflection on the relationship between his meditation and the weapons booming at Fort Knox in Merton, *A Vow of Conversation*, 117.

30. Rogers, "Sister Joan Chittister," in *Poverty, Chastity, and Change*, 300.

CHAPTER FIVE

1. Patricia Wittberg in "Outward Orientation in Declining Organizations: Reflections on the LCWR Documents," in *Claiming Our Truth: Reflections on Identity by United States Women Religious*, ed. by Nadine Foley (Washington, D.C.: LCWR, 1988), 89–105, documents this paradox and suggests that the outward focus of declining congregations may be dysfunctional for organizational survival. I find her sociological description and analysis very clarifying, but I am suggesting in this paper another kind of explanation of the phenomenon and a different response to it.

2. For statistics, see Marie Augusta Neal, *Catholic Sisters in Transition: From the 1960s to the 1980s* (Wilmington, Del.: Michael Glazier,

1984), 18–22, as brought up to date by Lora Ann Quiñonez and Mary Daniel Turner, *The Transformation of American Catholic Sisters* (Philadelphia: Temple University Press, 1992), 141, and Wittberg, "Outward Orientation," 89–90.

3. The patterns of behavior of organizations in decline are described by Helen Rose Fuchs Ebaugh, *Women in the Vanishing Cloister: Organizational Decline in Catholic Religious Orders in the United States* (New Brunswick, N.J.: Rutgers University Press, 1993), 30–45.

4. Anne Munley, "An Exploratory Content Analysis of Major Themes Present in Selected Documents of United States Women Religious," in *Claiming Our Truth*, 184–91.

5. Available in *Claiming Our Truth*, 173–81.

6. Constance FitzGerald, "Impasse and Dark Night," in *Women's Spirituality: Resources for Christian Development*, 2d ed., edited by Joann Wolski Conn (New York/Mahwah, N.J.: Paulist Press, 1996): 410–35. (This article first appeared in 1984 in *Living with Apocalypse: Spiritual Resources for Social Compassion*, edited by Tilden H. Edwards [San Francisco: Harper & Row, 1984], and is reprinted in the Conn volume with permission of the original publisher.) FitzGerald has continued and expanded her reflection on this topic in "Desolation as Dark Night: The Transformative Influence of Wisdom in John of the Cross," *The Way Supplement* 82 (Spring 1995): 98–105.

7. The legitimacy of the move from the original intention of an author to a current meaning of a text that has been resituated in a later context is the subject of textual hermeneutics. Very useful on this subject is the work of Paul Ricoeur, esp. his *Interpretation Theory: Discourse and the Surplus of Meaning* (Fort Worth, Tex.: Texas Christian University Press, 1976). I have developed a theory of hermeneutical actualization of biblical texts that would be applicable also to texts from the history of spirituality in *The Revelatory Text: Interpreting the New Testament as Sacred Scripture*, 2d ed. (Collegeville, Minn.: Liturgical Press, 1999), esp. chapter 5, section C, "The Text as Language."

8. I first delivered a full-length paper on this subject at the twenty-fifth anniversary celebration of the Ministry for Religious, and it appeared as "Contemporary Religious Life: Death or Transformation?" in *Religious Life: The Challenge of Tomorrow*, edited by Cassian J. Yuhaus (New York/Mahwah, N.J.: Paulist Press, 1994), 9–34. It was soon republished in *Cross Currents* 46 (Winter 1996/1997): 510–35, through which it has reached a much broader audience. The response to it has reassured me that what I am describing rings true for a significant number of women Religious.

9. It is, however, significant that one of John's major mystical treatises, *The Living Flame of Love*, was written for a lay woman, indicating that John did not consider his doctrine suitable only for enclosed nuns.

10. Because I am using John's spiritual theology as an heuristic device rather than as a literal description, it better suits my purpose to treat his material in the order in which he gives it, i.e., the active nights of sense and spirit in *The Ascent of Mount Carmel* (henceforth *A*) and the passive nights of sense and spirit in *The Dark Night* (henceforth *DN*) rather than in the order it is usually taught, i.e., the nights of sense followed by the nights of spirit. In other words, I am using a hermeneutical rather than a pedagogical arrangement.

11. Because John's vocabulary is technical and unfamiliar to many people, I am including as an appendix a schematic diagram of his writings on the dark night in relation to the topics discussed in this and the following chapter. (My thanks to Mary Milligan, R.S.H.M., for suggesting this addition.)

12. The commentary entitled *The Ascent of Mount Carmel* was written between 1581 and 1585; *The Dark Night* between 1584 and 1585; The *Spiritual Canticle* in 1584; *The Living Flame of Love* in 1584–85, and a second version in 1591, the year of John's death. The experience of the Dark Night of purification is dealt with in the first two treatises, both of which are commentaries on his poem, "Dark Night."

13. A very good introduction to John's work in general and to each of the treatises in particular, as well as the best available English translation of John of the Cross's work, is *The Collected Works of Saint John of the Cross*, revised edition, translated by Kieran Kavanaugh and Otilio Rodriguez, with revisions and introductions by Kieran Kavanaugh (Washington, D.C.: Institute of Carmelite Studies, 1991).

14. It is important to stay within John's vocabulary because the word *contemplation* has quite different meanings in different spiritual writers. In Ignatius of Loyola, for example, contemplation is a much more active practice.

15. Although widespread, this suppression of individuality was not universal. See, for example, the chapter by Margaret Brennan, " 'Not Two Exactly Alike,' " in *Building Sisterhood: A Feminist History of the Sisters, Servants of the Immaculate Heart of Mary* (Syracuse, N.Y.: Syracuse University Press, 1997): 95–109, recounting the encouragement of individuality in spirituality by the foundress of the order and the ways in which that tradition was honored in subsequent history.

16. Although this formulation, which was somehow embedded in virtually all Constitutions as the primary and secondary end of the Institute, is unacceptable to most congregations today because it is dualistic, other-worldly, and disembodied, it did express in the language of an earlier time the focus of Religious Life as the search for God.

17. For a brief history of the effect of the Sister Formation Movement on American Sisters, see Elizabeth Kolmer, *Religious Women in the United States: A Survey of the Influential Literature from 1950 to 1983* (Wilmington, Del.: Michael Glazier, 1984), 19–31, and Quiñonez and Turner, *Transformation*, 3–30.

18. I believe the position on the superiority of celibacy was always theologically erroneous. Wittberg regards it as sociologically essential to the ideological framework of the life. See Wittberg, *The Rise and Fall of Catholic Religious Orders: A Social Movement Perspective,* SUNY Series in Religion, Culture, and Society, edited by Wade Clark Roof (Albany, N.Y.: State University of New York Press, 1994), 213–14.

19. Cf. Kavanaugh, *Collected Works of St. John of the Cross,* 107.

20. John's beginners and proficients correspond respectively to the classical categories of those in the purgative and illuminative "ways."

21. Obviously, I am talking about Religious in renewing congregations as a cohort. There were congregations that, as a whole, resisted renewal, and individuals in every congregation who did so.

22. The most disturbing case was probably the destruction of the Los Angeles I.H.M. congregation by Cardinal McIntyre when the congregation refused to revert to a preconciliar lifestyle. Although no full-scale history of the event is yet available, it is described in Quiñonez and Turner, *Transformation,* 152–53.

The document concerning Institutes Engaged in Apostolic Works entitled, "Essential Elements in Church Teaching on Religious Life," intended to reign in the renewal, the letter to the U.S. bishops accompanying it, and the appointment of Archbishop John Quinn of San Francisco to chair a committee of bishops to implement it are available in *Origins* 13 (1983): 133–42.

23. See Quiñonez and Turner, *Transformation,* 107–12 and elsewhere for the story of a number of these conflicts between Church authorities and women Religious.

24. Patricia Wittberg in chapter 5 of *Rise and Fall* gives an excellent account of the types of resources needed for Religious orders to thrive and the ways in which these resources, historically, were mobilized.

In her recent article, "Ties That No Longer Bind," *America* 179 (September 26, 1998): 10–14, she discusses the problems that the loss of institutions presents for Religious orders.

25. The cases of Agnes Mansour, R.S.M. (documentation of this case is available in *Origins* 12 [1983]: 621, 676–79 and *Origins* 13 [1983]: 34–36, 197–206), who was forced from her congregation for exercising a ministry approved by her superiors, Carmel McElroy, R.S.M., and Barbara Fiand, S.N.D.deN, who were driven from their positions in Catholic Seminaries, were added to the already notorious incidents involving the revocation of canonical missions of Catholic theologians such as Hans Küng and Charles Curran, the pursuit of numerous other theologians, and the condemnation of theological positions.

26. See Carolyn Osiek, *Beyond Anger: On Being a Feminist in the Church* (New York: Paulist Press, 1986) and Sandra M. Schneiders, *Beyond Patching: Faith and Feminism in the Catholic Church*, The Anthony Jordan Lectures, Newman Theological College, Edmonton, 1990 (New York/Mahwah, N.J.: Paulist Press, 1991) on this subject.

27. A very hopeful development in the past few years has been the organization of younger Religious across congregational lines. This group held a meeting in 1997 entitled "Fertile Fields," which gave rise to a new publication, *Giving Voice: A Newsletter for Women Religious Under 50*, the first issue of which was published in March 1999.

The *National Catholic Reporter* (March 5, 1999) published a special report authored by Arthur Jones entitled, "Nuns Renew Vows: Mission, they say, not age, must drive today's congregations." It highlighted the approach of aging congregations to the challenges of the third millennium. Thus, at both ends of the age spectrum Religious themselves are recommitting themselves and their resources to the mission that has always energized the life.

28. Prejean's book, *Dead Man Walking: An Eyewitness Account of the Death Penalty in the United States* (New York: Vintage, 1994), was made into a critically acclaimed film in which Susan Sarandon played Prejean as the unassuming, remarkably effective minister who accompanied a condemned killer to execution and ministered to the relatives of his victims and the prison personnel at the same time. Her community life and relationships with Church authority as well as her ministry, aptly portrayed in the film, give a very realistic, unromanticized, but compelling picture of contemporary Religious Life.

29. The experience of deepened personal prayer and the skill in discernment that many Religious developed through directed

retreats and spiritual direction was undoubtedly influential in this growing respect for God's action in people's lives.

30. E.g., Mary Jo Leddy, *Reweaving Religious Life: Beyond the Liberal Model* (Mystic, Conn.: Twenty-Third Publications, 1990); Diarmuid Ó Murchú, *Reframing Religious Life: An Expanded Vision for the Future* (U.K.: St. Paul's, 1995).

31. E.g., Joan Chittister, *The Fire in These Ashes: A Spirituality of Contemporary Religious Life* (Kansas City: Sheed & Ward, 1995); Barbara Fiand, *Living the Vision: Religious Vows in an Age of Change* (New York: Crossroad, 1990) and *Wrestling With God: Religious Life in Search of Its Soul* (New York: Crossroad, 1996); Judith A. Merkle, *Committed by Choice: Religious Life Today* (Collegeville, Minn.: Liturgical, 1992); *Living in the Meantime: Concerning the Transformation of Religious Life,* edited by Paul J. Philibert (New York: Paulist Press, 1994); Sean D. Sammon, *An Undivided Heart: Making Sense of Celibate Chastity* (New York: Alba House, 1993); Evelyn Woodward, *Poets, Prophets, and Pragmatists: A New Challenge to Religious Life* (Notre Dame, Ind.: Ave Maria Press, 1987); *Religious Life: The Challenge of Tomorrow,* edited by Cassian J. Yuhaus (New York: Paulist Press, 1994).

CHAPTER SIX

1. By *totalitarian* I do not mean necessarily repressive or oppressive but rather that the institution governed all aspects of life. Religious had no "outside" life apart from community. Consequently, they did not seriously engage, as a personal issue, the modernity that surrounded them.

2. This often cited text is from Cyprian's treatise, *De Habitu Virgines* (The Conduct of Virgins), chapter 3 (*Patrologia Latina* 4: 439–64). It is available in English translation in Saint Cyprian, *Treatises,* translated and edited by Roy J. Deferrari, The Fathers of the Church Series 36 (New York: Fathers of the Church, 1958). He translates *habitu* as "dress," but this is doubtful. It would be better translated "conduct" or "manner of life."

3. The struggles with Church authorities over renewal are narrated by Lora Ann Quiñonez and Mary Daniel Turner in *The Transformation of American Catholic Sisters* (Philadelphia: Temple University Press, 1992), 141–64.

4. Obviously, there are religious geniuses who, even from childhood, have remarkably mature God-images. I am speaking here of the common path of religious development.

5. We would probably see what John is talking about less in terms of sinfulness than in terms of fixation in categories of thought and imaginative constructs that are totally inadequate to the reality of God.

6. An excellent description of this process of late adolescent religious doubt induced by the university atmosphere of critical thought is given by Shirley du Boulay in her biography of Bede Griffiths, *Beyond the Darkness: A Biography of Bede Griffiths* (New York: Doubleday, 1998), 17–29.

Marcus J. Borg, in *The God We Never Knew: Beyond Dogmatic Religion to a More Authentic Contemporary Faith* (San Francisco: HarperSanFrancisco, 1997) describes his own experience of this crisis that is typical of many young adults in modern society.

7. This is not, of course, the necessary or universal conclusion of scientists. John Polkinghorne, a celebrated physicist who is also an Anglican priest, offers a very sound (and eminently readable) alternative in his little book *Quarks, Chaos, and Christianity: Questions to Science and Religion* (New York: Crossroad, 1997).

8. For an excellent summary of classical theism's presentation of God and the critique of it to which contemporary theology is challenged, see Elizabeth Johnson, *She Who Is: The Mystery of God in Feminist Theological Discourse* (New York: Crossroad, 1992), 19–22.

9. I dealt with this issue in an address to the LCWR, available as "Congregational Leadership and Spirituality in the Postmodern Era," *Review for Religious* 57 (January–February, 1998): 6–33.

10. One of the most celebrated exponents of the distinction between God and the Godhead is Meister Eckhart. In Sermon 52 we hear his famous exhortation, "...let us pray to God that we may be free of 'God.'" This sermon is available in English in *Meister Eckhart: The Essential Sermons, Commentaries, Treatises, and Defense,* translated and introduced by Edmund Colledge and Bernard McGinn, C.W.S. (New York/Mahwah, N.J.: Paulist Press, 1981), 200.

11. A remarkable example of this experience is that of Thérèse of Lisieux's agony and death ending with her final words, "My God, I love you." The account can be found in Guy Gaucher, *The Passion of Thérèse of Lisieux,* translated by Anne Marie Brennan (New York: Crossroad, 1998), 91–95.

12. See Constance FitzGerald, "Desolation as Dark Night: The Transformative Influence of Wisdom in John of the Cross," *The Way Supplement* 82 (Spring 1995): 96–108.

13. John of the Cross's real descriptions of this transformation occur in *The Spiritual Canticle* in his commentaries on stanzas 20–40 and in *The Living Flame of Love,* in his commentaries on stanzas 3 and 4. Both of these works are available in *The Collected Works of Saint John of the Cross,* rev. ed, translated by Kieran Kavanaugh and Otilio Rodriguez, with revisions and introduction by Kieran Kavanaugh (Washington. D.C.: Institute of Carmelite Studies, 1991).

14. A touching testimony to this development in the spiritual life is Teresa of Avila's "Spiritual Testimony 65," written in 1581, when she was close to the end of her life, in her mid-sixties. See *The Collected Works of St. Teresa of Avila,* vol. 1, translated by Kieran Kavanaugh and Otilio Rodriguez (Washington, D.C.: Institute of Carmelite Studies, 1976), 363–65.

15. See Denys Turner, *The Darkness of God: Negativity in Christian Mysticism* (Cambridge: Cambridge University Press, 1995), especially his chapter on John of the Cross, 226–51.

16. Bernard McGinn seems not to agree with Turner on this point. See especially his book *The Flowering of Mysticism: Men and Women in the New Mysticism* (1200–1350), vol. 3 of *The Presence of God: A History of Western Christian Mysticism* (New York: Crossroad, 1998), which is devoted to the extremely experiential mysticism of the late medieval period. However, McGinn would agree that whatever extraordinary phenomena the mystic might experience, mysticism itself does not consist in such phenomena.

17. See the article by Constance FitzGerald on the development of the Jesus spirituality of Teresa of Avila as interpreted by John of the Cross, "A Discipleship of Equals: Voices from Tradition—Teresa of Avila and John of the Cross," in *A Discipleship of Equals: Towards a Christian Feminist Spirituality,* edited by Francis A. Eigo (Villanova, Pa.: Villanova University Press, 1988), 63–97.

18. I heard this analogy from Margaret Susan Thompson citing it from Ritamary Bradley, who developed it from a new article on the evolution of dinosaurs. In response to my inquiry she suggested consulting http://www.usmp.berkeley.edu/diapsids/avians.html where we learn that dinosaurs are not extinct. Dinosaurs are the biological ancestors of our birds. I found the metaphor for the evolution of Religious Life beautiful and hopeful.

19. Elizabeth Durkin and Julie Durkin Montague, "Surveying U.S. Nuns," *America* 172 (February 11, 1995): 11–16.

20. Tom Roberts, *NCR* (September 11, 1998), 19. See also the recent special report by Arthur Jones, "Nuns Renew Vows," *NCR* (March 5, 1999): 11–18. Carole Garibaldi Rogers in *Poverty, Chastity, and Change: Lives of Contemporary American Nuns,* Twayne's Oral History Series, edited by Donald A. Ritchie (New York: Twayne Publishers, 1996) records interviews with a wide range of women Religious who have lived through the renewal period and remained committed and joyful.

21. I do not think there is a contradiction between taking seriously the real problems in Religious Life, as Sean D. Sammon does in his recent article, "Last Call for Religious Life," *Human Development* 20 (Spring 1999): 12–27, and the interpretation I am suggesting. Much purification in the spiritual life takes place through our own real weaknesses and sinfulness.

22. This seems particularly urgent with regard to vocations. The continuation of Religious Life does not depend on large numbers but it does depend on some new vocations.

CHAPTER SEVEN

1. *L.G.* in Flannery, vol. 1 devotes the first chapter to "The Mystery of the Church," followed by chapter 2, "The People of God," and then goes on to speak of the hierarchical nature of the Church.

2. See Elizabeth A. Dreyer, *Earth Crammed with Heaven: A Spirituality of Everyday Life* (New York/Mahwah, N.J.: Paulist Press, 1994) for a full-length treatment of lay spirituality, including its personal and ministerial aspects.

3. *L.G.,* 10, in Flannery, vol. 1.

4. David Power in "Theologies of Religious Life and Priesthood," in *A Concert of Charisms: Ordained Ministry in Religious Life* (New York/Mahwah, N.J.: Paulist Press, 1997), 84, says, "...one of the questions that has continued to defy clear theological explanation is the council's statement—since then frequently repeated by the magisterium—that the ministerial priesthood and the baptismal priesthood differ not only in degree but in kind." He then enumerates several attempts to explain it, none of which seem to succeed.

5. *L.G.* I, 43, in Flannery, vol. 1.

6. Canon 207, 2 (cf. *CCL,* 1983) recognizes that Religious are drawn from both groups, have a special role in the Church, but emphasizes that "their state does not belong to the hierarchical structure of the Church."

7. On this phenomenon and its implications for the ordained and for Religious in general, see Paul K. Hennessy, "Introduction: The Parochialization of the Church and Consecrated Life," in *A Concert of Charisms,* 1–8.

8. St. Augustine, Sermon 340, 1, in vol. 38 of *Patrologia Latina,* 217 vols., edited by J. P. Migne (1878–1890), 1438.

9. For example, Elisabeth Schüssler Fiorenza and other feminist biblical scholars and theologians have argued that a "discipleship of equals" has much more convincing New Testament credentials than the hierarchical organization, which seems to be modeled more closely on the Roman Empire than on the practice or teaching of Jesus.

On the other hand, scholars such as Raymond Brown point out that the introduction of some kind of organization and leadership structure was necessary if the early Church was not to disintegrate in nonnegotiable irreconcilable conflicts of interpretation of the Gospel. This does not, however, entail subscribing to a theory that Jesus personally established the priesthood or ordained his disciples. One need not maintain that Jesus personally established the current version of the papacy and Vatican and divided the Church into ordained and unordained to recognize, as do many theologians, that the Holy Spirit was at work in the development of Church order and that this makes it something more than a purely human development.

10. *L.G.* III, beginning with par. 18, in Flannery, vol. 1.

11. The issue of the exercise of ecclesiastical jurisdiction and its relationship to ordination has been affected by the effort to include laypeople in the ministerial structure of dioceses. The question is very complex and not germane to the discussion in this chapter. However, a clarifying discussion of the topic in relation to clerical orders that have nonordained members can be found in R. Kevin Seasoltz, "Institutes of Consecrated Life and Ordained Ministry: Some Canonical Issues," in *A Concert of Charisms,* 139–68, esp. 149–53.

12. It is easy to see how these distinctions function, at least in principle, by looking at the organization of Canon Law (see *CCL*).

13. Doris Gottemoeller, in "The Priesthood: Implications in Consecrated Life for Women," in *A Concert of Charisms,* 129, and note 3, cites "NCCB National Study of the Diaconate," *Origins* 25 (1996): 501, as testifying to both permanent deacons' own questions about

whether ordination is required for what they do and the perception of permanent deacons as "incomplete priests" or "more advanced laity."

14. The best treatment I have found of Societies of Apostolic Life is a two-part address to the May 14, 1997, General Assembly of the Daughters of Charity by Miguel Perez Flores, "The Company of the Daughters of Charity, Society of Apostolic Life I, II," in *Echoes of the Company* (internal publication of the Daughters of Charity), 316–32, 373–478. According to Flores there are only nine such societies of women and twenty-seven of men.

15. It is important to recall here the extensive treatment of this issue of specificity vs. elite status or superiority in chapters 1 and 2.

16. The degree to which this pejorative connotation has infiltrated our understanding of Christian life is expressed by Seasoltz, "Institutes of Consecrated Life," in a paragraph with whose basic content and tenor I completely agree but in which he rejects the naming of the distinction between Religious and secular institutes because the latter term implies that there is in the life of some Religious (those in secular institutes) an "area of life that is secular or unredeemed by the death and resurrection of Jesus Christ" (146). As I will try to show, "secular" need not, in fact does not, imply unredeemed. It has to do with the location of whatever (redeemed or unredeemed) is being discussed, namely, "in the world" or "toward the world" (understood nonpejoratively) in a particular way.

17. Cf. esp. *L.G.*, 33–34, in Flannery, vol. 1.

18. However, members of Societies of Apostolic Life see their secular character as an important distinguishing feature of their life, and Secular Institutes fall canonically within the category of Institutes of Consecrated Life. In other words, the category of secularity is important and positive, and abolishing it seems neither possible nor desirable.

19. I dealt with this at some length in chapter 4 and will take it up again, in more explicit detail, in chapters 9 and 10.

20. Both clergy and laity, as well as many bishops, were distressed by the recent attempt of several Vatican offices (Congregation for the Clergy, Pontifical Council for the Laity, Congregation for the Doctrine of the Faith, Congregation for Divine Worship and the Discipline of the Sacraments, Congregation for Bishops, Congregation for the Evangelization of Peoples, Congregation for Institutes of Consecrated Life and Apostolic Life, Pontifical Council for the Interpretation of Legislative Texts) to restrict the terms *minister* and *ministry* to the

ordained or clerically appointed ("Some Questions Regarding Collaboration of Nonordained Faithful in Priests' Sacred Ministry," *Origins* 27 [1997]: 397, 399–409). In fact, the attempt has become a dead letter since few Church officials are inclined to enforce it and the laity in general has not accepted it.

In a strongly worded criticism of the document Bishop Reinhold Stecher of Innsbruck, Austria (*NCR,* online version, December 1997) said clearly, "The Decree on Lay Ministers is concerned entirely with defending the rights of the ordained. It shows no concern for the health of the community....*Everything is sacrificed to a definition of Church office for which there is no basis in revelation"* (italics in original translation).

21. See the very enlightening doctoral dissertation of Siddika P. Angle, *Angel to Apostle: Models of Spirituality for Single Catholic Laywomen in the United States, 1866–1965,* 2 vols. (Berkeley, Calif.: Graduate Theological Union Dissertation, 1995). Angle, stating that "this is a group that has not been studied in any fashion" (2:456), analyzes all the pertinent ecclesiastical documentation on the subject of the spirituality of laywomen between the First Council of Baltimore and Vatican II. She discerns five "models" proposed in various ways to such women: servant, virgin in the world, spiritual mother, New Christian Woman, and the Grail. Of these she concludes that only the last has some potential for contemporary lay women.

22. Two helpful reflections on the spirituality of the single person by Francine Cardman of Weston Jesuit School of Theology are the following: "On Being Single," in *The Wind is Rising: Prayer Ways for Active People,* edited by William R. Callahan and Francine Cardman (tabloid format) (Mt. Rainier, Md.: Quixote Center, 1978): 6–7, and "Singleness and Spirituality," *Spirituality Today* 35 (1983): 304–18. In the latter article Cardman supplies references to the few articles and books available on the subject.

23. Power, in "Theologies of Religious Life and Priesthood," 68–81, gives some of the main historical markers in this development.

24. Even greater confusion and considerable pain and anger is generated by the willingness of the Vatican to allow married Episcopal ordained ministers who become Catholic to be and function as ordained in the Catholic Church while continuing their married lives. This not only makes it clear that celibacy is not intrinsic to ordained ministry but makes the forced exclusion from ordained ministry of Catholics called to marriage, especially those who are ordained and would like to marry, especially galling.

25. A compassionate but very frank discussion, especially from the standpoint of clinical psychiatry and psychology, of the problems of clerical celibacy is offered by A. W. Richard Sipe, *A Secret World: Sexuality and the Search for Celibacy* (New York: Brunner/Mazel, 1990).

26. The story of this major clash between the Vatican and U.S. women Religious is recounted by Lora Ann Quiñonez and Mary Daniel Turner in *The Transformation of American Catholic Sisters* (Philadelphia: Temple University Press, 1992), 133–40.

27. It should be noted that the struggle between Religious and hierarchical authority in the Church has been a constant in the history of Religious Life. No institution can be expected to find the presence within itself of a loyal opposition maintaining an ongoing prophetic critique comfortable. On this ongoing tension, see Kevin Seasoltz, "A Western Monastic Perspective on Ordained Ministry" and "Institutes of Consecrated Life and Ordained Ministry," in *A Concert of Charisms*, 25–26 and 139–41, respectively.

28. This thesis is developed in detail with all the appropriate clinical data by A. W. Richard Sipe, *Sex, Priests, and Power: Anatomy of a Crisis* (New York: Brunner/Mazel, 1995).

29. The strangely ambivalent willingness in clerical circles to "look the other way" in regard to male-to-male sexual relations that has marked the unsavory history not only of clandestine homosexual activity among the clergy but also of clerical sexual abuse of boys underscores the deep repugnance for female sexuality that is quite different from the disapproval of sexual activity with males which, while regrettable, is seen more as a sign of weakness than a fundamental contamination.

30. The theological challenge to the exclusion of women from Orders began immediately after the publication of "Inter Insigniores," the Declaration on the Question of the Admission of Women to the Ministerial Priesthood, published by the Sacred Congregation for the Doctrine of the Faith on October 15, 1976 (cf. *Origins* 6 [1977]: 517–24), for example, in the volume of essays, *Women Priests: A Catholic Commentary on the Vatican Declaration,* edited by Leonard Swidler and Arlene Swidler (New York: Paulist Press, 1977) and continued through the publication of the CTSA's document questioning the 1995 Congregation for the Doctrine of the Faith's "Responsum ad Dubium," which maintained that the teaching of the 1994 document, "Ordinatio Sacerdotalis," that the Church could not ordain women, belonged to the "deposit of faith." (This document is

available as "Tradition and the Ordination of Women," *CTSA Proceedings* 52 [1997]: 197–204.)

The biblical challenge began with the vote of the Pontifical Biblical Commission in its April 1976 meeting, unofficially published in late June of 1976, that the New Testament does not settle in a clear way whether women can be ordained (while the prohibition in "Ordinatio Sacerdotalis" claims to be based on the "written Word of God"), that Scripture alone could not ground the exclusion of women from ordination and that Christ's plan would not be transgressed if women were ordained. The CBA published its reflection, concluding with, "The conclusion we draw, then, is that the NT evidence, while not decisive by itself, points toward the admission of women to priestly ministry," as "Women and Priestly Ministry: The New Testament Evidence," in *CBQ* 41 (1979): 608–13.

The discussion continues despite all efforts to suppress it, and the 1994 poll (reported by Dean Hoge of Catholic University of America) of Catholics showed 64 percent of Catholics in favor of women's ordination, with the numbers rising steadily since the 1970s.

31. The increasingly absolute postconciliar teaching on the exclusion of women from ordination began with "Inter Insigniores," the "Declaration on the Question of the Admission of Women to the Ministerial Priesthood," which declared that "the Church, in fidelity to the example of the Lord, does not consider herself authorized to admit women to priestly ordination." This was followed by the Apostolic Letter "Mulieris Dignitatem" (On the Dignity and Vocation of Women), published August 14, 1988, on the role of women, which does not and may not include a vocation to ordination (cf. *Origins* 18 [1988]: 261–83).

The resistance to the teaching continued, and Pope John Paul II issued "Ordinatio Sacerdotalis" (Apostolic Letter on Ordination and Women), on May 22, 1994 (cf. *Origins* 24 [1994]: 49–52), intending to end the discussion. This did not happen, and in 1995 the Congregation for the Doctrine of the Faith issued a "Responsum ad Dubium," entitled "Concerning the Teaching Contained in 'Ordinatio Sacerdotalis'" (*Origins* 25 [1995]: 401–5), strongly implying that the teaching was infallible.

In 1998 Pope John Paul II issued an Apostolic Letter, "Ad Tuendam Fidem" (To Defend the Faith, cf. *Origins* 28 [1998]: 113–16), inserting provision for a profession of faith into Canon Law, and Cardinal Ratzinger of the Congregation for the Doctrine of the

Faith followed it with a "Commentary on Profession of Faith's Concluding Paragraphs" (cf. *Origins* 28 [1998]: 116–19), in which he gave, as an example of a truth that must be held with the faith due infallible teaching, the exclusion of women from Orders. This amounted to an attempt to invest the exclusion with infallibility.

32. This is one of the problems with the oft-repeated assertion of the ontological distinction between the ordained and the lay.

CHAPTER EIGHT

1. The only partly humorous summary of the duties of the Catholic laity, "pray, pay, and obey," summed up this disempowered situation.

2. Catholic Action, as lay ministry was first called in modern times, was first suggested by Pope Pius X but very actively promoted by Pius XI. See Michael E. Engh, "Catholic Action," in *The Harper-Collins Encyclopedia of Catholicism,* edited by Richard P. McBrien (New York: HarperCollins, 1995), 240.

3. See *L.G.,* 33–38 in Flannery, vol. 1.

4. *P.O.* can be found in Flannery, vol. 1.

5. See the very enlightening analysis of this development and its effect on ordained Religious in John W. O'Malley, "One Priesthood: Two Traditions," in *A Concert of Charisms: Ordained Ministry in Religious Life,* edited by Paul K. Hennessy (New York/Mahwah, N.J.: Paulist Press, 1997), 9–24.

6. See, e.g., *L.G.* IV, 33–35 in Flannery, vol. 1.

7. Nygren and Ukeritis, in *FORUS,* p. 250: "The increasingly widespread insertion of members of religious orders into diocesan and parochial positions, to the point where such commitments take precedence over involvements in the lives of their congregations, is a growing phenomenon in the United States. This trend, which is known as parochial assimilation, has had a dramatic effect on most religious orders, probably most significantly among women. It easily can lead to a compromise of the prophetic role of members of religious life."

8. The first chapter of *G.S.* (in Flannery, vol. 1) is devoted to "The Dignity of Marriage and the Family." By abandoning the Tridentine claim (cf. Denziger 1810) of the intrinsic superiority of consecrated celibacy to matrimony and emphasizing that "consecration" and sending into the world in imitation of Jesus is foundational to

ordained, lay, and Religious mission, the Council implicitly recognized the equality of diverse vocations in the Church.

9. There has been a powerful movement in men's Religious communities since the Council to deal openly with this "class system" and to introduce genuine equality in at least some congregations. This has proved extremely difficult because of the Vatican insistence that, in clerical congregations, at least major superiors and formation directors be clerics. In speaking of monastic communities of men that have ordained ministers, Kevin Seasoltz, in "A Western Monastic Perspective on Ordained Ministry," in *A Concert of Charisms*, 48, says that despite postconciliar efforts to declericalize monastic life, there are still issues that must be resolved "if the monasteries are once again to be vibrant expressions of the charismatic, prophetic, and contemplative dimensions of the church rather than institutions that simply parallel the hierarchical church on the local level."

10. Patricia Wittberg, in *The Rise and Fall of Catholic Religious Orders: A Social Movement Perspective*, SUNY Series in Religion, Culture, and Society, edited by Wade Clark Roof (Albany, N.Y.: State University of New York Press, 1994), especially in chapters 13 and 14, regards the abandonment of the ideology of superiority as a, if not the, primary factor in the decline of Religious Life.

11. The Council of Trent (cf. Denziger 1810) declared that it is better and holier to remain in the state of virginity or celibacy for the sake of the kingdom than to marry. Vatican II, in *P.C.*, 12 (in Flannery, vol. 1), significantly, refrains from repeating or citing this Tridentine declaration and says only that such chastity "deserves to be esteemed as a surpassing gift of grace."

12. See notes 30 and 31 of chapter 7 for full documentation of the modern Vatican position and for discussion of the position by contemporary Catholic scholars.

13. This tension and its history is well detailed by R. Kevin Seasoltz, "Institutes of Consecrated Life and Ordained Ministry: Some Canonical Issues," in *A Concert of Charisms*, 139–68.

14. See Edward Schillebeeckx, *The Church with a Human Face: A New and Expanded Theology of Ministry*, translated by John Bowden (New York: Crossroad, 1985).

15. The effort for structural reform of the Church is now worldwide. In the United States it is spearheaded by the Association for the Rights of Catholics in the Church, which was founded in February 1980 and which developed a "Charter of the Rights of Catholics

in the Church," which has been endorsed or used as a model by analogous groups in many other countries. Numerous other groups and associations concerned with particular issues of justice and equality in the Church have arisen in the years since the Council, e.g., Priests for Equality, Women's Ordination Conference, Catholics Speak Out, Corpus, and Dignity.

16. For an exploration of the various dimensions of reform that many see as necessary, see *A Democratic Catholic Church: The Reconstruction of Roman Catholicism,* edited by Eugene C. Bianchi and Rosemary Radford Ruether (New York: Crossroad, 1992), which contains chapters by various authors on virtually all the issues mentioned.

17. The canonical description of Religious Life can be found in Canon 607 (cf. *CCL,* 1983): "A religious institute is a society in which members, according to proper law [i.e., their own constitutions], pronounce public vows either perpetual or temporary, which are to be renewed when they have lapsed, and live a life in common as brothers or sisters. The public witness to be rendered by religious to Christ and to the Church entails a separation from the world proper to the character and purpose of each institute."

18. See *L.G.,* 43 (in Flannery, vol. 1), which states that "This form of life has its own place in relation to the divine and hierarchical structure of the Church. Not, however, as though it were a kind of middle way between the clerical and lay conditions of life. Rather it should be seen as a form of life to which some Christians, both clerical and lay, are called by God so that they may enjoy a special gift of grace in the life of the Church and may contribute, each in his [sic] own way, to the saving mission of the Church." This conciliar position is reflected in Canons 573–74 and in Canon 207 (cf. *CCL,* 1983).

19. This is, in fact, what happened to the Los Angeles congregation of the Sisters, Servants of the Immaculate Heart of Mary and what has been chosen by such groups as Sisters for Christian Community.

There does not seem to be any complete history of the disastrous conflict between Cardinal McIntyre and the I.H.M.'s but there is a brief account in Lora Ann Quiñonez and Mary Daniel Turner, *The Transformation of American Catholic Sisters* (Philadelphia: Temple University Press, 1992), 152–53. Another brief account is provided by Dorothy Vidulich, "'Radical' IHMs pioneered religious community," *NCR* 31 (June 30, 1995): 19.

20. Congregations of men and women with simple vows were granted juridical status as Religious Institutes by Leo XIII's constitution *Conditae a Christo,* promulgated December 8, 1900. For an

excellent treatment of the history of Church law regarding apostolic, noncloistered Religious Life for women, see Lynn Marie Jarrell, *The Development of Legal Structures for Women Religious Between 1500 and 1900: A Study of Selected Institutes of Religious Life for Women* (Ann Arbor, Mich.: University Microfilms International, 1985).

21. Margaret S. Thompson, in "'Charism' or 'Deep Story'? Toward a Clearer Understanding of the Growth of Women's Religious Life in Nineteenth-Century America," in *Religious Life and Contemporary Culture,* Theological Education Process, Cycle II (Monroe, Mich.: Sisters, Servants of the Immaculate Heart of Mary, 1998), notes that between 1727 and 1917 there were at least 422 apostolic congregations of women active in the United States, most of which are still active today. Very few if any of these were canonically Religious before 1900, but neither they nor the people they served thought of them as anything other than Religious.

Probably the best, if not the only, attempt at a history of the foundations of women's Religious congregations in the United States is George C. Stewart, Jr., *Marvels of Charity: History of American Sisters and Nuns* (Huntington, Ind.: Our Sunday Visitor, 1994).

22. This tactic was employed to force Agnes Mansour, a Sister of Mercy, out of her community for exercising a ministry approved by her Religious superiors because the department of the State of Michigan in which she worked distributed abortion funds. The documentation of this case is available in *Origins* 12 (1983): 621, 676–79 and *Origins* 13 (1983): 34–36, 197–206.

23. It is, however, interesting to note that communities, such as the Sisters for Christian Community, which have never sought canonical approbation, seem to have little trouble being recognized by ecclesiastical authorities or laity in the areas in which they minister. There are about a dozen such communities at the present time that enjoy some kind of recognition by the ecclesiastical authorities of the dioceses in which they minister.

24. Patricia Ranft in her excellent historical treatment of the development of Religious Life through the Reformation period shows well how the de facto development of noncloistered Religious Life outstripped ecclesiastical legislation. See *Women and the Religious Life in Premodern Europe* (New York: St. Martin's Press, 1996), esp. 95–106.

25. It is extremely difficult to obtain statistical or other types of data on such "noncanonical communities" because they lack any

central agencies comparable to LCWR that could track numbers and other statistics. However, Patricia Wittberg, on the basis of research she is currently doing with the Center for Applied Research in the Apostolate, informed me of ten "noncanonical" groups that do not seem to be seeking approbation but are recognized in some way within their dioceses. The CARA research project in which she is involved is tentatively entitled "The CARA Directory of Emerging Religious Communities, 1999," and is scheduled for publication in June 1999. She tells me that there are some 168 new communities of various types in their research data base.

26. Although *L.G.* (see esp. ch. VI, in Flannery, vol. 1) and many other official documents insist that the hierarchical Church is solely competent to approve as genuine the charisms of Religious Institutes, to regulate the practice of the life, and to guard the fidelity of Religious to their way of life, the fact that most Religious congregations came into existence and discerned and practiced their own way of life, sometimes for centuries, prior to ecclesiastical approbation suggests that such statements reflect less a historical fact or a theological datum than an institutional claim to power over the form of life.

27. Andrew Greeley and Michael Hout, in "American Catholics and the Next Pope: A Survey Report" done in March–April 1996 found 65 percent of Catholics in favor of the ordination of women. The Time-CNN national poll done before the Pope's visit to the United States in 1996 found "overwhelming support among Catholics for the ordination of women" (internet summary). (For a press release detailing the results of the Greeley-Hout study, contact June Rosner in Chicago, Ill. at 312-664-6100.)

28. We now have a remarkable and convenient resource on the extent and depth of change in papal and Vatican positions in *Rome Has Spoken: A Guide to Forgotten Papal Statements, and How They Have Changed Through the Centuries,* edited by Maureen Fiedler and Linda Rabben (New York: Crossroad, 1998). The book is a collection of official Church teachings on such topics as infallibility, conscience, biblical interpretation, religious freedom, ecumenism, slavery, dissent, evolution, and so on, which amply documents such change.

29. See Doris Gottemoeller, "The Priesthood: Implications in Consecrated Life for Women," in *A Concert of Charisms,* 130, on the role of women Religious in WOC.

30. The Council, in *P.C.,* 8 (in Flannery, vol. 1), recognized explicitly that for such congregations "apostolic and charitable activity is of the very nature of religious life, as their own holy ministry and

work of charity, entrusted to them by the Church and to be performed in its name."

31. Elizabeth Durkin and Julie Durkin Montague, "Surveying U.S. Nuns," *America* 172 (February 11, 1995): 14.

32. The issue of whether women should seek ordination in the present system came to a head in the 1995 Women's Ordination Conference Gathering. The only account in print of that meeting is by Pamela Schaeffer, "WOC gathers to promote women's ordination amid conflicting visions, goals," *NCR* 32 (Dec. 1, 1995): 9–11, along with an unsigned editorial on p. 24. I consulted with Andrea Johnson, National Coordinator of WOC, who told me that WOC considered the *NCR* article sensationalistic and not truly reflective of the situation. WOC's own publication, *New Women, New Church* (Fall 1995) contains pre-Gathering papers on the subject that she feels give a better picture of the conversation.

33. The historical question of whether women deacons in the early Church were actually ordained and/or whether the order of deacons was at least a precursor of active Religious Life is too complicated to be broached here and would not materially affect the argument in which I am engaged.

34. Seasoltz, in "A Western Monastic Perspective," makes a persuasive case that the clericalizaton of male monastic life, if not every case of ordination of a monk, was not a positive development.

35. *Who Are My Brothers?*, edited by Philip Armstrong (New York: Alba House, 1988) is a collection of essays on the vocation of Brothers, especially in relation to clerics in mixed or clerical orders. It also contains excellent material on the history of the Brother vocation and an analysis of the results of a national sociological survey of Brothers.

36. Originally, male Religious (monks) were all lay, so Brothers, as distinct from ordained Religious, did not exist as a category. When Brothers as specifically lay Religious emerged it was as a support (if not servant) class in relation to choir monks and eventually to ordained Religious. Male Religious who opted for the lay state, i.e., Brothers in the contemporary sense, have seemed to many as men who have made a strange choice not to "be all they can be." This is changing as more men in clerical or mixed communities choose not to be ordained but even this development is confused by the desire to be ordained of an increasing number of men who originally entered to be Brothers and perhaps now see ordination as the path to first-class status. See Roland J. Faley, "An American Experience of Priesthood in

Religious Life," in *A Concert of Charisms*, 120–21, for a description of this development. For a good historical description and analysis, see Bruce Lescher, "Laybrothers: Questions Then, Questions Now," *Cistercian Studies* 23 (1988): 63–85.

37. Since I wrote the first draft of this chapter a clear example of this type of conflict has been playing itself out in the diocese of Rochester, New York. This tragic situation is still unresolved.

38. See Faley, "An American Experience of Priesthood."

39. *P.C.,* 15, in Flannery, vol. 1.

40. *P.C.,* 10 (in Flannery, vol. 1) suggests that institutes of Brothers could ordain some of their members "to meet the need for priestly ministration in their houses" without compromising their lay status. (Apparently the same need on the part of women is not recognized as equally urgent!) Brothers have been, wisely, slow to act on this suggestion. In paragraph 15 it is recognized that mixed congregations of men can admit lay and clerical members "on an equal footing and with equal rights and obligations, apart from those arising out of sacred orders." So, in effect, there are clerical orders, lay orders, and mixed orders among men. In the first inequality based on orders is intrinsic, in the second there are no clerics (although the suggestion is that there could be), and in the third equality is the basic presupposition but the distinction (and superiority) of clerical members derives from certain implications of ordination itself.

41. The provision is in Canon 588, "Ecclesiae Sanctae II," the "Norms for Implementing the Decree: On the Up-To-Date Renewal of Religious Life," published by Paul VI (August 6, 1966).

42. Cf. *P.C.,* 15, Flannery, vol. 1.

43. An interesting case study of an unsuccessful attempt at episcopal control is recounted by Gerald P. Fogarty, "The Bishops *versus* Religious Orders: The Suppressed Decrees of the Third Plenary Council of Baltimore," *The Jurist* 33 (1973): 384–98.

One of the most astonishing stories is that of the conversation between Bishop Ireland and Mother Alexia, general superior of the School Sisters of St. Francis in 1885, when the new motherhouse of the order was dedicated in Winona, Wisconsin. The Bishop, in a conversation following the celebratory dinner, set as conditions for the motherhouse existing in Winona that no further Sisters be accepted from Europe, no Sister be sent out to teach before completing her normal training, and that the community become a diocesan congregation. Mother Alexia refused, especially the last condition, and the long anticipated, just-dedicated motherhouse became, in one moment, an academy but not a motherhouse. This remarkable act of Religious autonomy is recounted by Sister Francis Borgia (Rothleubber), *He Sent Two: The Story of the Beginning of the School Sisters of St. Francis* (Milwaukee: Bruce, 1965), 88–94.

The tragic split in the Congregation of Sisters, Servants of the Immaculate Heart of Mary of Monroe, Michigan, deriving directly from episcopal interference, and duplicated in one way or another in a number of U.S. congregations, is told by Marita-Constance Supan, "Dangerous Memory: Mother M. Theresa Maxis Duchemin and the Michigan Congregation of the Sisters, I.H.M.," and Suzanne Fleming, "She Who Remained: Mother Mary Joseph Walker and the 'Refounding' of the I.H.M. Congregation," in *Building Sisterhood: A Feminist History of the Sisters, Servants of the Immaculate Heart of Mary* (Syracuse: Syracuse University Press, 1997), 31–67 and 68–92, respectively.

44. Particularly galling to some Orders is the requirement that professed Religious make a promise of celibacy and obedience to the bishop at the time of ordination to the transitional diaconate, effectively disparaging the vow of consecrated celibacy they have already made and setting up potential conflict between the authority of the superior and that of the bishop.

45. This was made abundantly clear at the time of the controversy in 1984 over the signing, by both male and female Religious, along with numerous secular laypeople, of an open letter in the *New York Times* calling for discussion of the abortion issue. When the Vatican demanded unqualified recantation from all the Religious involved, the men, who were clerics, immediately complied. The women, through their community leaders, spent over a year negotiating with Vatican authorities a solution that did not require the women Religious to compromise on their prophetic action but that "clarified" their position sufficiently to allow the Vatican to withdraw without loss of face.

46. See the exposition of the problems this involves in John W. O'Malley, "One Priesthood: Two Traditions," in *A Concert of Charisms,* 11–17.

47. *P.C.,* 8 (in Flannery, vol. 1): "In these institutes, apostolic and charitable activity is of the very nature of religious life, as their own holy ministry and work of charity, entrusted to them by the Church and to be performed in its name."

48. This dynamic was explored with sobering clarity by Leonardo Boff in *Church: Charism and Power: Liberation Theology*

and the Institutional Church, translated by John W. Diercksmeier (New York: Crossroad, 1985).

CHAPTER NINE

1. Cf. *P.C.,* 1 (in Flannery, vol. 1) on the gift of Religious Life to the Church, and 2, on the particular charism (though the word itself is not used) of each institute. *E.T.,* 11 (in Flannery, vol. 1) speaks of "the charisms of your founders" in commenting on *P.C.,* 2 and of "the charism of the religious life" itself. *L.G.,* 43 (in Flannery, vol. 1) speaks of the evangelical counsels as "a gift of God which the Church has received from her Lord..." and of the various types of Religious Life fostering not only the "progress in holiness of their members" but also "the good of the entire Body of Christ." It speaks also (46) of the choice of the life of the counsels by an individual as response to a "personal vocation" or charism.

2. Canons 487–681 (*CCL,* 1917, 479–687) deal minutely with virtually every aspect of Religious Life, creating uniform provisions for all Institutes. Compare with this voluminous treatment the entire section on Religious Life of the 1983 Code that comprises Canons 573–709 (*CCL,* 1983, 219–71), a brief 28 pages in English (with Latin on facing pages). The much greater conciseness of the revised canons, as well as their reduced number and specificity, confers on Institutes themselves the right to specify their life by particular law (i.e., their own constitutions) in many areas previously covered by Canon Law. This allows much more diversity among Institutes as well as more attention to their own traditions and practices.

English-speaking readers will find useful *A Handbook on Canons 573–746: Religious Institutes, Secular Institutes, Societies of the Apostolic Life,* edited by Jordan Hite, Sharon Holland, and Daniel Ward (Collegeville, Minn.: Liturgical Press, 1985). A briefer treatment than this four-hundred-page volume is *Light for My Path: The New Code of Canon Law for Religious–Digest, Source Material, Commentary,* edited by Austin Flannery and Laurence Collins (Wilmington, Del.: Michael Glazier, 1983).

3. For a fuller treatment of charism, both biblically and theologically, see Wilfrid Harrington, "Charism," *The New Dictionary of Theology,* edited by Joseph A. Komonchak, Mary Collins, and Dermot A. Lane (Wilmington, Del.: Michael Glazier: 1987), 180–83.

4. Paul, in 1 Cor 12:27–31, speaks of this variety of charisms (χαρίσματα) given for the upbuilding of the body of the Church and in 1 Cor 7:7 identifies the call to virginity specifically as a "gift from God" (χάρισμα); 1 Tm 4:14 and 2 Tm 1:6 refer to the gift Timothy received to lead the Church; 1 Pt 4:10–11 emphasizes that the various charisms are given to be stewarded for the Church. The term and the concept occur in a number of other places, but the basic sense is always a distinct gift given to an individual that graces the person him- or herself but especially fosters the good of the community.

5. Acts 2:1–4 describes this event: they were "all together" but the flame of the Spirit descended upon "each one of them." However, the effect was that they were "all filled with the Holy Spirit and began to speak in other tongues."

6. E.g., *L.G.*, 45, in Flannery, vol. 1.

7. Margaret Susan Thompson in "'Charism' or 'Deep Story'? Toward a Clearer Understanding of the Growth of Women's Religious Life in Nineteenth-Century America," in *Religious Life and Contemporary Culture,* Theological Education Process, Cycle 2 (Monroe, Mich.: Sisters, Servants of the Immaculate Heart of Mary, 1998) shows how, historically, Religious congregations were founded and flourished long before being approved by ecclesiastical authority and sometimes despite disapproval. In note 1 on p. 3 she refers to the claims of the hierarchy in conciliar and postconciliar documents and remarks, "These passages...raise some serious questions about the autonomy and integrity of religious charisms, since the implication is that they cannot be presumed to exist 'authentically' until those in (external) hierarchical authority say they exist. Certainly, this is a matter deserving of substantial consideration...."

8. Cf. *E.T.,* 11 (in Flannery, vol. 1): "...the charism of the religious life, far from being an impulse born of flesh and blood...is the fruit of the Holy Spirit, who is always at work within the Church."

9. Although it is convenient for historical reasons to refer to the "life of the evangelical counsels" and the conciliar documents use this as a virtual synonym for Religious Life, the term is highly problematic. As Francis J. Moloney in *A Life of Promise: Poverty, Chastity, Obedience* (New South Wales, Australia: St. Paul Publications, 1984), 15–16, says, poverty, chastity, and obedience insofar as they are Gospel values are neither "recommended" as somehow supererogatory or matters of choice nor are they demanded of only some members of the Church. They are Gospel imperatives demanded of all the baptized. Religious may live them differently but either they are

"evangelical" and therefore demanded of all or they are "counsels" for some, in which case they are not intrinsic to the Gospel. I avoid the term because I believe they are Gospel values, imperative for all Christians, lived in particular ways by different Christians. For example, chastity may be lived in marital fidelity; but to live it as consecrated celibacy is characteristic of Religious Life.

10. The best resource on this history of which I am aware is the dissertation of Lynn Jarrell, *The Development of Legal Structures for Women Religious Between 1500 and 1900: A Study of Selected Institutes of Religious Life for Women* (Ann Arbor, Mich.: University Microfilms International, 1985), which gives the history of premodern legislation on Religious Life for women and then shows how the movement toward the recognition of apostolic congregations and societies occurred.

11. Noncloistered apostolic congregations of simple vows were formally recognized as Religious by Leo XIII on Dec. 8, 1900, in his constitution, *Conditae a Christo*. Angelyn Dries, in "The Americanization of Religious Life: Women Religious, 1872–1922," *U.S. Catholic Historian* 10 (nos. 1–2): 24, gives a reference to an English translation: Ildephonse Lanslots, *Handbook of Canon Law for Congregations of Women Under Simple Vows* (New York, n.p., 1919), 246–58. The first part of the document, specifically recognizing as Religious both diocesan congregations subject to the bishop and congregations approved by the Holy See which transcend diocesan boundaries, both of which make simple vows, is more accessible in *The States of Perfection,* selected and arranged by the Benedictine Monks of Solesmes, translated by E. O'Gorman (Boston: St. Paul Editions, 1967), 164–65.

12. Dolores Liptak, in "Full of Grace: Another Look at the 19th-Century Nun," *Review for Religious* 55 (November/December 1996): 625–39, remarks on 627 that "[f]rom the start, bishops and priests [in the early years of American evangelization] tended to value sisters for practical reasons, speaking of them in terms of their 'immediate visible utility'....[S]ome bishops seemed to count upon them as interchangeable parts in the institutions they governed."

13. Liptak, "Full of Grace," 638 n. 17, calls attention to the number of early American foundations organized "around the themes of Mary's Presentation, Visitation, Immaculate Heart, and Seven Sorrows."

14. This is the point of Thompson's article, "'Charism' or 'Deep Story'?". (See note 7 above.)

15. The first attempt at a full-scale history of women's Religious Life is Jo Ann Kay McNamara, *Sisters in Arms: Catholic Nuns through Two Millennia* (Cambridge: Harvard University Press, 1996). Pages 695–740 offer a vast bibliography on the subject.

For the history of women's Religious Life in Europe from the beginning to its migration to the New World, see Patricia Ranft, *Women and the Religious Life in Premodern Europe* (New York: St. Martin's Press, 1996).

Elizabeth Kolmer, in "Women Religious in the United States: A Survey of Recent Literature," *U.S. Catholic Historian* 10 (1989): 87–92, provides a guide for studying the history of women Religious in the United States, and George C. Stewart, Jr., *Marvels of Charity: History of American Sisters and Nuns,* foreword by Dolores Liptak (Huntington, Ind.: Our Sunday Visitor, 1994) is a compendium of historical information on orders and congregations and, through several appendices on institutions, statistics, and other facts, makes available data that is very hard to extract from directories or other sources.

16. This designation intended to distinguish such congregations on the one hand from contemplative orders (which were not "apostolic" in this older understanding) and, on the other hand, from those orders (usually the same) whose members made solemn (as distinguished from simple) vows. *CCL,* 1983, has suppressed these distinctions, referring only to "institutes which are wholly ordered to contemplation" (674) and "institutes dedicated to works of the apostolate" (675), and there is no reference to solemn vows. Some older orders provide for solemn vows in their particular law, but the only distinction now in Canon Law is between public and private, and temporary and perpetual. Public vows (1192) are those "accepted in the name of the Church by a legitimate superior; otherwise [they] are private."

17. For the history of the development of the Brotherhood see Bruce Lescher, "Laybrothers: Questions Then, Questions Now," *Cistercian Studies* 23 (1988): 63–85.

18. Margaret Susan Thompson, "Discovering Foremothers: Sisters, Society, and the American Catholic Experience," in *The American Catholic Religious Life: Selected Historical Essays,* edited with an introduction by Joseph M. White (New York: Garland, 1988): 63–80 discusses the problem of unearthing the history of women Religious, due both to the ways in which women kept their own records and to the biases in historiography.

A Conference on the History of Women Religious was held at The College of St. Catherine, St. Paul, Minnesota, from June 25–28,

1989, some of the papers of which were published as a special volume of *U.S. Catholic Historian* 10 (1989). This initial conference and its successors are the project of the History of Women Religious Network, which was born in 1987 and continues to work on the subject. To follow the ongoing work of the group one could contact Karen Kennelly, 12001 Chalon Rd., Los Angeles, Calif. 90049-1599, for issues of *History of Women Religious News and Notes*.

19. An excellent exception that will go a long way toward reincorporating women into the history of Religious Life in the Middle Ages is Bernard McGinn, *The Flowering of Mysticism: Men and Women in the New Mysticism (1200–1350)*, vol. 3 of *The Presence of God: A History of Western Christian Mysticism* (New York: Crossroad, 1998). The bibliography on pages 465–505 of this volume is a valuable resource. McGinn supplies good sketches of the various forms of Religious Life that developed in the High Middle Ages, especially among women.

20. A good example of this type of presentation is the volume, still valuable in many respects, of Lawrence Cada, et al., *Shaping the Coming Age of Religious Life* (New York: Seabury, 1979), which lays out "The Evolution of Religious Life: A Historical Model" in chapter 1 as a background for a theory of life cycles in forms of Religious Life and in particular Institutes. The authors denote the years 200–500 as the Age of the Desert, 500–1200 as the Age of Monasticism, 1200–1500 as the Age of the Mendicant Orders, 1500–1800 as the Age of the Apostolic Orders, and 1800 to the present as the Age of the Teaching Congregations. While this is, in some respects, a helpful schema that has had enormous currency among contemporary Religious and has helped many realize the historicity of the lifeform, it has a number of notable defects. First, it begins in 200 C.E. with the desert monastics (predominantly men) rather than in the first century with the consecrated virgins and widows (predominantly women). Second, it equates apostolic congregations of simple vows with teaching congregations (which most Brothers' congregations are), thus rendering "invisible" the health care and social service congregations (overwhelmingly female) that also belong to this group. Third, it creates the impression of one type of Religious Life supplanting another, which I will call into question. The authors recognize the limitations of their schema and never intended it to be more than a convenient way of organizing voluminous data, but its oversimplification must be recognized if we are to move forward in our analysis of the life.

A much more ambitious example is the volume of Raymond Hostie, *Vie et mort des ordres religieux: approches psychosociologiques* (Paris: Desclée de Brouwer, 1972), which was never translated into English but was widely used in renewal efforts. Hostie made no claim to having investigated the history but used the historical studies available. His periodization and his decision to deal only with male orders, since he considered them normative, testifies to the problems I am discussing here.

21. Medieval women mystics, most of whom were in some form of Religious Life, were often virtuosos of asceticism and penance, but it was characteristically a unitive or spousal embrace of the suffering of Christ rather than the more "athletic" war against the flesh for purposes of self-mastery and progress in prayer that was more characteristic of male ascetics.

22. An excellent treatment of Beguine spirituality, which is being reexamined and newly evaluated after centuries of being seen as bordering on the heretical, is Saskia Murk-Jansen, *Brides in the Desert: The Spirituality of the Beguines*, Traditions of Christian Spirituality, edited by Philip Sheldrake (Maryknoll, N.Y.: Orbis, 1998).

23. See Mary Ann Foley, "Uncloistered Apostolic Life for Women: Marguerite Bourgeoys' Experiment in Ville-Marie," *U.S. Catholic Historian* 10 (1989): 37–44.

24. See Dries, "The Americanization of Religious Life," esp. the chart on p. 22.

25. Ranft, *Women and the Religious Life*, esp. chapters 6–8.

26. The Daughters of Charity founders, Louise de Marillac and Vincent de Paul, were adamant in claiming that the company was not a Religious Institute because, as Vincent said, being Religious meant being cloistered and thus unable to serve the poor. However, they were also clear about the consecration to Christ that was at the heart of the vocation to ministry, and the members of the Company made private annual vows of consecrated celibacy, poverty, obedience, and service of the poor.

27. See Ranft, *Women and the Religious Life*, 74–76.

28. Ibid., 121.

29. Ibid., 122.

30. See Mary Ann Foley, "Uncloistered Apostolic Life for Women."

31. See Ranft, *Women and the Religious Life*, 101–6, on the history of the order in Europe and Stewart, *Marvels of Charity*, 51–52, on the adaptation involved in their move to the New World.

32. See Margaret Susan Thompson, "Discovering Foremothers," for the high points of this development.

33. The struggle of these first congregations with early American anti-Catholicism and ecclesiastical lack of understanding and the eventual triumph of their witness and service over the opposition is recounted by Liptak, "Full of Grace."

34. From 448 members in 1830, numbers reached a high point of approximately 200,000 in 1965. Stewart, *Marvels of Charity*, 564–65, gives actual statistics but estimates that between 1790 and 1990 approximately 350,000 U.S. women were Religious.

35. See Stewart, *Marvels of Charity*, 516–48, for a list of hospitals founded by women Religious between 1829 and 1990.

36. See Stewart, *Marvels of Charity*, 549–56 for names and dates of colleges founded by women's Religious congregations.

37. Patricia Wittberg in "Ties That No Longer Bind," *America* (September 26, 1998): 10–14, discusses the role these institutions played in development of leadership among women Religious.

38. Ranft, *Women and the Religious Life*, 131.

39. Thomas Aquinas defended the "mixed life" as the highest form of Religious Life precisely because "even as it is better to enlighten than merely to shine, so it is better to give to others the fruits of one's contemplation than merely to contemplate" (*Summa Theologica* II, II, Q 188, Art. 6, available in English in *Summa Theologica*, 3 vols., translated by the Fathers of the English Dominican Province [New York: Benziger, 1947–1948]). Mendicant Religious Life of men embodied this conviction. The institutional Church did not recognize the validity of this form of life for women, insisting, with increasing vehemence, on enclosure and finally on papal cloister. However, it is interesting that Clare of Assisi, foundress of the female branch of the Franciscans and the first woman to write her own Rule, saw the cloistered life of her community as essentially apostolic. As McGinn puts it in *The Flowering of Mysticism*, 69, "Clare conceived of her commitment to Francis's *forma vitae* as involving a new public responsibility for the entire Church," a life of withdrawal but not of confinement. The bull of canonization of Clare lyrically celebrates the breadth of her apostolic zeal even in the cloistered life: "She was kept inside, and remained outside. Clare was hidden, yet her way of life was open. Clare kept silent, but her fame cried out. She was concealed in a cell, but she was taught in the cities."

40. Cf., for example, *P.C.*, 8 (in Flannery, vol. 1): "In these institutes, apostolic and charitable activity is of the very nature of religious life...," and elsewhere.

41. As I indicated in the introduction, my primary intended audience is apostolic Religious. Consequently, in what follows I will give a more detailed treatment of that form of life. The briefer treatment of contemplative life in no way implies that I think it less important but simply that it is not the primary subject matter of this work. It is also clear that I am less qualified to deal with the contemplative life form since I do not live it. My purpose in discussing it here is for contrast and to lay to rest certain misunderstandings about both forms of life, e.g., that contemplative life is nonapostolic or that apostolic Religious are less called to prayer, etc.

CHAPTER TEN

1. See Karl Rahner, "The Unity of Love of God and Neighbor," (no. 152) in *The Content of Faith: The Best of Karl Rahner's Theological Writings,* edited by Karl Lehmann and Albert Raffelt, translated by Harvey D. Egan (New York: Crossroad, 1992), 579–87 (taken from *Everyday Faith,* translated by Willliam J. O'Hara [New York: Herder and Herder, 1968], 106–17). Rahner says, e.g., "Love of God and love of neighbor are mutually inclusive" (580–81); "Where a person really abandons himself [sic] and loves his neighbor with absolute selflessness, he has already come to the silent, inexpressible mystery of God..." (582); "It is truly the case that we meet the incarnate Word of God in the other human being" (535).

2. An accessible discussion of Old Testament prophecy supplying a useful bibliography is Thomas W. Overholt, *Channels of Prophecy: The Social Dynamics of Prophetic Activity* (Minneapolis: Fortress, 1989).

3. Bernard McGinn, *The Flowering of Mysticism: Men and Women in the New Mysticism (1200–1350),* vol. 3 of *The Presence of God: A History of Western Christian Mysticism* (New York: Crossroad, 1998), 27.

4. This is very evident in Luke's presentation of the prophetic ministry of John the Baptist, who tells his hearers that being children of Abraham is no free pass to salvation but that they must "[p]roduce good fruits as evidence of your repentance," and in response to the question about what this means spelled out the

requirements to feed and clothe the poor, act honestly in business, and fulfill one's duties (Lk 3:8–15).

5. Cf. Matthew's presentation (Mt 27) of the role of the Jewish leaders in the arrest, trial, and condemnation of Jesus for disturbing the peace of the Roman province, and John's presentation of the leaders declaring themselves subjects of Caesar (Jn 19:12, 15).

6. See the excoriation of the practice of the religious leaders in Mt 23:1–36.

7. *G.S.*, 1, in Flannery, vol. 1.

8. See the excellent article of Constance FitzGerald, "Desolation as Dark Night: The Transformative Influence of Wisdom in John of the Cross," *The Way Supplement* 82 (Spring 1995): 96–108, esp. 105.

9. Margaret Brennan, "'A White Light Still and Moving': Religious Life at the Crossroads of the Future," in *Religious Life: The Challenge of Tomorrow,* edited by Cassian J. Yuhaus (New York: Paulist Press, 1994), 92–108.

10. See *U.R.*, in Flannery, vol. 1.

11. See *N.A.*, 2, in Flannery, vol. 1.

12. Several important efforts, however, have been made. A mapping of the terrain was Paul F. Knitter's book, *No Other Name? A Critical Survey of Christian Attitudes Toward the World Religions,* American Society of Missiology Series 7 (Maryknoll, N.Y.: Orbis, 1986). See also his *One Earth, Many Religions: Multifaith Dialogue and Global Responsibility* (Maryknoll, N.Y.: Orbis, 1995) and *The Uniqueness of Jesus: A Dialogue with Paul Knitter,* edited by Leonard Swidler and Paul Mojzes (Maryknoll, N.Y.: Orbis, 1997). A significant dialogue on the subject among Knitter, Monica Hellwig, Leonard Swidler, and the Protestant process theologian John B. Cobb was published as *Death or Dialogue? From the Age of Monologue to the Age of Dialogue* (Philadelphia: Trinity, 1990).

13. For a very good summary of the development of the intermonastic dialogue between Catholics and the world religions, see Pascaline Coff, "How We Reached This Point: Communication Becoming Communion," in *The Gethsemani Encounter: A Dialogue on the Spiritual Life by Buddhist and Christian Monastics,* edited by Donald W. Mitchell and James A. Wiseman (New York: Continuum, 1998), 3–17.

14. See Thomas Merton, *The Way of Chuang-Tzu* (New York: New Directions, 1965); *Zen and the Birds of Appetite* (New York: New Directions, 1968); *Thomas Merton on Zen* (London: Sheldon, 1976); his journals: *The Vow of Conversation: Journals,* 1964–1965 (New York: Farrar,

Straus, Giroux, 1988), and *The Asian Journal of Thomas Merton,* edited from his original notebooks by Naomi Burton, Patrick Hart, and James Laughlin, with consulting editor Amiya Chakravarty (New York: New Directions, 1973).

15. The story of Bede Griffiths, the Benedictine monk who spent decades in India living as a Hindu-Christian holy man, has been recently and competently told by Shirley du Boulay, *Beyond the Darkness: A Biography of Bede Griffiths* (New York: Doubleday, 1998).

16. Coff tells of her own involvement in the Monastic Interreligious Dialogue in "How We Reached This Point," 4–9.

17. See Hugo M. Enomiya-Lassalle, *Zen–Way to Enlightenment* (New York: Taplinger, 1966), in which he recounts how he started to practice Zen as part of his missionary preparation, in order to understand the Japanese character but came to see through practice "that Zen was a great help to my own spiritual life" (9). He went on to become a Zen master and to write a book on the practice of Zen for Christians, *Zen Meditation for Christians,* translated by John C. Maraldo (LaSalle, Ill.: Open Court, 1974).

18. See the dissertation of Peter Feldmeier, *Interrelatedness: A Comparison of the Spiritualities of St. John of the Cross and Buddhaghosa for the Purpose of Examining the Christian Use of Buddhist Practices,* 2 vols., Ph.D. dissertation (Berkeley, Calif.: Graduate Theological Union Dissertation, 1996), in which he sets out the problems and possibilities of interreligious practice and attempts to respond to them.

19. Raimundo Panikkar is perhaps the foremost Christian proponent of the theological interrelationship between Christianity and non-Christian (particularly Asian) religious insight. See his *The Silence of God: The Answer of the Buddha,* translated by Robert R. Barr (Maryknoll, N.Y.: Orbis, 1989) and *The Trinity and the World Religions: Icon-Person-Mystery* (Maryknoll, N.Y.: Orbis, 1973).

20. Unfortunately, the recent book by Diarmuid Ó Murchú, *Reclaiming Spirituality: A New Spiritual Framework for Today's World* (New York: Crossroad, 1998), is a good example of the kind of hasty analysis, overgeneralization, and facile solutions to which this discussion is prone.

21. I offer a brief history of the term *spirituality* in "Spirituality in the Academy," *Theological Studies* 50 (December, 1989): 676–97. See also Bernard McGinn, "The Letter and the Spirit: Spirituality as an Academic Discipline," *Christian Spirituality Bulletin* 1 (Fall 1993): 1–10.

22. Peter Van Ness, "Introduction: Spirituality and the Secular Quest," in *Spirituality and the Secular Quest,* World Spirituality: An

Encyclopedic History of the Religious Quest 22 (New York: Crossroad, 1996), 5.

23. I offer this definition in "The Study of Christian Spirituality: Contours and Dynamics of a Discipline," *Christian Spirituality Bulletin* 6 (Spring 1998): 1, 3–12, with the definition explained on pages 1 and 3.

24. The spread of Buddhism, first within Asia and then beyond, is a remarkable example of the inculturation of a culturally rooted tradition in new environments. An accessible account is available by Robert C. Lester, "Buddhism: The Path to Nirvana," in *Religious Traditions of the World*, edited by H. Byron Earhart (San Francisco: HarperSanFrancisco, 1993), 847–971.

25. There has been historically and continues to be to some extent an ethnic and even a quasi-national character to Judaism that has no parallels in other religious traditions. However, since conversion to Judaism is possible, the biological, ethnic, and/or national features are not absolutes.

26. The recent warning about the writings of Anthony de Mello by the Congregation for the Doctrine of the Faith, "Notification on Positions of Father Anthony de Mello," with a cover letter by Cardinal Ratzinger seeking the banning of his books is available in *Origins* 28 (1998): 211–14, and the current investigation of Jacques Depuis, a careful theologian of religions at the Gregorian University, are examples of such concern.

27. Both Michel Foucault in *The History of Sexuality*, vol. 1, translated by Robert Hurley (New York: Pantheon, 1978) and Hannah Arendt in *The Human Condition* (Chicago: University of Chicago Press, 1958) exposed the link between control of divine forgiveness and control of society. More recently, A. W. Richard Sipe, in *Sex, Priest, and Power: Anatomy of a Crisis* (New York: Brunner/Mazel, 1995), 98–100, has discussed the same dynamic, recalling Friedrich Nietzsche's analysis and connecting the sexual scandals that have undermined the credibility of the clergy to the decline of sacramental confession, through which such power to control access to divine forgiveness has traditionally been exercised.

28. Leonardo Boff, in *Church, Charism, and Power: Liberation Theology and the Institutional Church*, translated by John W. Diercksmeier (New York: Crossroad, 1985) applied the liberationist analysis of material monopoly to what he called the monopoly of symbolic resources through the sacerdotal control of the sacramental system.

29. Phil 4:8 seems to encourage such an open-minded approach to religious matters among Christians.

30. Two examples of this function, both ambiguous but striking, are the recently deceased theologian, Charles Davis, who not only resigned from the clergy but disaffiliated from the Roman Catholic Church shortly after Vatican II over the issue of papal power, and Mary Daly, the self-proclaimed post-Christian philosopher-theologian who became convinced that the sexism of the Church is irremediable and salvation will have to come from a society of women.

31. E.g., "Letter to the Bishops of the Catholic Church on Some Aspects of Christian Meditation," issued by the Congregation for the Doctrine of the Faith on Dec. 14, 1989 (available in *Origins* 19: 492–98), calling into question Christian use of eastern meditation.

32. A wonderful historical example of the vitality of contemplative spirituality in the face of institutional repression is the mystical conversations of Gertrude of Helfta (thirteenth century) with Christ while her monastery was under ecclesiastical interdict in 1296. When Gertrude expressed her fear of being "cut off from you by the excommunication" Jesus replies, "This excommunication which has been imposed on you will do you no more harm than would someone trying to cut you with a wooden knife...." This interchange occurs in *The Herald of Divine Love* III, 16, translated and edited by Margaret Winkworth, CWS (N.Y./Mahwah, N.J.: Paulist Press, 1993), 172.

33. Lora Ann Quiñonez and Mary Daniel Turner, in *The Transformation of American Catholic Sisters* (Philadelphia: Temple University Press, 1992), 107, recount that when they interviewed Archbishop Thomas C. Kelly, O.P., in March of 1988, they "asked him what he believed was the major objection of the Congregation for Religious to LCWR. Without a pause he answered, 'Feminism.'"

34. See Sandra M. Schneiders, *Beyond Patching: Faith and Feminism in the Catholic Church,* The Anthony Jordan Lectures, Newman Theological College, Edmonton, 1990 (New York/Mahwah, N.J.: Paulist, 1991).

35. Maria Riley, *Transforming Feminism* (Kansas City: Sheed & Ward, 1989), discusses the secular history of the movement and how it was transformed by religiously motivated women and transformed them.

36. The truly prophetic declaration of the 1971 Synod of Bishops, *C.U.* (in Flannery, vol. 2)—"[a]ction on behalf of justice and participation in the transformation of the world fully appear to us as a constitutive dimension of the preaching of the Gospel, or, in other words, of

the Church's mission for the redemption of the human race and its liberation from every oppressive situation" (introduction, 696)—involved an application of this call for justice to the Church itself. In chapter 3 the synod states: "While the Church is bound to give witness to justice, she recognizes that anyone who ventures to speak to people about justice must first be just in their eyes" (703).

37. One can trace the uneven development of the Church's official stance on liberation theology in the volume containing all of the major church documents to date on liberation theology: *Liberation Theology: A Documentary History,* edited by Alfred T. Hennelly (Maryknoll, N.Y.: Orbis, 1990/1992).

38. This is precisely what is happening in the reform movements growing in various segments of the Church. The Association for the Rights of Catholics in the Church, the We Are Church movement, Catholics Speak Out, Quixote Center, FutureChurch, Priests for Equality, and Women-Church are examples of groups active in the United States whose members are reimagining the Church as a community of equal discipleship. They have their analogues in other countries, especially in Europe. See also Andrew Greeley and Michael Hout, "American Catholics and the Next Pope: A Survey Report" done in March–April 1996. (For a press release detailing the results of this study, contact June Rosner in Chicago, Ill. at 312-664-6100.)

CONCLUSION

1. I am borrowing from the very accessible popular treatments of quantum physics of John Polkinghorne, *Quarks, Chaos, and Christianity: Questions to Science and Religion* (New York: Crossroad, 1997 [orig. 1994]) and Margaret J. Wheatley, *Leadership and the New Science: Learning about Organization from an Orderly Universe* (San Francisco: Berrett-Koehler, 1992) to construct this metaphor.

2. See Polkinghorne, *Quarks, Chaos, and Christianity,* 16–17.

3. Ibid., 68–69.

4. Wheatley, *Leadership and the New Science,* 121–37.

5. Ibid., 135.

Works Cited

Abbo, John A., and Jerome D. Hannon. *The Sacred Canons: A Concise Presentation of the Current Disciplinary Norms of the Church.* 2 Vols. St. Louis: Herder, 1951.

Angle, Siddika P. *Angel to Apostle: Models of Spirituality for Single Catholic Laywomen In the United States, 1866–1965.* 2 vols. Berkeley, Calif.: Graduate Theological Union Dissertation, 1995.

Aquinas, Thomas. *Summa Theologica.* 3 vols. Translated by the Fathers of the English Dominican Province. New York: Benziger, 1947–1948.

Arbuckle, Gerald A. *Out of Chaos: Refounding Religious Congregations.* New York/Mahwah, N.J.: Paulist Press, 1988.

Arendt, Hannah. *The Human Condition.* Chicago: University of Chicago Press, 1958.

Armstrong, Philip, ed. *Who Are My Brothers?* New York: Alba House, 1988.

Augustine of Hippo. *Patrologia Latina.* Vol. 38. Edited by J. P. Migne. 1878–90.

Bellah, Robert, et. al. *Habits of the Heart: Individualism and Commitment in American Life.* Berkeley, Calif.: University of California Press, 1985.

Bharati, Agahanda. "Sacred Offices and Orders—Monasticism." In the *New Encyclopaedia Britannica,* 15th ed., s.v. "monasticism," 981–87.

Bianchi, Eugene C., and Rosemary Radford Ruether, eds. *A Democratic Catholic Church: The Reconstruction of Roman Catholicism.* New York: Crossroad, 1992.

Billy, Dennis J. "'Objective Superiority' in *Vita Consecrata.*" *Review for Religious* 55 (November/December 1996): 640–45.

Boff, Leonardo. *Church: Charism and Power: Liberation Theology and the Institutional Church.* Translated by John W. Diercksmeier. New York: Crossroad, 1985.

Bolen, Jean Shinoda. *Goddesses in Everywoman: A New Psychology of Women.* San Francisco: Harper & Row, 1984.

Borg, Marcus J. *Meeting Jesus Again for the First Time: The Historical Jesus and the Heart of Contemporary Faith.* San Francisco: HarperSanFrancisco, 1994.

————. *The God We Never Knew: Beyond Dogmatic Religion to a More Authentic Contemporary Faith.* San Francisco: HarperSanFrancisco, 1997.

Borgmann, Albert. *Crossing the Postmodern Divide.* Chicago: University of Chicago Press, 1992.

Bowman, Douglas C. *Beyond the Modern Mind: The Spiritual and Ethical Challenge of the Environmental Crisis.* New York: Pilgrim, 1990.

Brennan, Margaret. "'Not Two Exactly Alike.'" In *Building Sisterhood: A Feminist History of the Sisters, Servants of the Immaculate Heart of Mary,* 95–109. Syracuse, N.Y.: Syracuse University Press, 1997.

————. "'A White Light Still and Moving': Religious Life At the Crossroads of the Future." In *Religious Life: The Challenge of Tomorrow,* edited by Cassian J. Yuhaus. New York: Paulist Press, 1994, 92–108.

Brown, Peter. *The Body and Society: Men, Women and Sexual Renunciation in Early Christianity,* Lectures on the History of Religions, vol. 13. New York: Columbia University Press, 1988.

Brueggemann, Walter. *The Prophetic Imagination*. Philadelphia: Fortress, 1978.

Cabrol, F. "Monasticism." In *Encyclopaedia of Religion and Ethics*, vol. 8, edited by James Hastings. Edinburgh: T. & T. Clark, 1980, 782.

Cada, Lawrence, et al. *Shaping the Coming Age of Religious Life*. New York: Seabury, 1979.

Cardman, Francine. "On Being Single." In *The Wind Is Rising: Prayer Ways for Active People*, 6–7. Edited by William R. Callahan and Francine Cardman. Tabloid Format. Mt. Rainier, Md.: Quixote Center, 1978.

———. "Singleness and Spirituality." *Spirituality Today* 35 (1983): 304–18.

Carlen, Claudia. *The Papal Encyclicals 1939–1958*, vol. 4. Wilmington, N.C.: McGrath, 1981.

Catechism of the Catholic Church. Collegeville, Minn.: Liturgical Press, 1994.

Catholic Biblical Association of America. "Women and Priestly Ministry: The New Testament Evidence." *Catholic Biblical Quarterly* 41 (1979): 608–13.

Chittister, Joan. *The Fire in These Ashes: A Spirituality of Contemporary Religious Life*. Kansas City: Sheed & Ward, 1995.

Code of Canon Law: Latin-English Edition. Translated by the Canon Law Society of America. Washington, D.C.: Canon Law Society of America, 1983.

Coff, Pascaline. "How We Reached This Point: Communication Becoming Communion." In *The Gethsemani Encounter: A Dialogue On the Spiritual Life by Buddhist and Christian Monastics*, 3–17. Edited by Donald W. Mitchell and James A. Wiseman. New York: Continuum, 1998.

Daly, R. J., et al., eds. *Religious Life in the U.S. Church: The New Dialogue.* New York/Mahwah, N.J.: Paulist, 1984.

Donahue, John. "A Tale of Two Documents." In *Women Priests: A Catholic Commentary on the Vatican Declaration*, 25–34. Edited by L. Swidler and A. Swidler. New York/Mahwah, N.J.: Paulist Press, 1977.

Donovan, Mary Ann. "Dancing Before the Lord: Theological Anthropology and Christian Spirituality as Graceful Partners." In *CTSA Proceedings* 53 (1998): 73–87.

Dreyer, Elizabeth A. *Earth Crammed with Heaven: A Spirituality of Everyday Life.* New York/Mahwah, N.J.: Paulist Press, 1994.

Dries, Angelyn. "The Americanization of Religious Life: Women Religious, 1872–1922." *U.S. Catholic Historian* 10, Nos. 1–2 (1989): 24.

Du Boulay, Shirley. *Beyond the Darkness: A Biography of Bede Griffiths.* New York: Doubleday, 1998.

Durkin, Elizabeth, and Julie Durkin Montague. "Surveying U.S. Nuns." *America* 172 (February 11, 1995): 11–16.

Dwyer, Judith A. "Appendix A: Tradition and the Ordination of Women." *CTSA Proceedings* 52 (1997): 197–204.

Ebaugh, Helen Rose Fuchs. *Women in the Vanishing Cloister: Organizational Decline in Catholic Religious Orders in the United States.* New Brunswick, N.J.: Rutgers University Press, 1993.

Eckhart, Meister. *Meister Eckhart: The Essential Sermons, Commentaries, Treatises, and Defense.* Translated and introduced by Edmund Colledge and Bernard McGinn. CWS. New York/Mahwah, N.J.: Paulist Press, 1981.

Engh, Michael E. "Catholic Action." In *The HarperCollins Encyclopedia of Catholicism*, 240. Edited by Richard P. McBrien. New York: HarperCollins, 1995.

Enomiya-Lassalle, Hugo M. *Zen Meditation for Christians*. Translated by John C. Maraldo. Lasalle, Ill.: Open Court, 1974.

———. *Zen: Way to Enlightenment*. New York: Taplinger, 1966.

"Essential Elements in Church Teaching on Religious Life." Congregation for Religious and Secular Institutes. *Origins* 13 (1983): 133–42.

Faley, Roland J. "An American Experience of Priesthood in Religious Life." In *A Concert of Charisms: Ordained Ministry in Religious Life*. Edited by Paul K. Hennessy. New York/Mahwah, N.J.: Paulist Press, 1997.

Feldmeier, Peter. *Interrelatedness: A Comparison of the Spiritualities of St. John of the Cross and Buddhaghosa for the Purpose of Examining the Christian Use of Buddhist Practices*. 2 Vols. Ph.D. Dissertation. Berkeley, Calif.: Graduate Theological Union Dissertation, 1996.

Fiand, Barbara. *Living the Vision: Religious Vows in an Age of Change*. New York: Crossroad, 1990.

———. *Wrestling with God: Religious Life in Search of Its Soul*. New York: Crossroad, 1996.

Fiedler, Maureen, and Linda Rabben. *Rome Has Spoken: A Guide to Forgotten Papal Statements, and How They Have Changed Through the Centuries*. New York: Crossroad, 1998.

FitzGerald, Constance. "Desolation as Dark Night: The Transformative Influence of Wisdom in John of the Cross." *The Way Supplement* 82 (Spring, 1995): 98–105.

———. "A Discipleship of Equals: Voices from Tradition—Teresa of Avila and John of the Cross." In *A Discipleship of Equals: Towards a Christian Feminist Spirituality*, 63–97. Edited by Francis A. Eigo. Villanova, Pa.: Villanova University Press, 1988.

————. "Impasse and Dark Night." In *Women's Spirituality: Resources for Christian Development*, 2d ed., 410–35. Edited by Joann Wolski Conn. New York/Mahwah, N.J.: Paulist Press, 1996.

Flannery, Austin P., ed. *Vatican Council II: The Conciliar and Postconciliar Documents*. 2 vols. Grand Rapids: Eerdmans, 1975 and 1984.

Flannery, Austin P., and Laurence Collins, eds. *Light for My Path; The New Code of Canon Law for Religious–Digest, Source Material, Commentary*. Wilmington, Del.: Michael Glazier, 1983.

Fleming, Suzanne. "She Who Remained; Mother Mary Joseph Walker and the 'Refounding' of the I.H.M. Congregation." In *Building Sisterhood: A Feminist History of the Sisters, Servants of the Immaculate Heart of Mary*. Syracuse, N.Y.: Syracuse University Press, 1997, 68–92.

Flores, Miguel Perez. "The Company of the Daughters of Charity, Society of Apostolic Life I, II," Address to the May 14, 1997, General Assembly of the Daughters of Charity. In *Echoes of the Company* (internal publication of the Daughters of Charity), 316–32, 373–478.

Fogarty, Gerald P. "The Bishops *Versus* Religious Orders: The Suppressed Decrees of the Third Plenary Council of Baltimore." *The Jurist* 33 (1973): 384–98.

Foley, Mary Ann. "Uncloistered Apostolic Life for Women: Marguerite Bourgeoy's Experiment in Ville-Marie." *U.S. Catholic Historian* 10, nos. 1–2 (1989): 37–44.

Foley, Nadine, ed. *Claiming Our Truth: Reflections on Identity by United States Women Religious*. Washington, D.C.: LCWR, 1988.

Foucault, Michel. *The History of Sexuality*. Vol. 1. Translated by Robert Hurley. New York: Pantheon, 1978.

Gaucher, Guy. *The Passion of Therese of Lisieux*. Translated by Anne Marie Brennan. New York: Crossroad, 1998.

Geden, A. S. "Monasticism (Buddhist)." In *Encyclopaedia of Religion and Ethics*, vol. 8, edited by James Hastings. Edinburgh: T. & T. Clark, 1980, 798.

Gertrude of Helfta. *The Herald of Divine Love*. Translated and edited by Margaret Winkworth. CWS. N.Y./Mahwah, N.J.: Paulist Press, 1993.

Goffman, Erving. "The Characteristics of Total Institutions." In *A Sociological Reader on Complex Organizations*. Edited by Amitia Etzioni and Edward Lehman. New York: Holt, Rinehart and Winston, 1980, 319–39.

Gottemoeller, Doris. "The Priesthood: Implications in Consecrated Life for Women." In *A Concert of Charisms: Ordained Ministry in Religious Life*. Edited by Paul K. Hennessy. New York/Mahwah, N.J.: Paulist Press, 1997.

Greeley, Andrew, and Michael Hout. "American Catholics and the Next Pope: A Survey Report." March–April, 1996. For a press release detailing the results of this study, contact June Rosner in Chicago, Ill. at 312-664-6100.

Griffin, David Ray. "Introduction: Postmodern Spirituality and Society." In *Spirituality and Society: Postmodern Visions*. Edited by David Ray Griffin. Albany, N.Y.: State University of New York, 1988, 1–31.

Harding, M. Esther. *Woman's Mysteries Ancient and Modern: A Psychological Interpretation of the Feminine Principle as Portrayed in Myth, Story, and Dreams*. New and revised ed. New York: Pantheon, 1955.

Harrington, Wilfrid. "Charism." In *The New Dictionary of Theology*. Edited by Joseph A. Komonchak, Mary Collins, and Dermot A. Lane. Wilmington, Del.: Michael Glazier: 1987, 180–83.

Hennelly, Alfred T., ed. *Liberation Theology: A Documentary History*. Maryknoll, N.Y.: Orbis, 1990, 1992.

Hennessy, Paul K. "Introduction: The Parochialization of the Church and Consecrated Life." In *A Concert of Charisms: Ordained Ministry in Religious Life*. Edited by Paul K. Hennessy. New York/Mahwah, N.J.: Paulist Press, 1997.

Heschel, Abraham J. *The Prophets*. Vol. 1. New York: Harper & Row, 1969.

Heyward, Carter. *When Boundaries Betray Us: Beyond Illusions of What Is Ethical in Therapy and Life*. San Francisco: HarperSanFrancisco, 1993.

Hite, Jordan, Sharon Holland, and Daniel Ward, eds. *A Handbook on Canons 573–746: Religious Institutes, Secular Institutes, Societies of the Apostolic Life*. Collegeville, Minn.: Liturgical, 1985.

Holland, Joe. "Family, Work, and Culture: A Postmodern Recovery of Holiness." In *Sacred Interconnections: Postmodern Spirituality, Political Economy, and Art*. Edited by David Ray Griffin. Albany, N.Y.: State University of New York Press, 1990, 103–22.

Hostie, Raymond. *Vie et mort des ordres religieux: approches psychosociologiques*. Paris: Desclée De Brouwer, 1972.

Hunt, Máire. "The Mystery of God in Celtic Consciousness." *The Mast Journal* 4 (Fall 1993): 14–20.

Ignatius of Loyola. *The Spiritual Exercises of Saint Ignatius Loyola: An American Translation from the Final Version of the Exercises, the Latin Vulgate, into Contemporary English.* Translated by Lewis Delmage. New York: Wagner, 1968.

Jaini, Padmanabh S. *The Jaina Path of Purification.* Berkeley, Calif.: University of California Press, 1979.

Jarrell, Lynn Marie. *The Development of Legal Structures for Women Religious Between 1500 and 1900: A Study of Selected Institutes of Religious Life for Women.* Ann Arbor, Mich.: University Microfilms International, 1985.

————. "The Legal and Historical Context of Religious Life for Women." *The Jurist* 45 (1985): 419–37.

John of the Cross. *The Collected Works of Saint John of the Cross,* rev. ed. Translated by Kieran Kavanaugh and Otilio Rodriguez, with revisions and introduction by Kieran Kavanaugh. Washington. D.C.: Institute of Carmelite Studies, 1991.

Johnson, Elizabeth. *She Who Is: The Mystery of God in Feminist Theological Discourse.* New York: Crossroad, 1992.

Jones, Arthur. "Nuns Renew Vows: Mission They Say, Not Age, Must Drive Today's Congregations." *National Catholic Reporter,* March 5, 1999, 11–18.

Jung, C. G. *Collected Works of C. G. Jung.* Vol. 9, part 1. Edited by Sir Herbert Read, Michael Fordham, and Gerhard Adler. Translated by R. F. C. Hull. Princeton, N.J.: Princeton University Press, 1968.

Knitter, Paul F. *No Other Name? A Critical Survey of Christian Attitudes Toward the World Religions.* American Society of Missiology Series 7. Maryknoll, N.Y.: Orbis, 1986.

————. *One Earth, Many Religions: Multifaith Dialogue and Global Responsibility.* Maryknoll, N.Y.: Orbis, 1995.

Kolmer, Elizabeth. *Religious Women in the United States: A Survey of the Influential Literature from 1950 to 1983.* Wilmington, Del.: Michael Glazier, 1984.

————. "Women Religious In the United States: A Survey of Recent Literature." *U.S. Catholic Historian* 10, nos. 1–2 (1989): 87–92.

Lakeland, Paul. *Postmodernity: Christian Identity in a Fragmented Age.* Minneapolis: Fortress, 1997.

Lanslots, Ildephonse. *Handbook of Canon Law for Congregations of Women Under Simple Vows.* New York: n.p., 1919.

Leddy, Mary Jo. *Reweaving Religious Life: Beyond the Liberal Model.* Mystic, Conn.: Twenty-Third Publications, 1990.

Lescher, Bruce. "Laybrothers: Questions Then, Questions Now." *Cistercian Studies* 23 (1988): 63–85.

Lester, Robert C. "Buddhism: The Path to Nirvana." In *Religious Traditions of the World.* Edited by H. Byron Earhart. San Francisco: HarperSanFrancisco, 1993, 847–971.

"Letter to the Bishops of the Catholic Church on Some Aspects of Christian Meditation." Issued by the Congregation for the Doctrine of the Faith. *Origins* 19: 492–98.

Liebert, Elizabeth. *Changing Life Patterns: Adult Development in Spiritual Direction.* New York/Mahwah, N.J.: Paulist Press, 1992.

Liptak, Dolores. "Full of Grace: Another Look At the 19th-Century Nun." *Review for Religious* 55 (November/December, 1996): 625–39.

Luther, Martin. *The Augsburg Confession.* Available in English as *The Book of Concord: The Confessions of the Evangelical Lutheran Church.* Translated and edited by Theodore G. Tappert. Philadelphia: Fortress, 1979.

MacCana, Proinsias. "Celtic Mythology." In *Library of the World's Myths and Legends*. New York: Peter Bedrick, 1985, 6–19.

McGinn, Bernard. *The Flowering of Mysticism: Men and Women in the New Mysticism (1200–1350)*. Vol. 3 of *The Presence of God: A History of Western Christian Mysticism*, 3 vols. New York: Crossroad, 1998.

———. *The Foundations of Mysticism*. Vol. 1 of *The Presence of God: A History of Western Christian Mysticism*, 3 vols. New York: Crossroad, 1991.

———. "The Letter and the Spirit: Spirituality as an Academic Discipline." *Christian Spirituality Bulletin* 1 (Fall, 1993): 1–10.

McNamara, Jo Ann Kay. *Sisters in Arms: Catholic Nuns Through Two Millennia*. Cambridge: Harvard University Press, 1996.

Merkle, Judith A. *Committed by Choice: Religious Life Today*. Collegeville, Minn.: Liturgical Press, 1992.

Merton, Thomas. *The Asian Journal of Thomas Merton*. Edited from his original notebooks by Naomi Burton, Patrick Hart, and James Laughlin, with consulting editor Amiya Chakravarty. New York: New Directions, 1973.

———. "The Inner Experience: Society and the Inner Self (II)." *Cistercian Studies* 18 (1983) and 19 (1984).

———. *Thomas Merton on Zen*. London: Sheldon, 1976.

———. *A Vow of Conversation: Journals 1964–1965*. Edited and Prefaced by Naomi Burton Stone. New York: Farrar, Straus, Giroux, 1988.

———. *The Way of Chuang-Tzu*. New York: New Directions, 1965.

————. *Zen and the Birds of Appetite.* New York: New Directions, 1968.

Merton, Thomas, and Rosemary Radford Ruether. *At Home in the World: The Letters of Thomas Merton and Rosemary Radford Ruether.* Edited by Mary Tardiff. Maryknoll, N.Y.: Orbis, 1995.

Mitchell, Donald W., and James A. Wiseman, eds. *The Gethsemani Encounter: A Dialogue On the Spiritual Life by Buddhist and Christian Monastics.* New York: Continuum, 1998.

Moloney, Francis J. *A Life of Promise: Poverty, Chastity, Obedience.* New South Wales, Australia: St. Paul Publications, 1984.

"Monastic Vows." In *The Augsburg Confession: A Confession of Faith Presented in Augsburg by Certain Princes and Cities to His Imperial Majesty Charles V in the Year 1530.* Translated from the German. Philadelphia: Fortress, 1980, 40–47.

Mott, Michael. *The Seven Mountains of Thomas Merton.* Boston: Houghton Mifflin, 1984.

Munley, Anne. "An Exploratory Content Analysis of Major Themes Present In Selected Documents of United States Women Religious." In *Claiming Our Truth: Reflections on Identity by United States Women Religious.* Edited by Nadine Foley. Washington, D.C.: LCWR, 1988.

Murk-Jansen, Saskia. *Brides in the Desert: The Spirituality of the Beguines.* Traditions of Christian Spirituality Series. Edited by Philip Sheldrake. Maryknoll, N.Y.: Orbis, 1998.

Neal, Marie Augusta. *Catholic Sisters in Transition: From the 1960s to the 1980s.* Wilmington, Del.: Michael Glazier, 1984.

Norris, Kathleen. *The Quotidian Mysteries: Laundry, Liturgy and "Women's Work."* Madeleva Lecture in Spirituality. New York/Mahwah, N.J.: Paulist Press, 1998.

Nygren, David J., and Miram D. Ukeritis. *The Future of Religious Orders in the United States: Transformation and Commitment.* Foreward by David C. McClelland. Westport, Conn.: Praeger, 1993.

O'Brien, T. C. "Virginity, Consecration To (Rite)." In *New Catholic Encyclopedia: Supplement: Change in the Church,* vol. 17. Washington, D.C./New York: Publishers Guild, 1979, 692.

O'Malley, John W. "One Priesthood: Two Traditions." In *A Concert of Charisms: Ordained Ministry in Religious Life.* Edited by Paul K. Hennessy. New York/Mahwah, N.J.: Paulist Press, 1997.

Ó Murchú, Diarmuid. *The Prophetic Horizon of Religious Life.* London; Excalibur, 1989.

———. *Reclaiming Spirituality: A New Spiritual Framework for Today's World.* New York: Crossroad, 1998.

———. *Reframing Religious Life: An Expanded Vision for the Future.* U.K.: St. Paul's, 1995.

Osiek, Carolyn. *Beyond Anger: On Being A Feminist in the Church.* New York/Mahwah, N.J.: Paulist Press, 1986.

Overholt, Thomas W. *Channels of Prophecy: The Social Dynamics of Prophetic Activity.* Minneapolis: Fortress, 1989.

Panikkar, Raimundo. *Blessed Simplicity: The Monk as Universal Archetype.* New York: Seabury, 1982.

———. *The Silence of God: The Answer of the Buddha.* Translated by Robert R. Barr. Maryknoll, N.Y.: Orbis, 1989.

———. *The Trinity and the World Religions: Icon-Person-Mystery.* Maryknoll, N.Y.: Orbis, 1973.

Philibert, Paul J., ed. *Living in the Meantime: Concerning the Transformation of Religious Life*. New York/Mahwah, N.J.: Paulist Press, 1994.

Polkinghorne, John. *Quarks, Chaos, and Christianity: Questions to Science and Religion*. New York: Crossroad, 1997 (orig. 1994).

Power, David. "Theologies of Religious Life and Priesthood." In *A Concert of Charisms: Ordained Ministry in Religious Life*. Edited by Paul K. Hennessy. New York/Mahwah, N.J.: Paulist Press, 1997.

Prejean, Helen. *Dead Man Walking; An Eyewitness Account of the Death Penalty in the United States*. New York: Vintage, 1994.

Quiñonez, Lora Ann, and Mary Daniel Turner. *The Transformation of American Catholic Sisters*. Women in the Political Economy. Edited by R. J. Steinberg. Philadelphia: Temple University Press, 1992.

Rahner, Karl. "The Unity of Love of God and Neighbor." In *The Content of Faith: The Best of Karl Rahner's Theological Writings*. Edited by Karl Lehmann and Albert Raffelt. Translated by Harvey D. Egan. New York: Crossroad, 1992, 579–87. Taken from *Everyday Faith*. Translated by William J. O'Hara. New York: Herder and Herder, 1968, 106–17.

Ranft, Patricia. *Women and the Religious Life in Premodern Europe*. New York: St. Martin's, 1996.

Rees, Elizabeth. "Autonomous Religious Life: The Consecrated Virgin in the World." *The Way Supplement* 50 (Summer, 1984): 122–24.

Ricoeur, Paul. *Interpretation Theory: Discourse and the Surplus of Meaning*. Fort Worth, Tex.: Texas Christian University Press, 1976.

Riley, Maria. *Transforming Feminism*. Kansas City: Sheed & Ward, 1989.

Ripinsky-Naxon, Michael. *The Nature of Shamanism: Substance and Function of a Religious Metaphor.* Albany, N.Y.: State University of New York Press, 1993.

Rogers, Carole Garibaldi. *Poverty, Chastity and Change: Lives of Contemporary American Nuns.* Twayne's Oral History Series, no. 24. Edited by Donald A. Ritchie. New York: Twayne, 1996.

Rothleubber, Sister Francis Borgia. *He Sent Two: The Story of the Beginning of the School Sisters of St. Francis.* Milwaukee: Bruce, 1965.

Saint Cyprian. *Treatises.* Edited by Roy J. Deferrari. Fathers of the Church Series, vol. 36. New York: Fathers of the Church, 1958.

Sammon, Sean D. "Last Call for Religious Life." In *Human Development* 20 (Spring 1999): 12–27.

———. *An Undivided Heart: Making Sense of Celibate Chastity.* New York: Alba House, 1993.

Sasaki, Joseph. *The Lay Apostolate and the Hierarchy.* Ottawa: St. Paul's University/University of Ottawa Press, 1967.

Schaeffer, Pamela. "WOC Gathers to Promote Women's Ordination Amid Conflicting Visions, Goals." *National Catholic Reporter* 32 (December 1, 1995): 9–11.

Schillebeeckx, Edward. *The Church With A Human Face: A New and Expanded Theology of Ministry.* Translated by John Bowden. New York: Crossroad, 1985.

Schneiders, Sandra M. *Beyond Patching: Faith and Feminism in the Catholic Church.* The Anthony Jordan Lectures, Newman Theological College, Edmonton, 1990. New York/Mahwah, N.J.: Paulist Press, 1991.

———. "Celibacy as Charism." *The Way Supplement* 77 (Summer, 1993): 13–25.

————. "Congregational Leadership and Spirituality in the Postmodern Era." *Review for Religious* 57 (January–February, 1998): 6–33.

————. "Contemporary Religious Life: Death or Transformation?" In *Religious Life: The Challenge of Tomorrow.* Edited by Cassian J. Yuhaus. New York/Mahwah, N.J.: Paulist Press, 1994, 9–34.

————. *New Wineskins: Re-Imagining Religious Life Today.* New York/Mahwah, N.J.: Paulist Press, 1986.

————. *The Revelatory Text: Interpreting the New Testament as Sacred Scripture.* 2d ed. Collegeville, Minn.: Liturgical Press, 1999.

————. "Spirituality in the Academy." *Theological Studies* 50 (December, 1989): 676–97.

————. "The Study of Christian Spirituality; Contours and Dynamics of a Discipline." *Christian Spirituality Bulletin* 6 (Spring 1998): 1, 3–12.

Seasoltz, R. Kevin. "Institutes of Consecrated Life and Ordained Ministry: Some Canonical Issues. In *A Concert of Charisms: Ordained Ministry in Religious Life.* Edited by Paul K. Hennessy. New York/Mahwah, N.J.: Paulist Press, 1997.

————. A Western Monastic Perspective on Ordained Ministry." In *A Concert of Charisms: Ordained Ministry in Religious Life.* Edited by Paul K. Hennessy. New York/Mahwah, N.J.: Paulist Press, 1997.

Silver, Ilana Friedrich. *Virtuosity, Charisma, and the Social Order.* New York: Cambridge University Press, 1995.

Sipe, A. W. Richard. *A Secret World: Sexuality and the Search for Celibacy.* New York: Brunner/Mazel, 1990.

————. *Sex, Priests, and Power: Anatomy of A Crisis.* New York: Brunner/Mazel, 1995.

The States of Perfection. Selected and arranged by the Benedictine Monks of Solesmes. Translated by E. O'Gorman. Boston: St. Paul Editions, 1967.

Stewart, George C., Jr. *Marvels of Charity: History of American Sisters and Nuns*. Foreword by Dolores Liptak. Huntington, Ind.: Our Sunday Visitor, 1994.

Supan, Marita-Constance. "Dangerous Memory: Mother M. Theresa Maxis Duchemin and the Michigan Congregation of the Sisters, I.H.M." In *Building Sisterhood: A Feminist History of the Sisters, Servants of the Immaculate Heart of Mary*. Syracuse, N.Y.: Syracuse University Press, 1997, 31–67.

Swidler, Leonard, et al. *Death or Dialogue? From the Age of Monologue to the Age of Dialogue*. Philadelphia: Trinity, 1990.

Swidler, Leonard, and Arlene Swidler, eds. *Women Priests: A Catholic Commentary on the Vatican Declaration*. New York/Mahwah, N.J.: Paulist Press, 1977.

Swidler, Leonard, and Paul Mojzes, eds. *The Uniqueness of Jesus: A Dialogue with Paul Knitter*. Maryknoll, N.Y.: Orbis, 1997.

Teresa of Avila. *The Collected Works of St. Teresa of Avila*. Vol. 1. Translated by Kieran Kavanaugh and Otilio Rodriguez. Washington, D.C.: Institute of Carmelite Studies, 1976.

Thompson, John B. *Critical Hermeneutics: A Study in the Thought of Paul Ricoeur and Jürgen Habermas*. Cambridge: Cambridge University Press, 1981.

Thompson, Margaret S. "'Charism' Or 'Deep Story'? Toward A Clearer Understanding of the Growth of Women's Religious Life in Nineteenth-Century America." In *Religious Life and Contemporary Culture*. Theological Education Process, Cycle 2. Monroe, Mich.: Sisters, Servants of the Immaculate Heart of Mary, 1998.

———. "Discovering Foremothers: Sisters, Society, and the American Catholic Experience." *The American Catholic*

Religious Life: Selected Historical Essays. Edited with an introduction by Joseph M. White. New York: Garland, 1988, 63–80.

Trimingham, J. Spencer. *The Sufi Orders in Islam*. Oxford: Clarendon, 1971.

Turner, Denys. *The Darkness of God: Negativity in Christian Mysticism*. Cambridge: Cambridge University Press, 1995.

Van Ness, Peter. "Introduction: Spirituality and the Secular Quest." In *Spirituality and the Secular Quest*. World Spirituality: An Encyclopedic History of the Religious Quest, 22. New York: Crossroad, 1996.

Vidulich, Dorothy. " 'Radical' I.H.M's Pioneered Religious Community." *National Catholic Reporter* 31 (June 30, 1995): 19.

Ward, Benedicta, trans. *The Desert Christian: Sayings of the Desert Fathers, the Alphabetical Collection*. New York: Macmillan, 1975.

Weber, Max. *From Max Weber: Essays in Sociology*. Translated and edited by H. H. Garth and C. W. Mills. New York: Oxford University Press, 1958.

Wheatley, Margaret. *Leadership and the New Science: Learning about Organization from an Orderly Universe*. San Francisco: Berrett-Koehler, 1992.

White, Joseph M., ed. *The American Catholic Religious Life: Selected Historical Essays*. New York: Garland, 1988.

Wilder, Amos N. *Early Christian Rhetoric: The Language of the Gospel*. Cambridge, Mass.: Harvard University Press, 1971.

Wittberg, Patricia. *Creating a Future for Religious Life: A Sociological Perspective*. New York/Mahwah, N.J.: Paulist Press, 1991.

———. "Outward Orientation in Declining Organizations: Reflections on the LCWR Documents." In *Claiming Our*

Truth; Reflections on Identity by United States Women Religious. Edited by Nadine Foley. Washington, D.C.: LCWR, 1988, 89–115.

———. *Pathways to Re-Creating Religious Communities.* New York/Mahwah, N.J.: Paulist Press, 1996.

———. *The Rise and Fall of Catholic Religious Orders: A Social Movement Perspective.* SUNY Series in Religion, Culture, and Society. Edited by Wade Clark Roof. Albany, N.Y.: State University of New York Press, 1994.

———. "Ties That No Longer Bind." *America* 179 (September 26, 1998): 10–14.

Woodward, Evelyn. *Poets, Prophets, and Pragmatists: A New Challenge to Religious Life.* Notre Dame, Ind.: Ave Maria Press, 1987.

Yuhaus, Cassian J., ed. *Religious Life: The Challenge of Tomorrow.* New York/Mahwah, N.J.: Paulist Press, 1994.

Index